Facial Recognition Surveillance

CLARENDON STUDIES IN CRIMINOLOGY

Published under the auspices of the Institute of Criminology, University of Cambridge; the Mannheim Centre, London School of Economics; and the Centre for Criminology, University of Oxford.

RECENT TITLES IN THIS SERIES:

Domestic Violence in Pakistan:
The Legal Construction of 'Bad' and 'Mad' Women
Kamal

Transforming Justice Responses to Non-Recent Institutional Abuses
McAlinden, Keenan, and Gallen

Mafia Expansion: The 'Ndrangheta in Established Democracies
Hauser

Constructing Victimhood: Beyond Innocence and Guilt in Transitional Justice
Lawther

Crime and Civilization: The Birth of Criminology in the Early Nineteenth Century
Kivivuori

Palestinian Political Organizations in Israeli Prisons
Bernstein

Victims and the Labour of Justice at the International Criminal Court: The Blame Cascade
Ullrich

Law and Personality Disorder:
Human Rights, Human Risks, and Rehabilitation
O'Loughlin

Policing Sport Mega-Events: Security, Spectacle, and Camouflage in Rio de Janeiro
Pauschinger

Character, Circumstances, and Criminal Careers: Towards a Dynamic Developmental and Life-Course Criminology
Wikstrom, Treiber, and Roman

Children in Police Custody: Adversity and Adversariality Behind Closed Doors
Bevan

Victims and Criminal Justice: A History
Cox, Shoemaker, and Shore

Rethinking Drug Laws: Theory, History, Politics
Seddon

Facial Recognition Surveillance

Policing and Human Rights in the Age of Artificial Intelligence

Pete Fussey

Professor of Criminology, Department of Sociology, Social Policy and Criminology, University of Southampton, UK

Daragh Murray

Senior Lecturer, Queen Mary University School of Law, UK

OXFORD
UNIVERSITY PRESS

OXFORD
UNIVERSITY PRESS

Great Clarendon Street, Oxford, OX2 6DP,
United Kingdom

Oxford University Press is a department of the University of Oxford.
It furthers the University's objective of excellence in research, scholarship,
and education by publishing worldwide. Oxford is a registered trade mark of
Oxford University Press in the UK and in certain other countries.

Published in the United States of America by Oxford University Press
198 Madison Avenue, New York, NY 10016, United States of America.

British Library Cataloguing in Publication Data
Data available

Library of Congress Control Number: 2025934512

ISBN 9780192883704

DOI: 10.1093/9780191979927.001.0001

The manufacturer's authorised representative in the EU for product safety is
Oxford University Press España S.A., Parque Empresarial San Fernando de Henares,
Avenida de Castilla, 2 – 28830 Madrid (www.oup.es/en or product.safety@oup.com).
OUP España S.A. also acts as importer into Spain of products made by the manufacturer.

Advance Praise

'Rapid AI developments propel anxious debates everywhere. But few are informed by the kinds of brilliant research on which this book depends. Years of painstaking observation and analysis, alongside police and publics in everyday contexts, flowers into detailed, thoughtful and accessible arguments. A model of thorough research, that queries 'humans-in-the-loop,' demonstrates that technology frames suspicion, and exposes a tragic neglect of human rights. And has wisdom regarding AI, well beyond police work.'

—David Lyon, Emeritus Professor,
Queen's University, Kingston, Ontario

'This book is a must read. Based on extensive ethnographic observations of one of the largest police forces in the world, the book undertakes two equally novel and important tasks. First, it conceptualises why the police's use of advanced surveillance technologies are capable of giving rise to compound human rights harms and sets out what a human rights due diligence framework to prevent such harms should look like. Second, it shows how algorithmic decision making undermines the exercise of police discretion with manifold consequences for human rights and policing culture. The result is a superb delivery of an evidence-based cautionary tale about the erosion of human rights based policing through the emergence of algorithmic classifications of suspicion.'

—Başak Cali, Professor of International Law, University of Oxford

'*Facial Recognition Surveillance* is a tour de force. Masterfully weaving together theoretical, doctrinal, and empirical data, Fussey and Murray have published a groundbreaking book that greatly advances the world's knowledge of the dangers and possibilities of facial recognition technologies and their use by law enforcement. Sharp observers of how these technologies are being used in practice, Fussey and Murray have produced an essential resource for anyone interested in the past, present and future use of biometrics in policing–and more generally, for anyone interested in the interplay of digital technologies and the protection of human rights in the digital age.'

—Alexa Koenig, Director,
Investigations Human Rights Center, UC Berkeley

Fussey and Murray's book on Facial Recognition Surveillance is thought-provoking and disturbing. The authors bring a human rights and empirical frame to what likely is the most extensive use of real time facial recognition by a democracy. They have thought deeply about how this extensive surveillance affects us all, something that should be understood better before proceeding. And it is disturbing because the UK has not done that; rather, we learn of disregard for the rule of law and insufficient care about the impact of this tool on society. If surveillance is your jam, this is a must read.

—Barry Friedman, Jacob D. Fuchsberg Professor of Law,
Affiliated Professor of Politics, Director, Policing Project,
New York University School of Law

This book dives deep into the world of facial recognition technology, thanks to the expert guidance of Professor Pete Fussey and Dr. Daragh Murray. Their combined knowledge of surveillance, policing, and human rights, coupled with their first-hand experience with the Metropolitan Police's trials, brings a unique perspective. The authors dissect the technology's historical roots, its actual use in operations, and, crucially, what it all means for our human rights in terms particularly of freedom of expression and assembly. This is no ordinary academic study; it's a vital exploration of how this technology is reshaping policing and is impacting on our fundamental rights.

—Lord Clement-Jones, Former Artificial
Intelligence Committee Chair, House of Lords

'In this ground-breaking book Pete Fussey and Daragh Murray provide a detailed examination of one of the most controversial AI-driven policing tools, revealing the diffuse harms associated with advanced surveillance technology and offering a compelling human rights framework that establishes the key questions law enforcement policies should be judged against. The rigorous analysis in *Facial Recognition Surveillance* could not be more timely or welcome. Criminology at its very best, warning us of the worst ahead. Essential, if occasionally disturbing, reading.'

—Eamonn Carrabine, Professor of Sociology, University of Essex

'For years, academics have warned we are sleepwalking into a surveillance state. With this book, Fussey and Murray ensure we are now wide awake. With an unrivalled combination of law and case studies, first-hand accounts of research on the ground and policy deliberations, coupled with the theoretical tools necessary to understand the implications for societies under surveillance, Fussey and Murray present the definitive account of facial recognition in policing.

Essential reading for anyone who wants to understand, and engage with, the debate that we must insist upon before the police expand their facial recognition capabilities further.'

—Carole McCartney, Professor of Law and Criminal Justice,
University of Leicester

'In *Facial Recognition Surveillance*, Pete Fussey and Daragh Murray shatter the illusions of frontier technology in policing. Their book explores the Metropolitan Police's experiments with 'live' surveillance and takes us on a rich ethnographic journey from government policy discussions into the interiors of unmarked surveillance vans. As the book unfolds, so too does a larger story about efforts to control cities and populations. Fussey and Murray show us the ground we have yielded and the ground that we must retake if liberty is to survive.'

—Mark Maguire, Professor of Anthropology,
National University of Ireland, Maynooth

'A cogent and compelling exploration of facial recognition technology. Written with great insight and clarity, this book unpacks the technology's role as a fundamentally intrusive mass surveillance tool that is increasingly transforming policing around the world, with implications for human rights. The book offers much-needed insight into the history, sociotechnical dynamics, and consequences of unregulated digital surveillance. It is an essential resource for anyone concerned about the human impact of policing with facial recognition technology.'

—Pam Ugwudike, Professor of Criminology, University of Southampton

'Facial recognition surveillance poses dire threats to human rights. Based on unprecedented access to police deployments of such technologies, this incisive book shows how facial recognition systems amplify both algorithmic and human biases. The outcome, more often than not, is augmented policing of poor and minoritized communities. This ethnographically rich book provides a guide for charting and contesting these disturbing transformations.'

—Torin Monahan, Professor in the Department of Communication at The
University of North Carolina at Chapel Hill

'This book is a must read for anyone working on technology policy issues, and it will be a crucial resource for policymakers. Fussey and Murray deliver a masterful breakdown of the operational realities surrounding facial recognition deployments, meticulously illuminating the far-reaching social and legal implications of this technology. Anyone seeking a deeper understanding of modern-day surveillance, should read this book.'

—Rashida Richardson, Distinguished Scholar of
Technology and Policy, Worcester Polytechnic Institute

To
Raquel Vazquez Llorente
and
Françoise Hampson

We see psychologically, cameras see geometrically.

David Hockney

Series Editors' Preface

The Clarendon Studies in Criminology series aims to provide a forum for outstanding theoretical and empirical work in all aspects of criminology and criminal justice, broadly understood. The Editors welcome submissions from established scholars, as well as manuscripts based on excellent PhD dissertations. The series was inaugurated in 1994, with Roger Hood as its first General Editor, following discussions between Oxford University Press and Oxford's then Centre for Criminological Research. It is edited under the auspices of three centres: the Institute of Criminology at the University of Cambridge, the Centre for Criminology at the University of Oxford, and the Mannheim Centre for Criminology at the London School of Economics. Each supplies members of the Editorial Board and, in turn, the Series General Editor or Editors.

In *Facial Recognition Surveillance*, Pete Fussey and Daragh Murray explore how AI-powered facial recognition technology impacts the work of police forces and the lives of citizens. They raise several questions about the use of such technology, both in terms of human rights and operational deployment on the ground. They see facial recognition technology as one of the most controversial forms of police surveillance. As it gets deployed more widely also in democratic societies, they offer a critical inquiry into the issues that it raises, ranging from suspicion formation, limitation, and biases to the legal/democratic grounds justifying its deployment.

This work combines two books into one. First, it retraces the origins and development of facial recognition in the context of policing and urban security. This is followed by a discussion of the human rights and legal implications of using facial recognition technology, particularly in democratic societies. In the second part of the book, the authors then bring us into the field to observe how this technology is deployed on the ground. This is based on a rich and unprecedented ethnographic observation of police operations carried out by the Metropolitan Police Service in London, United Kingdom.

Policing has consistently witnessed—and embraced—innovation throughout its history. Recent years have seen 'dramatic technological advancement', as Fussey and Murray put it. Questions about how advanced surveillance is governed and regulated in the digital age, and its human rights implications, have become increasingly pressing and urgent. This book offers some critical reflections in this space. We are pleased to include it in the Clarendon Studies in Criminology series.

Paolo Campana and Kyle Treiber
General Editors
Institute of Criminology, University of Cambridge
March 2025

Acknowledgements

This book is the product of extensive discussion, engagement, thinking, and research conducted over several years, the course of which has brought us into contact with many people who have supported this work in ways that are both direct and indirect. We are thankful to everyone who has been involved along the way and feel privileged to have had the opportunity to work with you all. Thank you. This research was supported by a UKRI Future Leaders Fellowship, Grant Number: MR/T042133/2 and the ESRC Human Rights, Big Data and Technology project ES/ M010236/1.

With apologies to those we have inevitably missed, first, we would like to thank all those involved in the Metropolitan Police Service (MPS) operational trials of live facial recognition technology for their willingness to engage in the research process that formed the basis of this book. In particular, we appreciate the MPS's openness and transparency in their engagement, their facilitation of access to the operations, and their support for the independent nature of our work. We also appreciate engagement with Jenny Gilmer and Andy Read (South Wales Police), Jennifer Housego (Essex Police), and Jan Ellerman (Europol).

The following were exceptionally generous with insights, feedback, challenge, their time, their knowledge, and their patience, all of whom sharpened our thinking on various aspects of this book: Tony Porter, Fraser Sampson, Paul Wiles, and Tony Eastaugh (former Biometrics and Surveillance Camera Commissioners); John Wadham (PSNI Human Rights Ombudsman); Diego Quiroz (Scottish Biometrics Commissioner's Office); David Reichel, Tamas Molnar, and Jo Goodey (EU Fundamental Rights Agency); Lord Clement Jones; Angus Cleary, Ariana Carrano, and Yara Ali-Adib (the Equality and Human Rights Commission); Clément Voule (former UN Special Rapporteur on Freedom of Peaceful Assembly and of Association), Gina Romero (UN Special Rapporteur on Freedom of Peaceful Assembly and of Association), and Sonya Merkova (UN Special Rapporteur's Office); Michael Wiener, Johan Olhagen, and Tim Engelhardt (UN Office of the High Commissioner for Human Rights); Wendy O'Brien and Anna Giudice (UN Office of Drugs and Crime); Nick Oakshott (UN High Commissioner for Refugees); Alexander Babuta (Turing Institute); Ilia Siatitsa and Tomaso Falchetta (Privacy

International); Carly Kind and Reema Patel (Ada Lovelace Institute); Amba Kak (AI Now Institute); Sadhbh McCarthy (CIES); Eric Kind, Ben Hayes, Mahdi Assan, and Aparna Surendra (AWO); Simon McKay (The Chambers of Simon McKay); Hannah Couchman, Sam Gritt, Emmanuelle Andrews, and Mark Wilding (Liberty/Liberty Investigates); Silkie Carlo and Madeleine Stone (Big Brother Watch); Ben Wizner (ACLU); Albert Fox Cahn (S.T.O.P.); Wairagala Wakabi (CIPESA); Amber Sinha and Elonnai Hickok (CIS); Matt Mahmoudi and Tanya O'Carrol (Amnesty International, Tech Team); and Olga Cronin (ICCL). Thanks are also due to Baroness Jenny Jones, Lord Strasburger, Carol Monaghan MP, Sian Berry MP, Lord Justice Fulford (former Investigatory Powers Commissioner), and colleagues at IPCO/OCDA.

Our work was substantially enriched by conversations with the media, where many insightful questions forced us to strengthen, sharpen, and better communicate our arguments. In this respect, particular thanks are due to Vikram Dodd, Shanti Das, and Rob Booth at *The Guardian/Observer*, Madhumita Murgia at the *Financial Times*, Geoff White at the BBC, Kashmir Hill and Adam Satariano at the *New York Times*, Julia Horowitz at CNN, Rowland Manthorpe and Alexander J. Martin at Sky, and Matt Burgess at *WIRED*.

Many ideas in this book have been shaped over years of conversations and friendship with other academics. These include but are not limited to Torin Monahan, David Lyon, Kirstie Ball, William Webster, Charles Raab, Claire Garvie, Rashida Richardson, Amy Stevens, Simone Browne, Keith Spiller, Daniel Marciniak, Lorna McGregor, David Murakami Wood, Azedeh Akbari, Marion Oswald, Joe Purshouse, Alan Dignam KC (Hon), Matthew Abbey, Sophie Kate Crowe, Vic Baines, Caroline Lequesne, Ahmed Shaheed, Katja Franko, Zuzanna Wojciak, Vivian Ng, Ronit Matar, Lorna Woods, Mark Maguire, Barry Freidman, Alexa Koenig, Ashley Deeks, Yuval Shany, Geoff Gilbert, Maurice Sunkin KC (Hon), Klaus McDonald-Maier, Carole McCartney, Rosamunde van Brakel, Ben Bradford, Jonathan Jackson, Kuda Hove, Otto Saki, Paul Kimumwe, Eamonn Carrabine, Chris Greer, Nigel South, Niclas Rautenberg, Noam Lubell, Kat Hadjimatheou, Pam Ugwudike, Jenny Fleming, Stephen Matthews, and the Surveillance and the City Network.

On a personal note, gratitude is due for the obscene fortune that allowed a life to be shared with Jai Fussey, Mia Fussey, and Raquel Vazquez Llorente.

This book is also dedicated to Françoise Hampson. Thank you for teaching me to be less like Moses and more like a plumber.

Errors of judgement and interpretation, of course, rest with the authors. Which one is up for debate.

Contents

Figures and Tables

Figures

Tables

Table of Cases

UNITED KINGDOM

UNITED STATES

EUROPEAN COURT OF HUMAN RIGHTS

Table of Legislation

Abbreviations and Glossary

ACE-V	Analysis, Comparison, Evaluation-Verification
ACPO	Association of Chief Police Officers
AI	artificial intelligence
ANPR	automatic number plate recognition
AVATAR	Automated Virtual Agent for Truth Assessments in Real-time
BSCC	Biometrics and Surveillance Camera Commissioner
BTP	British Transport Police
CBP	Customs and Border Protection
CNN	convolutional neural networks. A form of AI that, among other attributes, optimizes image analysis
CRIMINT	Criminal Intelligence database used by the Metropolitan Police Service to manage police intelligence
CRIS	Crime Report Information System database for managing offender and other crime records data
DPIA	Data Protection Impact Assessment
EAPPs (DP)	a federated platform used to merge different police databases
ECtHR	European Court of Human Rights
EU	European Union
EWMS	Emerald Warrant Management System. The Metropolitan Police Service system for processing and logging warrants. This logs/includes details of outstanding arrest warrants concerning individuals charged with crimes and wanted for not attending court, skipping bail, or non-compliance issues such as breaching court orders and being wanted for questioning
FAST	Future Attribute Screening Technology
FRT	facial recognition technology
FRVT	Face Recognition Vendor Test
GDPR	General Data Protection Regulation
HC	High Court
IC	Identity Code
ICAO	International Civil Aviation Organization
ICCPR	International Covenant on Civil and Political Rights
ICO	Information Commissioner's Office
LEDS	Law Enforcement Data Service

LFR	live facial recognition
MPS	Metropolitan Police Service
NGO	non-governmental organization
NIST	National Institute of Standards and Technology
NPCC	National Police Chiefs' Council
NPL	National Physical Laboratory (evaluators of Metropolitan Police Service facial recognition algorithms)
NSA	National Security Agency
OBSCC	Office of the Biometrics and Surveillance Camera Commissioner
OIFR	operator-initiated facial recognition
OSAC	Organization of Scientific Area Committees
PACE	Police and Criminal Evidence Act 1984
PNC	Police National Computer. Established in 1974, this holds formal records of encounters of individuals with the police and other criminal justice agencies. For example, it holds data on arrests, charges, court decisions, and a range of licensing records (such as driving and firearms)
PND	Police National Database. An intelligence database distinct from the Police National Computer. Established in 2011 as a recommendation of the Bichard Inquiry into the child protection issues following the double child murders of Holly Wells and Jessica Chapman in Soham, Cambridgeshire
POFA	Protection of Freedoms Act 2012. This established the role of the Surveillance Camera Commissioner and Biometrics Commissioner, both merged into the Office of the Biometrics and Surveillance Camera Commissioner in 2021
PSED	Public Sector Equality Duty
RFR	retrospective facial recognition
RIPA	Regulation of Investigatory Powers Act
SCC	Surveillance Camera Commissioner
SCOT	Social Construction of Technology
STS	science and technology studies
SWP	South Wales Police
UN	United Nations
VIIDO	Visual Images, Identifications and Detections Office
watchlist	reference database of images and test (such as names and offence type) used for facial recognition operations

Introduction

> A boy in school uniform is stopped on the street by four plainclothes officers. The size of the officers is accentuated by the diminutive stature of their target: a boy no more than 14 years old, in uniform eating takeaway chips on his way home from school. Clearly intimidated and visibly distressed, the child's hands are shaking as the officers crowd over him and demand to see a form of identification. Earlier that afternoon, an individual walking on the same street refused a request by these officers to produce identification documents. The officers proceeded to use force to physically unclasp the individual's hands, pull his fingers apart and place them onto a mobile fingerprint scanner.
>
> The same day saw multiple arrests, mostly for cannabis possession, after people were searched for avoiding the cameras in a 'suspicious manner'.
>
> **(Ethnographic fieldnotes, Romford, east London, 31 January 2019)**

The element connecting these discrete incidents is that the individuals had all, moments before, passed in the vicinity of a live facial recognition (LFR) deployment operated by the Metropolitan Police Service (MPS). Facial recognition technology (FRT) is more accurately described as a system, one that links digital and human forms of surveillance and connects image- and text-based data sources. During the London facial recognition operation described above, two highly powered cameras with exceptional optical capabilities, manufactured by Bosch and Axon, were positioned on the roof of a police van. These fed images of passersby into two high-spec laptops inside, each possessing market-leading image-processing capabilities. Using AI-driven algorithms, these machines identify, extract, and code the pertinent data from each image. Data from these street-based images is then compared to information held on a pre-prepared database, one created from police intelligence on 'wanted' individuals. If the algorithm assesses sufficient similarity between the image of a face captured on the street and an image held on the database, an alert is triggered. In the above operation each alert was issued twice: once to an intelligence unit monitoring laptops inside the van and simultaneously to street-based 'intervention teams' equipped with smartphone-sized devices. This operation was the first of its kind where officers routinely relied on these handheld devices, and it marked the initiation of a practice that has since defined how facial recognition operates on Britain's streets. These computer-generated alerts then triggered a more human-centric chain of events. The credibility of the matches was scrutinized by humans twice: by the intelligence unit in the van who—if they were satisfied that a match was accurate—radioed through confirmation and identifying features to street-based officers, who would again check images while searching for and apprehending any suspects.

This sequence outlines what has since become the template for police uses of 'live' facial recognition surveillance in the UK. Highlighting these constituent features reveals how 'facial recognition technology' is in fact misnamed. The technology only ever *suggests* rather than conclusively *recognizing*. Undercutting the hyperbole that often accompanies this technology, then, is the reality that FRT outcomes arise from a meeting point of suggestion, inference, and subjective judgement. Relatedly, FRT encompasses processes, practices, and outcomes that are not reducible solely to 'technology'. Human actors initiate the process by deciding who they are going to search for and compiling databases from intelligence logs. As this book shows, officers engage with the technology in complex ways throughout the lifecycle of an operation. Ultimately, FRT encounters are resolved through physical on-street interactions. As such, the practice of facial recognition surveillance is not solely technical but inexorably socio-technical.

Returning to the schoolboy, and the role of inference, the computer system assessed his face to sufficiently resemble a 'wanted' suspect on the database. The intelligence teams reviewing the camera feeds were not convinced. Following much-discussed human-in-the-loop protocols, these specialist officers correctly judged the computer suggestion to be inaccurate. On this occasion, the decision was not difficult: the child on the street appeared younger than the database image and so the computer match was not credible. In actions that would be repeated in future operations, these reservations were not shared by those on the street with access to the same information, who chose to ignore their colleagues' professional judgement (and the evident age disparity). They stopped him anyway.

The ensuing confrontation produced outcomes difficult to reconcile with the MPS's claims that facial recognition provides 'precise community-based crime fighting' (Science and Technology in Policing n.d.). Here, the technology was neither accurate nor deployed in the service of any community. Indeed, this inaccurate facial recognition match led directly to an escalated confrontation on the streets, one that would not have occurred otherwise. This included passersby shouting at the officers, berating them for 'bullying children' and 'straight-up racism'. Similar alienating effects were identified by director of London-based non-governmental organization (NGO) Big Brother Watch Silkie Carlo, whose representatives were also present and followed up the case. As she explained in an interview:

Silkie Carlo (SC): There was a fourteen-year-old boy who was misidentified and stopped and searched on the last day of the Romford deployment. I've seen the footage of it, and it makes me absolutely furious, to be honest with you.

Pete Fussey, author: I saw that, I was in the van that day and stepped out while it happened.

SC: Naturally, the child now has formed a completely negative view of the police and what he looks like to adults in general and police officers. I can't imagine how terrified I would be if four plain-clothed men appeared out of the blue and dragged me off by my wrists to one side, let alone as a fourteen-year-old child, and this is a gateway technology that allows police to conduct stop and search with the veil of this kind of objectivity of facial recognition cameras. That incident is a really a quite chilling representation of just how authoritarian this can be. You know, a case of mistaken identity of a fourteen-year-old, you know, like I say, over at scale so how many more young Black children or people like [redacted] who had his scarf over his face, how many more people are going to be subjected to arbitrary treatment by the police, because you're subjecting thousands of people every day to an automatic police line-up. (Interviewed April 2019)

This episode illustrates many significant questions pertinent to the introduction of advanced surveillance technology into everyday policing, many of which are interrogated in detail throughout this book. New symbioses arise. FRT can validate and amplify the biases of human decision-making.

And human decision-making can validate and amplify the biases of technology. This holds implications for human oversight which can serve not as an accountability measure but as something that reproduces the inaccuracies and inequalities of technology. Longstanding formulations of suspicion also become reconfigured in ways that are seemingly subtle yet are profound in their implications. Questions over accountability and explainability arise, as well as questions over where the origins of suspicion lie, the credence it is given, and how it is acted upon. This includes how design choices made in a Tokyo lab, where these facial recognition algorithms originate, affect determinations of suspicion on London's streets. The above also reveals how, behind the hype and hubris accompanying advanced technology, there are hidden, inconvenient, and potentially harmful consequences.

Often missing from selective audits of digital policing tools is their potential to impact negatively on other elements of policing. These include the threat to prized notions of police discretion (Joh 2016; Fussey et al. 2021). As the above account demonstrates, this also risks alienating already overpoliced and underserved communities, in a context where trust in the police has plumbed historic depths. Such contradictions were laid bare in the above operation in Romford, east London, which ultimately collapsed when officers became tied up processing people electing to avoid walking past the cameras; or, to put it another way, people refusing consent to AI-driven biometric processing as part of a police 'trial'. In almost all cases, those avoiding the cameras with 'something to hide' were in possession of small quantities of cannabis, an offence far below the threshold required for subjecting anyone to practically any other form of intrusive surveillance.

FRT uses machine learning techniques—most commonly, deep convoluted neural networks—to identify an individual, or individuals, within a digital image. This typically occurs on the basis of a three-stage process. First, the faces within an image are *detected*. Second, the biometric features are *extracted* from those faces. Third, the extracted biometric features are *compared* against a reference image or images. FRT itself is most typically deployed in either a '1:1' or '1:*n*' configuration that is to either verify or identify. In a 1:1 setup, a single individual's face (or, more accurately, a biometric template of their face) is typically compared against a single image. The purpose is to *verify* whether an individual is who they claim to be. Some of the most common examples of 1:1 verification are the use of facial recognition to unlock a phone or to gain access to a mobile banking app. In a 1:*n* setup, facial recognition is used to *identify* who an individual is. The probe template is checked against a larger database (a watchlist) to try and find a match. It is this configuration that is of most interest to police forces as it allows for the identification of previously unknown individuals. For the purposes of this book, the database of reference images is referred to as the 'watchlist', in line with MPS nomenclature. The watchlist contains the 'source' images that the camera-detected 'probe' images are matched against. The watchlist, therefore, is foundational to facial recognition operations and fundamental to realizing the surveillance potential of the technology.

Law enforcement adoptions of frontier technologies have generated some of the most significant controversies over the public impact of AI and other digital tools, and FRT has become the focal point of current debates. It is an issue residing at the sharp edge of debates over human rights in the digital era. Addressing an empirical gap, this book details the only independent empirical study in the world to date that accesses and examines operational police LFR deployments. The authors gained unprecedented access to the MPS's operational trial deployments of LFR technology in London, the course of which elicited data that allows several core tenets of policing research to be reconsidered for the digital age.

Taking a cue from the field of science and technology studies, empirical attention to LFR reveals how this advanced surveillance technology shapes and is shaped by the complex operational environments into which it is deployed. Linking to core traditions in the sociology of policing, digital law enforcement practices are analysed in their situated environments. Discourses of surveillance are routinely framed as a series of antagonistic binaries: 'rights versus security'; 'covert versus overt'; 'intrusive versus non-intrusive'; 'suspect versus non-suspect'; 'nothing to fear, nothing to hide'; 'utopian versus dystopian', and so on. Yet surveillance attains a more complex form when enacted. The book reveals how the use of advanced surveillance technologies subtly disrupts these binaries by introducing, for example, gradations of suspicion and a move from directed surveillance towards more ambient observation of the public at large. The analysis further demonstrates how FRT subtly frames suspicion formation, how human discretion becomes modified in relation to computational decision-making, and how unstructured intelligence becomes codified and concretized through operational surveillance databases. These varied and often discretionary practices raise pressing questions over how advanced surveillance is governed and regulated in the digital age. It is in this space that human rights considerations become more urgent.

Methodology

Three methodological approaches were adopted to generate the data that supports the analysis in this book. Much of this was facilitated by the authors' role as independent reviewers of the MPS trial deployments of FRT on London's streets. This academic review was cited in MPS public communications and highlighted several times in parliamentary debates (inter alia, House of Commons 2019). This afforded full and unprecedented access to the planning, live operations, and debriefing processes associated with these deployments. Central to this approach was ethnographic observation of operations, comprising access to the surveillance intelligence room (usually a van equipped with FRT stationed on a busy London street), accompanying street-based patrol teams, and presence at planning meetings, police intelligence meetings, and pre-operational briefings. Six full MPS facial recognition operations alongside one South Wales Police (SWP) deployment were observed, with initial access granted in March 2018 and continuing until the end of the operational trials in May 2019. The SWP observation fell outside of the scope of the review and, at attendance, felt like more of a curated showcase for visitors than a research event, so is not included in the analysis. Each MPS facial recognition deployment occurred within a broader process of planning, intelligence analysis, database development, legal determinations, public engagement, liaison with oversight bodies, operational briefings, post-deployment debriefings, and operational review. Qualitative interviews were also conducted with officers at strategic, tactical, and operational levels of responsibility and others with officers in adjacent investigatory roles. Added to meetings held at Scotland Yard and with officers involved in the deployments, this totalled around 200 hours of observation. Conversations would sometimes arise organically from long hours sitting together on surveillance operations, while others would adopt the format of direct and intentional briefings, with myriad variations in form. Formal semi-structured interviews were also conducted with oversight bodies and civil society groups active in this space. The MPS review also facilitated access to internal police documentation. These included internal legal briefings, trial methodology, and other internal planning documents.

This empirical phase took place amid a larger ecosystem of research and policy activity focusing on the human rights implications of advanced surveillance technology. Driven by an Economic and Social Research Council (ESRC)-funded project running from 2015 to 2023[1] and an ongoing UK

[1] 'Human Rights, Big Data and Technology', ES/M010236/1.

Research and Innovation (UKRI)-funded project[2]—both focusing on the international dimensions of human rights and emerging technology—relevant work included empirical research on the oversight of intelligence agencies (Murray and Fussey 2019; Murray et al. 2021) and on police operational uses of digital technology (inter alia, Fussey and Sandhu 2022). These activities helped frame a broader understanding of the form and human rights implications of digital technologies in policing environments and are cited where relevant.

Involvement in national and supranational policy development facilitated additional access to participants, knowledge, and expertise. Among other interventions, the authors co-drafted United Nations (UN) human rights standards on police uses of technology at protests (Model Protocol for Law Enforcement Officials to Promote and Protect Human Rights in the Context of Peaceful Protests 2024), in fulfilment of UN Human Rights Council Resolution A/HRC/RES/50/21. This was subject to a dedicated debate in the House of Lords (House of Lords 2024) which facilitated access to expertise from law enforcement, legal, and regulatory practitioners across the world. Other work at the supranational level involved collaboration with the European Union's (EU's) human rights body, the Fundamental Rights Agency, on the regulation of biometric surveillance. In the UK, one author led the human rights and ethics strand of the Biometrics and Surveillance Camera Commissioner's national strategy between 2018 and 2023, and both contributed to national guidance on the regulation of FRT (Surveillance Camera Commissioner 2020). The authors have been involved in several parliamentary processes focused on the regulation of surveillance in the UK and Ireland and supported an invited amicus submission to the England and Wales Court of Appeal in Britain's only legal case to date addressing the legality of FRT.[3]

The Book

This book is divided into two parts. Part I sets out the contextual, conceptual, and legal framework, developing three core areas of critical inquiry. It analyses, first, the origins and development of facial recognition in the

[2] 'What Does Artificial Intelligence Mean for the Future of Democratic Society? Examining the Societal Impact of AI and Whether Human Rights Can Respond', MR/T042133/2.

[3] *R (Bridges)* v *The Chief Constable of South Wales Police* [2020] EWCA Civ 1058.

context of digital policing and urban security, then assesses its form and impact before examining the human rights implications of this technology. Part II interrogates the empirical data that drives the analysis offered throughout the text.

Chapter 1 situates LFR in the context of law enforcement's long history of engagement with both technology and biometric identification techniques. Originating as far back as the 1880s and Parisian detective Alphonse Bertillon's innovative use of fingerprinting and custody images, policing has consistently embraced innovation. However, recent years have seen dramatic technological advancement, and by extension an expansion in law enforcement surveillance capability. Advanced computational innovations—such as AI-driven decision-making and algorithmic information management processes—have made detailed insight into individuals' day-to-day activities, attributes, and behaviours increasingly possible, rendering the invisible visible and available for analysis. FRT sits squarely in this process. Advances in AI-driven convolutional neural networks have transformed a once niche, gimmicky, and poorly performing technology into a viable and potentially powerful tool of police surveillance. Uses of LFR sit at the intersection of these processes and debates. In addition to offering radically new surveillance capabilities, LFR technology operates in different ways to existing surveillance architectures and subtly alters several longstanding aspects of policework, including the application of discretion and formulation of suspicion. Moreover, public uses of this technology constitute a meeting point where issues of citizenship, rights, law enforcement, and digital society intersect.

Chapter 2 explores the form, function, and impact of FRT in more detail. Emphasizing the complex interplay of technical and human-social elements, the chapter assesses the evidence typically presented to legitimate FRT and, in doing so, exposes a fragility in many technologically deterministic narratives that accompany the adoption of this and other advanced surveillance technologies. Particular attention is paid to one of the most controversial issues to have surrounded the public use of this technology, that of algorithmic bias with respect to race and gender. The chapter further examines how, despite specific limitations in efficacy, FRT can be regarded in other ways as a step change in surveillance practice. In particular, remote biometric measurement has significantly altered the ways individuals have become understood and managed. These profound shifts in surveillance practice are considered through three modalities: the ways the bodies and intentions of urban citizens have been apprehended and, separately, the specific forms of knowledge that arise from computational processes and how this becomes valorized and instituted into policing practice. These dramatic shifts in the form, function, and scope of surveillance underpin the analysis of the implications for human rights that follows.

Chapter 3 acts as an introduction to those rules of international human rights law relevant to the analysis of FRT. It begins by setting out the three-part test used to determine whether a measure engaging, or interfering, with a human right amounts to a violation of that right. This test is used to examine whether the police use of FRT is 'in accordance with the law', 'in pursuit of a legitimate aim', and 'necessary in a democratic society'. Particular attention is paid to the first and last components of this test as they constitute the principal human rights frame of analysis for this book. The second part of the chapter analyses the key relevant human rights law provisions, namely the rights to privacy, freedom of expression, freedom of assembly, and the prohibition of discrimination, as well as the newly claimed right to a human decision-maker.[4] In order to more fully understand the overall impact of facial recognition deployments, this chapter also introduces the concept of compound human rights harm. This is a frame of analysis intended to capture the multifaceted harm associated with the chilling effects of surveillance, which engages a number of human rights protections simultaneously.

Part II is anchored in the interrogation of empirical data. Determining whether the police's use of FRT will comply with human rights law is not a straightforward task for two key reasons. First, human rights law typically applies after the fact, and so adapting the law to proactively inform police decision-making requires a change in approach. Second, facial recognition is a novel and complex technology, and properly understanding its impacts—whether beneficial or harmful—is equally novel and complex. In order to address this challenge, Chapter 4 develops a due diligence framework specifically tailored to the police use of FRT. This framework unpacks the 'necessary in a democratic society' test and is centred around understanding and evaluating the 'competing interests' at play in any police FRT use; that is, the claimed utility and the potential harm. It sets out the key considerations that should be taken into account prior to, and in the evaluation of, any deployment.

[4] Several other rights are also relevant, notably freedom of association and freedom of religion. However, these rights are examined in a manner largely similar to freedom of expression and freedom of assembly, and so discussion is focused on those rights for illustrative purposes.

Drawing on this due diligence framework, Chapters 5 and 6 evaluate the policy documentation developed by the police, examining how utility and harm, respectively, are identified, evidenced, and approached. Chapter 5 surfaces a number of key issues, including the permissiveness of the policy framework with respect to the purposes for which FRT can be deployed. Of significance is the lack of detail with regard to how 'suspicion' is quantified, the absence of any real limitation regarding the type of offences for which FRT can be deployed, and the possibility of including persons 'of interest' to the police on the watchlist. Chapter 6 examines how the MPS conceptualize harm and incorporate a legal analysis of harm into the policy framework. Concerns are raised regarding the legal approach adopted, particularly vis-a-vis an inappropriate emphasis on the 'reasonable expectation of privacy' at the expense of privacy concerns related to the recording of information in public; the failure to examine context-dependent privacy intrusions and the downplaying of chilling effects; and the de-emphasis of privacy considerations vis-a-vis those on the watchlist but not subject to any court order. Taken together, Chapters 5 and 6 raise significant concerns regarding the overall approach taken to the preparation of the policy documentation. The documentation fails to critically engage with the issues at hand and so does not provide officers with the tools, information, or procedure by which to engage with the complex issues raised by FRT. The result is an imbalanced framework that resembles more an advocacy piece than a guide and which inevitably tilts in favour of authorization.

Chapter 7 analyses the deployment of LFR through unique empirical examination of authorization procedures, planning practices, operational briefings, uses of police intelligence, and the assembly and classification of data to construct suspect databases. The analysis reveals how surveillance deployments are shaped by the affordances of this technology, and belief in its capability, with intelligence often used in instrumental ways to support such decisions. Associated practices become further legitimized through discourses that reify the potential of technology and valorize partial information as 'actionable intelligence'. Additional ambiguities are revealed during the assembly of dispersed data and its inconsistent classification during the construction of suspect databases. Together, these practices reveal a paradox whereby perceived certainties brought about by technology become mediated through ambiguous and uncertain operational environments. Considered together, these practices hold profound implications for the conduct of police surveillance.

Chapter 8 draws on ethnographic research to empirically analyse human and technical interactions in live police operational settings. Meaningful human intervention is a legal requirement for police uses of algorithmic data-driven processes. Yet a crucial unresolved question with significant rights implications is not only *whether* human intervention takes place but also the *nature* of this adjudication. The analysis reveals how algorithmic classifications of suspicion have diverse and wide-ranging implications for the operation of police discretion. In particular, sites of human decision-making varied during police operations and included decisions made by intelligence units in a control room and, on other occasions, by street-based intervention teams. Yet across these assorted arrangements was a discernible 'presumption to intervene' whereby discretion became ceded to algorithmic identifications of suspicious individuals regardless of their accuracy.

Overall, the book analyses the active deployment by one of the world's largest police forces of one of the most controversial forms of public surveillance in use today. Empirical attention is centred at a critical moment in the trajectory of LFR use, at the tipping point of national adoption. This period of operational trials led to a transformation in how the technology became mainstreamed into policing practice. Prior to this, facial recognition was deployed experimentally, and with ephemerality. After this period, LFR spread beyond its isolated uses in London and South Wales and has since been deployed in Essex, North Wales, Northamptonshire, and elsewhere, while every police force in the UK now utilizes retrospective FRT. In London itself, the scale and frequency of deployments have escalated rapidly, with watchlists having grown over 600 per cent in size since the largest deployment studied here, and with over 3 million faces scanned in the capital between 6 April 2023 and 28 June 2024 (MPS 2024b). The operations studied here formed the template for how this now pervasive technology monitors the nation's cities.

PART I

SURVEILLANCE AND HUMAN RIGHTS IN CONTEXT

1
The Emergence of Advanced Biometric Surveillance

1.1 Introduction

Recent years have seen facial recognition technology (FRT) emerge as one of the most controversial forms of police surveillance. While the capabilities of this technology continue to advance and its uses expand, it is important to recognize that such developments do not take place in a vacuum. This chapter traces the context and trajectory from which digital surveillance generally, and FRT specifically, rose to become a prominent form of security technology. Yet while FRT and other advanced surveillance technologies are rooted in, and emerge from, clear enabling contexts, they also represent something new: a step change in the capability and potency of surveillance.

FRT constitutes a radically more intrusive form of surveillance. As this book will show, this claim can be justified on many grounds. Most obvious is that FRT extends the asymmetries of surveillance. It offers the capability to scan all individuals in a crowd unobtrusively and without their knowledge. FRT functions by processing biometric information, a special category of data, so designated by most data protection regimes on account of the heightened intrusion it enables. Facial recognition does not merely allow for the identification of an individual in the crowd, it enables the *remote* identification of *every* individual within the crowd, thus dramatically reconfiguring the right to privacy in public. FRT processes images at a scale far exceeding the capabilities of human observers or traditional surveillance cameras. The numbers of individuals processed as they passed through a camera's field of vision ran into the tens of thousands during the police operations observed for this book. The numbers of individuals sought out now regularly exceed 15,000 per operation. This remote surveillance power is unparalleled: to achieve identification at this scale using traditional methods would require both significant resources and unprecedented disruption to daily life. FRT further makes possible detailed insights

Facial Recognition Surveillance. Pete Fussey and Daragh Murray, Oxford University Press.
 DOI: 10.1093/9780191979927.003.0001

into individuals' day-to-day activities, attributes, and behaviours. It facilitates monitoring, tracking, and profiling at a city-wide scale, and in doing so renders the invisible visible, while offering this surveillance product up for further machine learning-driven analysis.

In terms of its digital architecture, the current moment in the technological development of FRT is significant. Advances in AI-driven convolutional neural networks—often applied, trained, and refined through social media platforms—have transformed a once niche, gimmicky, and poorly performing technology into an increasingly viable and potentially powerful police surveillance tool. Many less obvious yet similarly important differences exist and are explored below.

Many histories of FRT start in the mid- to late twentieth century (inter alia, Gates 2011; Andrejevic and Selwin 2022), appropriately contextualizing its growth with the quickening pace of innovation in the computational sciences. Yet, as recognized throughout this book, the application of FRT implicates complex socio-technical processes. Accordingly, it is also important to highlight that the core aspirations driving current uses of this technology have deeper technical, operational, and social origins. Policing ambitions to confirm suspect identities through biometric technology have famous ancestry in Parisian detective Alphonse Bertillon's innovative use of fingerprinting and custody images during the 1880s and, a century later, the development of DNA fingerprinting in Leicestershire, UK. Both advances served similar ends: to connect an individual's biometric information with police data records. While police uses of FRT can be connected to similar ambitions, the technology implicates another dimension, one that resonates with Victorian-era concerns over the 'problem' of the illegible crowd: the ability to remotely identify individuals within such congregations. The technology also promises to address a further policing priority: the location of offenders in their urban setting.

This chapter analyses the emergence of FRT from these contexts and connects its development with longstanding dilemmas facing urban policing. This discussion is intended to not only set out the enabling circumstances for how FRT came into being but also trace the confluence of technological development, urban security, and policing ambitions that drive its continued development. The adoption of advanced technology has long been commonplace in policework. The chapter argues that, similar to other contexts, such uses of technology do not advance purely for the sake of innovation but become implemented within an enabling context, one that is shaped by longstanding policing challenges and ambitions.

The rise of remote biometric identification technologies can therefore be considered amid specific trajectories of both technological innovation in policing and these persistent motivations of policework. Among the latter, the many histories and sociologies of policing have grasped a consistent thread. This connects the growth of modern policing with aspirations to bring visibility to acts and patterns of deviance; to accurately focus suspicion; and to recognize actual, potential, and perceived offenders in increasingly complex and dangerously imagined urban environments.

To chart the rise of FRT, and to appropriately situate this and other advanced surveillance technologies in the appropriate context, this chapter is divided into three areas of discussion. It will first emphasize transitions in the urban policing environment. As cities grew and diversified, so did the range of concerns that, in turn, inspired action to order and govern. This complex social milieu saw responses that sought to order and make legible the people, places, and processes at the root of emerging anxieties. Several companion processes relevant to the growth of FRT are highlighted here, including revolutionary attempts to render risk and hazards through data. Three processes central to the development of FRT in contemporary society are then examined: attempts to reconfigure the physical and social topography of the city; digital and data-driven ordering and categorizing processes; and the rise of overt surveillance. The third substantive area of discussion charts the introduction of facial recognition surveillance into urban spaces. As this analysis relays, the evolution of this technology was faltering and interrupted, with initial overhyped introductions being short-lived and replaced by other forms of human-driven recognition techniques. However, a step change in image processing brought about by advances in AI and mass consumption of social media shifted this pattern and enabled FRT to become a viable—and potent—tool of law enforcement. The chapter ends with consideration of the myriad conceptual approaches used to decipher such developments before setting out the theoretical position used to frame the analysis of this book.

1.2 Urban Legends: Rendering and Ordering Dangerousness through Surveillance

Rapid urbanization and the anxieties it brought provides an important framing for the applications of police technology discussed in this book. Indeed, nineteenth-century urban expansion, catalysed by the Industrial

Revolution, coincided neatly with the increasing formalization of policing functions through recognized law enforcement institutions, perhaps most famously incarnated by the creation of London's Metropolitan Police Service (MPS) in 1829 (see Hobbs 1988). Such changes occurred amid multiple and heightened anxieties that arguably persist to this day. As the impact of urban life on individuals and their psychology was being laid out in famous essays by Georg Simmel and Louis Wirth, policing began its enduring project of making the city legible. In the process, transgressive acts and actors became increasingly connected to specific locations and assigned (spatial) visibility. This practice emerged from a wider context in which myriad individual and social maladies became represented cartographically, perhaps most famously achieved by John Snow's early epidemiological cholera maps and Charles Booth's detailed mapping of London's poverty during the 1880s. Similar questions occupied social scientists, where landmark studies on the location of offenders (Shaw and McKay 1942) and their perceived movement through urban spaces (Brantingham and Brantingham 1981) bookended the mid-twentieth century and continue to influence today's preoccupations with digital crime mapping and predictive policing.

As urbanization developed through the nineteenth century, anxieties arose more broadly over the unknowability and threat brought about by new and growing congregations of urban citizens. Enduring fears involved sundry perceived threats against the social order, including the 'madness of crowds' popularized by Charles MacKay (1841 [1995]) and the loss of individual agency amid the 'popular mind' of the multitudes, as famously articulated by Gustave Le Bon (1895 [2018]). While such accounts have been rightly criticized for their oversimplistic, problematic, and often racialized characterizations of collective behaviour (Reicher 2001), their influence has endured. As industrialized cities expanded, so did the impulse to see them and their populations as problematic; phenomena to be mapped, managed, and made legible (Foucault 2007, 2008). Such concerns found increasing reflection in the arts. In literature, for example, it is perhaps no coincidence that, as Carrabine (2008) identifies, the mid-nineteenth century saw a rising prominence of fictional detectives bestowed with almost supernatural abilities to read the city. While Carrabine credits the intellectual genius of Edgar Allan Poe's investigative hero Auguste Dupin as typifying this trend, one could add the sequence of legendary detectives Bucket,

Porfiry, and Heat from the respective imaginaries of Dickens, Dostoevsky, and Conrad.

Generations of urban scholars have since added the central role of fear—particularly when emitted from the wealthy—as a primary shaper of the social and physical patterning of cities (inter alia, Jacobs 1961; Davis 1990, 1992; Zukin 1995; Smith 1996). These persistent concerns are reflected in the intellectual preoccupation with risk, anxiety, and fear in the sociological imagination. Among these, Pearson's (1988) genre-defining study of 'respectable fears' in England accurately located populist consternations of the 1980s within centuries-old cycles of class-based stereotypes. In a criminological descendent of Orwell's *Road to Wigan Pier*, this idea travelled through Taylor et al.'s (1996) canonical analysis of insecurities in northern England's post-industrial/post-Fordist cities.

As the millennium turned, another landmark passed, one that commemorated the majority of the world's population becoming urban dwellers (World Bank n.d.). At the same time, globalization brought the dual anxieties of transnational organized crime and international terrorism into considerations of domestic urban security. Unburdened by evidence, bellicose political and media discourse heavily linked—and still links—these concerns to the mobility of migrant populations who, despite being a feature of urban settings for millennia, became renewed objects of suspicion. Writing on the eve of 9/11, Bigo (2001) perceptively spotted this tendency, recognizing how (inter)national security concerns had infiltrated the domestic realm. International and domestic security concerns, traditionally addressed by distinct security agencies (MI5, MI6/FBI, CIA), had now become commingled, resulting in an 'everyday securitisation from the enemy within' (Bigo 2001: 112). The implication of 'homegrown' offenders in the 2004 Madrid Atocha station bombings and the 7/7 attacks on London's mass transit systems the following year, continuing through the multiple atrocities in France beginning in Nantes (2014) via the Paris and Nice atrocities of 2015 and 2016, and across England's cities in 2017, placed further emphasis on the interior. One meaningful consequence has been the way everyday policing discourse, and justifications for its methods, now routinely incorporate the language and practice of national security. As explored in this and later chapters, decades after 9/11, this has become a common justification for FRT yet was arguably less conspicuous during the wider spread of camera surveillance through the UK during the 1990s.

1.2.1 Pluralizing Control

Typified by the first major crime-related intervention by the Blair government, the 1998 Crime and Disorder Act, this domestication of the war on terror overlapped with the pluralization of crime control responsibilities across public authorities. Under section 17 of the Act, addressing crime and disorder became a statutory duty of all public bodies. Thus, as Fussey (2013: 352) noted in his analysis of the surveillance of Muslim communities in Birmingham, this proliferation of interests left 'local contexts overpopulated with competing frames of risk, scales of control and techniques of management co-existing simultaneously in the same "space"'. Over the past three decades, this pluralization of control has become a key interest for theoretical criminologists concerned with ideas of 'risk' and 'governance'. This complex and internally antagonistic body of work is difficult to synthesize into a single paradigm. Arguably, however, many key texts loosely cohere around Foucault's major project of 'governmentality' (Foucault 1991, 2007). For Foucault, and those considering his ideas in relation to security (inter alia, Fussey 2004; Mythen and Walklate 2006; Amoore 2007; De Goede and Randalls 2009; Anderson 2010), governmentality replaces traditional top-down power configurations with devolved, dispersed, and often ambiguously formed arrangements (see Rose et al. 2006). Emphasis becomes focused not just on formal risk management processes but on the heterogenous arrangements of power that are implicated in its delivery. Indeed, this latter observation links to a further important—yet perplexingly overlooked—theme in Foucault's studies of power: that power is *productive*. Here, Foucault (1982) argues that the analysis of power, therefore, should emphasize its exercise rather than its potential location. Power is a verb rather than a noun.

This plural *and* productive character of control holds several important implications for the analysis of urban FRT deployments. Taking these in turn, in criminology it has also become common to link ideas of governmentality (and heterogenous governance more generally) with neo-liberal processes, particularly emphasizing the diversification of security, the growing privatization of social control practices, and the commercial governance of urban spaces. While some have critiqued a tendency to incorrectly synonymize 'governmentality' with 'neo-liberalism' (Collier 2009; Fussey 2013), clear value lies in examining the myriad actors implicated in the production of urban security.

Particularly important for this context of advanced AI-driven surveillance is how commercial 'platform surveillance' (Murakami Wood and Monahan 2019) and other digital monitoring tools have become instrumental in elevating the role of commercial knowledge in the provision of security. Yet the novelty of this technology often invites innovative interpretations and the risk of ignoring enduring concerns. This is particularly evident in Zuboff's (2019) celebrated work on 'surveillance capitalism' that correctly emphasizes the growing power of Silicon Valley while problematically relegating the state to the point of near irrelevance. In such accounts, one behemoth (the state) becomes replaced with another ('big tech'). Needless to say, the supposed insignificance of state control may come as a surprise to those still subjected to it, particularly across huge swathes of the majority world. More accurately, state–commercial relationships are not easily partitioned into binaries or characterized by replacement of the former by the latter. Composite state–corporate arrangements have adopted a complex character and continue to evolve.

Drawing the above historical and conceptual threads together, the rise of today's advanced AI surveillance techniques such as FRT can be situated in several overlapping contexts. As urban areas grew, they brought anxieties and fears, characterized by concerns over their unknowability and the disorderly potential of their inhabitants. Key to this analysis of advanced surveillance is how such concerns become addressed. As the discussion above relays, surveillance measures are driven strategically through pervasive logics of risk management and, tactically, through an array of urban security techniques.

1.3 Physical and Digital Ordering of the City

Preoccupations with risk, post-millennium tensions over political violence, and enduring fears of unknown people and places provide important context for understanding the growth of urban surveillance. Yet, as set out in the discussion above, the complexity of such urban settings is matched by the complex ensembles of security agencies. This pluralization of control has also brought a diversification of priorities into the management of cities. The outcome can leave individuals subjected to multiple (and potentially competing) forms of regulation in the same space at the same time, a phenomenon variously described through theoretical lenses of 'perioptical' (Lianos 2012) or 'topological' (Fussey 2013) control. Amid this complexity, however, are several discernible themes. Among these, current ambitions to read the city through digital means, such as through FRT, can be located in relation to these more enduring attempts to physically order urban space.

1.3.1 Reordering the Physical and Social Landscape

Attempts to modify the fabric of the city to enhance security and surveillance have been constant features of human societies since antiquity (Sennett 1990). These approaches have taken a range of forms, many of which have been less than subtle. For example, the twenty-first century has seen a continued programme of displacing 'problematic' urban populations through financial, legal, and physical means. Relentless property speculation-led gentrification—often reselling the very symbols of urban 'edginess' to those craving the emblems but eschewing the reality of deprived urbanism (Hatherley 2010)—has been a principal driver. Such processes have been routinely companioned with the introduction of powerful surveillance tools, ostensibly to soothe the arriviste anxieties of these new, wealthier inhabitants (Fussey et al. 2012). Less subtle still was the reimagining of Paris's Haussmannized 'slum' clearances of the 1840s to bring new 'order' to urban spaces. These *tabula rasa* approaches to ordering the city persist today and take many forms. One echoes the St Louis Pruitt-Igoe 'death of modernity' moment (Jencks 1977), where progressive visions of the city, a commitment to social housing, and shelter for those seeking asylum become swept away under market-driven urban 'redevelopment'. Here, dangerously imagined urban spaces become remade in the image of neo-liberalism. Such extreme examples are particularly evident in the urban redevelopment of eastern neighbourhoods in Glasgow[1] and London, respectively for the 2014 Commonwealth and 2012 Olympic Games, under

[1] This appetite for destruction perhaps reached its nadir in Glasgow where livestreamed dynamiting of the city's Red Road housing project, an estate itself the subject of an eponymous 2006 surveillance-themed film, was originally slated as a centrepiece of the 2014 Commonwealth Games opening ceremony. This one act serves as a particularly powerful symbol of the consummation of the spectacle of 'celebration capitalism' (Boykoff 2014) with the speculation of real estate markets. This union was expressed by one Glasgow council official with a crassness as spectacular as the events it described: '[an] unforgettable statement of how Glasgow is confidently embracing the future' (The Guardian 2014). In a somewhat fitting postscript to this episode, two of the Red Road towers remained standing despite this explosion. Tempering Jencks's pessimistic prophesy here, despite attempts to decimate it, a symbol of modernity endured.

the spectacle of what Boykoff (2014) calls 'celebration capitalism'. The latter location has since become one of the sites for the most frequent urban facial recognition deployments anywhere in the world outside China.

Other ways of repatterning the social topography of the city have notably involved the displacement or ghettoization of 'problem populations' (see, inter alia, Wacquant 2007; Fassin 2013). Amid such approaches has been the recruitment of the harder edge of policing to blame and exclude the urban poor for the structural disadvantage they endure. Relevant initiatives included the ethically and empirically flawed 'broken windows' and 'zero tolerance' variants of policing. These schemes are perhaps most famously attributed to—and exemplified by—William Bratton and Rudolph Giuliani. Bratton and Giuliani also had the enormous fortune of implementing these practices in New York City, at a time with crime already on a precipitous decline following the explosion and then maturation of the city's early 1990s crack market (see, inter alia, Bowling 1999). These tactics, accurately described by Smith (1998) as 'revanchist' in their vindictiveness, did much to burnish the personal fortunes and unexamined reputations of macho 'law and order' proponents, yet brought significantly less in the way of enduring outcomes for social and criminal justice.

Taken together, and to repurpose Herbert Marcuse's (1964) legendary maxim, such examples highlight an iron fist of coercive practices concealed within the velvet glove of urban transformation. Taking a longer view, surveillance and other control strategies have become so integral to urban development that for centuries narratives of the latter have been articulated with vocabularies of the former.

This physical and digital enclaving of wealthy neighbourhoods against the urban realities into which they are placed has become a global phenomenon. Designed to reinforce economic inequalities across the US (Davis 1990) and majority world (Kaker 2014; Sumich 2023), such techniques were described by Davis (1992) as a form of constant low-intensity warfare against the urban poor. These approaches reinforced inequalities of security in areas of higher-intensity lethal conflict too, as documented in Baghdad's 'Green Zone' (Chandrasekaran 2007), Beirut (Fussey 2007), and Palestine (Weizman 2017). Some scholars saw this as the arrival of 'passage-point urbanism' where movement is heavily restricted by one's entitlement to pass physical and digital checkpoints (Graham 2010). While this enclaving of habitation, retail, commerce, and mobility is an unquestionable urban reality for many, in global cities such as London—the subject of this analysis—other urban segregation practices take more subtle and complex forms. Here, spaces are not exclusively ordered along simple binaries of entitlement and disqualification. Less obvious modulations of urban movements are also at play. Processes of filtration work to identify and siphon away those considered dangerous or undesirable. It is amid these subtler urban ordering practices that public facial recognition surveillance may be located; a shift from traditional assertions of territorial control to the separation of 'desirable' from 'undesirable' circulations, as Foucault (2007) put it.

Amid heightened anxieties over terrorism, the reshaping of London included the strategic placement of reinforced street furniture and public sculpture to impede vehicle-borne explosive attacks and the rerouting of traffic away from glass buildings for the same ends. As Coaffee's (2009) detailed analysis documents, the securitization of London's financial district after sequential Provisional IRA attacks during the early 1990s was anchored in advanced surveillance techniques and symbiotic in relationship to any manifestation of physical security. This included the metropolitan application of military surveillance, including London's hosting of the world's first civilian use of automatic number plate recognition (ANPR) surveillance technology. This application—one that has since spread across mundane applications, including traffic enforcement and car park management[2]—at once typifies two connected surveillance trends. First is the narrowing difference between military and civilian surveillance technologies (see Haggerty and Gazso 2005), exemplified in 2024 by Israel's adaptation of Google's commercially available AI-driven image search products to conduct facial recognition surveillance in Gaza and identify, arrest, and imprison hundreds of Palestinians (The New York Times 2024; see also Amnesty International 2023). Second, and relatedly, is how such military–civilian adaptations nuance longstanding conceptual notions of 'surveillance creep' (Marx 1989). Here, many advanced surveillance technologies no longer simply creep from one function to another. This dynamic is particularly relevant to the application of FRT. FRT mostly comprises a software (rather than hardware) that can be repurposed, reconfigured, and reapplied with ease and, image quality permitting, has equal application in new *and* existing surveillance architectures, on van-mounted cameras, body-worn video, drones, and social media screen grabs. Interoperability and adaptability are thus embedded from the design

[2] Such is the scale of ANPR surveillance that the then Biometrics and Surveillance Camera Commissioner estimates that by the end of 2023 more than 1 billion daily vehicle matches will be made in England and Wales (personal communication, June 2022).

stages. From conception, such technologies are not intended for fidelity to one function. They are inherently promiscuous.

1.3.2 Digitally Ordering the City

While these forms of advanced surveillance hold deep historical antecedents, the digital era has brought something new in terms of its nature, scope, and reach. Collectively, the abundancy of data and the visibility of digital footprints have dramatically enhanced police surveillance capabilities. The recent proliferation of digital information—or a 'data revolution' (Kitchin 2014)—has been further accelerated by recognition of the commercial value of data ('information capitalism'—Thrift 2005) and Silicon Valley's resultant efforts to extract and monetize increasing fine-grained detail from consumers of digital products ('surveillance capitalism'—Zuboff 2019). By necessity, individuals' reliance on data-dependent products for basic social and economic activity has created unparalleled opportunities for digital scrutiny. These in turn have significantly elevated opportunities for police surveillance and influenced the growth of cutting-edge surveillance tools (as famously revealed by Edward Snowden over a decade ago).

Amid these developments has been a growth in police uses of advanced technology which, concomitantly, attracted growing academic attention. Human geography's 'digital turn' of the early 2000s brought notable theoretical and empirical nuance to this enquiry. Much of this work has emphasized the role of technology in categorizing objects, subjects, and spaces. These include Graham's (2005) influential concept of 'software sorted geographies' which highlights the merger of the digital and geographical to shore up social and physical urban boundaries. Prominent variations on this theme include Lyon's (2003a) notion of 'social sorting' surveillance. Now instituted into the vernacular of surveillance studies, and itself an adaptation of Calhoun's (1998) earlier argument, social sorting refers to the data-driven processes of categorizing individuals due to their digital traces. For Lyon and others, these categories in turn enable or restrict access to health, welfare, and a range of life opportunities. Such data thus forms a foundation from which decisions are made, decisions that hold significant consequences and regularly turn on antagonistic binaries: they allow or restrict movement, render objects affordable or unobtainable, and confer benefits or restrict access to them. In the case of FRT, it denotes whether the police will attempt to intercept someone or not. The ubiquity of these practices—to the extent that such categorizing processes now shape and enable the transactions of everyday life—is no longer remarkable. Yet their effects are not diminished by our habituation.

Burrows and Gane's (2006) concept of 'code-space' extends these ideas by analysing both the 'social character' of software-categorized spaces and, crucially, their impact on individuals who become classified by such technology. Attention is paid to how individuals internalize such classifications and the consequences for the formation of subjective identities. Also of note to considerations of how FRT is used to denote suspicion is Burrows and Gane's (2006: 808) prescient emphasis on non-state (corporate) 'social *ascriptions* of identity'. Despite often being subjective and hidden, the impacts of surveillance and digital classification are therefore profound. As Norris and Armstrong (1999) argued in their landmark study of CCTV operators, the acts of monitoring and classification themselves communicate profound social message. This body of scholarship thus highlights both the inherent lack of neutrality in digital categorization processes and the significance of their impacts. Also notable is the way digital innovation continues to turn on the classification of subjects. As explored throughout this book, this principle is inherent in the operation of live facial recognition (LFR) technology, as these tools assign suspicion to individuals as they circulate through urban spaces.

This work also reminds us of the subtle and complex ways technology becomes recruited to classify, order, and securitize spaces and populations. Advanced technology opens possibilities for new forms of categorization and offers finer detail and dynamism to these endeavours. Innovative computational processes, particularly those driven by artificial intelligence and other forms of machine learning, allow for vast numbers of variables to become (re)assessed with increasing rapidity. Previously hidden relationships and associations between variables become surfaced, enabling classifications of risk, uncertainty, and danger to become reassessed anew. As Amoore (2014: 17) argues in a pointed critique of the more rigid classifications posited by many conceptualizations of 'software sorted geography', 'the norm is hyper-mobile'. Resonating more with ideas such as Gilles Deleuze's (1995) vision of control as a form of 'modulation', or Henri Lefebvre's (2004) attention to the calibrations of urban 'rhythms', AI-driven decision-making enables a shift from a more static world of binary classifications to something more agile. These technologies also allow the act of classification and removal of objects and subjects designated as 'harmful' without the blunt instrument of territorial control. Such unwanted phenomena are filtered as urban processes play out. As argued in the rest of this chapter, these two digitally enabled advancements—the hypermobility of the norm and the ability to delineate undesirable artefacts without asserting territorial dominance or disturbing the flow of urban processes—are important components of how FRT functions in contemporary cities.

1.3.3 Overt Urban Surveillance

The most recognizable and commented-on forms of urban surveillance are the open street surveillance cameras which have proliferated across urban spaces since the late 1980s. While ostensibly introduced as a crime reduction measure, surveillance cameras have acquired a wide range of applications and are central to the remote digital management of cities.

The UK has been at the forefront of debates over the efficacy and ethics of public surveillance technology. Indeed, since the 1990s it has been common to hear claims that UK citizens are more intensively surveilled than anyone else in the world (Graham et al. 1996), with Londoners subjected to observation by around 300 cameras a day (Norris and Armstrong 1999). Today, however, the range of different surveillance systems and their positioning across domestic, commercial, and public spaces has removed the possibility of any accurate census of camera coverage. As such, commonly articulated tropes such as 'British citizens most surveilled in the world'—regularly appended with lazy stereotypes of a nation populated by over-compliant, slumbering conformists and a startling ignorance of the political realities of life in, say, authoritarian Xingjian—probably should be given the credence they deserve.[3] Nevertheless, it is also true that public authorities in the UK

[3] Much of the hype over the UK's supposed 'surveillance capital of the world' status originates from a single source. In 2004 the media picked up a statistic published in a European Commission-funded piece of research claiming that UK citizens are observed by 4.2 million cameras (UrbanEye 2004). This statistic was derived from researchers walking along a London high street and counting the number of cameras in each 'institution'. This number was then multiplied by the number of registered businesses in London (on the precarious assumption they all possess premises with surveillance cameras). A ratio of cameras to Londoners was formulated and then extrapolated to the entire (urban and rural) UK population. Without detailed explanation, other numbers were added on the basis that surveillance cameras in schools, hospitals, and other public institutions would not be represented in this original statistic, and a figure of 4.2 million was arrived at. Putting it somewhat mildly, the authors later described this statistic as a 'guesstimate' (Norris and McCahill 2006: 102). These evident statistical shortcomings have not stopped this figure being widely reported as 'fact'.

were enthusiastic and early adopters of overt urban surveillance (see, inter alia, Norris and McCahill 2006).

The precipitous expansion of urban camera surveillance during the 1990s and 2000s was driven by many factors. Chief among these were the political capital to be gained from law and order politics; assumed public support; faith in their effectiveness; the alignment of surveillance cameras with established 'administrative criminological' practices of capable guardianship; generous government capital funding; and the visible symbolism of cameras to show that authorities were 'doing something about crime' (Fussey 2007).

In an argument routinely applied across most technological forms of social control, part of the further appeal of surveillance cameras for public authorities was the ability to offer non-falsifiable arguments over utility: if crime drops, it is because cameras are effective deterrence measures; if crime increases, it is because they detect more crime. Yet, like other populist forms of crime control (harsher sentencing, increased visible policing, etc.; see Reiner 2007), an inability to evidence this impact undermines this argument. Indeed, at the height of UK camera surveillance expansion during the early 2000s, the Home Office commissioned two major studies to evaluate their effectiveness in reducing crime. The first, a meta-analysis of existing studies, concluded that for every study claiming the efficacy of street-based surveillance cameras, another study exists establishing inconclusive or negative effect (Welsh and Farrington 2002). The second study pointed to an indeterminate impact on crime and challenged claims that surveillance cameras reduced 'fear of crime' (Gill and Spriggs 2005). Indeed, a contrary argument is that excessive surveillance architecture may exacerbate urban fears through the heavy symbolism of 'fortress' aesthetics (Davis 1990; Christopherson 1994) and visible, hostile, 'architectures of enmity' (Amoore 2009). This lack of an appropriate evidence base underpinning the deployment of surveillance persists with respect to claims made over FRT, and forms a central theme of this analysis.

The ubiquity of surveillance cameras, and their routine incorporation with other security measures, means it is now probably impossible to quantify their precise contribution to public safety. More relevant with respect to FRT, and police uses of technology more generally, however, is the way surveillance cameras became deployed with great alacrity without knowledge of their potential capabilities or harms. Added to this is an unevidenced discourse of technological determinism that 'common sense' dictates how surveillance measures will inevitably reduce crime, a hubris that quietly ebbs as the reality of modest performance emerges. The performative and symbolic drivers of surveillance expansion, and the habit of deployment in the absence of appraised capabilities, are evident across other areas of digital policing and resonates strongly with the development of facial recognition surveillance in the UK. As the ethnographic data shows, this dynamic is present in the accelerated deployment of FRT in London without a meaningful evidence base indicating why FRT is needed, all coupled with hyperbolic claims heralding a 'transformation' in policing (The Guardian 2023c).

During the late 1990s and early 2000s, a substantial academic literature emerged to consider the speed and impact of urban surveillance camera deployments (see, inter alia, Webster 2004). Although large and diverse, scholarship on surveillance cameras tends to cohere around four prominent themes: efficacy; social justice, fairness, and rights; ethnographic studies of operational practice; and theoretical accounts.

Taking these in turn, key landmarks in surveillance camera evaluations are highlighted above. Added to these are more focused studies of camera effectiveness in addressing more routine forms of crime including bus vandalism (Poyner 1992), car parks (Tilley 1993), and in urban centres (inter alia, Brown 1995). One of the earliest published evaluations was Musheno et al.'s (1978) examination of camera surveillance and fear of crime in New York City which failed to identify any positive impact of the cameras in this regard. A companion literature also emerged to question the epistemological and methodological foundations of published evaluative research, variously critiquing the limited temporal scope of studies (Tilley 1993; Short and Ditton 1995); failure to account for crime displacement (Fyfe and Bannister 1996; Skinns 1998); and the use of leading questions in acceptability studies (Ditton 1998).

Other research has emphasized the social costs arising from far-reaching surveillance camera deployment. Across the European Union, and including societies with living memory of authoritarianism, public opposition to surveillance camera deployment was identified in Denmark (Wiecek and Sætnan 2002), Belgium (Information Commissioner's Office 2006), Germany (Töpfer 2006), France (Germain 2007), and Poland (Waszkiewicz 2007), among others. Other work stressed the ways surveillance cameras operated to reinforce inequality. Writing a quarter of a century ago, Fiske (1998: 85) highlighted enduring concerns of current racial justice campaigning, when identifying how, in the US, surveillance cameras became implicated in massive 'over-surveillance' of Black men and the racist ways 'information' is translated into 'knowledge' (or 'intelligence').

Using quantitative observations to examine the targeting preferences of surveillance camera operators, Norris and Armstrong's (1999) classic study revealed how cameras were disproportionately trained on young Black males in the UK. The same study also revealed the voyeuristic use of cameras to observe and objectify female citizens. Browne's (2015) research further highlights the intersectionality of surveillance-driven disadvantage by emphasizing the racialized and gendered gaze. Despite such work, and the fact that the gendered gaze is a prominent concern in parallel fields such as analyses of visual culture (Mulvey 1975), gender remains an underused lens through which to view surveillance impacts. In the small field of gender-specific analyses, Brown's (1998) work serves as a rare feminist analysis of surveillance cameras, while Bailey and Steeves's (2015) research is widely considered a touchstone of gender-focused literature in the wider surveillance studies canon.

Studies of surveillance-driven inequality have mostly focused on class and other forms of socio-economic disadvantage. Many commentaries have emphasized how surveillance cameras were introduced as part of large-scale urban redevelopment by making them more attractive for retail consumption and real estate investment. Work in this field largely focuses on how surveillance infrastructure operates to exclude homeless people, groups of youths and individuals drinking in public, other non-consumers (see, inter alia, Davis 1990, 1998; Bannister et al. 1998; Coleman and Sim 1998, 2000; Norris and Armstrong 1999; McCahill 2002; Fyfe 2004), or 'flawed consumers' (Bauman 1998).

Others have pointed to the use of surveillance as a core component of the hard-edge security companioning the gentrification of urban spaces and the promotion of investor-friendly visions of social order. This includes attempts at urban branding amid contrived 'culture-led' (Palolen 2011) or 'celebratory capitalism' forms of gentrification (Boykoff and Fussey 2014). Others have similarly emphasized the role of surveillance as a means of inviting wealthier inhabitants into gentrifying neighbourhoods previously associated with 'dangerousness' (Raco 2003; Coaffee 2005; Atkinson and Helms 2007; Fussey et al. 2012). Relatedly, Coleman (2004) reported on how surveillance cameras were integral to Liverpool's urban renaissance ahead of the city's designation as European Capital of Culture in 2008. Here, municipal laws were adapted to optimize surveillance practices and ban certain (youth-orientated) headgear, a process that simultaneously facilitated the surveillance of people's faces while prohibiting expressions of youth culture. Such studies demonstrate how surveillance-backed 'regeneration' consistently privileges high-income groups. These processes have been memorably, and caustically, described by Zukin (1995) as 'domestication by cappuccino culture', whereby diversity 'has been supplanted by a purified and suburbanite sense of public space' (Atkinson 2003: 1841) and, to extend the metaphor, spaces became invested with blandness and whiteness.

Several ethnographic studies have sought to understand the operational uses of surveillance cameras and variously assess how the potential of technological surveillance becomes realized in practice, their impact on individuals, and the unintended consequences of their deployment. Perhaps most important for this study of facial recognition is the way these earlier studies reveal an important contrast between a supposed neutrality of technology and the subjectivities that shape its operation. Norris and Armstrong's (1999) ethnography of surveillance camera operators is the most recognized contribution to this field and evidences the reproduction of racial bias through the targeting activities of camera operators. Adopting a similar conceptual and empirical approach, McCahill's (2002) ethnography of camera operators demonstrated how visceral, affective, and emotional properties including boredom, distaste, and other bigotry shape surveillance practices. Goold's (2004) work showed how individual and organizational differences result in dramatically varied practices despite the use of similar surveillance infrastructure in Britain. Similarly, Smith's empirical study revealed surveillance to be 'an ambiguous pursuit: as much about managing external disturbances on the street as managing internal discomposure within the self' (2015: 4).

Detailed ethnographic analyses such as those discussed above allow us to apprehend unanticipated issues that arise from surveillance practices and serve to shape the scope of surveillance. Such contributions are important not least because they challenge the technological determinism that populates much discourse on police technology and assumes the potential of technology automatically becomes realized on deployment. Moreover, as discussed in what follows, such detailed qualitative attention to the sociotechnical environments into which surveillance technologies are deployed is crucial to understanding their form and impact.

1.4 The Growth, Practice, and Theory of Facial Recognition Surveillance

While the expansion of open street camera surveillance in the UK was swift, highly visible, and much commented on, less obvious were the initial public experiments with FRT occurring around the same time. While their developmental trajectories differed, the expansion of surveillance cameras is, in many ways, proleptic to the growth of public FRT. This is particularly apparent at the current moment, at the cusp of mass adoption. The widespread adoption of surveillance cameras throughout the 1990s and early 2000s established certain conditions of possibility that enabled today's accelerating FRT deployments. For example, the speed and scale of street-based camera expansion brought a habituation to surveillance technology that, in turn, arguably conferred FRT with a political and public palatability barely imaginable as recently as twenty-five years ago. The development of an extensive surveillance camera network also created the infrastructure to which live facial recognition *can* be adapted and to which retrospective facial recognition (RFR) *is* now routinely being applied. As argued above, these public cameras elevated the role of visual surveillance—and recourse to surveillance camera footage—across security, social control, investigatory, and criminal justice practices. The growth of FRT also shares historical antecedents in the longer project of rendering visible the city, its disorder, and its supposed maladies. Yet perhaps the most significant driver of FRT expansion would have been difficult to predict, even at the time cameras were first installed on London's streets. This is the conjunction of ubiquitous social media platform use and step changes in AI-driven image analysis.

However, in acknowledging the almost symbiotic relationship between FRT and surveillance cameras, it is important not to lose sight of the radical changes brought about by this newer technology. FRT holds significantly more advanced, and more intrusive, surveillance capability. While facial recognition advocates are keen to draw parallels between LFR and human and analogue forms of street-based surveillance (House of Commons 2019)—thereby softening the vocabulary of surveillance intrusiveness—crucial differences in form, scope, and impact exist. This book charts these differences, the specific potencies of FRT, and their impact on human rights and social justice in detail.

Underpinning these differences lies something more fundamental. This concerns the significance of the face as a marker of our identity. The face also constitutes the public iteration of our selves. FRT does not just differ from other forms of surveillance but also other forms of biometric identification. This point is reflected in Gates's (2011) important contribution to the field, where she sets FRT apart from other forms of biometric monitoring due to the intimate and cultural meaning of our faces. The European Court of Human Rights (ECtHR) has echoed this sentiment, referring to the face as 'one of the key attributes of a person's personality'.[4] Such observations point to the fundamental personal and social value held by 'the face'. It is paradoxical: on the one hand, it is a unique yet intimate part of our identity; on the other, it acts as our main public representation of self. These observations also stand on a solid philosophical grounding. Perhaps most notable is the resonance with Levinas's (1985) assessment of the unique significance of 'the face' as something that 'orders and ordains' our selves and our relationships.

Also reflecting on how the social meanings of the face connect with surveillance activities, Andrejevic and Selwyn (2022) perceptively note how FRT allows 'issues of identification [to] slip into social judgement', an act that 'mimics aspects of sociality'. This digital mimesis of social function also points to an anthropomorphism apparent across many narratives of FRT. Here, much like the Victorian-era fictional detectives, FRT is bestowed with human-like attributes, differing only in their enhancement.

Any audit of the emergence of FRT requires a note of caution. Understanding the historical development of such an eye-catching and highly politicized security technology is fraught with difficulties. Reliable information is difficult to source and many accounts arise from unverified journalistic, commercial, or grey literature. Such afflictions are present on all sides of the debate. For example, and as documented in what follows, evangelists regularly make unevidenced claims over the huge security gains that would inevitably follow FRT deployments. Dystopian accounts also commonly rely on varied standards of evidence. Moreover, aside from narrowly conceived technical evaluations, empirical studies of FRT deployments are almost entirely absent. Nevertheless, the following draws on available information plus published academic commentary and government evaluations to trace the development of FRT in public places.

1.4.1 Origins

For a technology that is widely considered to be at the cutting edge of law enforcement, FRT has a surprisingly long history. Gates (2011) identifies the 1970 World's Fair in Osaka as a key moment in the public introduction of this technology. Here, Japanese technology company NEC—the supplier

[4] *Glukhin* v *Russia*, Judgment, ECtHR, App. No. 11519/20, 4 July 2023, para. 66.

of the technology later used by the London MPS and South Wales Police in the first major public deployments of LFR—showcased an early version of this technology. This early iteration of FRT performed poorly. As Fussey et al. (2021: 328) note, 'the technology had greater success in capturing the public's imagination than their faces'. Irrespective of these failings, such public experimentation can be seen to perform another role. Drawing on Langdon Winner's critique of World's Fairs as a mechanism to present experimental technology as a *fait accompli*, investing it with a sense of permanence and legitimacy, Gates (2011: 25–26) considered how in

> promoting a model of closed, corporate-sponsored research and development of which ordinary people need only be in awe . . . [i]t is no stretch to say that the NEC Computer Physiognomy attraction conveyed this implicit message. One can imagine that in 1970, the experience of having a computer scan and analyze one's face might have impressed on the sitter a powerful sense of her own future subjugation to information processing machines.

This prescient observation recognizes dual process at play. One sets a path for technical refinement with clear lines traceable to today's police FRT experiments. The other confers a sense of materiality, durability, and inevitability to fledgling technology. This sense of inevitability, and technologically deterministic suggestions of inherent legitimacy, is evident throughout today's discourse on FRT. Despite such initial bombast, however, little discernible happened in the decades immediately following the World's Fair.

Information on FRT deployments in the UK is patchy to say the least. In a polemical monograph, Davies (1996) claimed that a rudimentary form of FRT was piloted at Manchester City Football Club's former Maine Road stadium during the mid-1990s. In a foreshadowing of technical difficulties that continue to plague the operational uses of the technology decades later, Davies argued that problems in processing large uncompressed files severely limited computer processing capability and led to officers manually overriding the system by physically matching photographs to surveillance camera feeds. Common to FRT-related policing experiences of today, the security promises of a much-hyped technology are contrasted by the operational realities of modest technological performance, limited policing 'success', and significant levels of hidden human work. Such concealed labour-behind-the-lens resonates with analyses of other AI systems that seemingly offer system efficiencies yet are predicated on enormous human toil (Taylor 2018; Murgia 2023) and, as later chapters show, is essential to today's use of FRT in policing.

1.4.2 Capital Experiments

As with other forms of advanced video surveillance—such as surveillance cameras, ANPR, and advanced video analytics[5] for transport hubs—early public experiments with facial recognition were trialled on the citizens of London, particularly those residing in the east of the city. Writing over a decade ago, Fussey et al. (2011) highlighted how the east London borough of Newham became the site for one of the first open street deployments of FRT in the country. Public communication was minimal, although the positioning of public signs (see Figure 1.1) indicated that the technology was deployed in the centre of Stratford and thus situated only metres away from the site of numerous subsequent Metropolitan Police LFR operations, including two of those empirically analysed in Chapters 7 and 8.

Figure 1.1 'Criminals Beware Smart CCTV in Operation' sign placed during the UK's first public FRT experiments. Stratford High Street, Newham, London. Photograph by Pete Fussey, 2002.

[5] 'Video analytics' refers to software tools that analyse video feeds. Many forms and functions exist but examples include the use of computers to issue alerts for unattended baggage, loitering individuals, or crowd densities, or to automatically track items or people as they move, such as digitally 'tagging' a logo on a sweater so its wearer can be followed.

The introduction of FRT and other advanced forms of video surveillance in this location (NIJ 2003) is connected to successive programmes of urban redevelopment in this once-maligned part of London. This began with the 'Stratford City Challenge' regeneration and transport infrastructure scheme and culminated in the development of the 2012 Olympic site. According to journalistic sources and claims made by those managing the cameras at the time, Newham's FRT capability was provided by 'visual electronics company' Visionic's FaceIT scheme. Ostensibly deployed to tackle a range of crimes and threats of political violence from Irish Republican groups, proponents attributed many successes to FRT. For example, Newham's CCTV manager at the time (a council employee) claimed in a 2003 media interview that a three-hour deployment at a local Underground station identified twelve 'targeted individuals' ahead of a football match between West Ham United and Leeds United. A spokesperson from Visionics also told *The Guardian* (2002) that the system was responsible for 'referring' ninety-three faces to the police on a single day in August 2001. Echoing later claims made in the police FRT policy framework between 2018 and 2024 (see Chapter 5), he further stated that 'humans alone could not easily have accomplished such a massive task' (NIJ 2003: 20). Visionics also offered the unevidenced claim that their technology had led to a 40 per cent reduction in crime across the borough (Milone 2001). Dismantling such flimsy evangelism is not difficult. Crime did not decrease by 40 per cent over that period and no evaluation research exists to support any claim of FRT effectiveness (see also Langstone 2009 for commentary on how FRT is regularly conflated with other technologies to claim effectiveness).

Consistent across these accounts is the absence of any detail on how these 'identifications' were resolved and on the veracity of matches. For example, were the 'referrals' true positives, resulting in arrests indicative of an effective system? If so, why is this important detail unsaid? In this context, 'referrals' could equally be false positives, indicating that the system performed badly, with up to ninety-three people wrongly stopped by the police. If these industry claims were true, the technology would have performed significantly better than the systems deployed by the Metropolitan Police decades later, systems that have benefitted from decades of AI-driven innovation. Moreover, unnecessary citations of operational secrecy are often a red flag when conveniently used to avoid evaluative scrutiny. More problematic for Visionics is that their claims were also contradicted by local senior police officers who stated they were unaware of a single successful identification (*The Guardian* (2002). That FRT was not reintroduced into Newham until 2018 indicates its initial technical performance was more modest than these industry and local council claims suggest.

Of longer-term significance is the way language was used to justify FRT and to infer, rather than evidence, effectiveness. Such rhetorical devices have endured and remain commonplace in the heated discourse surrounding this technology. Indeed, a significant critique presented in Chapter 5 is that UK police forces have failed to provide any evidence supporting the claimed utility, or effectiveness, of current LFR deployments. Instead, justification is based either on unevidenced claims or hyperbolic public statements, such as this in 2020 by the then MPS commissioner:

> In an age of Twitter and Instagram and Facebook, concern about my image and that of my fellow law-abiding citizens passing through LFR and not being stored, feels much, much, much smaller than my and the public's vital expectation to be kept safe from a knife through the chest. (Reported in *The Guardian* 2020)

Such refrains are common. Yet their frequency does not translate into accuracy. The logical fallacy of technological determinism is matched by an imagined causal link between surveillance and gruesome victimization. Little place exists for human rights in such discourse, at least outside of the legally illiterate 'what about the human rights of victims?' narrative.

From a human rights perspective, of particular importance here is the contrast between the vagueness and inexactitude of language used to justify FRT use and the precision needed to hold it to account. The degree to which this vagueness is intentional is open to question. However, as later chapters show, such ambiguity serves a range of strategic purposes and, crucially, inhibits the application of human rights law constraints. Particularly concerning here is how, in the absence of evidence supporting the claimed utility of a FRT deployment, meaningfully evaluating the potential human rights harm linked to that deployment is virtually impossible (see Chapter 4).

Around the same time as the initial Newham deployments, public deployments of FRT were also taking place in Florida. In another linkage between major sporting events and experiments with emerging surveillance technology, FRT was deployed in January 2001 during the XXXV Super Bowl at the Raymond James Stadium in Tampa. In a prelude to many current uses, FRT was used here to scan the faces of spectators as they accessed stadium turnstiles. According to the *Los Angeles Times* (2001), nineteen individuals were flagged from a crowd of over 100,000 spectators. However, like London, such claims were also based on the hardly impartial statements of industry representatives. Also echoing the exaggerated claims of FRT performance heard in London, a Freedom of Information request by the ACLU (2002) revealed that many of these alerts were false positives and, among the 'true positive' matches, none had committed an offence more serious than ticket touting. These outcomes not only challenge the overall efficacy of these FRT applications, they also question whether the deployments could be considered 'necessary' from a human rights law perspective. The same year and same city also saw FRT deployed in Ybor City, the ethnically diverse hub of Tampa's night-time economy. Notable is how, despite the fervent claims of its supporters, both experiments were short-lived. The Ybor City experiment, for example, failed to identify a single individual on its watchlist, leading to the technology being abandoned within three months (ACLU 2002). However, the ephemerality of turn-of-the-century FRT uses was dramatically recontextualized by the magnitude of what was to follow.

The fallout from the Al-Qaeda attacks on New York and the Pentagon on 11 September 2001 dramatically changed the climate of urban security. An intensified atmosphere of surveillance (Lyon 2003b) was accompanied by a technologically solutionist narrative which held that future atrocity could be averted through investment in ever-more advanced security technology. As Gates (2006) identified, a common claim across corporate and political discourses of the time was that 9/11 could have been prevented *if only* FRT had been deployed at Washington Dulles and Boston Logan airports. Leaving aside the most obvious shortcoming of this argument—that many of the hijackers' identities were already known, it was their intentions that were not—the fact that subsequent public deployments of FRT took so long to emerge is highly significant. Such delays are indicative of an overhyped technology that, once installed, had underdelivered. That FRT was not deployed during the Olympic Games held in the US just a few months after 9/11—noting the tendency for sporting megaevents to serve as testing grounds for urban surveillance technology (Fussey et al. 2012)—reaffirms this point. Despite the loud evangelical claims of FRT performance in both London and Florida, actions, it would seem, speak louder than words.

While the decade following 9/11 saw continued shortcomings in the digital architecture of FRT (Introna and Wood 2004; Fussey 2010), interest in video analytics grew apace. Two events can be identified as particularly significant for the UK context: the terrorist attacks of 2005 and the riots of 2011. Both originated in London, the empirical site of analysis for this book.

The 2005 7/7 terrorist attacks on the capital's mass transit systems revealed many deficiencies in the city's urban resilience. Among these, the interoperability of integration of emergency planning and the digital and telecommunications infrastructure it relied on were particularly exposed (HM Coroner 2011). Related to this was an acute awareness within the MPS of the limited (human) capacity to collect and process surveillance camera footage during the investigation into the bombings (interview with former Association of Chief Police Officers (ACPO) lead for CCTV, 2011). Indeed, to take an example from just one of London's thirty-two boroughs, Hackney, on the day of the bombings the Metropolitan Police's Anti-Terrorism Branch (SO15) requested all public surveillance camera footage from that area for the hours between midnight and 1 pm. According to Hackney's deputy CCTV manager of the time, 'this translated into 22 015 hours of footage, equivalent to around 56 000 CDs of data' (interviewed June 2007). Such deluges of visual data generated significant problems in the form of what was then characterized in intelligence communities as 'haystacking'—the sheer volume of data ('hay') made finding the needle a virtual impossibility. Such realizations stimulated heightened attention to, and investment in, automated 'video analytics', the digital processing of images to identify subjects and objects—the needle in the haystack—beyond the scale of human capacity. It is against this context that digital tools capable of analysing enormous quantities of image and text data can be seen as providing a solution.[6]

[6] The authors explored this issue in a research interview with then UK independent reviewer of terrorism legislation, Lord Anderson. Following the 2013 Snowden revelations, Anderson was commissioned to conduct the most detailed investigation in history into MI5, MI6, and GCHQ surveillance practices and intelligence-handling procedures, and given unprecedented access to do so (Anderson 2015). Anderson confirmed this trajectory of digital analysis and, interestingly, argued that such advances in data analytics had largely addressed the 'haystacking' issue:

> What people sometimes say is, you are not going to make it any easier by adding hay to the haystack. I spoke to a lot of intelligence and ex-intelligence people . . .

1.4.2.1 Human and digital recognition

While unknown at the time, the 2011 urban riots that began in north London and spread to several other English cities mark an important juncture in the development of FRT in the UK. Over three days in August the riots played out before both the world's media and the capital's extensive surveillance camera network, while witness or participant footage was continuously replayed on social media platforms. Like the investigations following the 7 July bombings, tackling the enormous quantities of video footage became a primary investigatory challenge. Unlike the investigations into the 2005 terrorist attacks, however, the abundance of surveillance camera data provided an opportunity. In response, a different type of facial recognition practice gained prominence where, in the absence of viable digital FRT, the problems of tackling copious data were overcome by attempts to use human resources more effectively.

'Operation Withern', the MPS operation to prosecute those involved in the civil disturbances, became innovative for both its use of diverse visual media to track individuals and its use of what seemed a novel approach to identifying suspects in crowds. The operation led to over 4,000 arrests of those suspected of involvement in the 2011 disturbances with, according to investigating officers, 2,500 charged and an 82 per cent conviction rate (interview with MPS detective with senior Operation Withern role, 2015). Central to this activity was the development of new human surveillance processes to intended to meet the demand of analysing abundant video material.

Detectives responsible for tracking suspects implicated in the 2011 riots had requisitioned over 150,000 hours of public surveillance camera footage (interview with MPS detective with senior Operation Withern role, 2015). Added to this was that, contrasting with riots of the past, these disturbances also played out on social media. Smart telephony was on the

and I concluded that was wrong. The best way I have found of explaining it is if you think of doing a Google search, in the early days of Google and there wasn't a large amount on the internet and you might get lucky, you might not get lucky. Now everything is on the internet. If you can formulate your search appropriately, you will always find what you are looking for. Huge amounts of data do not make life more difficult for you, so long as you have intelligent ways of interrogating that data. And that is what I saw in the ways that GCHQ and MI5 have developed for interrogating that data intelligently, and therefore making good use of it. (Interviewed July 2017) cusp of mainstream adoption by 2011,[7] leading to incalculable volumes of public-generated video footage being posted on the internet. According to this same participant, this quantity of material led to a quarter of suspected rioters being identified through images posted in media reports rather than formal municipal surveillance cameras.

The other former disadvantage concerned how surveillance footage was framed. There had been a longstanding tension over different policing objectives, namely that between the need for a close-cropped image for identification purposes and a wide-angle view for situational awareness and subject tracking. As a counter-terrorism police officer relayed to Fussey (2013: 364), 'The standard policing use of CCTV is for evidential level . . . You want a close up, clear and unambiguous image. For [counter-terrorism] it's different, there's less of a requirement on clarity, more on coverage and tracking ability.' During the riots, these conflicting aims were apparent, and compounded, through what one MPS detective explained as surveillance camera operator tendencies to '(a) focus on something "exciting" but not necessarily the offending behaviour—i.e. a fire or (b) random focusing because too much is going on, there was too much imagery' (interviewed June 2012). The same participant also identified an overall tendency for operators 'to focus on close-ups in the belief it offered prospects for identification evidence, while the police actually wanted a wide angle, a big picture, to see what was happening'. Identification came at the expense of wider situational awareness. Yet, for the MPS, this renewed requirement for identifying people in a crowd provided an opportunity to develop a new approach, one with direct lineage to today's applications of digital FRT.

Faced with the challenge of isolating the 'signal' of identifiable individual suspects from the 'noise' of increasingly abundant visual data, the MPS set up a specialized unit to hone the practice of identification: the Visual Images, Identifications and Detections Office (VIIDO) unit based in Southwark, south London. While those involved in the unit have

[7] Accentuating how these events occurred at a turning point in the use of smartphone telephony, many MPS officers interviewed for this research still referred to the 'Blackberry Riots'. This was on account of perpetrators using the 'Blackberry Messenger' function to communicate, which essentially operated as a closed network between 'daisychained' devices, therefore not reliant on public networks, thus remaining beyond the scrutiny of the police. Connecting mobile devices 'off-grid', such as via Bluetooth, has become a more widespread strategy in public protests with examples ranging from the 'Sukey' app that alerted student protestors to police 'kettling' tactics in London during 2010 and the 'Firechat' app that concealed protestors' communication from Chinese state surveillance during Hong Kong's 'Umbrella Revolution' of 2014.

attested to the use of RFR to identify suspects, the technology was widely considered to have been ineffective at the time (interviewed June 2012). Nevertheless, what was significant about this development was the way identification activities became specialized and, crucially, valorized through narratives of epistemic scientific knowledge. Notable was the creation of a new role, a new identity, one attracting status and again evoking the literary imagery of the preternatural Victorian urban detectives: the 'super recognizer'.

The 'super recognizer' denotes trained police officers considered to have above-average abilities in identifying and matching individuals and facial characteristics from video footage. Since 2011, super-recognition has grown into a lucrative industry, with a designated training programme underpinned by applied psychology (inter alia, Davis et al. 2016) and self-proclaimed merits that are ventriloquized through international media reporting. In essence, super-recognition involves the selection and training of police officers perceived to have higher-level aptitudes for facial identification. Those selected and enrolled in super-recognizer programmes undergo training to test and finesse recall, image matching, and perception of facial geometry (interview with police 'super recognizer', 2018). Like many persuasive narratives, individual stories matter. According to the VIIDO lead, 3 per cent of all identifications of those implicated in the riots were made by one officer who worked in the Custody Suite of central London's Charing Cross police station (Neville 2012). It is not stated how many individuals were already known to this officer. Ranked second was Constable Gary Collins who identified 180 suspects and proclaimed somewhat immodestly in a *New York Times* profile that 'as a kid you don't know you have a gift; you just think everybody is like you' (*New York Times* 2015).

Proponents have attributed impressive-sounding claims to the work of police super recognizers. These include assertions of decisive involvement in murder convictions and the implication that super recognizers were involved in supporting the identification of those perpetrating the Cologne 2015 New Year's Eve mass sexual assault (*The Guardian* 2016). The effectiveness of super-recognition has also been asserted across different fields of policing (such as counter-terrorism—Neville 2012). It has also been monetized. The latter involves consultancies with police forces and private security firms in jurisdictions with poor human rights records including Singapore and Hong Kong (Super Recognisers n.d.; South China Morning Post 2015).

1.4.2.2 'It's bullshit': seeking Bertillon, finding Bachelard

Two important caveats temper the enthusiasm for this 'revolution in policing' (*The New Yorker* 2016). The first concerns the downstream implications of the measures. For example, much of the sentencing for those identified in the 2011 riots was both symbolic and severe. This included attempts to 'make examples' of individuals, and communicate deterrence, where sentences were double the average sanctions for similar infractions with fewer discretionary reductions for first-time offenders (Ministry of Justice 2012). Notable among such punishments is the six-month custodial sentence handed to a twenty-three-year-old electrical engineering student with no previous convictions for stealing £3.50 worth of bottled water from a Brixton supermarket. The point here is that exceptional events often catalyse and heighten surveillance infrastructures. These exceptional events also intensify the punitive climate. Those identified by the former become processed through the latter.

The second concerns issues of efficacy. When asked by Patrick Radden Keefe of *The New Yorker* about the merits of FRT, then Metropolitan Police Bronze Commander for CCTV and VIIDO lead during the investigation into riots, Detective Chief Inspector Mick Neville, replied simply: 'It's bullshit' (*The New Yorker* 2016). Although such 'human-triumphs-over-technology' narratives are compelling and attractive, and while much media and other coverage has tended towards the fawning and uncritical (inter alia, *The New Yorker* 2016), acute shortcomings afflict human 'super-recognition'. Some people inevitably possess a greater ability to recognize faces than others. Yet considerable scientific critique has been levelled at the enterprise of super-recognition as a means of codifying this ability and also at its role in the investigation and prosecution of crime. These less favourable appraisals focus on methodological, procedural, and, in both scientific and criminal justice senses, evidential grounds.

Among these, the tests for determining individuals' aptitude as 'super recognizers' have been criticized as narrow, deficient, and inaccurate. For example, several critics have noted that such tests may screen in individuals who scored highly by chance rather than by ability (Boback et al. 2016; Bate et al. 2018). Reflecting problems with other biometric techniques are issues of contamination.[8] In the case of super-recognition, such impurity

[8] Contaminated biometric evidence has been implicated in many miscarriages of justice. Perhaps most notable among these are the unsafe conviction of Sean Hoey, accused of a Real IRA bombing in Omagh, Northern Ireland, during Britain's largest mass murder trial in 2007. Evidence relied on as decisive in the original trial but later deemed unreliable concerned 'Low

appears routine and makes it difficult to discern the distinction between cause and effect. For example, Edmund and Wortley (2016: 489) ascertain how high numbers of identifications associated with the 2011 riots involved officers 'with prior personal familiarity with those identified'. The false equivalencing of police super recognizers deployed to identify suspects with expert witnesses has been tested in court several times. One crucial theme of such cases has involved the degree to which officers were 'primed' in advance, for example by receiving a suggestion of the suspect's name before viewing an image.[9] 'Confirmation' is clearly different to 'recognition'. Another issue involves the metaphorical 'upgrading' of poor-quality surveillance video when accompanied by a confident police identification, regardless of whether an officer's claims are, in fact, accurate.[10] Despite this, the courts have largely remained deferential to police opinions. Yet these instances demonstrate how the epistemic scientific vocabulary of 'super-recognition' is undermined by the subjective ontological conditions of its practice. Relatedly, the likelihood of confirmation bias may moderate some of the grander claims for super-recognizer effectiveness. As Edmund and Wortley (2016: 492) also note, '[k]nown errors by police super-recognisers and police familiars are not disclosed'.

Perhaps the most damning assessment has come from successive reports of the (then) Forensic Science Regulator who, following the collapse of a legal case in which evidence from a 'super recognizer' was demonstrably flawed, argued that the practice has no forensic or evidential merit (Forensic Science Regulator 2018: 20). Here, the regulator made a key distinction between super recognizers' 'investigative' and 'evidential' value and dismissed the validity of giving super recognizers any 'expert witness' status during court procedures.

Her argument is based on several grounds. These include the role of super recognizers in an 'operational policing unit, with no separation to ensure independence and impartiality'; inherent conflicts between the roles of investigating officer and expert witnesses; lack of safeguards against cognitive bias; and, fundamentally, that opinions of 'super-recognizers' would

Copy Number' DNA techniques that used very small numbers of human cells to compile a genetic profile yet are highly sensitive to cross-contamination. Much like controversies over expert testimony, such events provide a reminder of the fallibilities associated with some scientific epistemologies, and that excessive faith in the objectivity of scientific method can have devastating consequences.

[9] For example, *R* v *Moss* [2011] EWCA Crim 252.
[10] *R* v *Doherty* [2016] EWCA Crim 246.

fail basic evidential standards for expert evidence because it 'is not based on scientifically validated methodology, nor are error rates known' (Forensic Science Regulator 2018: 20). One could add to this list the lack of ecological validity, where claims that may hold some foundation and testing in very narrow 'lab' conditions deplete once they become deployed in wider settings. Such observations also align with US-based research testing the face-matching capabilities of law enforcement professionals and finding poor performance across all categories, including among 'super recognizers' (National Academics Press 2024).

Returning to computational facial recognition, vague and unevidenced claims were again repeated at the next publicly documented UK police use of the technology: at the 2015 'Download' rock festival attended by 90,000 festivalgoers in Leicestershire, UK. Employing now familiar evangelical, deterministic, and performative language, a police spokesperson told the BBC that 'the software provided an efficient and effective way of picking known offenders out of a crowd'. The same spokesperson also continued the tradition of neglecting to offer any evidence to justify such claims, adding that 'it is too early to give definitive crime figures' (BBC 2015).

Common across both forms of human and technological facial recognition is a discernible tendency where the further claims of effectiveness stretch, the further they become shorn of the evidence to support them. In place of meaningful evidence sits an often-bellicose discourse that is variously normative, value-laden, and interest-driven. As demonstrated throughout later chapters, these narratives are not consigned to the past events discussed above; they remain very much in evidence today. Speculative knowledge continues to be decorated with scientific discourse in an attempt to claim legitimacy, justify unproven surveillance, and close down critique. It is a practice that recalls philosopher of science Gaston Bachelard's longstanding warning to regard scientific knowledge as polemical (see Foucault 1994).

1.4.3 Inception and 'The AI Revolution' in Policing

The growth of 'super recognition' in policing exemplified an enduring ambition to isolate specific faces from the anonymity of the crowd, coupled with the recognition that significant quantities of video footage could be turned to the police's advantage. Further pursuit of this longstanding ambition has continued in the more recent phase of police FRT deployments.

Separating the tranche of policing FRT experiments in the 1990s and early 2000s from current deployments was a new technological advancement which brought a step change in the accuracy and viability of facial recognition for policing: convolutional neural networks (CNN). The initial development of CNN[11] is largely attributed to former Sorbonne computer scientist and one of the three 'godfathers of AI', Yann LeCun.[12] Its rapid expansion is credited to its adoption by internet search engines and social media platforms to drive its facial identification software (e.g. Google's reverse image searching function[13] or the Facebook feature that allowed users to 'tag' friends). In essence, CNN is a method of digital analysis that, in the context of FRT, maximizes the efficiency of computational processes to enable image processing to occur at enormous speed and with escalating complexity. Key to this activity is the triaging out of redundant content contained in an image but not required for facial analysis ('downsampling') and the layering of tasks to allow multiple processing activities to occur simultaneously. Working with smaller quantities of relevant data—where template file sizes are typically a few kilobytes (see NIST 2018) rather than the many megabytes of a standard image file—confers many benefits for facial recognition processing. Among them, this allows for higher-resolution source images to be analysed with greater efficiency. One result is that existing computer power can be leveraged to perform increasingly complex tasks. It also opens possibilities for standard consumer hardware to perform higher-order tasks. It is this architecture of supercharged CNN image processing that drove the current public proliferation of FRT.

Demonstrating how decisive the adoption of CNN was for the development of FRT, the US Department of Commerce's National Institute of Standards and Technology's (NIST's) evaluation of 127 commercially available FRT algorithms revealed that, 'between 2014 and 2018, facial recognition software got 20 times better at searching a database to find a matching photograph' (NIST 2018). As one senior NIST researcher noted, by 2018 most of the FRT industry had transitioned to deep CNN AI approaches

[11] CNNs are sometimes referred to as deep convolutional neural networks (DCNN) or 'deep neural networks'. Slightly confusingly, all are accurate descriptors. The difference is that CNNs are one of many forms of deep neural networks. For the purposes of non-specialist consideration, CNN and DCNN are largely interchangeable phrases.

[12] The other two being Yoshua Bengio and 2024 Nobel Prize winner Geoffrey Hinton.

[13] Google was key to driving the advancement of CNN through its 'Inception' product, first introduced in 2014 and now in its third iteration.

(Grother 2019). This transition was reflected in the massive adoption of FRT products by industry, across social media platforms,[14] and in online retail environments.[15] It is these innovations in image analysis and the attendant processing efficiencies that enabled FRT to become a more affordable and viable policing tool.

During this new phase of AI-driven facial recognition capability, the US Customs and Border Protection (CBP) agency became one of the first enthusiastic early adopters of the technology. In 2016 CBP started trialling FRT to verify the identifies of travellers between Atlanta and Japan. A subsequent partnership was made with Metropolitan Washington Airport Authority for a more advanced system. This used cloud-based authentication systems to boost the throughput of (trusted) passengers at borders and reduce the reliance on paper documents. FRT is now a core component of the agency's 'CBP One' app, the use of which is mandatory for those seeking asylum at the southern US border.

Despite such examples, it is important to note that policing uses of FRT tend to differ in fundamental ways. Most notable is the way border verification processes generally match footage of an individual to a 'source' image of themselves (such as their passport) as a means of *verifying* rather than *establishing* identity. The latter is a much higher-order computational task and also requires a larger database of potential matches. Accordingly, clear human rights differences exist between consenting to present a face against an image of oneself (a database of one person) to open a smartphone or cross an international border compared to being unknowingly surveilled by the police and matched against a database of several thousand 'suspects'.

It is at this point that FRT was reintroduced into UK policing. This new era can be dated to 28 August 2016 and the MPS's deployment of LFR technology at London's Notting Hill Carnival.[16] This phase of FRT deployments

[14] Facebook initially trained their CNN-driven software on 4,000 users. By 2016, and assisted by millions of volunteers helping to train the algorithms by tagging their online friends, it had become the principal software engine for the platform's facial identification features (interview with Facebook data scientist, 2020).

[15] Online retailers including Amazon use CNN image recognition to analyse online browsing activities and algorithmically suggest similar or complementary products through microtargeted advertisements (interview with Amazon data scientist, 2019). Such uses demonstrate the importance of computer vision image analysis in the algorithmic microtargeting economy.

[16] The same NEC S17 algorithm was also deployed by South Wales Police in May 2017 and was used again by the MPS at that year's Notting Hill Carnival.

marked a turning point. Prior to this, facial recognition was a niche and poorly performing technology that would only ever operate in speculative and episodic deployments, and thus never gained traction. Following the AI revolution and the groundswell of experimental adoption by state agencies, the technology reached a tipping point. From 2016 onwards, the pace of adoption accelerated and once-ephemeral deployments started to become routine. It is this decisive period of police FRT adoption that forms the empirical focus of this book. Many deployments around this time were conducted with a technological evangelism. A desire to extend FRT use was accompanied by a belief that any poor performance was temporary, and that inherent qualities of the technology would eventually prevail. In such framings, the absence of evidence ceased to become an impediment to deployment. It is through such discourse that Derbyshire Police could attribute enormous success to FRT without evidencing discernible impact at the Download rock festival; that US borders agency CBP could use facial recognition for scheduling asylum determinations at its southern border without their iProov system ever being independently tested; and, as explored throughout this book, that the MPS could describe poorly performing technology as a 'precise' 'revolution in policing' only matched in recent times by the impact of DNA profiling (*The Guardian* 2023c). Later chapters also show how adaptations of logic, science, and law became recruited to support this gospel. Public consultation became converted into PR; poor performance was redeemed through technical evaluations that inflated and successes; faulty statistics denied racial and gender bias; and superficial human rights law assessments promoted faith in its utility while erasing the spectre of harm.

This book analyses a technology on the cusp of mass adoption. Parallelling this wave of policing experiments was the growing introduction of FRT into privately administered public spaces in the UK's major cities. These largely focused on spaces of retail and leisure consumption. A notable example includes the Trafford Centre in Manchester, where shoppers were monitored without notification or consent for six months in 2018 prior to the intervention of the then Surveillance Camera Commissioner (interview with (then) Surveillance Camera Commissioner, 2019). During summer 2019, *Financial Times* reported on the non-disclosed use of LFR in gentrified areas near London's King's Cross station (*Financial Times* 2019). The private governance of both this space and its security infrastructure meant it escaped the regulatory scrutiny that would otherwise apply to public spaces.[17] Significant here is the way public bodies including London's MPS and the British Transport Police were reported to have fed suspects' images to and, in turn, received intelligence products from the LFR scheme's private security operators. This occurred during the MPS's own trials of LFR and was never disclosed to the public. Such arrangements demonstrate the instrumental use of private security by public bodies in a way that reduces their exposure to regulatory scrutiny. Shortly after the story broke, the UK Information Commissioner's Office (ICO) publicly announced it was launching an investigation into this case. However, in a denouement increasingly typical of the way highly intrusive forms of advanced surveillance are governed in the UK, and signalling the continued inactivity of the ICO in this space, six years on, the regulator has yet to report on this case or take any discernible action.

Other reported episodic uses of FRT—including the gentrified Hays Galleria arcade on London's South Bank (*Evening Standard* 2019)—were soon replaced by widespread uses across the UK's retail and entertainment spaces sector. One of the most prominent UK operators, Facewatch, boasts relationships with many major high street retailers. Another major UK retailer, Southern Co-op, has also been an enthusiastic adopter of the technology, reserving its most extensive deployments in areas with the highest socio-economic deprivation (*The Observer* 2024). The interoperable functionality and software-based form of FRT means its applications are unlikely to remain restricted to distinct functions. For example, in October 2024 Michigan Congresswoman Rashida Tlaib wrote to the CEO of Kroger's 120 grocery stores in the state to appeal against their decision to use facial recognition classification technology to alter pricing on electric labels displayed on supermarket shelving.[18]

[17] As argued throughout this book, current oversight arrangements for FRT are fragmented, complex, and, ultimately, wholly deficient. Issues of data protection and compliance with the Data Protection Act 2018 are overseen by the ICO and cover public and private entities alike. However, other relevant forms of surveillance oversight such as those falling under the remit of the Surveillance Camera Commissioner and the Biometrics Commissioner (two roles that have since merged) were mandated in the Protection of Freedoms Act 2012 to only apply to public bodies.

[18] A small yet important distinction is important to note here, however. The text of the letter reveals the congresswoman as referring to 'classification' rather than 'recognition' technologies. In this setting, the tool would classify age, gender, and race and, she claims, alter pricing accordingly. This is a different computational task to identifying an individual from a database, as FRT does in the strictest definition. This difference between classification and identification has wider resonance and is commonly conflated in discussions of FRT.

In 2023, South Wales Police's use of FRT to scan the faces of attendees at a Beyoncé concert attracted significant media attention. Yet ambitions to use the technology in spaces of entertainment and celebration have been apparent since its earliest public experiments. For example, *Rolling Stone* (2018) magazine reported how Taylor Swift's predominantly young and female fans were deceived into clandestine facial recognition scans via a kiosk masquerading as a 'selfie station'. Aside from the lack of any transparency or accountability for these actions, such uses reveal deeper issues at play. One is how the elevated price of refusal changes the dynamics of consent for FRT in spaces of entertainment. A further issue, present across FRT use more generally but especially visible here, concerns how this technology amplifies asymmetries of surveillance. This growing disparity of knowledge and accountability—where subjects explain and account for their actions but watchers do not—allows unrestrained adaptations of FRT to new applications.

The gentrification of Tottenham Court Road, metres from the police surveillance operations analysed in Chapters 7 and 8, demonstrates such a dynamic. Here, monuments of London's storied musical heritage—including the nursery of punk and venues formative in the careers of Hendrix, Jagger, Dylan, Bowie, and Elton John—were bulldozed to make way for corporate tenants, bringing cutting-edge surveillance technologies in their wake. Garish digital art, described by architecture critics as 'crass, ad-laden [and] . . . as if Times Square had collapsed in on itself' (*The Guardian* 2022), draws the gaze to the 150 facial recognition-equipped cameras embedded in the fabric of gentrification. In that critic's reference point, New York City, another use of FRT is similarly anchored in entertainment and demonstrates similar adaptability. Here, the Madison Square Garden Entertainment (MSGE) company installed FRT at the city's iconic venues to disqualify attendees on the vaguest of pretexts. This included barring entry to a mother chaperoning her daughter's Girl Scout troop to a show at Radio City Music Hall on the grounds that she was employed by a law firm engaged in litigation against MSGE (*The New York Times* 2023). Such encounters highlight two components of surveillance asymmetry: the way, once instituted, that the addition of new criteria allows FRT practices to effortlessly creep into new domains; and the absence of information available to surveillance subjects prior to their rights being engaged. Figure 1.2 demonstrates this lack of meaningful information presented to attendees at the time such exclusionary practices were revealed by *The New York Times* with the standard vague declarations of public safety offered to conceal these deeper asymmetrical surveillance practices. These twin themes, of creep and transparency, are identifiable as consistent features of FRT activities and were prominent in the operations studied in later chapters. Here, purposes became adapted, people were added to databases, and information was obscured, activities that directly intersect with human rights law concerning questions of necessity, purpose limitation, and consent.

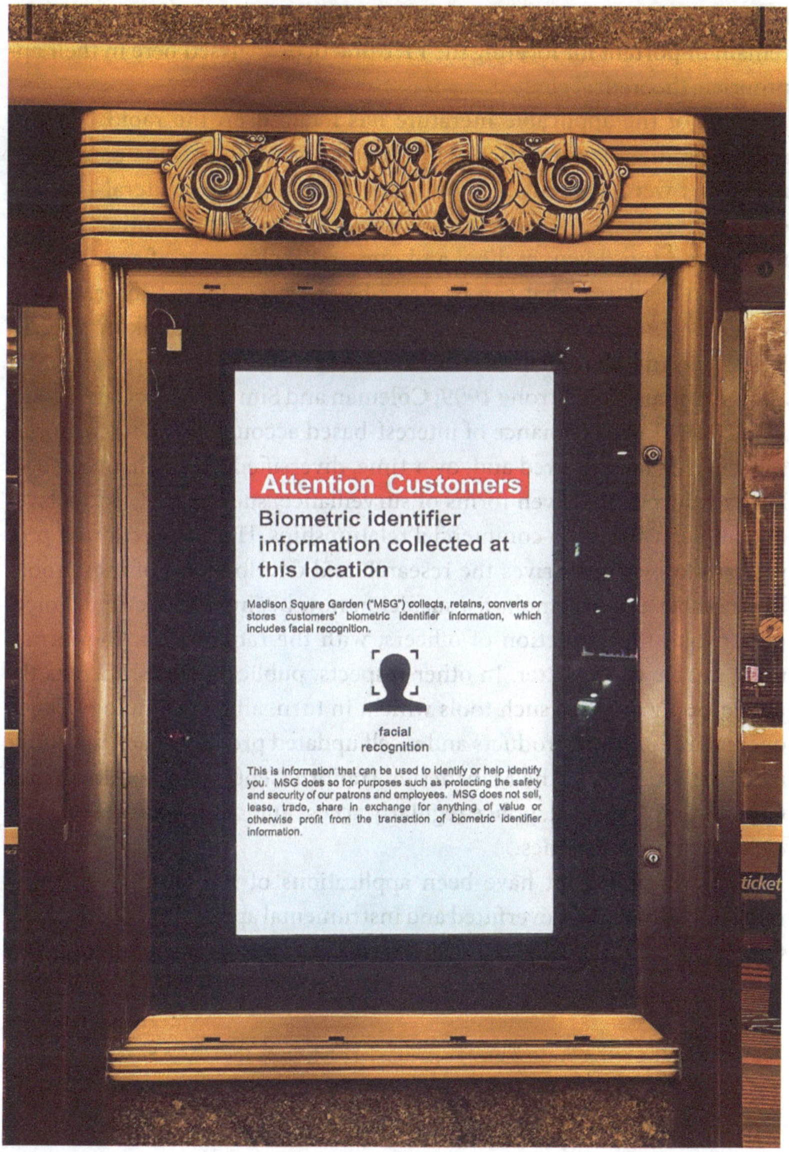

Figure 1.2 Facial recognition notification issued by Madison Square Garden Entertainment at Radio City, New York City. Photograph by Pete Fussey, 2023.

1.4.4 Conceptualizing the Growth of Surveillance

A comprehensive audit of how such surveillance practices have been theorized would necessarily be selective. It would also replicate existing work (inter alia, Lyon 2006). Nevertheless, acknowledgement of relevant conceptual landmarks, and recent theorizing on human–technology interactions, remain important for locating the FRT practices analysed here in their appropriate theoretical context.

Much of the applicable literature has focused on the rapid proliferation of camera surveillance, which occurred when specific conceptual narratives were particularly dominant. Among these, a literal—yet literarily inaccurate[19]—'Orwellian' vocabulary has been commonly used to denote a top-down, malign, and oppressive character of surveillance. Closely related are what can be described as neo-Marxist-informed accounts, or those emphasizing toxicities of neo-liberalism, linking surveillance with the aforementioned commodification of public spaces (inter alia, Norris and Armstrong 1999; Coleman and Sim 2000; McCahill 2002; Fyfe 2004). The dominance of interest-based accounts of state-corporate surveillance has endured and, over time, diversified. Later chapters show how advanced AI-driven forms of surveillance, such as FRT, add a layer of complexity to state–commercial relationships. Highly specialized proprietary knowledge drives the research and development of these tools. In a notable shift in emphasis, suspicion now begins with design choices rather than the discretion of officers, with the rationale for the former unattainable to the latter. In other respects, public agencies, such as the police, apply and test such tools which, in turn, allow technology developers to refine their products and resell updated products back for public use. Furthermore, as the Manchester Trafford Centre and London King's Cross examples reveal, police regularly access and query privately run facial recognition schemes.

Similarly dominant have been applications of Foucauldian thought, most notably an often overfitted and instrumental application of Foucault's (1977a) Benthamite metaphor of the panopticon to contemporary

[19] Literarily incorrect because many accounts lack fidelity to the source material. That surveillance is most heavily trained on the poor, marginalized, and minoritized is in little doubt. Yet Orwell's novel does not detail surveillance of the dispossessed. Rather, it was the politically active middle classes of Winston and Julia that were monitored with such intimacy.

surveillance practices. These discussions have been rehearsed extensively elsewhere (see Haggerty 2006 for a review) and warrant only brief elaboration here. In his most famous iteration of the concept, Foucault emphasized how the *suggestion* of surveillance induces compliance. Because surveillance is everywhere, anyone might be watched, and so we self-police. Common to other foundational concepts, while Foucault's argument appears elegant in its simplicity, it also captures intriguing layers of complexity. Panoptic surveillance is therefore a technique—something Foucault calls a 'technology of power'—rather than *an end in itself*. Moreover, it is a technique that is highly portable. In one of the most quoted passages of *Discipline and Punish*, and one that captures a central argument, Foucault (1977a: 298) traces how panoptic surveillance was a technique finessed in penal institutions and then 'transported . . . to the entire social body'. It is in this transportation of surveillance techniques from the prison to wider society—via factories and education institutions through to the fabric of everyday life—that the link is made to surveillance cameras.

Over time, the theory has become considered as ubiquitous, imposing, and inescapable as the panopticon itself (Haggerty 2006). Perhaps inevitably, such growth attracted significant criticism. Some of this is fair; for example, the suggestion that surveillance impacts are uniform and universal. However, much criticism either focuses on how the panopticon has been interpreted by others or overlooks Foucault's own refinements in subsequent writing. Regarding the former, as Fussey (2013) charts, the tedious regularity with which the 'opticon' suffix[20] became applied to descriptions of surveillance has worked to trivialize the concept. Regarding the latter, Foucault made many refinements to the idea that anticipated much of the puzzling criticism since levelled at him. For example, Foucault himself warned against the over-literal application of the panopticon metaphor within the same pages of *Discipline and Punish* in which the concept was introduced. Moreover, Foucault's astonishing intellectual journey meant his own development, adaptation, and revision of prior ideas was perhaps inevitable. This occurred barely months after *Discipline and Punish* had been translated into English during his *Security, Territory, Population* lectures at the Collège de France in Paris during the winter of 1977–1978.

[20] For example, the 'superpanopticon' (Poster 1990), 'synopticon' (Mathiesen 1997), 'oligopticon' (Latour 2005), 'ban-opticon' (Bigo 2008) et cetera.

Here Foucault (2007) unambiguously abandoned the idea that power solely operated at micro-level (disciplinary) scales ('Well, I think I was wrong'—Foucault 2007: 48).

These ideas find continued relevance in other regards too. The pandemic-era growth of public protest and other social movements at a time of advanced AI-driven surveillance has elevated the importance of surveillance chilling effects as an area of pressing enquiry. In such contexts, analyses of how the suggestion of surveillance may impact participation in such movements holds sustained value. In other respects, Stan Cohen's (1979, 1985) studies of 'social control' (he disliked the term) sought to apply Foucault's ideas to the increasingly civic character of penal sanctions. Alternatives to custody were deemed nothing of the sort; they were additions, an accumulation of control. Reflecting his talent for translating sociological ideas into everyday vernaculars (e.g. 'folk devils', 'moral panics', 'states of denial'), Cohen famously described such developments in terms of 'widening the net, thinning the mesh'. The debt to Foucault is explicit. As Cohen acknowledged, '[t]o write today about punishment and classification without Foucault is like talking about the unconscious without Freud' (1985: 10).

These late twentieth-century ur-texts on classification and power also had their progenitors. Among them is Arendt's (1973 [1951]) detailed examination of post-war refugee movements. In an account highly relevant to the puerile victim-blaming that stains today's political discourse on asylum seekers, Arendt observed how legally unclassified individuals (and actions) become governable by placing them into legal categories that *do* exist (notably, criminality). Also considering the theme of classification, Douglas's (1966) classic analysis interrogated how uncategorizable matter becomes characterized as disorderly and repugnant. By extension, such matter becomes in need of ordering and sanitizing. It is to such texts that twentieth-century conceptualizations of surveillance-driven classification—such as social sorting (Lyon 2003a)—owe their lineage. Such ideas also acquire renewed relevance when considering the sorting and filtering functions of FRT.

More recent conceptualizations of advanced surveillance have grappled with the relationship between human and non-human (e.g. technology) elements. Important among these were adaptations of the Social Construction of Technology (SCOT) approach. This approach focuses on how cultural, political, and social contexts shape technology-driven practices. While not unique to this perspective, this recognition also conveys a subtle yet important shift in our consideration of technology; that technologies are inseparable from society; they are 'fully inscribed into the political, economic and social relations of capitalism' (Graham and Marvin 1996: 94).

The last two decades, however, have seen the replacement of SCOT analyses with more nuanced approaches drawn from the philosophy of science, most notably variants of science and technology studies (STS) and, within this field, actor–network theory (e.g. Latour 2005; Callon et al. 2009). Although an internally antagonistic body of work, put most simply, actor–network theory-informed analyses maintain that, while practitioners do indeed shape the application and potential of technology, these social environments are simultaneously shaped and conditioned by these technologies (inter alia, Latour 1987). STS has therefore been crucial in addressing and resolving the dualism between technologies and the social. As Dyb and Halford (2009: 235) observed, 'STS shows that scientific facts are made in practice and, indeed, in particular locales'. This emphasis on social action gave rise to a widening field of constructivist study detailing how the form, meaning, and outcomes of technology become shaped during its passage through social settings (e.g. Bijker and Law 1992). Such observations are particularly relevant to much of the policy discourse surrounding AI-driven law enforcement tools, particularly the 'human-in-the-loop' accountability mechanisms that assume humans are sufficiently objective and capable of correcting digital processes (see below).

More recent developments have built on these foundations to theorize human and non-human relationships through ideas of 'new materialism'. Among them has been a concerted reclamation of Foucauldian thought (e.g. Lemke 2021; Olssen 2021), notably through concepts of 'dispositif' and 'milieu' (Foucault 2007). Others have attempted to tackle the holy grail of theoretical physics, linking the 'rules' of quantum subatomic relationships with larger-scale phenomena to comprehend human and non-human relationships. While a complex and nascent field, this approach commonly analyses digital and human relationships with reference to complex subatomic particle behaviour. Notable among this proliferating literature is the recent growth of 'entanglement theory' (Wendt 2015; Kydd 2022). It is difficult to draw commonality or coherence from such a rich and diverse literature. However, together, these approaches consider the human as submerged in networks and relationships that are non-human in character, and thus 'post-human' (Braidotti and Bignall 2019). They also erode boundaries between the human and digital realms.[21]

Overall, and put simply, human and non-human elements are brought together and something new becomes generated. Such observations have a clear debt to Heidegger's foundational work on 'being' and its emphases on how substance and meaning arise through action. However, within the context of human engagement with complex AI-driven surveillance technologies, these ideas hold resonance with concepts of emergence advanced by Deleuze and Guattari (1987) and different forms of assemblage theory (De Landa 2018). Indeed, Deleuze (1988) cited 'emergence' as Foucault's great unfinished project (also see Foucault 1977b).

Such analyses implicate further ontological debate over the degree to which technology and other artefacts possess any features (pre)existing outside of these relationships; a form of 'techno-essentialism' (see Bradford and Fussey 2023). In this sense, technology is considered to only generate outcomes through interrelationship with social contexts, processes, and relations. Technological outcomes do not necessarily exist independently of their social context. For example, constructivists such as Grint and Woolgar (1997) disagreed that objects held (essential) properties outside of these relationships. For them, technology has no autonomy outside its social relations. Furthermore, if technology has no autonomy outside its social relations, what does this mean for increasing human reliance on automated and semi-autonomous digital processing and the creation of suspicion? Such imbrications of human and digital are essential to understanding the outcome of advanced surveillance practices such as FRT.

While such debates are difficult to resolve conclusively, theoretical attention to notions of 'affordance' provides some resolution and frames the analysis of data presented in this book. Originating in the field of psychology (Gibson 1977), and then instituted into the field of STS, affordances similarly addresses issues of technological determinism while avoiding becoming excessively bogged down in such ontological debates. In brief, affordances stress how objects *invite*—and not dictate—actions and outcomes. In this sense, specific technologies provide conditions of possibility and opportunity rather than directly impelling certain outcomes. In the

[21] In response, Barad (2003) further argues that the entanglement of the human and non-human leaves the separation of epistemology from ontology redundant and advances the idea of 'onto-epistem-ology'.

context of digital policing, this leaves space for operational contexts, institutional cultures, and human discretion to assert themselves.

Such theorizations matter to considerations of FRT for several reasons. As Chapter 8 relays, a common refrain by advocates is that humans provide a robust form of adjudication for digital processes. A similar narrative is that these measures constitute a 'decision support rather than decision-making' mechanism, or that human decision-making is somehow objective and separate from the technologies it conjoins with. Here, human monitors are assumed to understand and curb the excesses of algorithmic bias through considered review of technological decisions, the 'human in the loop'. This logic was central to claims that LFR systems were being held to account in operational settings and is now a feature of the police's policy framework. Yet this argument, and the AI accountability structures built upon it, relies on a positivist ontology, a clear delineation between human and digital worlds, a distinction dismantled by the theoretical ideas discussed above. Simplistic human–machine binaries ignore the complex relationship between technology and its environment. It also ignores the subtle ways technology shapes and is itself shaped by practice. Acknowledgement of these complex imbrications, framed through concepts of affordance, enables deeper inquiry into considerations of human-in-the-loop adjudication of digital processes as a mechanism for bringing accountability, and into the complex human–technical co-construction of suspicion brought about by advanced surveillance technologies. As such, this book argues that detailed attention to the operational microenvironments in which digital policing occurs is crucial to understanding the impact and uses of such technologies.

1.5 Conclusions

This chapter has located the development of FRT in relation to longstanding urban ordering processes emerging from industrialization. Such recent digital forms of policing thus arose at a confluence of several longstanding processes. As cities grew in size and complexity through the twentieth century, continuing anxieties over unknowable and dangerously imagined populations became implicated in attempts to govern such spaces. The deployment of this technology in itself, from its first public—although ineffective—demonstrations to the current AI-driven manifestations deployed on London's streets, resonates with a longstanding preoccupation of attribution, of identifying people amid the anonymous urban milieu. Accordingly, the growth of specific digital policing tactics such as FRT may be situated in a broader context where policing ambitions to identify and recognize 'dangerousness' persist.

While manifestly different from other forms of surveillance, points of connection also exist between FRT and other forms of digital security. To take one seemingly recent policing approach, social media surveillance, law enforcement analyses of text-based and database sources have lengthy histories, even predating the histories of formal policing itself (Higgs 2011). Parallels also exist between FRT adoption and the trajectory of more familiar open street surveillance cameras. This often invites the view that FRT is merely another variant of existing—and more accepted—surveillance technologies. Indeed, this view was forwarded by South Wales Police to the High Court in a 2019 legal challenge over LFR use in Wales, with the court accepting the argument.[22] However, as recognized by the Court of Appeal in overturning this finding a year later,[23] significant differences exist. Such differences, and the impacts that follow, form a central focus of this book. To develop this analysis, the discussion moves from tracing the development and enabling contexts surrounding the growth of FRT to examine the form and impact of this technology in more detail. It is to these fundamental changes brought about by biometric surveillance that the analysis now turns.

[22] *R (Bridges) v Chief Constable of South Wales Police* [2019] EWHC 2341 (Admin), para. 75.
[23] *R (Bridges) v The Chief Constable of South Wales Police* [2020] EWCA Civ 1058, para. 85.

2
The Form, Function, and Fallibilities of AI-Driven Surveillance

2.1 Introduction

Chapter 1 traced the emergence of facial recognition technology (FRT) through enabling contexts. In this chapter, attention turns to the form and impact of FRT. Examining this complex and dynamic technology requires consideration of both the technical and human-social elements of its application, in addition to reflection on the complex relationships between them. Exploration of these issues is guided by two overarching lines of argument: shining a critical light on the evidence presented to legitimate FRT exposes the fragility of its supporting arguments; and, despite this, FRT can be regarded as a step change in surveillance practice.

This chapter is divided into two main parts. Section 2.2 considers aspects of the technical performance of facial recognition systems, drawing on literature from the computer and social sciences. In particular, the technical and social elements of FRT bring different ways of seeing together. From a technical perspective, the chapter first highlights how different forms of computational image analysis are overlayered to modify each other. This analysis shines a light on several otherwise concealed and underacknowledged shortcomings of the technology. Such limitations challenge the many techno-evangelist and technologically determinist discourses that accompany the adoption of advanced surveillance technologies. Of particular importance here is the argument that, contrary to what is often claimed, these weaknesses are not necessarily resolved through the improvement and finessing of technology. As the discussion shows, innovation may actually work to reproduce and multiply such deficiencies.

Facial Recognition Surveillance. Pete Fussey and Daragh Murray, Oxford University Press.
 DOI: 10.1093/9780191979927.003.0002

Section 2.3 explores the wider implications arising from the growing use of FRT in law enforcement settings. Human rights law is the principal lens through which the impact of FRT is analysed in this book and, as such, is explored over the chapters that follow. As a foundation for this rights-focused analysis, Section 2.3 focuses on how remote biometric measurement has significantly altered the ways individuals have become understood and managed. These profound shifts in surveillance practice are considered through three modalities. The first two consider the ways the bodies and souls of urban citizens have been apprehended. The third concerns the role of FRT in cultivating knowledge of suspicion, and the way this knowledge is valorized through technology.

2.2 Falsehoods and Fallibilities

Facial recognition processes require several distinct phases of extracting, processing, and codifying information from the 'source' (or 'enrolled') image; extracting, processing, and codifying information from a subject (a 'probe' image); and digital comparison of both sets of data. The biometrics industry has now formalized this approach as the Analysis, Comparison, Evaluation-Verification (ACE-V) process. Also significant is that computational processing of facial images extracts partial and specific data. This technological production of images shapes the degree to which important context is retained in any image or, in Walter Benjamin's (1968) famous lamentation, becomes stripped away.

FRT describes a collection of different hardware and software. These technological tools designed to map and match faces are themselves based on complex and diverse approaches. At its most fundamental level, significant differences exist in how machines interpret faces when compared to humans. This difference is significant for several reasons. First, psychological research has established how faces tend to be conceived in more general and affective terms, for example whether someone appears 'friendly' or 'attractive' (see Ainsworth 1998). Humans therefore process and interpret multiple features simultaneously. These more impressionistic 'holistic' forms of human perception are contrasted by facial identification processes operating in policing and criminal justice settings. Techniques such as artist impressions, photofits, e-fits, and the questioning of eyewitnesses emphasize recall of specific features such as eye colour, hair, and the shape and size of facial features. Current facial recognition tools replicate these differences between human and computational analysis of faces.

Obviously, the process of *comparing* faces is a key purpose of FRT, and it is for this distinct task that computer science has developed several possible approaches. Exploring these differences in approach reveals how computer-based face-mapping techniques are themselves highly diverse and subject to limitations. The foundational approach is 'photo anthropometry'. As the name suggests, this seeks to establish baseline measurements of the geometry of human faces (e.g. the length and angles of features extracted from each image). Many popular discussions of FRT assume the technology to work on such Euclidian principles. However, as the relevant US federal standards agency, the Organization of Scientific Area Committees (OSAC) for forensic science, points out in their national guidelines, photo-anthropometric approaches are deeply compromised when applied to real-world digital facial recognition *and* comparison. As they state, the quality of comparison is critically compromised by issues of 'resolution, focus, [lens] distortion, obscuration, viewpoint, lighting, and pose'. They continue that, without complete understanding of photographic data including 'focal length, lens distortion and subject distance', it is impossible to calibrate similarity between images (OSAC 2021: 6). Supporting this assessment, the forensic science literature has long disputed the shortcomings of photo anthropometry even when applied to high-quality source images (see, inter alia, Kleinberg et al. 2007).

This approach has largely been abandoned in favour of more sophisticated 'morphological analysis'. Put simply, morphological analysis seeks to mitigate the more unreliable aspects of digital facial comparison. This includes addressing how the linear measurements central to the anthropometric approach may be distorted by camera optics and other environmental and technical factors. Morphological analysis examines factors such as the shape and symmetry of features and identifies facial characteristics like scars and tattoos. Crucially, the approach also assesses the proportions *and* relationships between such data points. In recognition of its superior performance, morphological approaches are recommended by most technical standards on facial comparison (e.g. FISWG 2018). However, the morphological approach may be critically undermined by poor image quality. This is likely the reason that South Wales Police (SWP) invested significant funds in upgrading the digital quality of their custody images ahead of their live facial recognition (LFR) deployments in 2017 (observation of SWP facial recognition operation, July 2019).

2.2.1 Digital Deficiencies and the Reproduction of Error

FRT system performance is also afflicted by limitations that affect biometric identification more generally. For example, false identifications, while often attributable to deficiencies in a specific algorithm, may also arise due to *systemic limitations in biometric identification itself*. This phenomenon has long been recognized in computer science scholarship and was memorably articulated in the animalistic imagery of 'Doddington's Zoo' (O'Connell and Elliot 2014). In essence, 'Doddington's Zoo' concerns the categorization of individuals depending on the way biometric technologies may misidentify them. Included in this menagerie are 'wolves' (as in 'sheep's clothing'; individuals that score highly against other people but not themselves, and thus stimulate false positives), 'lambs' (who indiscriminately raise alerts, generating false positives), and 'doves' (who score highly against themselves and low against everyone else). Particularly important for the study of FRT, and any consideration of its human rights implications, is the role of 'lambs' and 'wolves'. Both 'lambs' and 'wolves' can exert a significant influence on the effectiveness of a FRT deployment and the extent of any rights interferences. 'Lamb' alerts will result in people being incorrectly identified—and therefore subject to police scrutiny—as they pass a camera's field of vision, while the inclusion of wolves on a watchlist will stimulate greater numbers of false positives, again resulting in inappropriate police engagements. It is important to note that such interferences arise from the way remote biometric technologies work rather than any physical or behavioural characteristic of a suspect. None of the facial recognition operations studied in this book included any tangible consideration of how individuals may be wrongly identified through their inherent susceptibility to biometric identification.

Compounding these limitations are a host of environmental factors that affect all optical methods, practices, and tools. For example, FRT performance is contingent on adequate lighting. Lower light reduces the available detail of an image and the contrast of any given scene. Both digital and celluloid forms of photography may compensate for poor lighting, although this often produces an image with a 'grainy' or pixelated quality. These factors combine to reduce FRT performance. This is also one reason why FRT used at borders, where stable and controlled lighting conditions are more feasible, tends to have higher efficacy rates (National Academies Press 2024). These limitations are widely recognized by users of FRT. For example, the Metropolitan Police Service (MPS) attributed reduced LFR performance on one London operation to poor lighting brought about by inclement weather. Elsewhere, a security manager at one US airport explained in a research interview that they were 'flooding the area' with infra-red light, imperceptible to humans, in an effort to optimize FRT performance (interviewed February 2020). In the context of UK policing, misalignment between optimal conditions for FRT performance and the police intelligence case justifying its deployment is also notable. As highlighted in Chapter 7, a common justification for deploying LFR in London was to address violence and disorder in the night-time economy (MPS Operational Mandate for LFR 2018d). Notwithstanding the fact that deployments actually occurred during the daytime, using LFR to address offences related to the night-time economy places the technology in an environment where it is least likely to be effective. Beyond issues of efficacy, depleted performance also affects the human rights necessity calculation by impairing the utility associated with a deployment, while potentially increasing the harm through false positives.

In both law and policy, a common corrective to technical fallibility is the introduction of human scrutiny and adjudication (the 'human in the loop'). This adjudication typically applies to the comparison of the probe and source images. However, the manner in which this information is presented can invite and influence how it is read. For instance, 'superimposition' is a facial comparison technique that involves the layering of two images on top of each other. Perhaps the most recognizable form of this technology is evident in mobile consumer technologies, such as the 'Face Swap Lens Effect' feature in Snapchat and the many portrait-blending apps where facial images can be merged by dragging a slider across the screen. However, superimposition techniques hold significant implications for law enforcement facial comparison activities, particularly in suspect identification processes. As one UK-based police officer half-jokingly expressed in a research interview,

> if I'm showing someone the images of two people on my tablet I have some choices: I can drag the slider slowly. The image changes gradually and the two faces look similar. Or I can do it fast to emphasize the differences. (Interviewed November 2018)

While clearly intended with dark humour, this comment underlines how the human operation of digital face comparison technology can be manipulated to reinforce a prior assumption of guilt. Indeed, the influence of human interference is backed up in the scientific literature on individual perception, something well understood in expert practitioner communities:

> a very slow fade [between images] may give the illusion of a perfect match as one image is almost imperceptibly replaced by another. In this practice, the human eye is led from one image to another blending the two together, reducing the ability to perceive differences. A fast fade may emphasize differences. In general, wipes and fades promote the appearance of similarities; whereas, toggling between images promotes the appearance of differences. It is for this reason that wipes, fades, and toggles can mislead naïve observers and even the improperly or untrained practitioner. If superimposition is used, these limitations must be fully understood and explained to any third parties. (FISWG 2012: 10)

Rather than ameliorating flaws, the introduction of multiple elements into facial comparison activities may draw new biases into the process. The deficiencies of one approach are not necessarily erased by the application of another. Instead, initial errors may become replicated and, in their validation, become more *durable*.

2.2.2 Bias in the Machine

Writing presciently about algorithmic bias long before the term was invented, Introna and Wood (2004) presented an early social science analysis of disparate facial recognition performance across age, race, and gender. While this analysis drew heavily on the periodic National Institute of Standards and Technology (NIST) facial recognition evaluations of the time, and flagged certain forms of bias that have since become outdated, notable is how, two decades later, debates over inequitable FRT performance have not abated. In fact, such debates have intensified *despite* the step change in the technology driven by the adoption of AI-driven digital architecture. The durability of this issue also challenges the argument that algorithmic bias will be eliminated once a few remaining technological refinements have been accomplished.

Most recent commentary on bias in FRT has focused on race and ethnicity. Recent years have seen this issue acquire similar prominence to debates over privacy. Like privacy (and data protection), bias may be considered in relation to long-instituted legal standards and frameworks. These include its connection to the prohibition of discrimination (Article 14 of the European Convention on Human Rights; Equality Act 2010) and the Public Sector Equality Duty (Equality Act 2010). Although these debates resonate with more longstanding concerns regarding discriminatory policing practices (e.g. The Lammy Review 2017; Casey 2023), bias in the context of FRT implicates additional socio-technical factors. Discrimination may arise across many points in the operational lifecycle and may include issues relating to input data, watchlist composition, or the focus of a deployment. From a technological perspective, concerns have been raised regarding biases embedded in LFR technologies which mean that the technology may perform inconsistently across different demographic groups. Particularly problematic is how performance varies in relation to different protected characteristics—notably an individual's sex, age, or ethnicity—which may thereby give rise to (indirect) discrimination (see Chapter 3).

Assessing the relationship between FRT, bias, and discrimination is complex. Part of this complexity lies in the way 'facial recognition' covers a diverse range of technologies, practices, and purposes. Strong performance in one application (such as matching images taken in controlled lighting conditions in a lab) may not translate to another (such as identifying faces from 'wild' sources such as social media video or footage captured during a LFR deployment). Image processing and recognition software engines also differ, as do sources of data and the means by which they are captured. These variances may complicate analysis of biased FRT performance, particularly when testing and comparison criteria is unclear. Different algorithms and different applications assert biases in different ways.

Leaving aside this caveat, that FRT capability varies across different demographic characteristics is an established scientific fact. One of the most heavily cited sources of algorithmic bias in FRT is Buolamwini and Gebru's (2018) evaluation of three widely used gender classification algorithms. The central finding was that 'all classifiers performed best for lighter individuals and males overall. The classifiers performed worst for darker females' (p. 12). Highlighting the often-overlooked issue of intersectionality in debates over algorithmic bias, race was identified as a key variable in exaggerating gender-based disparities in algorithmic performance. It is perhaps unsurprising that such a hard-hitting intervention in two highly contested fields—technological bias and racial justice—stimulated debate. Amazon, whose face recognition system ('Rekognition') has been sold to law enforcement agencies across the US and who have acute commercial interest in this debate, argued that Buolamwini and Gebru's analysis was compromised because the study focused on 'facial analytics' (i.e. gender classification) rather than 'face recognition'. This criticism has been echoed by others on the basis that the research did not run against *facial recognition* algorithms, which require the comparison of two images. Rather, it is argued that Buolamwini and Gebru's (2018) study focused on the analysis of only the single image required for gender classification (Grother 2019).

While this debate continues (e.g. Buolamwini 2019; Wood 2019), it is important that reducing the argument to this single technical point does not detract from the durability of the core arguments presented by Buolamwini and Gebru and, since then, Birhane (2022): that the capabilities of digital facial analytics vary across demographic groups, that they perform less accurately for some minoritized groups, and, consequently, that they may serve to compound existing social disadvantage.

A significant body of evidence supports such arguments (see, inter alia, Introna and Nissenbaum 2010; Kloppenburg and van der Ploeg 2018). Among these are several leading independent scientific assessments. Since the 1990s, NIST has been the most authoritative source for independent technical evaluation of face recognition algorithms. These evaluations have been collected in various reports and most comprehensively in the periodic Face Recognition Vendor Test (FRVT). One recent iteration of this test (2019) assessed 189 commercially available face recognition algorithms from 99 separate suppliers on a bank of over 18.27 million images of 8.49 million people. This comprehensive study found that *all* facial recognition algorithms performed unevenly across different demographic groups. Notable findings include significantly higher rates of false positives among West and East African and East Asian populations and lower rates for eastern Europeans. Conversely, algorithms developed in China had much lower false-positive rates on East Asian faces. Perhaps most significant was the finding that the algorithms used by US domestic law enforcement produced the highest false-positive rates among Native American, African American, and Asian populations. The same evaluation also found higher rates of false positives in women when compared to men across all algorithms and datasets. Regarding age, facial recognition algorithms performed worse on the faces of children and the elderly (NIST 2019).

Algorithmic racial bias plays out in multiple ways. Most explicit are the above cases where FRT performance varies across different ethnicities. The higher likelihood of a false match means an increased chance of a police encounter based on inaccurate information for some visible ethnic minorities. That this problem of algorithmic bias is recognized in the biometrics industry is reflected in the behaviour of commercial actors. For example, Apple, among others, invested heavily in demographically diverse training data for the 'Face ID' biometric algorithm used to unlock their iPhone X generation of mobile devices (Apple Corp 2017).

This weight of expert and scientific knowledge documenting the existence of algorithmic bias is contrasted by the MPS's own and commissioned research that claims its absence in their systems. Two significant pieces of research into algorithmic bias have been conducted by UK public users of FRT. The first was conducted by the MPS and National Physical Laboratory (NPL) over a year after their operational trials of the technology concluded and covers the same police operations observed for this book (NPL and MPS 2020). In March 2023, and accompanied by a significant public relations campaign, the MPS announced that a second, independent, report had been published, which found no 'statistically significant' bias in their facial recognition algorithm. This second report adopts a largely similar methodology to the first and is described as an independent review of FRT bias in all MPS public discourse since (NPL 2023). Standing in opposition to the extensive scientific knowledge documenting algorithmic bias set out above, both the MPS evaluation and its commissioned research claim bias is either absent or not 'significant' in their FRT systems.

These studies represent highly significant interventions in the public, political, and legal debates concerning FRT. The MPS have cited the latter NPL study as grounds to rapidly accelerate their FRT deployments through 2023 and 2024. One representative quote is expressed by the MPS director of intelligence, head of the MPS facial recognition strategy, and the National Police Chiefs' Council (NPCC) lead on FRT, who told the *Financial Times* in 2024 that their FRT operates 'at a threshold where testing has shown there to be zero bias' (*Financial Times* 2024).

The centrality of these studies, both to the public legitimation of FRT and police demonstrations of legal compliance, makes the analysis of these claims and their supporting research particularly important. As set out below, both studies are critically weakened by methodological shortcomings. Moreover, it is difficult to reconcile the public claims associated with the research with a more detailed analysis of the conclusions.

According to both studies, MPS FRT was judged to have no statistically significant difference in performance across different visible ethnicities, while some minor disparity on gender was acknowledged in the first evaluation. These claims were consistently repeated in the public arena to justify further LFR deployments (Dick 2020; *The Guardian* 2020). One of the principal problems affecting the first study (NPL and MPS 2020) is the inadequacy of its underpinning methodology. For example, claims of demographic neutrality are generalized on the basis of just nine cases in which individuals from perceived ethnic minorities were identified by FRT (NPL and MPS 2020: 24) and therefore do not withstand the most basic statistical scrutiny. In addition, the MPS used two different datasets, 'blue list' data (where police volunteers were sent past the cameras to measure their effectiveness) and 'watchlist' data (the database of suspects where no certainty existed regarding whether individuals would be present). Sometimes these data sources are conflated and at other times used selectively depending on the point being argued. In each case, the specific dataset used presents FRT performance in the best light.

Turning to the second evaluation, in which the MPS commissioned their former co-authors to conduct an independent study, the MPS website argues that the

> NPL report gives us an impartial, scientifically underpinned and evidence-based analysis of the performance of the facial recognition algorithm currently used by the Met [which] can be operated at where there is no statistical significance between demographic performances. (MPS 2023b)

Consistent with wider debates over FRT narratives, language is important here. Of particular note is how the language of 'science' is politicized to legitimate FRT and obfuscate the weaknesses in the underpinning evidence.

In the first instance, the NPL evaluation draws all of its conclusions from just thirty-three FRT matches. The conclusions relied on most heavily by the MPS arguments—that bias is 'not statistically significant'—are drawn from just seven cases. That such wide-ranging conclusions are drawn from such scant underpinning evidence clearly undermines the claim of 'scientifically underpinned and evidence-based analysis' articulated above.

Added to this is the issue of ecological validity, concerning the degree to which the NPL study replicates facial recognition operations in real life. The NPL study analyses one distinct part of FRT operation. While the study claims to use a watchlist size of 178,000 people, closer inspection reveals this to be a statement that invites misleading interpretation. The NPL study indeed uses this larger database 'in the background' but it is largely irrelevant to the study. Instead, those individuals matched were drawn from new images of 686 volunteer police officers who supplied images captured in entirely different conditions and who were instructed to pass before the cameras. All test days were also 'bright and sunny' (NPL 2023: 11) and tests were therefore conducted in conditions most optimal for FRT performance. Moreover, the FRT algorithms were tested on recorded footage rather than in real time and therefore deviate from real-life operational conditions.

Understanding why claims that police facial recognition algorithms are free of racial and gendered bias are unsubstantiated requires attention to several issues, namely facial recognition threshold sensitivity and the use of statistical significance. Regarding threshold sensitivity, LFR systems allow users to calibrate the system's sensitivity. Many systems, including the NEC system, give a 'similarity score' between 0.0 and 1.0. This is often misinterpreted as the percentage of similarity the computer calculates as existing between two images. In reality, the number is more akin to a 'correlation coefficient', where 0.0 represents no match at all (apples and oranges) and 1.0 is a confident match (apples and apples). The increments between numbers seem small but are often significant. Operators set this threshold to determine the sensitivity of systems for alerting to potential matches. They can set the threshold high, which will result in alerts with high confidence scores but fewer matches overall. Alternatively, the threshold can be set very low, which will generate higher numbers of alerts but many will be incorrect.

The NPL study tested bias at different threshold settings. Although the baseline statistics are not presented with exceptional clarity, it appears that the study tested just thirty-three matches. Of these, all but six matches occurred below the 0.6 threshold level. The report explicitly acknowledges that the facial recognition algorithms used by the MPS *do* contain inherent biases:

> At face-match thresholds of 0.58 and 0.56 we observe that false positives are not uniform between demographic groups. In particular, the number of false positives is disproportionately higher for black subjects than for Asian or white subjects; this demographic variation in FPIR [false-positive identification rate] is statistically significant. (NPL 2023: 19)

What is notable is how this finding can be used to claim the opposite, that no bias exists in the algorithms used by the police. This claim rests on the argument that if the system threshold is set sufficiently high, then such bias is eliminated. For example, when set at a 0.6 threshold, the facial recognition system incorrectly matched seven individuals; at 0.62, only one person was wrongly matched; and above 0.64, no such matches were made. The MPS argument turns on the point that if their system threshold is set to 0.60, then any racial or gender bias is not 'statistically significant'. For example, as stated by the MPS at the launch of the report:

> When [LFR is] used at a threshold setting of 0.6 or above, any differences in matches across groups were not statistically significant. This means performance was the same across race and gender . . . *the study was certainly large enough to ensure that any demographic differences would be seen*. We understand how we can operate to ensure the technology's performance across race and gender is equal. (Quoted in Security Matters 2023, emphasis added)

However, the main reason this is not 'statistically significant' is because the entire argument is based on just seven matches. Moreover, the claim that 'the study was certainly large enough to ensure that any demographic differences would be seen' is simply, and factually, incorrect.

Also of note are claims that no demographic bias is discernible above the 0.64 threshold. This is because no false positives occurred at this level. Put another way, no bias was observed because the system was not adequately tested in this range. Notable here is that such arguments rest less on how FRT operates and more on how statistics work. A suitable analogy would be the claim that 90 per cent of car accidents occur within a quarter-mile of home. This is less because such locales are inherently hazardous and more because almost all car journeys happen within a quarter-mile of home. Fewer journeys occur 600 miles away so accidents in that category are rarer.

Between 6 April 2023 and 28 June 2024, the MPS conducted 112 LFR operations with the system set at 0.6. A further ten deployments were conducted the following month, with the threshold set at 0.62, and twenty-five more between July and September 2024 with a threshold set at 0.64 (adapted from police operational statistics in MPS 2024b). Collectively, the MPS estimates that more than three million faces were scanned by their facial recognition cameras across the 137 deployments in London during this period. These operations were predicated on police claims of algorithmic neutrality derived from just seven cases.

2.2.3 Measuring Performance

Claims and counterclaims over FRT effectiveness are commonplace. One factor animating this debate is that different standards and measurements are used to ascertain effectiveness. This section seeks to bring further clarity to the discussion by highlighting the range of FRT evaluation approaches and, consequently, considering how these relate to the human rights implications arising from this technology.

Understanding this debate requires familiarity with four evaluation terms. These are false positives, when a computer *incorrectly matches* an individual to a database entry; true positives, when a computer *correctly matches* an individual to a database entry; false negatives, when a computer *incorrectly fails to match* an individual to a database entry; and true negatives, when a computer *correctly fails to match* an individual to a database entry. In a perfectly functioning system, every facial recognition assessment would either be a true positive or a true negative.

Taking a broad view of this debate, three prominent issues emerge. The first is that different evaluations may measure different things yet make similar claims to overall effectiveness. For example, some studies may measure true positives while others emphasize false positives and are therefore not necessarily comparable. The second issue concerns which population is being measured. For example, evaluation methodologies tend to highlight the larger number of people *processed* by FRT-equipped cameras (e.g. everyone passing the cameras, whether matched to the database or not), while other approaches are more tightly focused on individuals *identified* by cameras. The third consideration centres on whether a human or computer facial recognition match is being measured. This element becomes more complex in situations where a human adjudicates a computer-suggested match. These issues are elaborated in turn.

Taking the first two issues together, standard FRT evaluation methodology generally compares the overall number of faces scanned by a computer against the number of false alerts issued (e.g. NIST 2018; NPL and MPS 2020). While this may serve a purpose for assessing a general level of technical performance, it is inadequate for ascertaining the human rights implications of poorly performing technology. This approach normally signifies a very low percentage of false positives because the cameras normally scan many thousands of faces per hour as people pass their 'zone of recognition' and alerts occur very rarely. This measurement is normally used to justify claims of very high efficacy rates, such as those claiming effectiveness above 99 per cent (see NPL and MPS 2020). In addition, the baseline figure of the actual numbers of people passing the cameras is rarely known. Often these are based on estimates extrapolated from an analysed sample of footage.[1] Even when a computer logs how many matches it makes, any processing failures (such as when faces are not analysed) are not known. Computer processor overload and screen freezing were not uncommon in the LFR operations studied for this research. Moreover, it is not known when someone on a watchlist is incorrectly ignored by the system as they pass the cameras (a false negative).

Perhaps most significantly, this evaluative approach de-emphasizes the impact on individuals wrongly identified by FRT systems. Instead, systems can be portrayed as effective regardless of significant fluctuations in performance. The following provides an example of how this latter measure shapes an evaluation of LFR performance: if 20,000 people pass a camera within an hour and one person is incorrectly matched, this could be presented as an error rate of 0.005 per cent or that cameras were 99.995 per cent effective. If 500 people were wrongly identified, stopped, and identity-checked by the police, this could be presented as a 2.5 per cent error or a 97.5 per cent accuracy rate. By comparing numbers of matched individuals to large numbers of people irrelevant to any surveillance operation, this methodology dramatically de-emphasizes the impact of LFR on those tagged by the system (a highly significant 500 incorrect matches), while at the same time presenting what appears to be a very significant indicator of effectiveness (over 97.5 per cent). In this sense, facial recognition optics matter in more ways than one.

Another issue complicating evaluations of facial recognition performance is that policing operations combine computer and human decision-making in complex ways. Measuring only computer performance artificially separates out one element of an entire operation. Studies also vary regarding whether it is a computer or human decision being measured. This is significant for several reasons. For example, two prominent studies of police LFR uses judge effectiveness on the basis of whether a human operator accepts or discards a computer-suggested alert (Big Brother Watch

[1] This approach was confirmed to the authors by MPS staff during one of the observed deployments. Poor-performing LFR technology meant that an accurate census of the people passing the cameras was not possible for this specific operation. MPS evaluators developed a workaround by manually measuring crowd density by taking screenshots, counting the number of individuals in the image, and then extrapolating across the entire operation.

2018; Davies et al. 2018). In the review of the South Wales Police LFR trials, the research closest aligned to that presented in this book, the authors defined 'false positives' as 'a possible match suggested by the [LFR] system that is assessed incorrect by the human operators'. Correspondingly, 'true positives' were defined as 'a possible match suggested by the [LFR] system that is judged by the human operators'. As such, the decisions of *human adjudicators* in determining the accuracy of computer-generated alerts constitute the central unit of analysis. While a valid approach, it ultimately measures human interpretations of computational alerts and does not test the underlying quality of the algorithmic decision. For example, a human could erroneously discard a correct computational match. A human could also erroneously confirm an incorrect computational match.

The reality of LFR operations means this issue is far from hypothetical. The ethnographic observations of MPS operations discussed in Chapter 8 reveal how human adjudication of computational decisions varies enormously in complexity. In real operational settings, many matches are not clear-cut and are ultimately resolved through subjective judgement. As the discussion below reveals, these human decisions are also conditioned, and often compressed, by myriad temporal and environmental factors, the affordances of the technology, affective states, and other influences. Human judgement of computer-generated matches therefore constitutes an imperfect measure of overall FRT system accuracy. Moreover, reducing FRT evaluation to matters of technical performance represents a selective audit of its operational capability.

A further example of why such precision is important became evident in the ninth MPS test deployment of LFR. As the following ethnographic fieldnotes demonstrate, the human resources surrounding LFR are vital to its functioning in a law enforcement context and therefore need to be included in any evaluation thereof:

> 31/1/2019 13:46pm, Romford town centre: Growing concern among the operations team that high numbers of arrests (mainly following searches of those avoiding the cameras) are diverting officers from the operation; 'the trial is in danger of collapsing' due to limited 'resources on the ground'.
>
> 16:30pm operation ended because of depleted resources. Many officers originally assigned to the LFR trial now diverted to other tasks, mostly processing individuals deemed suspicious for avoiding the cameras. Support was offered and expected from a violent crime unit within

> the MPS but never arrived. When I asked what happened, a senior officer on the operation said, 'they forgot'.

This account surfaces many issues affecting how the technical performance of FRT is measured, including how FRT operation is contingent on human and institutional resources and contexts. In such settings, exclusively technical calculations of algorithmic performance constitute a fragment of overall system functioning and are thus deficient as a measure of overall capability. A challenge here, then, is to develop an approach that seeks to cut through this complexity, address issues of true- and false-positive conflation, resolve tensions between human and computer outcomes, and, most significantly, emphasize the impact of FRT on individuals in order to facilitate an assessment of relevant human rights considerations. Indeed, because both human and technical elements are central to FRT functioning and its human rights implications, they require acknowledgement in any assessment of performance.

2.3 New Frontiers of Surveillance: Biometric Data and the Production of Meaning

Despite contestations over effectiveness, FRT nonetheless brings transformative changes to the way surveillance is enacted. This book demonstrates how this transformative capability has a seismic impact on human rights. However, these changes are also predicated on a series of deeper transformations. FRT, as a form of remote biometric identification, alters the modalities by which subjects are observed and the meanings attached to the data extracted from them. The discussion below argues that these changes exist because of the foundational differences between biometric surveillance and other forms of video monitoring. These shifts include those of capacity and scale and the ability to penetrate new spaces, transgress the boundaries of the human body, and give form to what was once hidden. Not only do these distinctions set facial recognition apart from other forms of surveillance, facial recognition is also predicated on an altogether more invasive mode of observation. Put another way, heightened intrusion is encoded into the DNA of biometric surveillance.[2] Understanding these

[2] The impact of this enhanced intrusion is analysed from a human rights law perspective in Chapter 3.

principal differences is therefore instructive for revealing the wider individual and societal implications arising from the accelerated deployment of facial recognition in policing today.

In 1981, palaeontologist Stephen Jay Gould published a text that became a landmark for both the history and philosophy of science. Ostensibly positioned as an evidence-based dismantling of the 'scientific' theories that underpinned enduring racist tropes of his day (and of this[3]), Gould offered many arguments to criticize the way that physical attributes are understood by 'science' and to challenge how such 'knowledge' became politicized. Particularly relevant here are the suppositions and inferences made from measurements of the human body, an issue central to the practice of biometric surveillance. Among Gould's contributions are three observations that hold sustained relevance for analyses of biometric surveillance and its politicized deployment. These are the spurious connotations attached to physical characterizes (biological determinism), the value-laden nature of such scientific enquiries, and the very specific forms of knowledge they elicit. As Gould stated, particular caution should be exercised regarding how inferences are made from data, how they are justified through appeals to scientific knowledge, and how such discourse is politicized:

> one . . . fallac[y]—reification, or our tendency to convert abstract concepts into entities . . . We recognize the importance of mentality in our lives and wish to characterize it, in part so we can make the divisions and distinctions among people that our cultural and political systems dictate. (Gould 1981: 3–4)

Echoing Foucault's (1972) *archaeology of knowledge*, Gould critiqued how scientific discourses are used to valorize and politicize inferences that arise from studies of the human body. Resonant with Douglas's (1992) observations on the politics of fear, Gould was particularly concerned with how such knowledge becomes recruited into the sordid politics of blaming minorities. Relatedly, as Ruha Benjamin (2019: 8) convincingly argues in her analysis of how racial injustice becomes reproduced through technology—a process she characterizes as a *New Jim Code*—'the language of "progress" is too easily weaponised against those who suffer most under oppressive systems, however sanitised'.

[3] E.g. see Rutherford's (2020) recent intervention, this time through the lens of genetic science, in a debate that, depressingly, endures.

2.3.1 The Body: Towards a New 'Corporeality'?

In a 2008 essay, philosopher Giorgio Agamben warned of the growing deployment of 'biopolitical tattoos', state-driven 'technological apparatus [that] identifies and registers bare life' (2008: 202). Agamben's essay ostensibly serves as a manifesto against state overreach and conveys several warnings. These include the unprecedented incursion of state power, the subversion of the public sphere, and, crucially, the conversion of citizen to suspect through technologies that catalogue the body. Indeed,

> History teaches us how many such practices, initially reserved for foreigners, are soon applied to every citizen alike. What is at stake here is none other than the new and 'normal' biopolitical relation between citizens and the State. This relation no longer has to do with free and active participation in the public sphere, but instead concerns the routine inscription and registration of the most private and most incommunicable element of subjectivity—the biopolitical life of the body . . . The State, which ought to constitute the very space of public life, instead has made the citizen into the suspect par excellence—to the point that humanity itself has become a dangerous class. (2008: 202)

When considering advanced biometric surveillance tools such as FRT, however, such arguments do not go far enough. What is at stake is something more than bodily inscriptions, the idea that bodies are 'branded' so they can be monitored. Biometric surveillance does more than this. FRT, for example, functions by drawing inferences from the subcutaneous structure of bones and arrangements of cartilage and muscle in any given face. For Agamben, bio*political* tattoos become imposed from outside the body to within. Yet bio*metric* practices simultaneously assert themselves in the opposite direction: from within the body to the 'outside'. Data points are extracted from the interior and become externally visible. An *exteriorization* thus takes place. A bidirectional process may therefore be observed: categories, identities, and identifiers are simultaneously *imposed onto* and *extracted from* the body.

Over the last two decades, analysis has increasingly emphasized how data extracted from the body becomes reassembled and reinterpreted in new contexts. This process is perhaps most famously captured by the concept of 'data doubles' (Haggerty and Ericson 2000; Lyon 2001), which has acquired vernacular status in surveillance studies. This translation of the human form into digital code has, as Van der Ploeg (2012: 179) asserts, both redefined the body and generated 'new ontologies of the self'. Among many such accounts, however, it is possible to discern traces of lamentation, where life itself becomes depicted as reduced to digital fragments and thereby stripped of its humanity. This approach may emerge from a longer theoretical heritage, resonating with Walter Benjamin's (1968) observations over the cheapening of meaning through 'the mechanical reproduction of art' and, further still, to impoverished representations of the Platonic ideal. Concepts of the datafied body, however, take these ideas further. Here, it is not only that something is diminished by digital portrayal but that the referent, the human body, becomes *replaced* by its representation. As if moving beyond Baudrillard's (1994) hyperreality, the postmodern becomes the posthuman. In an important intervention in this debate, Akbari (2025) challenges such obituaries of the embodied self through her concept of 'code/body'. Rather than its erasure, biometric technologies reinstate and reconfigure the body in larger assemblages and data ecosystems. Artefacts such as cash, identity cards, and timesheets all become inscribed into flesh, where 'the body *becomes* the payment system, the surveillance machine, the border. It is integrated into the datafied society's infrastructure. It is platformised humanity' (2025: 199, emphasis in original).

The body therefore endures. Yet recent advances in remote biometric surveillance technologies extend beyond the confirmation of an identity. A shift occurs from *confirmation* to the *determination* of an identity; its traits and signifiers are predicated on analytics of both the interior *and* exterior of the human body. By extension, such techniques complicate the boundary of what is external *to*, and what is internally *of*, the human body. Increasing the reach of surveillance beyond the boundaries of the body creates radical possibilities for the monitoring and interpretation of individuals. As Van der Ploeg highlights, '[o]nce translations of bodily characteristics into digitally processable data have been made, these bodies become amenable to forms of analysis and categorisation in ways not possible before' (2012: 177). As such, surveillance practices can be seen to extend beyond the corporeal and temporal boundaries of a human life. Focus no longer rests solely on the individual as subject; surveillance allows observation of what lies *within and beyond* us. This fundamental principle upon which advanced biometric surveillance is predicated necessarily renders it more intrusive.

It is therefore possible to talk of biometric surveillance in terms of multiple coexisting processes. As Amoore (2014: 95) argues, 'the governing of species life, one might say, takes place through the exteriorization of intimate and corporeal elements of life itself, of a subject in formation'. These advanced biometric surveillance tools, then, become implicated in the generation of new forms of knowledge, a form of digitally mediated corpo*reality*.

Additional to considering how advanced biometric surveillance impacts its subjects, these innovations bring profound changes for their *users*. Most obviously, the computational architecture driving today's FRT systems allows processing to exist on previously unimagined scales. For example, biometric surveillance technologies sell the ability to scan and identify faces across huge crowds to a degree that surpasses the possibilities of human perception. Perhaps paradoxically, technologies designed to read the human body also potentially confer surveyors with abilities that extend beyond their own human capabilities.

As the next section elaborates, recent years have seen these processes of exteriorization intensify. Among these, one of the most hyped recent developments in biometric surveillance technology has attempted to deepen the reach into the inner realm of the individual: that of emotion recognition and sentiment analysis.

2.3.2 The Soul: Revealing Hearts of Darkness

In June 2024, the UK media reported on a two-year operation by Network Rail,[4] where eight major urban train stations were blanketed with Amazon's AI-driven surveillance cameras. Commuters passing through some of the UK's busiest transport hubs—including Manchester Piccadilly and London's Euston and Waterloo stations—were subjected to biometric scanning to elicit a dizzying range of data points (Wired 2024). Notable among these was the attempt to identify travellers' emotions. As Network Rail's internal documentation states, 'the customer emotion metric could be used to measure satisfaction [and] . . . could be utilised to maximum [sic] advertising and retail revenue' (CISCO 2023: 24). The pervasiveness of this system notably contrasted with the absence of public information over its use.

[4] The publicly owned body that manages most of the UK's rail infrastructure.

This episode of non-consensual remote biometric data extraction reveals much about the direction in which the biometrics industry is heading. Behaviour as a form of biometric data has attracted significant research and investment in recent years. Notable here is the commercial value of data collected on emotional states, regardless of the efficacy of such systems or the rights implications that arise. Attention is increasingly focused on the automated 'identification' and distillation of behavioural characteristics. These include classifying the way people walk (Forensic Science Regulator 2019), the aggregated 'behaviour' of crowd dynamics (Motsch et al. 2018), analysis of handwriting, and the elicitation of 'suspicious' emotions (see European Commission 2012). It is this latter context, security and suspicion, that has driven the development of technologies to identify and infer behavioural information ('affect technologies'). As the above example of advanced surveillance at Britain's rail hubs relays, advanced AI-driven surveillance systems are open ended and interoperable.

Facial recognition capability can be integrated into existing surveillance architecture. Affect technologies that attempt to classify emotions, behaviours, and sentiments are increasingly integrated into facial recognition systems. In an attempt to address the conundrum identified in Chapter 1 and posed to surveillance operators after 9/11, faces are monitored for identification but ambitions continue to observe subjects to decipher *intent*. In so doing, digitally informed pictures of suspicion become coloured with additional data points and layers of speculation.

Behavioural biometrics have been increasingly hosted at border crossings and highly securitized transportation hubs. Pioneered in the US, examples include the Automated Virtual Agent for Truth Assessments in Real-time (AVATAR) and Future Attribute Screening Technology (FAST). AVATAR takes the form of a digital kiosk that triages travellers on the grounds of suspicion through assessments of users' physiological and behavioural responses to questions. Those deemed to fall below a threshold of credibility are then filtered towards further (human) scrutiny. First deployed at the US–Mexico border, AVATAR achieved approval from Frontex, the European Union (EU) border-control agency, who, starting in Bucharest, began piloting and rolling out the programme in 2014 (National Center for Border Security and Immigration 2014). FAST, a US Department of Homeland Security-initiated programme, also operates at borders and scrutinizes individuals to a range of physiological measurements, including heart rate and eye movement. Such readings are then used to inform inferences over suspicion and an individual's supposed malintent. In some respects, these techniques mark a curious inversion of Foucault's (1977a) famous genealogy of the shifting locus of power from the body to the soul. Here, observation of the soul implicates rather than replaces the body.

Particularly striking about these initiatives is the degree of subjectivity required to classify such behaviours, and how such inferences depart from more familiar biometric identification techniques. Longstanding biometric systems designed to measure physical characteristics, such as fingerprinting and DNA profiling, draw from accepted scientific epistemologies and thus entail a degree of certainty. Yet the elicitation of meaning from behavioural cues draws on less established forms of knowledge. This in turn creates a space for normative, value-laden, and often culturally specific assumptions to frame the uses of such technology. As biometric identification techniques become more remote, so the degree of inference increases.

Embedded in affect technologies are highly normative assumptions about emotional states and their supposed physiological expression. These epistemologies reflect generations of neo-Darwinian claims, much rehearsed in Victorian-era criminology: that signs of deviance are visible and discernible. Additionally prominent is, again, how scientific language is recruited to justify such pseudoscience. Here, the lexicon of social psychology is deployed in the search for 'cognitive leakage', the belief that signs of malintent may spill from the psychological load of its bearers. Unencumbered by evidence, pseudoscience becomes repackaged by remote biometric identification technologies; the old wine of identifying and 'outing' wrongdoers comes in new bottles of digitally verified knowledge. Common to the rapid deployment of other biometric surveillance initiatives, affect technologies and digital behavioural analytics persist despite the continued absence of meaningful evidence to support them (see Matsumoto et al. 2011; GAO 2017; Maguire and Fussey 2016).

These shortcomings have afflicted the range of behavioural biometric identification. To take one biometric technique, the identification and categorization of individuals through their gait, the scientific community is united in its scepticism. For example, the national Forensic Science Regulator stressed in 2019 that the approach 'predominantly relies on observational analysis and comparison, rather than measurable objective techniques' (Forensic Science Regulator 2019: 7). In scientific guidance written for courts, the Royal Society earlier warned that

> there is no evidence to support the assertion that gait is unique within current or foreseeable limitations of measurements used in forensic gait

> analysis; There is no credible database currently that permits assessment of the frequency of either normal or abnormal gait characteristics. (The Royal Society 2017: 6)

Resonating with the growth of FRT, this informed critique has not prevented its adoption in law enforcement settings (Macoveciuc 2020).

As discussed throughout this book, absences of evidential basis, and the lack of credible methodology to establish that evidence, rarely serve as an impediment to the deployment of biometric identification technologies in policing. Particularly striking, then, is the contrast between the casual way scientific language is recruited to legitimize these approaches and the profound impacts of disqualification and injustice for those subjected to them. Digital automation of these security practices further deepens this tension. As mathematician Cathy O'Neil (2016) argues in her critique of digital society, those negatively affected by automated decisions are obliged to justify themselves to a higher standard than the algorithms that judge them.

The above discussion illustrates how biometric identification technologies have become deployed in the absence of meaningful evidence attesting to their performance. As the discussion above demonstrates, justifications for such activities are regularly decorated with scientific discourse. This has served to confer legitimacy on highly speculative surveillance practices that vary in both quality and impact. While the motivations for such practices invite simple explanations of technological evangelism, human–technical relationships are rarely straightforward. The discussion in the rest of this book explores how these technologies implicate and promote very specific forms of knowledge that are not easily discounted. In this setting, human responses to technology—such as the human deference to computer-issued FRT matches detailed in later chapters—acquire further meaning.

2.3.3 The Mind: Digital Truth Claims and a World Shaped through Technology

Biometric surveillance technologies represent people in highly specific ways. These representations are then invested with credibility precisely because of their technological origins. Such representations are, however, incomplete. The way digital representations of the social world strip away vital nuance and context is a commonly rehearsed critique in the computer and social sciences. One foundational expression of such debates occurs in the ur-text on postmodernism, where Francois Lyotard (1984) offers important insights that remain relevant for how digital technology is understood today. Foreshadowing many arguments later advanced in the field of science and technology studies, Lyotard reflected on how computerization reduces *knowledge* into highly specific and partial forms of *information*, an argument that digitally nuances T. S. Eliot's (1934: 7, emphasis added) lamentation, '[w]here is the wisdom we have lost in *knowledge* . . . Where is the *knowledge* we have lost in *information*?'.

Important here is how such optical statements claim authenticity through the validating discourse of technology, particularly in the context of policing practice. It can be argued that computational logics become reinforced through their reproduction. That which lies outside of such models, their externality, is gradually subjugated by the internal ontologies of the computational system. The reproduction of selective digitally produced 'evidence' further legitimizes the continued existence of these approaches and tools. In such settings, truth becomes that which is rendered, calculable, and actionable, 'a multiplicity of regimes of existence constantly stifled by algorithmic governmentality through the closing in of (digital) reality on itself', as Rouvroy and Berns (2013: 4) elegantly state.

It is here that another of Foucault's intellectual projects—one largely overlooked in criminology—holds particular value: that concerning questions of truth and the institution of 'regimes of veridiction'. Such concerns rose to become a persistent feature of his work throughout his career, and since at least the late 1960s (e.g. Foucault 1972, 1977c). In later iterations of these ideas, Foucault remarked that his focus was shifting away from associations with disciplinary power, the area of his thought most prominent in criminological and surveillance studies. Here he emphasized the importance of a shift from 'a site of jurisdiction' to a 'site of veridiction' (Foucault 2008: 30). In one of his most precise articulations of the concept, and relevant for analyses of computer-generated knowledge, for Foucault, regimes of veridiction, or 'truth', not only refer to 'types of discourse . . . harbour[ed] and cause[d] to function as true'. At stake is how such discourse is produced and instituted in highly specific ways, 'the way in which each [truth] is sanctioned' and the 'techniques and procedures which are valorised for obtaining truth' (Foucault 1977c: 13). These reflections on how particular truth claims emerge and are configured, and the outcomes they assert, hold deep significance in the digital era.

In the context of urban policing, risk and danger are increasingly encountered through digital technology. Technologies, we could argue, become lauded as a vital tool in the production of knowledge and, given the subjectivities and biases of their development and use, render dangers in their own image. Indeed, as Mary Douglas noted with discernible sarcasm,

> Somehow, it was thought that science had really made things different for us. We were supposed to be able to recognize real dangers, whose causes were objectively defined, backed by the authority of valid experiment and theory. Chance, mystery and malice lurked in small corners not yet claimed by science but, generally speaking, thanks to our accurate knowledge of the world and our powerful technology . . . 'real blaming' was possible . . . guaranteed by its objective basis in knowledge. (1992: 7)

Note, again, the persistence of the view that truth was still something reached through a process of incremental discovery. Through continued perseverance and refinement, science will inevitably shine its light into the dark spaces of uncertainty. In this context, facial recognition is positioned as something that will only improve, and its inherent biases will one day be removed. Yet such assertions not only ignore the biases and subjectivities embedded in technology, they also overlook the paradigm shifts and dramatic reversals within histories of science. Crucially, they also disregard the inevitable clashes between ascendent forms of knowledge. These are processes Foucault (1984) identifies (with a debt to both Nietzsche and Kuhn) as the cyclical replacement of new forms of 'truth telling'.

2.4 Conclusions

This chapter has argued that FRT represents a profound change in the way humans are surveilled, bodies are rendered, and intentions are deciphered. Accordingly, these changes constitute a step change in police capability, nuancing the practice of surveillance and altering its scope, form, and reach. Analysis of this shift is developed through later chapters, where FRT is not only more intrusive in a direct sense but it also subtly alters several longstanding aspects of policework, including the application of discretion and formulation of suspicion. Such extensions should not be interpreted as a synonym for technological determinism, however, and conceal a more complex picture of surveillance capability. Technological fallibilities and failings, and particularly inconsistent performance across ethnicity and gender, are buried under layers of technical discourse that requires attentive scrutiny to challenge.

The following chapters build on two core themes discussed here. The first concerns how this enhanced policing capability translates into harm. These compound and multiplicative harms are framed and captured through the lens of human rights law. Following this is a detailed empirical examination of police justifications for FRT ahead of active operations in London. Just as the above details how legitimating FRT narratives adapt and instrumentalize the discourse of science, once deployed in operational settings, such narratives adapt and instrumentalize the discourse of law.

3
Human Rights Law Considerations Brought into Play by Public Surveillance

3.1 Introduction

Significant academic interest has focused on the form and impact of advanced urban surveillance. As discussed in Chapters 1 and 2, much of this literature has centred on the range of potential harms brought about by surveillance practices. These include specific attention to how surveillance techniques exacerbate existing inequalities and bring new asymmetries of power and control. This chapter builds on and advances such implications of facial recognition technology (FRT) deployments by examining them through the lens of human rights law. Rights-based analysis provides an opportunity to build on the existing literature and to establish a more universal understanding of harm, to render these harms visible,[1] and to provide a means to address their impacts (McGregor et al. 2019). With respect to the latter, while traditional human rights law can be used to provide an after-the-fact remedy for those affected by FRT, human rights law mechanisms can also be adapted to intervene in, and inform, the decision-making processes surrounding FRT deployment; that is, before harm occurs.

This chapter sets out the key human rights law protections relevant to the deployment of facial recognition systems. Although framed around FRT—and in particular live facial recognition (LFR)—this discussion is relevant to surveillance practices generally, particularly in light of the move towards more advanced, and indeed more pervasive, surveillance architectures (as evidenced, for instance, by the incorporation of multiple surveillance databases into surveillance platforms such as Palantir).

[1] The idea that 'harm' itself is a socially constructed concept—as interrogated through sociologies of 'deviance' (e.g. Sumner 1994) and, more latterly, 'zemiology' (Canning and Tombs 2021)—is acknowledged here.

Facial Recognition Surveillance. Pete Fussey and Daragh Murray, Oxford University Press.
 DOI: 10.1093/9780191979927.003.0003

Analysing the human rights implications of FRT is complex and multifaceted. As a starting point, it must be recognized that different rights may be brought into play depending on the overall context within which a facial recognition system is used. For example, the right to liberty and security may be engaged if an individual is stopped by police following a facial recognition match, while the right to a fair trial will be engaged if facial recognition matches are used in court proceedings. This chapter, however, focuses squarely on the rights brought into play by FRT deployments themselves (rather than on rights engaged by any follow-up activities, such as the use of FRT in court). As such, it addresses those rights brought into play by the use of FRT in public spaces and how these rights implications should be considered and addressed by law enforcement officials.

The chapter commences with a brief introduction to international human rights law analysis by setting out the process by which interferences with human rights protections are determined to be lawful or not. Key rights brought into play by FRT are then examined in more detail. The rights discussed are the right to privacy, the right to freedom of expression, the right to freedom of assembly, the prohibition of discrimination, and the right to a human decision-maker.[2] In light of the surveillance capability made possible by facial recognition outlined in earlier chapters, and the chilling effects this may induce, the way in which these rights interact to protect individuals' ability to develop their (political) identity and to engage in democratic processes is also of significant interest.

The analysis herein draws primarily on the rights established in the European Convention on Human Rights and the case law of the European Court of Human Rights (ECtHR). This is because the operational trials that form the empirical basis of this book took place in the UK, and the European Convention on Human Rights is the most relevant human rights law treaty, by virtue of its incorporation into domestic law via the Human Rights Act (1998). That said, the approaches adopted under other international human rights law treaties—and in particular the International Covenant on Civil and Political Rights, the most broadly ratified relevant treaty—are largely similar, and the analysis presented herein should therefore have global relevance.

[2] It is noted that other rights, such as the right to freedom of religion or the right to freedom of opinion, may also be engaged. However, the manner in which these rights operate, and the manner in which they are likely to be engaged, are broadly similar to those discussed in the main text.

3.2 Determining Whether a Human Rights Interference Is Lawful

To facilitate a detailed analysis of the intersection between FRT and human rights, it is important to first set out key relevant human rights law terminology. In the first instance, it is important to note that most rights relevant to the operation of FRT—namely, the rights to privacy, freedom of expression, and freedom of assembly—are non-absolute rights,[3] meaning that they can be lawfully limited, or restricted, under certain conditions (see Section 3.2.2).[4] Equally, not all activities engage human rights protections. For example, and as explained below, the mere observation of an individual in public does not engage their right to privacy. Being observed is a natural consequence of being in public and so no human rights protections are brought into play. However, this dynamic alters if that individual's activities are recorded instead of merely being observed; then their right to privacy is engaged, again for reasons discussed below. Key here is the precision of terminology: an activity that engages a human rights protection is classified as constituting an 'interference' with that right. This does not automatically mean that the right in question is violated. It means that the right is brought into play, thereby triggering the requirement for a further test to determine whether the interference constitutes a violation of the human right. A human rights violation is, of course, unlawful. The test to determine whether such interferences are lawful—or constitute an unlawful violation—is clearly established in human rights law.[5] To be legitimate, an interference must be:

- in accordance with the law;
- in pursuit of a legitimate aim; and
- necessary in a democratic society.

[3] The rights to freedom of association and freedom of religion—which are both relevant to the police's use of facial recognition—are also non-absolute rights.

[4] The prohibition of discrimination is, of course, also relevant. However, this is an absolute right in that it straightforwardly prohibits detrimental treatment on the basis of any of the protected characteristics. No exceptions on the basis of, for example, national security are permissible.

[5] The test referred to here draws on the case law of the ECtHR, but this approach is reflected in other human rights systems. With respect to the International Covenant on Civil and Political Rights, the most widely ratified relevant human rights instrument, see, for instance, Article 21 and the discussion on limitations in General Comment 37, paras. 36–69, Human Rights Committee, General Comment No. 37, UN Doc. CCPR/C/GC/37, 17 September 2020.

This framework provides an important counterpoint to much prevailing surveillance discourse which often frames the legitimacy of a surveillance measure as a 'balancing' exercise, with 'security interests' on one side of the equation and the right to privacy on the other. From a human rights law perspective, there is no simple 'balancing'. States have an obligation to provide both security and privacy. While, under very specific circumstances, the latter may be limited to promote the former, this can only occur in prescribed circumstances *and* if the above three-part test is satisfied. This statutory reality also reveals the legal illiteracy of the 'nothing to hide, nothing to fear' argument. The apotheosis—and plainly wrong assumption—of this position is that state power may be unlimited and exercised arbitrarily. The inadequacy of these tropes for addressing the complex implications of public surveillance is underlined further by their grounding in overly subjective and ill-defined criteria and their failure to acknowledge the full extent of human rights protections. Human rights considerations cannot simply be 'balanced' against security or public order interests. Instead, and more accurately, human rights law evaluates whether any interference is 'in accordance with the law' and 'necessary' in light of the 'legitimate aim' pursued, on the basis of established objective criteria. In doing so, it ensures that both the potential utility of a surveillance measure, from a law enforcement perspective, and the potential harm of that measure, from a human rights perspective, are taken into consideration. Of additional note is how different aspects of the three-part human rights test have been interpreted by those seeking to deploy surveillance technologies. For example, socio-legal analyses and sociologies of policing have recognized a repeated tendency for the 'legitimate aim' and 'necessity' elements of the three-part test to become conflated and for 'necessity' to be misconstrued in a way that reduces its meaningfulness (Bullock and Johnson 2012; Fussey and Sandhu 2022; Harfield and Harfield 2023; see also Chapters 5 and 6). To enable meaningful assessment of the human rights implications of FRT, and the degree to which police uses of this technology accord with statutory human rights obligations, each component of the three-part test is now examined in more detail.

3.2.1 In Accordance with the Law

The purpose of the 'in accordance with the law' requirement is to ensure a legal framework capable of appropriately limiting officer discretion and preventing the arbitrary exercise of state powers. In the context of UK policing, this is particularly important, as facial recognition deployments currently occur in the absence of an explicit legal basis. The 'in accordance with the law' test requires (a) that a legal basis to oversee a rights interference exists and (b) that the overall legal framework is of *sufficient quality* to protect against arbitrary rights interferences; specifically, it must be sufficiently precise and 'foreseeable' as to its effects. In sum, it is not simply the case that a law needs to exist to permit surveillance; the law also needs to be of sufficient quality to protect the rights of those subjected to it.

In relation to the first component, human rights law requires that a measure giving rise to a human rights interference—such as the deployment of FRT by law enforcement agencies, other forms of intrusive surveillance, or, indeed, the arrest of an individual—must have 'some basis in domestic law'.[6] Typically, this legal basis is established by means of dedicated legislation. In the UK, for example, the Police and Criminal Evidence Act 1984 establishes a legal basis for police powers to stop and search, arrest, and detain, while the Investigatory Powers Act 2016 authorizes the use of advanced surveillance techniques such as equipment interference and the retention of communications data. An *explicit* legal basis is said to exist in cases such as these where dedicated legislation authorizes particular acts. However, under certain circumstances police activity may be authorized on the basis of *implied* powers. Under the common law, for example, the police are authorized 'to take all steps which appear . . . necessary for keeping the peace, for preventing crime or for protecting property from public damage'.[7] This has been held to establish an implicit legal basis for the collection and retention of personal information, including photographs of individuals, for the purposes of preventing and detecting crime.[8]

Based on a particular interpretation of the caselaw, UK police forces assert that the implied powers established under the common law, combined with a publicly accessible policy framework, are sufficient for uses of FRT to satisfy the 'in accordance with the law' test (MPS 2020b: 3.9). However, the degree to which such implied powers hold sufficient quality to protect against arbitrary rights interferences with respect to FRT has been a source of considerable debate (e.g. Fussey and Murray 2019).

[6] *Kennedy* v *the United Kingdom*, Judgment, ECtHR, App. No. 26839/05, 18 May 2010, para. 151.

[7] *Rice* v *Connolly* [1966] 2 QB 414 at 419B–C.

[8] *R (Catt)* v *Commissioner of Police of the Metropolis* [2015] UKSC 9, 4 March 2015, para. 7.

In *Bridges*, the initial High Court judgment found that common law policing powers provided an 'amply sufficient' basis for the police's use of LFR and that no new legislation was required.[9] This meant that facial recognition could be deployed on the basis of implied legal powers absent an *explicit* legal basis. In line with this conclusion, the High Court found that South Wales Police's (SWP's) use of facial recognition was 'in accordance with the law'.[10]

However, the *Bridges* judgment was subject to a successful appeal and the subsequent Court of Appeal decision was somewhat more nuanced. The Court of Appeal found deficiencies in the policy framework prepared by SWP, resulting in the conclusion that their use of LFR was not 'in accordance with the law'[11] and therefore constituted a violation of the right to private life. However, the Court of Appeal did not engage directly with the High Court's finding that the common law was 'amply sufficient'. As such, the possibility that an implied legal basis is sufficient remains open. As stated by the Court of Appeal:

> *in principle* a police force's local policies can constitute relevant 'law' in the present context, provided they are published. The critical question, in our view, is how much discretion the policies in this case leave to the police, particularly in relation to the question who can be put on a watchlist and the question of the location where AFR Locate can be deployed.[12]

Purshouse and Campbell (2021: 216) have noted that this 'finding is significant'. In effect, it suggests that police forces' own policies may be sufficient to satisfy the 'in accordance with the law' requirement, provided they are framed with sufficient precision.[13] However, the analysis below challenges this conclusion.

[9] *R (Bridges)* v *Chief Constable of South Wales Police* [2019] EWHC 2341 (Admin), para. 78.

[10] *R (Bridges)* v *Chief Constable of South Wales Police* [2019] EWHC 2341 (Admin), para. 96.

[11] *R (Bridges)* v *Chief Constable of South Wales Police* [2019] EWHC 2341 (Admin), para. 130.

[12] *R (Bridges)* v *The Chief Constable of South Wales Police* [2020] EWCA Civ 1058, para. 121 (emphasis added). AFR Locate is the LFR tool used by SWP.

[13] Interestingly, the Court of Appeal also stated that 'it is now common ground that SWP have the power to deploy AFR Locate' (para. 38). It is not clear that SWP's power to deploy FRT was in fact accepted by the appellant; there may not have been 'common ground'. Rather, it may be the case that this issue was not contested as it was not relevant to the appeal. For example, the appellant's skeleton grounds of appeal focused on the overall quality of the legal framework rather than any specific authority—or lack thereof—under the common law (Liberty 2020).

Under UK law, a key question is whether FRT can be considered 'intrusive' or not. In a prior ruling, *R (Catt)* v *Commissioner of Police of the Metropolis*, the Supreme Court held that:

> At common law the police have the power to obtain and store information for policing purposes, i.e. broadly speaking for the maintenance of public order and the prevention and detection of crime. These powers do not authorise intrusive methods for obtaining information, such as entry upon private property or acts (other than arrest under common law powers) which would constitute an assault. But they were amply sufficient to authorise the obtaining and storage of the kind of public information in question on these appeals.[14]

Essentially, according to the Supreme Court's reasoning, to satisfy the 'in accordance with the law' requirement, *non-intrusive* measures need not have an explicit legal basis, 'provided that they operate within a framework of law and that there are effective means of enforcing them'.[15] This of course implies that intrusive measures do require an explicit legal basis.

In *Catt*, collecting and storing pictures or videos of an individual in public was held to be non-intrusive and contrasted with intrusive methods such as entry upon private property, physical coercion, bugging, or DNA sampling.[16] The *Bridges* Court of Appeal confirmed the relevance of this distinction—between intrusive and non-intrusive methods of surveillance—in the context of facial recognition.[17] However, it has been argued that limiting 'intrusive' measures to those that encroach upon private property or involve a physical element of coercion, as per *Catt* and then *Bridges*, is no longer valid given the significant changes in surveillance capability made possible by facial recognition (Purshouse and Campbell 2021; Murray 2024). FRT has fundamentally changed *how* intrusion into private

[14] *R (Catt)* v *Commissioner of Police of the Metropolis* [2015] UKSC 9, 4 March 2015, para. 7. Interestingly, when *Catt* came before the ECtHR, the issue as to whether the police's implied common law policing powers were sufficient to satisfy the 'in accordance with the law' test was raised. Ultimately, the Court did not reach a conclusion in this regard as it instead found a violation of the right to private life with respect to the 'necessary in a democratic society' test. However, the Court did note that it had 'concerns about the ambiguity of the legal basis for the collection of the applicant's personal data'. See *Catt* v *The United Kingdom*, Application No. 43514/15, Judgment, 24 January 2019, para. 105.

[15] *R (Catt)* v *Commissioner of Police of the Metropolis* [2015] UKSC 9, para. 11.

[16] *R (Catt)* v *Commissioner of Police of the Metropolis* [2015] UKSC 9, paras. 1, 7.

[17] *R (Bridges)* v *The Chief Constable of South Wales Police* [2020] EWCA Civ 1058, para. 77.

life can occur. As detailed in Chapter 2, the advent of remote biometric identification has changed police surveillance in highly significant ways: it is no longer necessary to physically engage with an individual to identify them. Or, indeed, to track and profile them.

In *Bridges*, the Court of Appeal held that LFR technology exists on a spectrum of intrusiveness. At one end of the spectrum is *Catt*, which involved the 'non-intrusive' recording of images in public. No explicit legal basis was required for this 'non-intrusive' application. At the other end of the spectrum is *S* v *The United Kingdom*, which involved the 'intrusive' physical collection and retention of fingerprints and DNA profiles, for which an explicit legal basis was required.[18]

It is suggested that placing facial recognition on a spectrum *between* these two poles is inappropriate. Although FRT operates remotely and is not therefore equivalent to fingerprinting or DNA testing in terms of physicality, it does give rise to an interference with the right to private life that is equivalent to these other forms of biometric surveillance. The surveillance capability facilitated by FRT reveals at least as much about an individual as their fingerprint (i.e. it can identify them), with the potential to reveal far more (i.e. by facilitating inferences about their day-to-day life, movement, associations, political opinion, etc.). It is highly significant that, in a 2023 decision made subsequent to *Bridges*, the ECtHR classified FRT as 'highly intrusive'.[19]

Given both its designation under human rights law as 'highly intrusive' and its dramatic impact on the scope of police surveillance, facial recognition should, at minimum, be placed on a level with *S and Marper* in terms of its intrusiveness. As such, any use should require an explicit legal basis. Indeed, recognition of FRT as a highly intrusive surveillance technology suggests that it is inappropriate to allow its deployment, solely on the basis of implied powers, which are subject to internal regulation via police policy.

However, despite this line of reasoning, at the time of writing the question as to whether an explicit legal basis is required for FRT remains open in

[18] *R (Bridges)* v *The Chief Constable of South Wales Police* [2020] EWCA Civ 1058, para. 85. The Strasbourg ruling on *S and Marper* v *The United Kingdom* had seismic implications for the oversight of biometric surveillance in the UK. Most notably, this led to the establishment of a Biometrics Commissioner under the Protection of Freedoms Act 2012 who, along with other statutory functions, determined the legality of retaining biometric materials in individual cases.

[19] *Glukhin* v *Russia*, Judgment, ECtHR, App. No. 11519/20, 4 July 2023, para. 90.

the UK. This point is likely to feature in any future facial recognition-related litigation.

Turning to the second component of the 'in accordance with the law' requirement, the legal basis underpinning the police's use of facial recognition—whether implicit or explicit—must be of sufficient quality to limit officer discretion and protect against arbitrary rights interferences. Clarity in the legal or policy framework is necessary if longstanding concerns regarding the 'creep' of surveillance from one stated rationale to another are to be addressed (see Chapter 6). The 'quality' component has two elements. First, the law must be accessible; second, its consequences must be foreseeable.[20]

Taking these in turn, the requirement that the law be accessible is a core component of the rule of law: an individual should know the extent of the state's powers and the rules that they are bound by. This is why the discussion above referred to the existence of a publicly accessible policy framework. In the absence of dedicated legislation (as is the case with FRT), it is required that the extent of the police's powers be set out in police policy.

The foreseeability requirement relates to the precision with which the law (or policy framework) is formulated. Essentially, an individual should be able to foresee the consequences that certain acts may entail so that they can regulate their behaviour accordingly.[21] Foreseeability itself is subject to further definition. As reflected in ECtHR caselaw, the law need not 'be foreseeable with absolute certainty, as experience show[s] that to be unattainable'.[22] In the context of surveillance, for example, foreseeability 'cannot mean that an individual should be able to foresee when the authorities are likely to intercept his communications so that he can adapt his conduct accordingly'.[23] Instead, there must be clear and detailed rules on *how* surveillance occurs. The level of precision required will depend on factors such as the nature of the police power in question and the number of people affected by that power.[24] This suggests that a high degree of precision is required for

[20] *Roman Zakharov* v *Russia*, Grand Chamber, ECtHR, App. No. 47143/06, 4 December 2015, para. 228.

[21] *Perincek* v *Switzerland*, Grand Chamber, ECtHR, App. No. 27510/08, 15 October 2015, para. 131.

[22] *Perincek* v *Switzerland*, Grand Chamber, ECtHR, App. No. 27510/08, 15 October 2015, para. 131; *Lindon, Otchakovsky-Laurens and July* v *France*, Grand Chamber, ECtHR, App. Nos. 21279/02, 36448/02, 22 October 2007, para. 41.

[23] *Szabo and Vissy* v *Hungary*, Judgment, ECtHR, App. No. 7138/114, 12 January 2016, para. 62.

[24] *Gillan and Quinton* v *The United Kingdom*, Judgment, ECtHR, App. No. 4158/05, 12 January 2010, para. 77.

facial recognition deployments given FRT's highly intrusive nature and the significant numbers of people that will be subject to biometric scanning. As such, the extent of the police's powers and how they are to be exercised must be set out in a clear and detailed way.[25] This is important as a lack of clarity generates space for discretion and the arbitrary exercise of police power.

To date, this issue of precision has been one of the most contested regarding the legal basis for FRT. For example, the precision of SWP's policy framework was one of the key points of contention in *Bridges*, the only judicial review addressing the legality of FRT in the UK. Here, the conclusion that SWP's policy framework was overly broad was central to the Court of Appeal's finding that the use of LFR was not in accordance with the law.[26] The Court highlighted deficiencies regarding the 'who' and the 'where' questions, concerning who may be placed on a watchlist and where LFR may be deployed. These are important criteria and they should appropriately feature in any legal or policy framework regulating FRT. On their own, however, they may not be capable of placing adequate limits on officer discretion, particularly when other facial recognition applications, such as retrospective facial recognition (RFR), are considered. Other relevant criteria might include 'what' the basis for using facial recognition should be, such as the type or seriousness of the crime in question (this is, of course, linked to 'who') and 'when' facial recognition may be applied, as this may be relevant with respect to how far back in time the use of RFR may extend.

The extent to which current police FRT policy frameworks satisfy the 'in accordance with the law' requirement is analysed in detail in Chapter 5.

3.2.2 In Pursuit of a Legitimate Aim

To be lawful, any interference with the rights to privacy, expression, or assembly must be 'in pursuit of a legitimate aim'. The legitimate aims are set out in the text of the relevant rights and are broadly similar. For the right to privacy, the legitimate aims are:

> the interests of national security, public safety or the economic well-being of the country, the prevention of disorder or crime, the protection

[25] *Catt* v *The United Kingdom*, Judgment, ECtHR, App. No. 43514/15, 24 January 2019, para. 94.

[26] *R (Bridges)* v *The Chief Constable of South Wales Police* [2020] EWCA Civ 1058, para. 91.

of health or morals, or the protection of the rights and freedoms of others.[27]

It is generally accepted that policing activity pursues the legitimate aim of preventing disorder or crime, protecting the rights and freedom of others, protecting public safety, or—depending on the nature of the police operation—protecting national security.[28] As such, good-faith police deployments of FRT are unlikely to generate significant concerns for this specific criterion and this element of the three-part test is typically dealt with summarily by the courts.

However, socio-legal and criminological research has consistently highlighted how authorization processes for police surveillance consistently conflate 'legitimate aim' and 'necessity', such that a measure is considered necessary if it is in pursuit of a legitimate aim (Bullock and Johnson 2012; Sandhu and Fussey 2020). This misconstruction is replicated in the context of LFR. In practice, UK police policy documents treat necessity as synonymous with utility, meaning that the necessity test is inappropriately reduced to an analysis of whether the use of facial recognition is useful in pursuit of a legitimate aim. This misconstruction therefore leverages the least challenging test—the legitimate aim—to offer the appearance of 'satisfying' more stringent human rights law requirements. This is discussed in greater detail in Chapter 5.

3.2.3 Necessary in a Democratic Society

Necessity is one of the most extensively discussed issues when it comes to the deployment of advanced surveillance technologies. It is arguably also one of the most misunderstood. Later chapters evidence how these misconceptions can be identified throughout the entire deployment process. Under human rights law, the necessity test is intended to ensure the overall human rights compliance of a measure; that is, can it be considered 'necessary in a democratic society'? It is not, as commonly construed, intended to determine whether a measure is necessary (or useful) to a particular

[27] Article 8(2), European Convention on Human Rights. See also Article 10(2), European Convention on Human Rights; Article 11(2), European Convention on Human Rights.

[28] See, for instance, *Catt* v *The United Kingdom*, Judgment, ECtHR, App. No. 43514/15, 24 January 2019, para. 108; *Glukhin* v *Russia*, Judgment, ECtHR, App. No. 11519/20, 4 July 2023, para. 84.

operation. The 'democratic society' suffix to 'necessity' holds particular importance for articulating the level of accordance with the values associated with such a society.[29] Particularly relevant to applications of surveillance technologies, a core objective of the necessity test is the resolution of the 'competing interests' at play.[30] That is, the potential benefit to human rights associated with a surveillance measure, on the one hand, and the potential harm to human rights associated with that measure on the other. In the context of a facial recognition deployment, the competing interests may be the potential benefit to public order or the prevention of crime contrasted with the potential harm to privacy, freedom of expression, freedom of assembly, and so on. This means that, to conduct the necessity test effectively, both the potential utility and the potential harm associated with a particular surveillance measure must be identified (and clearly articulated in any authorization documents).

In *S and Marper* v *The United Kingdom*—a landmark case concerning police use of biometric data—the ECtHR addressed the competing interests arising between police retention of a large-scale DNA database (based on the claim that it was useful for the prevention and detection of crime) and competing-interest factors such as privacy, the risk of stigmatization, and so on (all falling under the right to a private life). In reasoning equally applicable to facial recognition, the Court expressed its approach to this issue as follows:

> The Court cannot, however, disregard the fact that, notwithstanding the advantages provided by comprehensive extension of the DNA database, other Contracting States have chosen to set limits on the retention and use of such data with a view to achieving a proper balance with the competing interests of preserving respect for private life. The Court observes that the protection afforded by Article 8 of the Convention would be unacceptably weakened if the use of modern scientific techniques in the criminal-justice system were allowed at any cost and without carefully balancing the potential benefits of the extensive use of such techniques against important private-life interests.[31]

[29] *Klass and Others* v *Germany*, Judgment, ECtHR, App. No. 5029/71, 6 September 1978, para. 55.

[30] *S and Marper* v *The United Kingdom*, Judgment, ECtHR, App. Nos. 30562/04 and 30566/04, 4 December 2008, para. 112.

[31] *S and Marper* v *The United Kingdom*, Judgment, ECtHR, App. Nos. 30562/04 and 30566/04, 4 December 2008, para. 112.

Importantly, evaluating competing interests is not equivalent to a straightforward balancing exercise. It is not the case that, if the utility outweighs the harm, then the measure will be considered necessary and therefore lawful. Nonetheless, this is a common misconception. Within surveillance discussions, and as noted above, necessity is often framed as a balance between privacy and security. This is inappropriate. The necessity test must engage with the overall rights impact of a measure *and* be consistent with democratic values. In a surveillance context, this will often involve a three-stage process. As underscored in the Strasbourg *Catt* judgment, a measure may be considered necessary in a democratic society 'if it answers to a "pressing social need", if it is proportionate to the legitimate aim pursued and if the reasons adduced by the national authorities to justify it are relevant and sufficient'.[32]

In order for a 'pressing social need' to be established, it is not necessarily required that the measure in question be 'indispensable' but it must be more than 'reasonable', 'desirable', or 'useful'.[33] The ECtHR has clearly stated that, for surveillance capabilities as intrusive as facial recognition, a high level of justification is required. This clearly translates as raising the threshold for deployment away from using FRT merely because it is 'desirable' or 'useful', instead requiring that its use align closer with being 'indispensable'.

A proportionality test is not set out explicitly in the European Convention on Human Rights but instead has been read into the necessity test; that is, a measure must be necessary in a democratic society and proportionate to the legitimate aim pursued. As such, proportionality refers to the relationship 'between the means used and the aim sought to be achieved'.[34] This requires an examination of alternative, less rights-intrusive means,[35] which must of course also independently satisfy the necessity test. The provision of 'relevant and sufficient' justification for a surveillance measure is necessarily dependent upon the establishment of an appropriate evidence base.

[32] *Catt* v *The United Kingdom*, Judgment, ECtHR, App. No. 43514/15, 24 January 2019, para. 109.

[33] *Handyside* v *The United Kingdom*, Judgment, ECtHR, App. No. 549/72, 7 December 1976, para. 48.

[34] *Perincek* v *Switzerland*, Grand Chamber, ECtHR, App. No. 27510/08, 15 October 2015, para. 228.

[35] *Nada* v *Switzerland*, Grand Chamber, ECtHR, App. No. 10593/08, 12 September 2012, para. 183.

This non-equivalence between 'necessity' and 'utility' is a crucial detail that should be emphasized. Observations of police FRT planning in London revealed significant confusion and conflation in this regard. In several pre-operational meetings ahead of deployments in east and central London, necessity was repeatedly framed incorrectly as whether the technology was useful to the investigation and proportionate in light of the underlying crime.[36] This misunderstanding is repeated throughout Metropolitan Police Service (MPS) policy documents, as discussed in Chapter 5. This understanding, however, is reflective of only a subset of the overall necessity test, substituting proportionality for necessity, failing to take into consideration the importance of respect for democratic values, and neglecting the harm to human rights side of the equation.

Not only does such confusion and conflation reflect similar findings in other analyses of police surveillance authorizations (inter alia, Harfield and Harfield 2018; Fussey and Sandhu 2022), it also frames the necessity calculation in ways that almost always extend the range of surveillance operations and limit the weight given to human rights considerations. These incomplete formulations also hold a performative function. Framing necessity in this way expresses a sense that the procedure and symbols of legal accountability are addressed while leaving crucial considerations of harm unresolved.

Ultimately, the necessity test requires a clear understanding of both the potential utility and the potential harm of a measure. If the necessity test is to be applied effectively and properly, it is essential that appropriate evidence be presented by the authorities: the pressing social need must be appropriately demonstrated and relevant and sufficient reasons justifying a measure provided. This is where the human rights due diligence framework developed below comes into play. Instead of waiting for an after-the-fact remedy, our framework adapts existing human rights law mechanisms to front-load human rights compliance, ensuring that as much of the necessity evaluation as possible is undertaken prior to any decision to deploy. We will return to this in Chapter 4.

Discounting the potential harm of FRT, as these misformulations of necessity do, generates further, compounded downstream implications. As

[36] This echoes the comment in the previous section regarding the legitimate aim being substituted for necessity. If the focus is only on proportionality, then a police decision will inevitably prioritize the investigation of prevention of crime over an individual's right to privacy.

the next section demonstrates, uses of FRT bring a complex range of rights into play. Many of these intersect with each other and amplify the potential impact of surveillance. The past thirty years have brought heightened understandings of how different forms of disadvantage inter-relate, most notably through concepts of intersectionality and, in the context of surveillance, of 'cumulative disadvantage' (Gandy 2009). Considering the range of rights brought into play, and their interrelationships with respect to FRT, reveals an important dimension to the impact of surveillance. Multiple surveillance harms are not additive; they are multiplicative.

3.3 Rights Brought into Play by Facial Recognition Technology

The right to privacy is the most typical entry point when discussing surveillance harms, as illustrated by the 'security versus privacy' dichotomy that dominates much of the discussion on surveillance and which is referenced above. However, privacy is an inappropriately narrow lens through which to view the effects of surveillance, particularly advanced surveillance technologies such as FRT. The impacts of surveillance are much broader and it is therefore necessary to analyse these broader rights impacts in order to properly take into account the overall impact of FRT, and to avoid the understatement and concealment of significant rights implications.

The link between facial recognition surveillance and bias—particularly on grounds of race, sex, or age—constitutes one of the most heated areas of discussion relating to this technology. The uneven performance of FRT algorithms across different demographic groups—and protected demographic characteristics—is established scientific fact. As such, the prohibition of discrimination is a key consideration when assessing the impact of FRT. The right to a human decision-maker is then addressed, given its centrality to police deployments, its role in street engagements, and the claims made by FRT advocates that it brings accountability to computer-driven processes. The use of surveillance technologies may also give rise to chilling effects, whereby individuals modify their behaviour due to the fear of surveillance. Any such chilling effects necessarily bring into play the rights to freedom of expression and freedom of assembly. The simultaneous impact that chilling effects may exert across multiple rights—that is, the compound harm they may give rise to—is then highlighted.

3.3.1 The Right to Privacy

The right to privacy is codified in Article 17(1) of the International Covenant on Civil and Political Rights as follows:

> No one shall be subjected to arbitrary or unlawful interference with his privacy, family, home or correspondence, nor to unlawful attacks on his honour and reputation.

Similar protections are established in Article 8(1) of the European Convention on Human Rights. This is the version encoded into UK law via the Human Rights Act (1998):

> Everyone has the right to respect for his private and family life, his home and his correspondence.

The scope of the right to privacy is broad and 'not susceptible to exhaustive definition',[37] and therefore it may be adapted and widened over time. At the heart of the right, however, is respect for personal autonomy[38] and for an individual's right to freely develop their personality and identity.[39] These are essential components of the right as they protect individuals' ability to be, or at least to become, their 'true selves'.[40] Privacy is sometimes characterized as something less fundamental, a luxury that is accessible to the rich or something readily traded for convenience. Indeed, the suggested expendability of privacy is inherent in the 'nothing to hide, nothing to fear' couplet and in the commercial convenient proclamations of Mark Zuckerberg's 'privacy is no longer the social norm' (*The Guardian* 2010) and former Google CEO Eric Schmidt's 'if you have something you don't want anyone to know, maybe you shouldn't be doing it in the first place' (EFF 2009).[41] While such basic binary conceptions of privacy are simplistic

[37] *Pretty* v *The United Kingdom*, Judgment, ECtHR, App. No. 2346/02, 29 April 2002, para. 61.

[38] *A, B and C* v *Ireland*, Grand Chamber, ECtHR, App. No. 25579/05, 16 December 2010, para. 212.

[39] *Mikulic* v *Croatia*, Judgment, ECtHR, App. No. 53176/99, 7 February 2002, para. 54.

[40] See, e.g., *A.-M.V.* v *Finland*, Judgment, ECtHR, App. No. 53251/13, 23 March 2017, para. 76. We will return to this in the next section in the context of the chilling effect. *Von Hannover* v *Germany*, Judgment, ECtHR, App. No. 59320/00, 24 June 2004, para. 69.

[41] Zuckerburg and Schmidt were less casual when it came to their own privacy. To avoid his house being overlooked, Zuckerberg purchased his neighbours' properties in Palo Alto

(Bauman and Lyon 2012) and, from a human rights law perspective, irrelevant, a deeper principle is at stake. Rather than being a luxury, privacy is central to an individual's formation of identity.

The development of relationships with others, and the outside world in general, is also recognized as a key element in individuals' identity development.[42] Accordingly, human rights law confirms that there is a 'zone of interaction of a person with others, even in a public context, which may fall within the scope of private life'.[43] This gives rise to the question as to what 'public' activity falls within the scope of the right to privacy. The starting point is a recognition that an individual must expect to be seen when they are out in public. This means that the observation—also often referred to as the monitoring—of an individual's public activities does not give rise to an interference with the right to privacy.[44] This includes situations where monitoring/observation occurs using technical means, such as when a security guard monitors a live surveillance feed.[45]

This equation changes, however, if a record of 'public' activity is captured; that is, if surveillance is initiated. While it is reasonable to expect to be observed while in public—indeed, this is almost inevitable—it is also reasonable to expect that this observation is fleeting, and that no records of actions are maintained. As such, surveillance—that is, the act of establishing a record, or analysis, of an individual's public activities—is a decisive turning point.[46] This issue becomes particularly important with respect to images of an identified person. Here, a recent ECtHR ruling recognized that a person's image constitutes 'one of the chief attributes' of their personality because it reveals their unique characteristics and distinguishes them from their peers.[47] The right to privacy is engaged as soon as any systematic or permanent record of public activities becomes established. This means that the recording or storage of surveillance camera footage—in and

(Greenwald 2014), while Schmidt banned journalists associated with organizations that had previously published his personal details online (EFF 2009).

[42] *Peck* v *The United Kingdom*, Judgment, ECtHR, App. No. 44647/98, 28 January 2003, para. 57.

[43] *Von Hannover* v *Germany (No. 2)*, Judgment, ECtHR, App. Nos. 40660/08 and 60641/08, 7 February 2012, para. 95.

[44] *Glukhin* v *Russia*, Judgment, ECtHR, App. No. 11519/20, 4 July 2023, para. 66.

[45] *P.G. and J.H.* v *The United Kingdom*, Judgment, ECtHR, App. No. 44787/98, 25 September 2001, para. 57.

[46] *Lopez Ribalda and Others* v *Spain*, Grand Chamber, ECtHR, App. Nos. 1874/13 and 8567/13, 10 October 2019, para. 89.

[47] *Glukhin* v *Russia*, Judgment, ECtHR, App. No. 11519/20, 4 July 2023, para. 66.

of itself—will engage the right to privacy.[48] Any processing of data—for example, using LFR or RFR—will then give rise to an additional interference with the right to privacy.[49]

As such, both the recording of video or photographic footage and the analysis of that imagery using FRT will give rise to separate interferences with the right to privacy (Human Rights Committee 2020: 62). FRT, then, implicates privacy in ways that are more profound and complex than for more traditional forms of public video surveillance. Moreover, in *Glukhin v Russia*—the first ECtHR decision directly addressing the use of FRT—the Court held that both RFR and LFR are 'highly intrusive' when it comes to the right to privacy.[50] This suggests that the Court considers the threshold for justifying police use of facial recognition to be high.

3.3.2 The Prohibition of Discrimination

Bias and discrimination are perhaps the issues on which the most significant controversy over facial recognition turns, at least in terms of the accuracy of the technology (see Chapters 2 and 8). The prohibition of discrimination is codified in Article 26 of the International Covenant on Civil and Political Rights:

> All persons are equal before the law and are entitled without any discrimination to the equal protection of the law. In this respect, the law shall prohibit any discrimination and guarantee to all persons equal and effective protection against discrimination on any ground such as race, colour, sex, language, religion, political or other opinion, national or social origin, property, birth or other status.

Although the International Covenant on Civil and Political Rights (ICCPR) does not define discrimination as such, the United Nations (UN) Human Rights Committee has authoritatively clarified:

[48] *Catt* v *The United Kingdom*, Judgment, ECtHR, App. No. 43514/15, 24 January 2019, para. 93.

[49] *Gaughran* v *The United Kingdom*, Judgment, ECtHR, App. No. 45245/15, 13 February 2020, para. 70. This was also confirmed by the UK Court of Appeal in *Bridges*.

[50] *Glukhin* v *Russia*, Judgment, ECtHR, App. No. 11519/20, 4 July 2023, para. 88.

> that the term 'discrimination' as used in the Covenant should be understood to imply any distinction, exclusion, restriction or preference which is based on any grounds such as race, colour, sex, language, religion, political or other opinion, national or social origin, property, birth or other status, and which has the purpose or effect of nullifying or impairing the recognition, enjoyment or exercise by all persons, on an equal footing, of all rights and freedoms. (Human Rights Committee 1989: 7)

In the UK, a similar right is established in the Equality Act 2010. A prohibition of discrimination is also established in Article 14 of the European Convention on Human Rights. This prohibition is somewhat narrower than that in the ICCPR and UK law as it only prohibits discrimination in relation to one of the Convention rights—that is, discrimination impacting the right to privacy—and not discrimination generally.

All prohibitions of discrimination, however, address both *direct* and *indirect* discrimination. Respectively, this is intended in the Human Rights Committee's above reference to 'purpose' and 'effect'. Direct discrimination relates to intentional discrimination on the basis of one of the prohibited grounds. Demonstrating direct discrimination requires proving that others are treated differently on the basis of a protected characteristic when they are in a comparable situation.[51] Indirect discrimination occurs when an act may appear neutral but has the *effect* of discriminating. The ECtHR described indirect discrimination as follows:

> a difference in treatment may take the form of disproportionately prejudicial effects of a general policy or measure which, though couched in neutral terms, discriminates against a group . . . such a situation may amount to 'indirect discrimination', which does not necessarily require a discriminatory intent.[52]

Applied to the use of FRT, the prohibition of discrimination requires that all those subject to the technology be treated in the same manner and that there be no difference in treatment—either directly or indirectly—on the basis of one or more of the protected characteristics. Concerns regarding

[51] See *Lithgow* v *The United Kingdom*, Judgment, ECtHR, App. Nos. 9006/80, 9262/81, 9263/81, 9265/81, 9266/81, 9313/81, and 9405/81, 8 July 1986, para. 177.

[52] *D.H. and Others* v *The Czech Republic*, Judgment ECtHR, App. No. 57325/00, 13 November 2007, para. 184.

discrimination arise in at least two ways, relating to technical performance and the nature of police deployments. First, as detailed in Chapter 2, concerns have been raised regarding bias built into FRT itself (often referred to as 'algorithmic bias'). This means that the technology may behave differently depending upon an individual's sex, race, or colour, thereby giving rise to indirect discrimination. Here, even if the purpose may not be intended to be discriminatory, the algorithm operates in such a way that it results in discriminatory outcomes. Second, FRT may be deployed in a manner that gives rise to concerns regarding directly discriminatory policing practices (Fussey 2013; BBC 2023). Such concerns have arisen, for example, in the context of the police's exercise of stop-and-search powers and in the use of surveillance cameras to monitor entire neighbourhoods.

In the UK, the Public Sector Equality Duty (PSED) requires that public authorities—which include the police—have 'due regard' to the need to eliminate discrimination (Equality Act: §149(1)). This is a positive duty meaning, in this instance, that the police must take reasonable steps to ensure that the FRT it uses—and indeed each facial recognition deployment—does not discriminate on the basis of one or more of the protected characteristics. This can be carried out either directly by the police force themselves or by way of independent verification (the MPS's efforts in this regard are discussed in Chapters 5 and 6). The PSED is a duty of process, not of outcome, hence the focus on 'reasonable steps'. The *Bridges* Court of Appeal confirmed that all police forces that intend to use facial recognition should satisfy themselves 'that everything reasonable which could be done had been done' in order to make sure that the software does not demonstrate bias.[53] The Court of Appeal also asserted that the presence of a human adjudicator, a 'human failsafe', is not sufficient to discharge the PSED.[54] Importantly, the *Bridges* Court of Appeal also held that the PSED applies irrespective of commercial confidentiality.[55]

To date, any discrimination-related discussion has typically focused on the performance of the algorithm itself.[56] However, and as discussed further in Chapters 7 and 8, facial recognition surveillance combines both human and technical elements. Determining the potentially discriminatory impacts of facial recognition, therefore, should also involve an evaluation of

[53] *R (Bridges)* v *The Chief Constable of South Wales Police* [2020] EWCA Civ 1058, para. 199.
[54] *R (Bridges)* v *The Chief Constable of South Wales Police* [2020] EWCA Civ 1058, para. 185.
[55] *R (Bridges)* v *The Chief Constable of South Wales Police* [2020] EWCA Civ 1058, para. 199.
[56] *Bridges*, NPL (2023).

other factors such as watchlist composition and the nature of the deployment. Moreover, to ensure human rights compliance, police forces themselves should take measures to ensure that neither the facial recognition algorithm itself nor how FRT is deployed give rise to discrimination. This is addressed further in the context of human rights due diligence (Chapter 4).

3.3.3 The Right to a Human Decision-Maker?

Under data protection law, the police may not take a significant decision about an individual, based solely on automated processing, unless that decision is authorized by law. In the UK, this obligation is established under section 49 of the Data Protection Act 2018, while at the European Union level it forms part of the Law Enforcement Directive, a companion to the General Data Protection Regulation (GDPR). In effect, this obligation codifies the right to a 'human in the loop' or, framed differently, the right to a human decision-maker. It should be noted, however, that this is a right under data protection law. A right to a human decision-maker does not exist under human rights law per se, although arguments exist to indicate that such a right may be emerging (Shany 2023; Huq 2020).

Section 49 of the Data Protection Act (and the Law Enforcement Directive) applies to the processing of biometric data undertaken as part of police facial recognition deployments. As no legislation exists authorizing the use of facial recognition for the automated identification of individuals, this means any decision to engage an individual cannot be made solely on the basis of a computer-generated alert. Such alerts must be subject to human adjudication, and this human adjudication must form the basis of the decision to engage the individual (or not). This role of the human decision-maker in operational settings represents a complex area of FRT deployments and is discussed in detail in relation to the ethnographic data in Chapter 8.

3.3.4 The Right to Freedom of Expression

Privacy and discrimination are the themes on which much of the debate surrounding facial recognition has so far focused. However, analysis of the broader rights impacts of this technology reveals potential longer-term harm to individuals' ability to freely develop and express their (political) identity and to democratic functioning. This is where the rights to freedom of expression and freedom of assembly become relevant. The right to freedom of expression is codified in Article 19(1) of the ICCPR:

> Everyone shall have the right to freedom of expression; this right shall include freedom to seek, receive and impart information and ideas of all kinds, regardless of frontiers, either orally, in writing or in print, in the form of art, or through any other media of his choice.[57]

Similar protections are established in Article 10(1) of the European Convention on Human Rights:

> Everyone has the right to freedom of expression. This right shall include freedom to hold opinions and to receive and impart information and ideas without interference by public authority and regardless of frontiers. This Article shall not prevent States from requiring the licensing of broadcasting, television or cinema enterprises.[58]

The right to freedom of expression is broad. It protects the right not only to express oneself but also to receive information, whether in person or through any other form of communication. It is widely regarded as central both to the effective functioning of democratic society[59] and—like the right to privacy—to the processes by which individuals develop their identity.[60] The UN Human Rights Committee clearly stated this in General Comment No. 34:

> Freedom of opinion and freedom of expression are indispensable conditions for the full development of the person. They are essential for any society. They constitute the foundation stone for every free and democratic society. The two freedoms are closely related, with freedom of expression providing the vehicle for the exchange and development of opinions. (Human Rights Committee 2011: 2)

[57] Article 19(2), International Covenant on Civil and Political Rights.
[58] Article 10(1), European Convention on Human Rights.
[59] *Centro Europa 7 S.R.L. and Di Stefano* v *Italy*, Grand Chamber, ECtHR, App. No. 38433/09, 7 June 2012, para. 129.
[60] *Axel Springer AG* v *Germany*, Grand Chamber, ECtHR, App. No. 39954/08, 7 February 2012, para. 78.

A key element is the role that freedom of expression plays in facilitating the free exchange of ideas. This allows individuals to access and evaluate different ideas and philosophies and, in doing so, to freely develop their own identity and political beliefs (Human Rights Committee 2011: 2, Joseph and Castan 2013: 18:01). In turn, freedom of expression facilitates the effective functioning and evolution of democratic society. As Bhagwat (2008: 994) argues,

> [w]ithout speech, democracy would be impossible because citizens would have no way to discuss and form their views, including their views about the conduct and competence of public officials.

Political speech is therefore subject to specific protections and, as reflected by the ECtHR, there is 'little scope . . . for restrictions on political speech or debate on questions of public interest'.[61]

If surveillance disrupts the free exchange of ideas and information, this will give rise to an interference with the right to freedom of expression (Murray et al. 2024). Freedom of expression becomes a clear concern with respect to police deployments of FRT given the ability to monitor a wide range of activities and identify those involved, both during *and* after an event. Potential interferences with the right are likely to be accentuated in circumstances, or within communities, where there is a distrust of police or where the scope of police powers is unclear. For facial recognition, interferences are particularly likely to occur when the technology is deployed in contexts where political expression occurs. The most obvious example of this is a protest or political meeting, but it is important to recognize that political expression occurs in a variety of different contexts. The ECtHR has explicitly recognized the possibility that—at least in the context of protests—the use of facial recognition may give rise to chilling effects in relation to the rights to both freedom of expression and assembly.[62] The chilling effects of surveillance are discussed in greater detail below.

[61] *Mariya Alekhina and Others* v *Russia*, Judgment, ECtHR, App. No. 38004/12, 17 July 2018, para. 212. See also Human Rights Committee, 'General Comment No. 34: Article 19: Freedom of Opinion and Expression', UN Doc. CCPR/C/GC/34, 12 September 2011, para. 23.

[62] *Glukhin* v *Russia*, Judgment, ECtHR, App. No. 11519/20, 4 July 2023, para. 88

3.3.5 The Right to Freedom of Assembly

The right to freedom of assembly is codified in Article 21 of the ICCPR:

> The right of peaceful assembly shall be recognized. No restrictions may be placed on the exercise of this right other than those imposed in conformity with the law and which are necessary in a democratic society in the interests of national security or public safety, public order (*ordre public*), the protection of public health or morals or the protection of the rights and freedoms of others.

A similar protection is established in Article 11 of the European Convention on Human Rights:

> Everyone has the right to freedom of peaceful assembly and to freedom of association with others, including the right to form and join trade unions for the protection of his interests.

The right to freedom of assembly guarantees the right to gather peacefully. This encompasses both indoor and outdoor gatherings of any nature, whether public or private, online or offline,[63] and can therefore include, for example, 'political, economic, artistic and social gatherings' (McGoldrick 2018: 228). The ECtHR has held that: 'the right to freedom of assembly is a fundamental right in a democratic society and, like the right to freedom of expression, is one of the foundations of such a society'.[64] In this regard, the right to freedom of assembly is seen as central to the effective functioning of democratic life[65] and to 'effective participation in civil and political society' (Joseph and Castan 2013: 19.01). The UN Human Rights Committee stated this clearly in General Comment No. 37:

> The fundamental human right of peaceful assembly enables individuals to express themselves collectively and to participate in shaping their societies. The right of peaceful assembly is important in its own right, as

[63] *Kudrevicius and Others* v *Lithuania*, Grand Chamber, ECtHR, App. No. 37553/05. 15 October 2015, para. 91.

[64] *Navalnyy* v *Russia*, Grand Chamber, ECtHR, App. Nos. 29580/12, 36847/12, 11252/13, 12317/13, and 43746/14, 15 November 2018, para. 98.

[65] *Kudrevicius and Others* v *Lithuania*, Grand Chamber, ECtHR, App. No. 37553/05. 15 October 2015, para. 91; *Lee* v *Republic of Korea*, 1119/02, para. 7.2.

> it protects the ability of people to exercise individual autonomy in solidarity with others. Together with other related rights, it also constitutes the very foundation of a system of participatory governance based on democracy, human rights, the rule of law and pluralism. Peaceful assemblies can play a critical role in allowing participants to advance ideas and aspirational goals in the public domain and to establish the extent of support for those ideas and goals. When they are used to air grievances, peaceful assemblies may create opportunities for the inclusive, participatory and peaceful resolution of differences. (Human Rights Committee 2020)

The UN Special Rapporteur on the Rights to Freedom of Assembly and Association has also emphasized the role played by freedom of assembly in fighting for human rights and challenging the status quo (UNSR 2014: 72). As such, the right to freedom of assembly is considered to 'form part of a collective exercise of freedom of expression'[66] and, further, '[t]he protection of opinions and the freedom to express them is one of the objectives of the freedom of assembly and association'.[67] As with privacy and expression, the right to freedom of assembly similarly protects the process by which individuals develop their identity. These formulations demonstrate important interconnections between these rights.

The centrality of the right to freedom of assembly to democratic life means the scope of any permissible limitation is narrow, whereby 'only convincing and compelling reasons can justify restrictions'.[68] Permissible interferences to this right are typically limited to 'cases of incitement to violence or rejection of democratic principles'.[69] This citation of violence has been a common justification used by those seeking to limit protest (and justify police violence against protestors) (Foot and Livingstone 2022). Importantly, isolated or sporadic acts of violence do not deprive the protest of a whole of its peaceful character, and (non-violent) individual participants retain protection under the right to freedom of assembly.[70]

[66] *United Communist Party of Turkey and Others* v *Turkey*, Grand Chamber, ECtHR, App. No. 19392/92, 30 January 1998, para. 43.

[67] *Socialist Party and Others* v *Turkey*, Grand Chamber, ECtHR, App. No. 21237/93, 25 May 1998, para. 41.

[68] *Gorzelik and Others* v *Poland*, Grand Chamber, ECtHR, App. No. 44158/98, 17 February 2004, para. 88.

[69] *Kudrevicius and Others* v *Lithuania*, Grand Chamber, ECtHR, App. No. 37553/05. 15 October 2015, para. 145.

[70] *Frumkin* v *Russia*, Judgment, ECtHR, App. No. 7456/12, 5 January 2016, para. 97.

The restriction of expression or assembly falling below this threshold is considered to endanger democratic functioning regardless of whether the aims of those protesting may be shocking or appear unacceptable to the authorities.[71] Importantly, the right to freedom of assembly is a positive right. It is not simply the case that the authorities must not interfere with the right to peacefully assembly, they must work to actively facilitate the exercise of the right (UNSR 2014: 72). This has implications with respect to how law enforcement agencies police protests and their decision-making vis-à-vis the deployment of surveillance tools (UNSR 2024). This is particularly relevant to the potential chilling effects for participants and the evidence that significant numbers of Londoners would be deterred from attending events monitored by FRT (London Police Ethics Panel 2019).

Turning to the link between the right to freedom of assembly and facial recognition, it is first important to highlight that assembly participants have a legitimate expectation of anonymity unless their conduct presents reasonable grounds for arrest (Human Rights Committee 2020: 60). In this light, the Human Rights Committee have noted that the use of facial recognition—and other technologies that can identify assembly participants—may infringe the right to privacy (Human Rights Committee 2020: 62), while the EU Fundamental Rights Agency (2020: 34) have stated that '[i]t is difficult to imagine situations where the deployment of facial recognition technologies on people participating in demonstrations may be necessary and proportionate'. This conclusion is reinforced in the UN Model Protocol for Law Enforcement Officials to Promote and Protect Human Rights in the Context of Peaceful Protest (2024: 60(c), 61, 63, 90) which highlights the chilling effects associated with police technology and requires that '[f]acial recognition technologies and other biometric technologies must not be utilized to identify individuals who are peacefully participating in a protest' (2024: 71(b)).

Any facial recognition deployment that disrupts individuals' right to peacefully assemble will give rise to an interference with the right.[72] As the right to freedom of assembly protects the collective exercise of the right to freedom of expression,[73] the circumstances which give rise to an

[71] *Kudrevicius and Others* v *Lithuania*, Grand Chamber, ECtHR, App. No. 37553/05. 15 October 2015, para. 145.

[72] See, e.g., *Glukhin* v *Russia*, Judgment, ECtHR, App. No. 11519/20, 4 July 2023, para. 88.

[73] *United Communist Party of Turkey and Others* v *Turkey*, Grand Chamber, ECtHR, App. No. 19392/92, 30 January 1998, para. 43.

interference with the right to freedom of assembly are likely to be similar, albeit they must relate to some form of collective action.

3.3.6 Compound Human Rights Harm

The use of facial recognition will rarely engage only one of the rights just discussed. Facial recognition typically has a diffuse impact, and it is likely that multiple rights will be brought into play simultaneously. Surveillance studies have long focused on the intersectionality and accumulation of disadvantage through monitoring and classification of individuals (Gandy 2009). Indeed, this multidimensional impact is a feature of digital technology generally. For example, building on Deleuze and Guattari, Van Brakel and Govaerts (2024) have referred to the 'rhizomatic' harms linked to predictive policing, while Marjanovic et al. (2021) have referred to 'algorithmic pollution'.

The chilling effects of surveillance constitute the paradigmatic example of the broader, more diffuse harm linked to FRT. Chilling effects concern the modification of behaviour due to concerns over surveillance and its potential consequences. The impacts are diverse and may, for example, influence the websites a person visits (Penney 2016; Stoycheff 2018), what they read, where they go, what they say (Townend 2017; Stevens Griffin 2021), what events they attend (Kendrick 2013, who they meet (Lashmar 2016; Waters 2017), what organizations they join (Murray et al. 2024), whether they take part in a political protest (Starr et al. 2008; Ali 2016), or if and how they engage in political activities (Stevens et al. 2023). Importantly, chilling effects are not binary but are nuanced and often intersectional in their impacts. That is, a chilling effect does not necessarily mean that a person will not engage in political activities when ordinarily they would have, but rather that the degree of engagement and other behaviour becomes modified. By interfering with otherwise normal, or desired, behaviour, chilling effects can interfere with the process by which individuals develop their (political) identity, which can in turn impact on their political participation and on democratic functioning more generally. Of further note is the resonance of such behavioural modifications with ideas of deterrence. For example, surveillance tools and other control initiatives are often justified on the grounds of providing a deterrent impact (see Tilley 1998). It is therefore inconsistent to claim—or, more commonly, assume without evidence—that activities are modified in the way intended (e.g. deterrence), yet other behavioural adjustments (e.g. chilling effects) do not arise.

Existing research clearly establishes that surveillance can give rise to identifiable chilling effects. For example, quantitative studies conducted following the 2013 Snowden revelations (which served as a useful comparator of behaviour) revealed 'statistically significant' reductions in searches for 'privacy-sensitive' terms both on Wikipedia (Penney 2016: 161) and in Google Search trends (Matthews and Tucker 2015). A study by PEN America (2013: 3) found similar results, including that 24 per cent of journalists interviewed 'have deliberately avoided certain topics in phone or email conversations' and '16% have avoided writing or speaking about a particular topic'. This is particularly concerning given the importance of freedom of expression and public debate and the central role played by journalists as a 'public watchdog'.[74]

Qualitative studies have tried to understand the contours of the chilling effect in more depth. Post-Snowden studies reinforced the quantitative research findings referred to above, demonstrating changes in journalistic practices affecting the relationship between journalists and their sources—'chilling' sources' willingness to speak—and prompting increased security measures (Lashmar 2106; Waters 2017). Recent research in Uganda and Zimbabwe documented how the chilling effect of surveillance prompted individuals to self-censor and interfered with political groups' ability to organize and mobilize (Stevens et al. 2023; Murray et al. 2024). Ali's (2016) study conducted in light of the New York Police Department's surveillance of Muslim communities revealed significant self-disciplinary effects, including self-censorship with respect to political discussions. A large study of social movement surveillance, also in the US, revealed similar results. Interestingly, this research highlighted the reputational damage which can arise when an organization is targeted by police surveillance, and which can affect individuals' willingness to engage with that organization (Starr et al. 2008). Similar effects have been documented in the UK. For instance, Aston (2017: 10) notes that the presence of police surveillance affected perceptions of legitimacy and that 'it made those already involved wary of continuing because of real or perceived harms and rendered newcomers less likely to become fully involved'. These studies clearly demonstrate the impact of chilling effects on the rights to freedom of expression and assembly.

[74] *Jersild* v *Denmark*, Grand Chamber Judgment, App. No. 15890/89, 23 September 1994, para. 31.

As highlighted above, the rights to privacy, freedom of expression, and freedom of assembly are all implicated in protecting the development of an individual's (political) identity.[75] Identity development is typically regarded as a dynamic, ongoing process, which is dependent on factors such as experimentation, discussion, challenge, debate, and peer support (Bauman 2004). Moreover, decades of research in social psychology, sociology, and cultural studies have emphasized the range of individual, social, and cultural factors that are key to influencing identity formation. Among these are studies that evidence the role of social movements in forming *both* individual and collective identity (Brewer and Silber 2000; Polletta and Jasper 2001; Davis et al. 2019). Connecting such ideas with human rights law, because identity formation develops through both individual and social processes,[76] the rights under discussion cannot exist, or operate, in isolation from each other. For example, it is recognized that a cloak of anonymity (protected by the right to privacy) is essential in order to enable individuals to experiment with different ideas—including by reading books, talking to different people, or attending talks or rallies (protected by the rights to freedom of expression and assembly)—thereby contributing to the formation of their identity/political opinion (e.g. Richards 2013).

This entitlement to anonymity can persist even in public spaces. The Human Rights Committee has asserted, for example, that participants in a public assembly have a certain expectation of anonymity precisely because they are in a crowd (Human Rights Committee 2020: 71). This position marks a significant point of friction between the application of human rights practice and the longstanding ambitions of urban policing. Chapter 1 detailed how the anonymity of 'the crowd', the anxieties it provoked, and the centuries-old project of making the city legible have been enduring concerns for urban policing. Indeed, these were the foundry from which surveillance tools such as FRT gained form. Standing in contrast are decades of international human rights law that asserts the right to anonymity in public, particularly in the case of political protest.[77] Surveillance narratives

[75] The rights to freedom of opinion and freedom of religion are equally relevant in this context, but are not discussed in detail here.

[76] In social psychology, these approaches have largely been addressed respectively through the perspectives of 'identity theory' and 'social identity theory'. In simplified form, these approaches have variously analysed the internalization of identity through the significance an individual attaches to their uniqueness, roles, status, social location, relationships, affiliations, and collective identities, among others.

[77] See, e.g., *Peck* v *The United Kingdom*, Judgment, ECtHR, App. No. 44647/98, 28 January 2003; Human Rights Committee, 'General Comment No. 37', UN Doc. CCPR/C/GC/37, 17

are often characterized through antagonistic binaries ('nothing to fear, nothing to hide', 'liberty vs. security', etc.). While these reductive framings often strip nuance from complex surveillance-mediated relationships, FRT introduces another couplet to this lexicon: public anonymity versus individual identification.

Once facial recognition becomes deployed, the identification of everyone within a crowd becomes possible. If anonymity is removed, this will immediately engage the right to privacy. Reflecting the intersecting—and intersectional—nature of surveillance-related rights considerations, this may impact simultaneously upon individuals' willingness to talk to certain people (engaging the right to freedom of expression) or even to attend the protest itself (engaging the right to freedom of assembly). Equally, any interference affecting an individual's ability to attend a protest (freedom of assembly)—or impacting on the nature of their participation in that protest (freedom of expression and assembly)—may prevent them from engaging with a community in support of new ideas (freedom of expression).

Since Goffman's (1968) landmark analysis of 'the total institution', social science research has repeatedly evidenced how individuals modify behaviours in the presence of monitoring and authority—whether through compliance or resistance—particularly in the presence of the potential for coercive power (see Marx 2016). Accordingly, if every mistake, misstep, or rush of curiosity is recorded and analysed, and if every public encounter has the possibility for future analysis, it is highly likely that human behaviour will become moderated.[78] Moreover, as Norris and Armstrong (1999) convincingly argue in their classic study of CCTV surveillance, the act of watching communicates subtle yet unequivocal messages to the observed, notably in terms of inclusion, eligibility, and suspicion. If individuals are not free to experiment and to engage with the world, on their terms, the free development of their identity will inevitably be constrained, interfering not only with the right to privacy but also with the exercise of rights such as freedom of expression and freedom of assembly.

September 2020; 'Model Protocol for Law Enforcement Officials to Promote and Protect Human Rights in the Context of Peaceful Protests', UN Doc. A/HRC/55/60, 31 January 2024.

[78] See McGrath (2004) for a novel take on this dynamic through his analysis of the performativity of subjects before the surveillance gaze. While not framed in terms of coercion, McGrath's analysis demonstrates the enduring connection between surveillance and behavioural modification.

Chilling effects also exert a broader impact, as research indicates that in such situations individuals tend to be pushed towards more mainstream positions, reflective of the status quo (see Penney 2016). This process could, in effect, be argued to constitute a 'regression to the mean', in many senses of the phrase. Building on this theme, Richards (2008: 404) has noted that an absence of surveillance is a prerequisite for diverse and innovative thought:

> When there is protection from surveillance, new ideas can be entertained, even when they might be deeply subversive or threatening to conventional or orthodox views. If we value a pluralistic society or the cognitive processes that produce new ideas, then some measure of intellectual privacy, some respite from cognitive surveillance, is essential.

The importance of privacy to pluralism is also underlined by Julie Cohen (2000: 1425):

> The point is not that people will not learn [or, in this context, develop] under conditions of non-privacy, but that they will learn differently, and that the experience of being watched will constrain, ex ante, the acceptable spectrum of belief and behavior. Pervasive monitoring of every first move or false start will, at the margin, induce choices towards the bland and the mainstream.

The negative impact on pluralism and the emergence of new ideas is exacerbated by the fact that chilling effects are most likely to be felt by non-majority groups, often at the margins of society, and by those outside—or in opposition to—the status quo. It is also precisely these communities who are often most active in challenge mainstream opinion, pushing for political change, and facilitating the emergence of new ideas and ways of thinking. If these components of society are chilled, it is not only individuals who are affected at a personal level but also society as a whole: without challenge to the status quo, there is a real danger that democracy will stagnate. The potential harm associated with the chilling effects of surveillance is therefore significant. Any increase in surveillance capacity—particularly a move towards the type of pervasive city-wide surveillance made possible by facial recognition, both in real time and retrospectively (Murray 2024)—will accentuate these potential harms.

Importantly, the rights brought into play as a result of FRT-related chilling effects are not affected independently or in isolation from each other. The nature of chilling effects means that these rights are all affected simultaneously: surveillance impacts on the complex processes of human interaction. It is for this reason that we refer to chilling effects as giving rise to *compound* human rights harm. Recognizing this compound, multiplicative harm is therefore essential when properly accounting for the human rights impact of surveillance technologies like facial recognition. Examining each right in isolation simply cannot capture the true impact of the rights interference. Understanding the overall harm linked to facial recognition therefore requires engaging with the interconnected, intersectional, and interdependent nature of the rights to privacy, freedom of expression, and freedom of assembly (McGoldrick 2018: 208).

These imbrications pose a problem for traditional human rights law analysis which is typically conducted on a right-by-right basis, whereby each right affected is examined discretely and in isolation from other impacted rights.[79] This separation is appropriate in many cases. If there are allegations that an individual was tortured while pending trial, it may be perfectly appropriate to first determine if there has been a violation of the prohibition of torture, before then turning to examine the impact on the right to a fair trial. To date, the ECtHR has followed this segregated approach and only looked at the impact of chilling effects on specific rights. The Court has, for example, separately noted the existence of chilling effects in relation to the right to privacy (arising from the unregulated retention of protest participants' personal data),[80] the right to freedom of expression (through the imposition of a criminal sanction for expression voiced as part of a debate on the judicial system),[81] the right to freedom of assembly (via a prior ban on a political rally),[82] and the right to freedom of religion (by means of disciplinary punishment on a prisoner for worshipping at night time, outside prescribed hours).[83]

The difficulty arises when multiple rights are engaged simultaneously. The ECtHR approach in *Glukhin* v *Russia* provides an on-point example of the complexities that arise. Here, the Court first examined the arrest of a protestor in light of the right to freedom of expression, before separately

[79] The caselaw of the Inter-American Court of Human Rights is an exception in this regard. See Matar and Murray (2025).

[80] *Catt* v *The United Kingdom*, Judgment, ECtHR, App. No. 43514/15, 24 January 2019, para. 123.

[81] *Morice* v *France*, Grand Chamber, ECtHR, App. No. 29369/10, 23 April 2015, para. 127.

[82] *Navalnyy* v *Russia*, Grand Chamber, ECtHR, App. Nos. 29580/12, 36847/12, 11252/13, 12317/13, and 43746/14, 15 November 2018, para. 103.

[83] *Korostelev* v *Russia*, Judgment, ECtHR, App. No. 29290/10, 12 May 2020, para. 64.

examining the use of facial recognition in light of the right to privacy, primarily through a data processing lens.[84] By not examining the overall impact linked to the police's use of facial recognition—that is, the simultaneous impact on the rights to privacy, freedom of expression, and freedom of assembly of both the protestor and other members of society—the Court missed out on the cumulative and compound harm connected to facial recognition. While the Court acknowledged that the use of facial recognition could exert a chilling effect on the rights to freedom of expression *and* of assembly, it did not engage in any substantive way with this possibility. This means that the opportunity to examine the actual overall harm linked to facial recognition was not taken, and so no real guidance on police use of facial recognition was provided. Similar difficulties are evident in the post-Snowden mass surveillance litigation before the ECtHR. Here, the Court looked only at the impact on the right to privacy, or the right to freedom of expression in situations involving journalists, and did not consider the overall chilling effects that a system of mass surveillance may engender, despite this being explicitly raised by the applicant and the intervenors.[85]

3.4 Conclusions

This chapter set out those human rights law provisions most relevant to the police use of FRT, namely the rights to privacy, freedom of expression, and freedom of assembly, as well as the prohibition of discrimination and emerging discussion around a newly claimed right to a human decision-maker. Significantly, the right to privacy and the 'freedoms' are not absolute rights, meaning that they can be limited under certain conditions. To be lawful, all such limitations must satisfy a three-part test. They must be 'in accordance with the law', 'in pursuit of a legitimate aim', and 'necessary in a democratic society'.

The 'in accordance with the law' requirement holds that a legal basis for a rights interference must exist, and this legal basis must be of sufficient quality to prevent arbitrary rights interferences (and must, therefore, appropriately limit officer discretion). In the UK, the police assert that the common law, coupled with a publicly accessible policy framework,

[84] *Glukhin* v *Russia*, Judgment, ECtHR, App. No. 11519/20, 4 July 2023, para. 92.

[85] See, e.g., *Big Brother Watch and Others* v *The United Kingdom*, Grand Chamber, ECtHR, App. Nos. 58170/13, 62322/14, and 24960/13, 25 May 2021.

is sufficient to establish an appropriate legal basis for the use of FRT. In Section 3.2 we argued that, in light of the ECtHR's classification of FRT as 'highly intrusive' coupled with the remote but invasive nature of the surveillance capability made possible by the technology, an explicit legal basis in UK law should be required. This is likely to be the subject of future litigation efforts. As it stands, however, it is clear that the minimum requirement is that police develop a publicly accessible policy framework that appropriately limits officer discretion.

The 'necessary in a democratic society' test is centred around resolving the competing interests at play, namely the potential utility and the potential harm associated with FRT deployment. Section 3.3 discussed the chilling effects of surveillance and developed a compound human rights harm approach as a means of encapsulating the complex, multifaceted, and multi-rights impact of this phenomenon. The MPS's efforts to identify and evaluate utility and harm (including compound harm), by means of their policy documentation, are evaluated in Chapters 5 and 6, respectively.

PART II

BIOMETRIC SURVEILLANCE AND HUMAN RIGHTS THROUGH POLICY, LAW, AND ACTION

4
A Due Diligence Framework for Facial Recognition Technology

4.1 Introduction

Having set out the rights considerations brought into play by the police use of facial recognition technology (FRT), the next step is to evaluate whether—and, if so, how—facial recognition can be deployed in a human rights-compliant manner. This is not a straightforward task, primarily as a result of two complicating factors. First, FRT brings new asymmetries of surveillance. As detailed in Chapter 1, facial recognition represents a step change in police surveillance capability and may result in a decisive shift in the delicate balance of power between the state and those subject to its jurisdiction. As such, determining the human rights impact linked to facial recognition is both novel and complex. The chilling effects demonstrate this point. Although the existence of surveillance-related chilling effects are acknowledged, identifying their precise impact in order to inform the 'necessary in a democratic society' test is difficult. At the moment, no clear solution to the problem exists, and further interdisciplinary research is clearly required to document these complex harms. As made clear through the analysis below, police processes are not equipped to capture this complexity. As a corollary, such harms are inevitably downplayed in authorization processes. Second, human rights law—the body of law we typically turn to when regulating police activities—does not offer concrete guidance. This issue stems from a fundamental issue in how the law and practice of human rights are established. Our understanding of how the law applies, and what the content of different rights in different contexts is, primarily derives from *after-the-fact* accountability mechanisms. Such after-the-fact accountability mechanisms invite action only once a harm has occurred. A change in thinking is required if human rights law is to move from an emphasis on after-the-fact review to something that is capable of informing decision-making processes from the outset (Murray 2020). Part of this need to develop more robust human rights approaches that better anticipate the

Facial Recognition Surveillance. Pete Fussey and Daragh Murray, Oxford University Press.
 DOI: 10.1093/9780191979927.003.0004

range of potential complex harms is evident in the European Union's 2023 AI Act that, in the course of its implementation, will require technology users to undertake human rights impact assessments. However, such initiatives are nascent and have yet to be tested with respect to FRT.

In responding to this challenge, this chapter builds on Chapter 3's analysis of the human rights implications arising from FRT to set out a proposal for how this change in thinking could be achieved. This is a novel contribution in that it adapts the typical approach to human rights law, based on after-the-fact assessment, so that it is capable of informing before-the-fact decision-making. It unpacks core human rights law features in order to understand how the 'necessary in a democratic society' test could be applied *before* the fact instead of after. In doing so, it develops a due diligence framework setting out the questions that should be taken into consideration before any deployment (or, indeed, when evaluating the lawfulness of any deployment). The framework itself depends on a clear articulation of the 'competing interests' at play and is structured around evidencing the potential benefit of a deployment on the one hand, and identifying the potential harm on the other. It is based on the understanding that, because of the multiplicity of harm and the range of potential deployment applications, there cannot be a formulaic, 'one-size-fits-all' approach to facial recognition. Evidently, the benefit and harm linked to the use of facial recognition at a border post to identify suspected terrorists will differ significantly from that linked to the use of facial recognition in a city centre to identify those 'of interest' to the police. Such plurality of deployments and their associated implications therefore highlight how a comprehensive and tailored due diligence process should be undertaken for *each* deployment in light of the specific aims of *that* deployment. To effectively engage with the 'necessary in a democratic society' test, this process must engage with the overall rights impact, where the compound harms addressed above are addressed. The due diligence framework itself is intended to embed appropriate human rights standards into the facial recognition approval and authorization process, and could map onto police processes in this regard. It is directed at identifying those questions the police should ask in order to facilitate human rights compliance.

Section 4.2 discusses the legal arguments in support of a mandatory human rights due diligence process, while noting that the specifics as to what this framework should look like are sparse. Accordingly, Section 4.3 assesses the application of the United Nations (UN) Guiding Principles on Business and Human Rights to FRT to interrogate the prospects of integrating longstanding corporate-focused due diligence approaches and processes.[1] Section 4.4 builds on this analysis to unpack the ways the necessary in a democratic society test can be optimized and appropriately applied to the use of advanced AI-driven surveillance. This discussion identifies the key elements of the necessity test, as established in caselaw, and considers how those elements currently applied in an 'after-the-fact' manner can be adapted to constitute a 'before-the-fact' pre-deployment due diligence framework. This proposed human rights due diligence framework will then be applied to inform the 'utility versus harm' calculation required if using advanced surveillance technologies in public. This discussion will first detail how the claimed 'utility' of police facial recognition operations should be demonstrated and, second, examine how the potential human rights harm of an operation may be identified. This is essential for the identification of any 'competing interests' at play and to the evaluation of whether a facial recognition deployment can be considered 'necessary in a democratic society'.

4.2 The Implied Legal Basis Underpinning a Human Rights Due Diligence Framework

In proposing the adoption of a human rights-based due diligence framework to inform pre-deployment decision-making, it is important to establish whether a legal basis for this framework exists. This will help to clarify whether the approach proposed here could be considered to form part of the obligations imposed on the police or whether it is merely recommendatory. As a first step, it must be acknowledged that human rights due diligence is not an explicit obligation established in any of the relevant human rights law treaties. However, it is suggested here that it *should* be regarded as an implicit, and therefore legally binding, obligation. Specifically, a due diligence framework should be recognized as a means (a) of giving effect to states' obligation to respect and (b) of facilitating compliance with the 'necessary in a democratic society' test. This concept of a legally binding set of principles also coheres with other detailed reviews of law enforcement

[1] The UN Guiding Principles on Business and Human Rights is the leading international framework setting out the measures that states must take, and corporations should take, to comply with human rights law. They set out a human rights due diligence process centred around the proactive identification of potential harm to human rights.

uses of remote biometric surveillance that call for the immediate development of legally binding codes of practice informed by human rights law (Ada Lovelace Institute 2022).

The 'obligation to respect' requires that states not undertake any measures that will give rise to a human rights law violation.[2] This has typically been thought of as a 'negative' obligation, such that compliance simply requires not acting in a particular way. This is arguably true in a limited number of situations. For example, compliance with the prohibition of torture requires that states not subject an individual to 'severe pain or suffering'.[3] Here, the consequences of an action are foreseeable with relative clarity. Other situations, however, are more complex. For example, a decision to allocate slots on a limited-bandwidth radio spectrum to particular broadcasters may have consequences that are not immediately foreseeable. It may, for instance, result in the prioritization of particular voices or groups over others, impacting on individuals' ability to freely access a diverse range of opinions, or perhaps undermining the public watchdog role of the press, both of which are components of the right to freedom of expression. Ensuring that the allocation of radio frequencies does not result in a human rights violation therefore requires a 'positive' act. Some form of impact assessment is required to evaluate the consequences of an action and to ensure that rights are not violated. Depending on the results, this may require either the modification or the cancellation of the original plan. In complex situations—a feature both of modern life and of surveillance assemblages—maintaining a distinction between 'negative' and 'positive' obligations is increasingly artificial. State activities, such as the use of surveillance tools, will inevitably cause ripples across society that are difficult to predict at first glance. Ensuring that these ripples do not result in human rights violations therefore requires evaluating their potential to do so before such tools are deployed. In such circumstances, compliance with the 'obligation to respect' is impossible without undertaking some form of impact assessment.

A prior impact assessment is also required in order to effectively assess whether a particular measure can be considered 'necessary in a democratic society'. As noted previously, the necessity test relevant to facial recognition

[2] The obligation to respect is established in, among other treaties, Article 1, European Convention on Human Rights, and Article 2, International Covenant on Civil and Political Rights.

[3] Convention Against Torture, Article 1.

is dependent on resolution of the competing interests at play; that is, the potential benefit to human rights of a measure compared to the potential harm to human rights of that measure. As just discussed, an impact assessment is required to assess the potential harm. The UK Surveillance Camera Commissioner (2019: 9) reached a similar conclusion when evaluating police live facial recognition (LFR) deployments:

> It should be a fundamental consideration of any relevant authority intending to deploy [LFR] that a detailed risk assessment process is conducted and documented as to the operational risks, community impact risk, privacy and other human rights risk and other risks associated with its use prior to any deployment of the capability is made. Such risks should be considered as part of the decision making processes associated with the necessity and proportionality of its use.[4]

However, it is important to emphasize that from a human rights law perspective, the focus should not be exclusively on potential risk: the potential utility of a measure is equally relevant. The competing interests at play cannot be addressed effectively unless both utility and harm are identified, and so any impact assessment should also examine the benefit to human rights of a deployment. Impact assessments are perhaps best understood as forming part of an overall human rights due diligence framework. In the context of new and emerging technologies, there is an increased onus on those deploying the technologies to conduct such assessments with a high standard of rigour. This framework should examine the proposed facial recognition deployment as a whole, include the potential impact on human rights in terms of benefit and harm, and then evaluate whether the proposed deployment is human rights-compliant or not. Importantly, this approach may also indicate what steps should be taken in order to facilitate a deployment's human rights compliance.

States are required to ensure the obligation to respect and to satisfy the 'necessary in a democratic society' test. Human rights due diligence is one way of meeting these obligations. In situations where the effects of a police deployment are not clear—which will be true in relation to the majority

[4] The precise contours of this risk assessment are discussed further in Surveillance Camera Commissioner, 'Facing the Camera: Good Practice and Guidance for the Police Use of Overt Surveillance Camera Systems Incorporating Facial Recognition Technology to Locate Persons on a Watchlist in Public Places in England & Wales', November 2020, paras. 3.84–3.91.

of surveillance activities, particularly those using experimental technologies such as facial recognition—human rights due diligence (or another approach capable of achieving the same objectives) should be regarded as an implicit legal obligation. The finding of the European Court of Human Rights (ECtHR) in *S and Marper* is pertinent. Here, the Court noted that 'any State claiming a pioneer role in the development of new technologies bears special responsibility for striking the right balance' between the potential benefit and the potential harm associated with such technologies.[5]

As noted above, drawing on human rights law to inform before-the-fact decision-making is not straightforward, and the contours of what human rights due diligence should look like are not clearly set out. However, the UN Guiding Principles on Business and Human Rights (the UN Guiding Principles) are a notable exception to this general approach to human rights as they focus explicitly on before-the-fact processes. The UN Guiding Principles set out a human rights due diligence framework for corporate actors intended to prevent human rights violations that may arise as a result of commercial activity. However, the Principles have wider relevance and may be translated to state processes. Indeed, the complex public–private relationships surrounding advanced police technologies[6] highlight the further implication of commercially focused standards to state police practices. Accordingly, the UN Guiding Principles are examined here in order to identify any lessons that can be used to inform police decision-making.

4.3 The UN Guiding Principles on Business and Human Rights

The UN Guiding Principles were unanimously endorsed by the UN Human Rights Council in July 2011. They were established to address corporate actors' human rights impact and represent a landmark on the road to both promoting corporate accountability for human rights violations and providing more effective before-the-fact human rights guidance. They address states' obligations to protect against human rights violations committed by

[5] *S and Marper* v *The United Kingdom*, Grand Chamber, ECtHR, App. Nos. 30562/04 and 30566/04, 4 December 2008, para. 112.

[6] For example, police uses of commercial algorithms that are unaccountable due to restrictions of sharing proprietary knowledge (although see discussion regarding the PSED in Chapter 3).

corporate actors, as well as corporations' responsibility to respect rights. Elements of states' obligation to protect against human rights violations by third parties include establishing regulatory frameworks to govern corporate activity. Corporations' responsibility to respect human rights are analogous to states' obligation to respect, as discussed above. However, they are referred to as a 'responsibility' because international human rights law does not place direct legal obligations on corporate actors. The corporate responsibility to respect is therefore an 'expectation' of the international community. While this responsibility may not be legally binding, the UN Guiding Principles do set out those steps that corporations must take if they are to act in line with international human rights law. The Principles themselves are an internationally recognized benchmark for the assessment of corporate activity.

Human rights due diligence is the means by which corporations give effect to their responsibility to respect. It is an ongoing process 'for identifying and assessing, preventing and mitigating, tracking, and accounting for (communicating and reporting) the adverse potential or actual human rights impacts with which a business is involved' (Danish Institute for Human Rights 2020: 17). Impact or risk assessments are sometimes treated as synonymous with human rights due diligence, but these elements should more accurately be seen as essential components within the overall due diligence framework (Danish Institute for Human Rights 2020: 18). Impact assessments are a means of identifying potential harm—and indeed potential utility—but the evaluation of those assessments, and the decision as to what related course of action to take, falls squarely within the due diligence framework. To encapsulate these wider range of concerns, we use the term human rights due diligence throughout this book.

Most relevant for public use of facial recognition technologies are Principles 15, 17, and 18 of the UN Guiding Principles which establish, and then develop, the corporate due diligence responsibility. The pertinent parts of Principle 15 set out the responsibility to establish a due diligence process:

> to meet their responsibility to respect human rights, business enterprises should have in place policies and processes appropriate to their size and circumstances, including:
>
> . . .
>
> (b) A human rights due diligence process to identify, prevent, mitigate and account for how they address their impacts on human rights

Principle 17 then adds further detail, setting out the parameters of a human rights due diligence process:

> to identify, prevent, mitigate and account for how they address their adverse human rights impacts, business enterprises should carry out human rights due diligence. The process should include assessing actual and potential human rights impacts, integrating and acting upon the findings, tracking responses, and communicating how impacts are addressed: Human rights due diligence:
>
> (a) Should cover adverse human rights impacts that the business enterprise may cause or contribute to through its own activities, or which may be directly linked to its operations, products or services by its business relationships;
>
> (b) Will vary in complexity with the size of the business enterprise, the risk of severe human rights impacts, and the nature and context of its operations;
>
> (c) Should be ongoing, recognizing that the human rights risks may change over time as the business enterprise's operations and operating context evolve.

Several elements contained within this Principle hold key relevance to police facial recognition deployments. The first is that human rights due diligence should be an effective process, capable of changing how an actor operates. This is emphasized by the requirement that the outcome of impact assessments should be integrated and acted upon, and is intended to avoid the risk that surveillance authorization procedures serve as vehicles to legitimate and extend such practices. These stipulations that processes should be capable of restricting the actions of surveillance operators is significant when considering how surveillance regulations have historically worked to *legitimate and extend* monitoring practices. As observed in the application of processes designed to regulate other surveillance practices, compliance measures risk becoming a symbolic means by which due diligence can be 'evidenced' in superficial ways. As Fussey and Sandhu (2022: 9) observed in their analysis of operational uses digital policing tools,

> compliance is consistently gestural and symbolic, operating as a bureaucratic process that enables officers to repackage existing activities

> without any meaningful engagement with fundamental rights issues. Such accounts see RIPA [Regulation of Investigatory Powers Act]—and its 'parent', the [Human Rights Act]—as, 'allowing officers to justify their decision making' amid a legitimating discourse of rights, thus providing 'a safety net in the event that they are asked to account for their actions.' (Bullock and Johnson 2012: 632)

A second consideration of Principle 17 is the recognition that not all human rights harms may be mitigated. In this regard, it is important to acknowledge that human rights law establishes clear 'red lines': if a particular activity will result in a human rights violation—even after efforts at mitigation—then it simply should not be undertaken. A clear example of a 'red line' occurs where a facial recognition algorithm is known to produce biased results that will give rise to indirect discrimination during deployments. This will violate the prohibition of discrimination, and so deployment is not legally permissible (McGregor et al. 2019). A third consideration is that human rights due diligence constitutes an ongoing process, one that extends across the entire lifecycle of an operation (Principle 17(c)). This is particularly important in the digital context, given the need to monitor for algorithmic bias, and in a policing context, given the need to monitor—in a robust and auditable manner—for operational effectiveness and any potential adverse human rights impacts, including indirect discrimination.

Principle 18 provides further guidance as to how a human rights due diligence process should be conducted:

> to gauge human rights risks, business enterprises should identify and assess any actual or potential adverse human rights impacts with which they may be involved *either through their own activities or as a result of their business relationships*. This process should:
>
> (a) Draw on internal and/or independent external human rights expertise;
>
> (b) Involve meaningful consultation with potentially affected groups and other relevant stakeholders, as appropriate to the size of the business enterprise and the nature and context of the operation. (Emphasis added)

Several elements of relevance emerge from this Principle. First is the emphasis on human rights expertise. This is particularly important with respect to complex operations and new and emerging technologies or practices, where the human rights impacts are not clear, and dedicated expertise is necessary if impacts are to be effectively evaluated. This is arguably a task that most police forces are not qualified to undertake on their own, highlighting the essential role that partnerships with external entities, including in industry and academia, can play in this space. This is particularly important given how sociologies of policing have revealed how human rights considerations are routinely misunderstood by law enforcement officers seeking to deploy intrusive surveillance measures (Bullock and Johnson 2012; Loftus et al. 2016; Fussey and Sandhu 2022). As the data for this research reveals, such misunderstandings were present in decisions affecting the deployment of facial recognition surveillance in London (see Chapter 7). Second is the emphasis on stakeholder consultation. Dependent upon the circumstances of deployment, this may be particularly important in a law enforcement context, given the emphasis on community policing and the importance of establishing trust. This point was elaborated upon by the national Surveillance Camera Commissioner during the time of the researched operations. Here he compared the Metropolitan Police approach to consultation over FRT with his experience as a senior counter-terrorism officer:

> what I think is appropriate is akin to what they refer to as consequence management in the world of counter-terrorism policing operations. Because it was recognized from the get-go that there was amazing sensitivity with broad swathes of community . . . So what was put in place [in respect of counter-terrorism measures] was almost an in-depth checklist of key components of a community strategy. MPs, local councillors, business people, residents in the area, communication that was evidenced and detailed. And was capable of gathering feedback. Prior to the deployment of a counter-terrorism operation, there would be a time scale where these things would hit. I did say to the Met, you need to operate at that level of engagement as you would in a consequence management operation of a highly sensitive policing operation. Now, they may say they've done that. I haven't seen that rigorously evidenced.
>
> I would have had the MPs, the councillors, I would have had civic leaders, I would have had resident association leaders, I would have had the businesses in the area. I would have had representatives of gangs and crimes, I would have had the high-profile groups, not just Liberty. I would have at least let them know and I would have had tick lists. I would have

let the minister be aware [and the] Home Office . . . given its sensitivity, I think that was exactly what was required. (Interviewed May 2019)

A third area of relevance to the due diligence process outlined in Principle 18 concerns relationships with third parties and the consideration of human rights impacts, '*either through their own activities or as a result of their business relationships*'. The mainstreaming of FRT across both public and private (mainly retail and entertainment) spaces elevates the significance of this point. As the undisclosed collaboration between the Metropolitan Police Service (MPS), British Transport Police (BTP), and the security company managing the privatized areas near King's Cross in London exemplified, public–private actors are not easy to separate. Here, in an arrangement that escaped public and regulatory scrutiny, police were feeding images to facial recognition systems operated by private contractors and then receiving associated intelligence arising from commercially run surveillance. Such relationships matter—particularly given the exemption of private actors from oversight by the Biometrics and Surveillance Camera Commissioner's Office in England and Wales—and should be analysed as part of a due diligence process prior to the initiation of any joint activity.

The UN Guiding Principles are some of the most detailed principles directed towards ensuring a human rights-compliant decision-making process, and should serve as an important reference point for law enforcement agencies. Key areas of relevance include emphasis on dedicated expertise and stakeholder consultation prior to police deployments and an evaluation of any police/private security actor relationships involving FRT or other forms of advanced technology.

4.4 Reverse Engineering the 'Necessary in a Democratic Society' Test

The starting point when developing a human rights due diligence framework for police uses of facial recognition is the 'necessary in a democratic society' test. The purpose of a due diligence process is to draw out the competing interests at play and thus determine whether a police facial recognition deployment is 'necessary'. When developing a human rights-compliant framework to inform FRT use, it is therefore appropriate to work backwards from this point. As set out in Section 3.2.3, five requirements of the necessity test are particularly relevant to deliberations over facial recognition deployments: (a) that it answers to a pressing social need; (b) that the use of facial recognition remains faithful to democratic principles; (c) that it is proportionate to the legitimate aim pursued; (d) that alternative means capable of achieving the same objective are considered; and (e) that 'relevant and sufficient' reasons for using facial recognition are provided, so that the justification for deployment can be 'convincingly established'.[7] As the due diligence framework is directed towards resolving the competing interests at play, it should be built around an articulation of the intended benefit and the potential harm.

The five requirements set out above can be translated to shape the overall process. Taking these components of the necessity test in turn, the requirement that the use of facial recognition answers to a pressing social need demands that the purpose of the deployment—'what' it is intended to achieve—be clearly articulated. The requirement to remain faithful to democratic principles advocates that a human rights framework should take into account the overall impact associated with the proposed use of facial recognition. This includes a detailed consideration of the context into which it will be deployed. Fidelity to democratic principles cannot be assessed in the abstract and so any analysis should address the specifics of each facial recognition deployment, including factors such as the operational setting and purpose (and whether minoritized communities will be targeted disproportionately, for example); data storage, retention, and sharing; whether facial recognition will be deployed as part of a broader assemblage of surveillance measures; the application of additional analysis software to captured images; and so on. This means that the parameters of the deployment—'how' it will be deployed—should be set out with a high degree of precision. Determining whether a deployment is 'proportionate to the legitimate aim pursued' requires clear articulation of the parameters of the deployment. This again links to 'how' FRT will be deployed. The consideration of alternative means indicates that a human rights-compliant due diligence framework should include an assessment as to the availability and suitability of other less intrusive means capable of achieving the same objective. Lastly, the requirement that 'relevant and sufficient' reasons be provided so that the justification for the deployment can be convincingly

[7] See *Klass and Others* v *Germany*, Judgment, ECtHR, App. No. 5029/71, 6 September 1978, para. 55; *S and Marper* v *The United Kingdom*, Judgment, ECtHR, App. Nos. 30562/04 and 30566/04, 4 December 2008, para. 112; *Catt* v *The United Kingdom*, Judgment, ECtHR, App. No. 43514/15, 24 January 2019, para. 109; *Nada* v *Switzerland*, Grand Chamber, ECtHR, App. No. 10593/08, 12 September 2012, para. 183.

established demonstrates the need for an appropriate evidence base. As justification is ultimately dependent on resolution of the competing interests, an evidence base is required to support analyses of both intended utility ('why' is a deployment necessary) and potential harm. How the establishment of utility and harm is approached will each be addressed in turn below.

4.4.1 Demonstrating Utility

The preceding discussion and analysis reveal four factors that should be taken into account in establishing the utility of a police facial recognition deployment. First, the intended objective should be clearly articulated (*what* is the deployment intended to achieve?). Second, the justification for that objective should be set out (*why* is the deployment necessary?). Third, the circumstances in which FRT would be deployed and operated should be clearly defined. This element brings the first two components together: the police justification should draw on the available information to evidence *how* the identified objective will be achieved. Such considerations are crucial in articulating and substantiating the specific role that facial recognition will play in achieving the identified objective, and therefore in ensuring that the means adopted are connected to the (legitimate) aim. Finally, the possibility of deploying alternative measures should be considered. In essence, this constitutes the 'why facial recognition?' question. The due diligence process proposed here is therefore built around four questions: 'what', 'why', 'how', and 'why FRT'.

This proposed framework maps broadly onto the '5WH' facial recognition deployment process (what, who, why, when, where, and how) developed by the UK Surveillance Camera Commissioner (2020: 3.39–3.54), a national framework to which the authors provided drafting and other expert input. The due diligence framework we propose here builds on this approach, while incorporating some slight modifications. Most significantly, we combine the Surveillance Camera Commissioner's first two criteria—the motivation underpinning a deployment (i.e. 'what' it is intended to achieve) and 'who' a deployment is intended to identify—into one criterion. This is because the nature of FRT, as a technology directed towards the identification of specific individuals, means that the 'what' and the 'who' are inextricably linked. To demonstrate using an example favoured by proponents of FRT: an operation aimed at identifying individuals suspected of active involvement in terrorist activities will be altered significantly if all individuals 'wanted' in relation to counter-terrorism efforts are sought. As later chapters show, definitions of 'wanted' vary significantly and include being wanted on the basis of an outstanding warrant or because they are of interest to an investigation, with 'of interest' being itself a very widely defined category. In the case of FRT operations, any change to the category of persons included on the watchlist will fundamentally alter the nature of a deployment and what it is capable of achieving.

Our second component, the justification for a deployment, maps directly to the 'why'[8] question presented by the Surveillance Camera Commissioner. Our third component, setting out the circumstances of a deployment (the 'how'), combines the Surveillance Camera Commissioner's 'when'[9] and 'where'[10] questions. This is because the two are inextricably linked, and a change to either one will inevitably change the nature of the deployment as a whole. For example, an operation deploying fixed facial recognition cameras at a specific location for a limited time period is markedly different from using a city-wide surveillance camera network, even if the time period remains the same; changing from a limited deployment time to deployment on a rolling basis has an equally significant impact. The Surveillance Camera Commissioner's (2020: 3.54) 'how' question—'[h]ow is it intended to conduct the use of LFR in the circumstances described and how will risk be managed?'—is partly folded into our 'how' component and partly of relevance to the overall due diligence framework. Each of the components of our proposed framework for the articulation of intended utility will now be unpacked.

4.4.1.1 Establishing 'what' the objective underpinning a facial recognition deployment is

Establishing the objective underpinning a FRT deployment is the necessary first step to substantiating any claimed utility for the technology. This articulation should be specific. As highlighted throughout this book, overly broad language undermines an accurate assessment as to the utility of a deployment, allows symbolic compliance, and enables function creep. For example, the objective of 'preventing crime and protecting public order', or

[8] 'Why is it considered to be necessary and proportionate to conduct surveillance by means of a surveillance camera system enhanced with LFR technology against known individuals in the context of what the police seek to achieve?'

[9] 'When is it intended to operate LFR in terms of times/days of the week etc. and what is the duration/lifespan of the intended operational conduct?'

[10] 'Where is it intended that the police conduct using LFR will take place?'

claims that technology is deployed 'for policing purposes', are commonly cited in police documentation (see Chapter 5), yet are overly broad. These objectives are essentially reflective of all policing activity and so do not provide any foreseeability as to the specific activities that will be undertaken,[11] making it impossible to determine specific human rights impacts. This tension between the generalities of 'policing purposes' and the specificities of human rights considerations also lies at the heart of legal challenges against police uses of the common law as a source of legal authority for FRT use.

Examples of more focused objectives could include, for instance, the identification of individuals suspected of belonging to a proscribed terrorist organization at border posts so that they may be stopped or questioned or the identification of individuals subject to an outstanding arrest warrant (for certain specified crimes) as they pass through a particular location.[12] As facial recognition is deployed specifically to identify individuals, the composition of the watchlist necessarily plays a key role in defining the objective being pursued. This importance of the watchlist can be demonstrated by modifying the second example. Changing the watchlist composition to include individuals 'of interest' to the police (say, for the facilitation of an investigation), as regularly happens in practice, changes the nature of the deployment. It fundamentally alters 'what' it is intended to achieve. This dynamic reinforces the importance of combining the first two categories in the Surveillance Camera Commissioner's framework, namely the 'what' (e.g. the prevention of terrorist movement, the apprehension of individuals subject to outstanding arrest warrants) with the 'who' (e.g. individuals suspected of belonging to a proscribed terrorist organization, individuals subject to arrest warrants for specific crimes).

Caselaw from the ECtHR indicates that, in light of their 'highly intrusive' nature, both retrospective and live facial recognition require a 'high level of justification' to be considered 'necessary in a democratic society'.[13] This promulgates the requirement that the issue facial recognition is tasked with addressing should be of a serious nature. Determining whether this threshold is satisfied depends upon a clear articulation of the 'what'. For instance, the justification linked to using FRT to identify an individual

[11] See, e.g., *Catt* v *The United Kingdom*, Judgment, ECtHR, App. No. 43514/15, 24 January 2019, para. 97.

[12] The examples discussed here are presented as hypotheticals in order to discuss the types of issues that may arise and to draw out relevant questions. They are not intended to endorse (or not) particular approaches.

[13] *Glukhin* v *Russia*, Judgment, ECtHR, App. No. 11519/20, 4 July 2023, para. 86.

suspected of homicide will be significantly higher than that linked to the investigation of petty robbery. No minimum threshold of severity has been set for FRT use in the UK, but in *Glukhin* the European Court found that the use of facial recognition in the context of administrative offence proceedings could not be regarded as necessary in a democratic society.[14]

4.4.1.2 Demonstrating 'why' achieving the identified objective is necessary

Specifying 'why' a particular facial recognition deployment is necessary is central to determining its claimed utility and to demonstrating whether using the technology 'answers to a pressing social need'. The requirement that any justifications for an interference with human rights be 'relevant and sufficient' and 'convincingly established' is pertinent here,[15] as this indicates that any justification provided should be evidence-based. Evidence should relate both to the need to address the identified objective and to the role of FRT in achieving that aim. In this sense, the 'why' should be used to justify the 'what'. This link between 'what' and 'why' is important. Presenting or justifying the 'what' in isolation conveys a form of technological determinism, where facial recognition is presented as inherently effective, irrespective of its links to a specific application.

Developing the above examples further demonstrates the inseparability of the 'what' and 'why' of FRT use. Terrorism is clearly an issue of public concern and is an example often used by proponents to justify the technology, particularly to patrol borders. Yet in the case of LFR, any terrorism-related deployment requires evidence that those targeted by the surveillance would be likely to be present at specific locations (such as entering the country through border posts). With respect to the second example, the identification of those with an outstanding arrest warrant, factors relevant to the evidence base here could include the severity of the offence individuals are wanted for; the number of individuals subject to outstanding warrants; the level of threat posed by such individuals; whether there is typically significant difficulty in apprehending such individuals or not; and whether they

[14] *Glukhin* v *Russia*, Judgment, ECtHR, App. No. 11519/20, 4 July 2023, para. 90.

[15] *Klass and Others* v *Germany*, Judgment, ECtHR, App. No. 5029/71, 6 September 1978, para. 55; *S and Marper* v *The United Kingdom*, Judgment, ECtHR, App. Nos. 30562/04 and 30566/04, 4 December 2008, para. 112; *Catt* v *The United Kingdom*, Judgment, ECtHR, App. No. 43514/15, 24 January 2019, para. 109; *Nada* v *Switzerland*, Grand Chamber, ECtHR, App. No. 10593/08, 12 September 2012, para. 183.

are likely to pass through a particular location and, hence, the facial recognition system's field of vision.

As highlighted in Chapter 5, surveillance operations generally, and FRT specifically, are regularly justified in abstract terms and often unencumbered by evidence. As set out here, however, to be human rights-compliant, the supporting evidence must be sufficient to justify the rights intrusion. Attaining this quality threshold requires a level of rigour, including with respect to the methodology, analysis, and use of statistics (as appropriate).

In certain circumstances, the evidence base underpinning a facial recognition deployment may be restricted, say for reasons of operational necessity or national security, making it difficult to independently assess. Several additional factors are relevant here, however. First, such restrictions are not relevant internally, and the inclusion of appropriate evidence presented as part of a due diligence process should be integral to any internal authorization. Second, transparency should be the rule and restrictions the exception. It may well be the case that the underlying evidence can in fact be made public (or at least elements thereof). This is particularly true after a deployment as the risk of undermining the deployment is obviously negated. Moreover, such moves towards transparency have been discernible in the oversight of other forms of intrusive surveillance, as evinced in reporting by the Investigatory Powers Commissioners Office that oversees UK intelligence agencies since 2017. By extension, if modes of transparency can be established for national security activities, this should be achievable in less sensitive policing contexts. Third, given the highly intrusive nature of FRT, independent oversight is a core requirement (see Murray et al. 2021). Any such body should have the authority to evaluate all underlying documentation, and should perhaps also have a role in determining what information can and cannot be released as part of efforts to foster public trust.

4.4.1.3 Setting out 'how' facial recognition technology will be deployed

The third step is to specify 'how' FRT will be deployed to achieve the specified, evidence-supported objective. This brings the 'what' and the 'why' together into an operational plan. Clarity around the intended circumstances of use is essential for several reasons. First, such clarity enables evaluation of the human rights-related impact of a deployment—both in terms of utility and harm—as these impacts will vary (potentially significantly) dependent on the form and scope of the deployment. Clarity in this area also allows an assessment of whether the deployment is proportionate to the legitimate aim pursued.

A number of factors are potentially relevant to setting out how FRT will be deployed. For example: will the deployment run for a set period, at particular intervals, or on a more continuous, long-term basis? Will the deployment be limited to a specified geographical area or will it be deployed across a wider surveillance camera network? Will the captured image feeds be stored for future examination, for instance through retrospective facial recognition (RFR) technology? Will the image feeds be subject to (automated) analysis, for instance to identify individuals at a particular event (as opposed to looking for specific individuals), or to track individuals' movements (and activities) over time? Alternatively, will the captured image feeds be fed into a larger algorithm to inform police intelligence pictures or decision-making (by means of pattern-of-life analysis or relationship mapping)?

Changes in 'how' facial recognition is deployed generate different human rights impacts. These may be demonstrated by returning to the previous examples. In the case of counter-terrorism, the specificity of the objective—identification of terrorist suspects at border posts—already sets broad parameters in relation to how LFR may be deployed, although some scope for interpretation remains. Significantly more scope for variance exists in the arrest warrant example. For example: where will LFR cameras be placed and how long will they be in place for? What will happen to any data captured during a deployment? Is such data deleted according to specific procedures or will it be fed into a larger intelligence database? Who may access retained data and on what basis? Is subsequent access restricted to the purposes of the initial operation or can footage be accessed—and potentially subjected to RFR analysis—if deemed relevant to a separate investigation? Importantly, if information is retained, will it be used to create profiles of individuals, establishing a record of their movements, and interactions, across time?

Depending on how LFR is deployed, the human rights impacts and level of intrusion may vary significantly. This will affect both the rights brought into play—moving from an interference with the right to privacy at passport control to potentially include the rights to expression, association, assembly, and religion in other permutations—and the severity of any interference. Tracking individuals, or their activities, or generating pattern-of-life profiles significantly increases the intrusiveness of facial recognition deployments. This is important to bear in mind when calculating the necessity of any use of this technology, noting that the 'basic' use of retrospective and live facial recognition has already been classified by the ECtHR as 'highly intrusive'.[16]

4.4.1.4 Why FRT?

The final element when evaluating the utility of a specific LFR deployment is a consideration of whether other less intrusive approaches may be used to achieve the same aim.[17] This assessment forms part of the necessity calculation established by international human rights law and is required to determine whether a deployment is 'proportionate to the legitimate aim pursued'.[18] It is also reflected in UK domestic law, where the third prong of the *Bank Mellat* proportionality test asks 'whether a less intrusive measure could have been used without unacceptably compromising the achievement of the objective'.[19] Put simply, this element speaks to the 'why facial recognition?' question.

The two terrorism and urban surveillance examples used throughout this discussion reveal further considerations with regard to the 'why' question. In the first example, LFR was used at a border post to identify suspected members of proscribed terrorist organizations. The obvious alternative measure in this instance is to rely on border officials to conduct the relevant checks. All individuals passing through a border post undergo an identity check, which may also involve initial questioning. At this point, an individual's identity can be checked against a database and an alert raised in the event of a match. Additionally, at airports, the International Civil Aviation Organization (ICAO) requires that border officials monitor for 'suspicious' behavioural or travel patterns. These may be used to flag an individual for more detailed questioning. Whether these measures will be effective in achieving the required objective, however, is unclear. A member of a proscribed organization may travel on falsified papers, deliberately obscure their travel route, or be trained not to raise suspicions on initial questioning (MPS 2018a: 5). In these circumstances, facial recognition may provide an 'added value' as it has the potential to counteract these

[16] *Glukhin* v *Russia*, Judgment, ECtHR, App. No. 11519/20, 4 July 2023.

[17] *Nada* v *Switzerland*, Grand Chamber, ECtHR, App. No. 10593/08, 12 September 2012, para. 183.

[18] *Roman Zakharov* v *Russia*, Judgment, ECtHR, App. No. 47143/06, 4 December 2015, para. 260. This statement was made in the context of secret surveillance but is regarded as equally applicable to the current discussion in light of the reasoning adopted in *Catt*. See *Catt* v *The United Kingdom*, Judgment, ECtHR, App. No. 43514/15, 24 January 2019, para. 114.

[19] *Bank Mellat* v *Her Majesty's Treasury* [2013] UKSC 38, para. 74.

two techniques. Alternatively, FRT may merely duplicate existing surveillance functions, bringing greater intrusion for little operational difference. Resolving this question rests on the specific added value associated with facial recognition compared to the alternative means. Relevant considerations may include whether sufficiently high-quality pictures of suspected individuals are available, or whether such persons are typically tracked on the basis of visual identification rather than other factors such as known aliases or patterns of movement.

In the second example, LFR is used to identify individuals subject to an outstanding arrest warrant. In this case, frequently used alternative means also exist. These include, for example, identity checks when individuals come into contact with law enforcement, targeted covert surveillance on specific individuals, visits to places typically frequented by the individual, or interviews with associates and/or family members. In considering the effectiveness of these alternative means, several factors are likely to be relevant. These include the nature of the underlying offence; existing success rates and time frames regarding apprehension of individuals subject to an arrest warrant; and rates of reoffending during the time period that individuals are at large, including the gravity of any offences. In determining the added value of facial recognition in this context, consideration should also be given to the likelihood of a wanted individual passing through a facial recognition camera system.

To summarize, if human rights harm is to be evaluated effectively, then it is essential that the intended utility of a particular LFR deployment, including the 'what', 'why', and 'how', be set out as precisely as possible. This is necessary both to limit the scope for officer discretion (and to ensure 'foreseeability') and because without specificity, any effective examination of the human rights-based harm is simply impossible. An evaluation of alternative means should also be conducted as this is a key component of the necessity test.

4.4.2 Identifying Harm

The second component of the 'necessary in a democratic society' test requires that the potential harm to human rights be identified. As with the determination of intended utility, there is no one-size-fits-all approach. Ultimately, the degree of human rights harm will depend upon the nature of the facial recognition deployment in question. This is precisely why the process to articulate intended utility is so important: this is where the objective, the evidence base, and the parameters of deployment are established (i.e. the 'what', the 'why', and the 'how'), and it is these parameters by which harm is assessed. The calculation of potential harm is particularly important with respect to surveillance technologies, such as facial recognition, which may bring multiple interconnected human rights considerations into play, and which have the potential to shift the traditional balance of power between state and citizen. The nature of these potential harms, however, often makes their identification and incorporation into evaluation processes difficult—and potentially unexamined—as demonstrated in the chilling effects discussion below.

This section focuses on three potential human rights harms, the identification of which are essential to the pre-deployment process:[20] (a) interferences with the prohibition of discrimination, (b) interferences with the right to privacy, and (c) compound harms associated with a surveillance-related chilling effect. It is important to highlight that these harms may exist either independently or simultaneously, depending on factors such as the nature of the deployment and the specific FRT used. For illustrative purposes, we focus on these three harms here, but an effective human rights due diligence process requires that all potential harms linked to a particular deployment be examined. These may include, for example, harms to freedom of assembly—if facial recognition is used in the context of a protest; harms to freedom of religion—if a facial recognition deployment occurs near a place of worship; or harms to freedom of association—if a facial recognition deployment occurs near where an association is established.

4.4.2.1 The prohibition of discrimination

Concerns regarding the accuracy of FRT, and in particular the potential for biased results, are well known, and are discussed in greater detail in Chapter 2. For present purposes it is sufficient to highlight that evidence exists that facial recognition capabilities shift on the basis of visible ethnicity, age, and gender. These findings are a key concern in relation to law enforcement facial recognition deployments as—if unaddressed—these performance characteristics may give rise to a violation of the prohibition of

[20] It is not suggested that this is an exhaustive list of harms. Rather, it is illustrative of some of the key issues involved, and the general approach presented here can be applied to other harms.

discrimination.[21] The principal risk is of indirect discrimination whereby, for example, a particular facial recognition tool returns higher false positives or false negatives across different protected characteristics. This may result in discriminatory policing practices, which not only constitute a human rights law violation but also have the potential to fracture community relations and undermine trust in the police more generally. The controversy and fallout surrounding discriminatory 'stop-and-search' practices in London illustrate the issues at play.[22] The only difference is that, here, the initial order to 'stop' comes from the facial recognition algorithm rather than the officer on the ground.

To protect against this, the prohibition of discrimination requires that positive measures be undertaken to determine whether the use of FRT will result in discriminatory outcomes. This emerges from the obligation to respect, which, as noted by Moeckli, 'requires states to refrain from any discriminatory action and to ensure that all their laws *and practices* comply with the right to non-discrimination' (Moeckli 2018: 161). In the UK, this obligation is reinforced by the Public Sector Equality Duty (PSED) (Equality Act: 149(1)), which establishes a non-delegable duty requiring public authorities (in this instance, police forces) to take reasonable steps to identify the impact of a particular measure—such as the deployment of FRT—on persons with protected characteristics.[23]

Police forces may fulfil their obligation to protect against discrimination in at least two ways, by (a) engaging with the developer or (b) conducting an assessment of the algorithm's performance, either themselves or by engaging an independent authority. The developer of a facial recognition algorithm should be able to provide appropriate information regarding the algorithm's performance across the range of protected characteristics, as well as other information relevant to performance during deployment, such as how well the algorithm performs in different light conditions or at different angles. Of course, the information provided must be sufficient to allow a determination as to possible discrimination vis-à-vis the operation of the algorithm. If the developer cannot, or will not, provide such information, then there is a strong argument to suggest that their algorithm should

[21] This was a significant component in the Court of Appeal's finding in *Bridges* vis-à-vis the Equality Act. See *Bridges* v *South Wales Police* [2020] EWCA Civ 1058, August 2020, Ground 5.

[22] *Gillan and Quinton* v *The United Kingdom*, Judgment, ECtHR, App. No. 4158/05, 12 January 2010.

[23] This is discussed in the context of facial recognition by the Court of Appeal in *Bridges*. See paras. 163–202.

not be used by any public authority, as the authority will be unable to ensure that use of the algorithm will not violate the prohibition of discrimination. As noted, in *Bridges* the Court of Appeal held that factors such as commercial confidentiality, or a developer's unwillingness to release detailed information on the algorithm's performance, did not negate the police's PSED.[24] In such circumstances, the police force cannot use the tool as is, and so another option is for the force to conduct their own evaluation of the algorithm. Human rights law does not provide explicit guidance as to how this evaluation should be conducted, but the point of the exercise is to identify any differential performance in relation to any of the protected characteristics. This assessment should ideally be auditable, as transparent as possible, and involve external independent expertise. UK police forces' evaluation of the facial recognition algorithm currently being used are discussed further in Chapter 2.

Ultimately, the prohibition of discrimination establishes a 'red line' vis-à-vis potential facial recognition deployments. If information as to how an algorithm performs in relation to protected characteristics cannot be obtained, then in light of known issues with respect to bias, the tool should not be deployed until such information is available and can be evaluated. Equally, if the data indicates that the deployment of a FRT will result in indirect discrimination, then it cannot be deployed until that bias is addressed (McGregor et al. 2019: 335).

4.4.2.2 The right to privacy

The right to privacy is arguably the right most associated with digital surveillance, and an evaluation of potential harm to this right should be central to any facial recognition due diligence process. As noted previously, facial recognition deployments engage the right to privacy at least twice: once when an image is recorded and again when that image is subject to biometric processing. Importantly, the right to privacy of all individuals subject to biometric processing is engaged. That is, the right to privacy of each and every individual passing through a facial recognition camera's field of vision is brought into play, irrespective of whether they are on a watchlist or not.[25] The extent—or severity—of the interference with the right to privacy must then be evaluated.

[24] *R (Bridges)* v *The Chief Constable of South Wales Police* [2020] EWCA Civ 1058, para. 199.

[25] This was confirmed by the UK High Court in *Bridges* v *Chief Constable of South Wales Police* [2019] EWHC 2341 (Admin), 4 September 2019, para. 59.

As a starting point, the ECtHR has held that the identification and location of an individual—using retrospective and live facial recognition, respectively—is 'particularly intrusive, especially in so far as live facial recognition is concerned'.[26] From this starting point, determining the actual degree of intrusion will depend primarily on 'how' facial recognition is deployed. There are no defined criteria by which to assess intrusion, but a non-exhaustive list of factors relevant to facial recognition may be identified:

- How is surveillance footage, to which FRT may be applied, obtained? For instance, is footage obtained at specific events (as is the case with current LFR deployments in the UK) or is all public surveillance footage with a city stored and made available to police?
- For what purposes may FRT be used? For example, can it be used for the investigation of specific crimes or to establish an intelligence picture? If it is for specific crimes, what categories of crime are relevant? If it is for intelligence purposes, what type of activities may be investigated (i.e. is it limited to national security matters or broader)?
- Who may be identified using facial recognition? Is it persons who are wanted by the courts (and who have therefore been subject to some form of judicial procedure) or is it persons of interest to the police? If the latter, what is the nature of that interest? Does it concern individuals suspected of committing a crime, witnesses to a potential crime, or others?
- Is facial recognition used to look for known persons or to identify unknown persons?
- What type of information may be revealed by the use of facial recognition? For instance, might it reveal sensitive personal information, such as that relating to an individual's health, sexual orientation, or political opinion?
- Is facial recognition deployed around locations that may be entitled to enhanced protection? For example, is it deployed at a protest, at a political meeting, or in the vicinity of a religious site?
- Is facial recognition used to develop profiles of individuals' activities, for instance by monitoring and tracking their movements?
- Is facial recognition combined with other data sources in order to develop a more complete picture of individuals' lives?

[26] *Glukhin* v *Russia*, Judgment, ECtHR, App. No. 11519/20, 4 July 2023, para. 86.

- Is facial recognition used to generate alerts if, for example, an individual enters or leaves a particular location, meets a particular person, or attends a particular event?
- How long is surveillance footage retained for and who has access to that footage?

These factors have been identified as they will have an impact on the overall number of people affected, the categories of persons targeted, and the nature and extent of personal information that might be revealed. They are illustrative and not exhaustive.

4.4.2.3 Compound harms associated with a surveillance-related chilling effect

The discussion in Chapter 3 makes clear that chilling effects linked to police use of facial recognition are a distinct possibility, and that they may result in significant harm to human rights. The difficulty is that mapping out the likely chilling effects prior to deployment is complex. Facial recognition is a completely new surveillance capability and its impacts are, at the moment, unknown. Further research is required to better understand the chilling effects of facial recognition, across a variety of different deployments, so that this information can effectively inform the potential harm strand of the 'competing interests' evaluation. That said, because the impact of the chilling effect can be so severe, both in terms of individuals' ability to freely develop their personality and the evolution of democratic society, caution on the part of those considering the deployment of facial recognition may be appropriate. Until the chilling effects are better understood, the risk may outweigh the reward, and a moratorium may be the most appropriate decision.

4.4.3 Due Diligence Framework Conclusion

The above advances the core components of a due diligence framework for police facial recognition deployments that is rooted in international human rights standards. Analysis of existing caselaw surfaces a number of questions that police forces should address to determine whether a proposed facial recognition deployment could be considered necessary in a democratic society and, ultimately, in accordance with international human rights standards. As such, this due diligence framework could be mapped onto the police's internal authorization process and linked to external oversight arrangements. It helps to frame the application for approval by identifying the questions to be asked, and facilitates an effective review of this application by ensuring that the authorizing officer has the information required to evaluate the application in light of the necessity test.

4.5 Conclusions

Human rights due diligence is a well-established concept at the international level. However, this chapter makes a novel contribution by moving beyond an articulation of principle to develop a detailed due diligence framework tailored specifically to the police's use of FRT. The framework itself is centred around the identification and articulation of the potential utility and potential harm of a FRT deployment, and as such it is a means of proactively engaging the 'necessary in a democratic society' test. It sets out the questions police must ask, and address, if they are to deploy facial recognition in a human rights-compliant manner and provides the frame of reference for the analysis in Chapters 5 and 6.

5
Identifying the Utility Linked to Facial Recognition Deployments

5.1 Introduction

London's Metropolitan Police Service (MPS) has been deploying facial recognition technology (FRT) with increasing regularity since summer 2016. MPS deployment records indicated a dramatic increase in live facial recognition (LFR) deployments, from 9 deployments between 2020 and 2022 (MPS 2022) to 146 deployments between 2023 and September 2024 (MPS 2024b). A 2023 investigation by UK human rights organization Liberty revealed that the MPS now conduct more than 24,000 retrospective facial recognition (RFR) searches each year (Liberty Investigates 2023). More recently, UK Prime Minister Kier Starmer announced a commitment towards 'a wider deployment of facial recognition technology' in response to the far-right riots across England and Northern Ireland during August 2024 (*The Independent* 2024). Such events denote a quickening pace of FRT use both by the MPS and across UK policing, and a trajectory towards mainstream adoption of the technology.

Contrasting this accelerated deployment is a more ponderous approach to regulation and oversight of the technology. Indeed, at present, only the UK's data protection authority, the Information Commissioner's Office (ICO), holds any remit for regulatory oversight of the technology. The last successful ICO investigation into public surveillance technology was in 2013 (Fussey and Webster 2023). Added to this have been attempts to erase scant oversight and external accountability mechanisms that exist in pockets of other public bodies. Perhaps the clearest example of this was the proposal to abolish the national Biometrics and Surveillance Camera Commissioner (BSCC) roles under the Data Protection and Digital Information Bill (no. 2) of 2023. The Bill failed due to then Prime Minister Rishi Sunak's dissolution of parliament before the tabled legislation had

Facial Recognition Surveillance. Pete Fussey and Daragh Murray, Oxford University Press.
 DOI: 10.1093/9780191979927.003.0005

completed its passage through the House of Lords. The Office of the BSCC limps on, yet no commissioner is in post at the time of writing.

This tension—between accelerating FRT use and the absence of meaningful regulation and external oversight—means that internal police processes and authorization procedures play a key role in setting out the justification for, and necessity and human rights implications of, facial recognition use. Amid this regulatory vacuum, this chapter analyses the legal and policy frameworks developed by the MPS to govern their LFR deployments. Here, the human rights due diligence framework developed in Chapter 4 is used to structure this more legally focused assessment. The analysis itself draws on both the 'in accordance with the law' test and the 'necessary in a democratic society' test. Regarding the former—'in accordance with the law'—particular attention is placed on the requirement that police policy be drafted with sufficient precision to limit officer discretion and ensure 'foreseeability'. Although the focus here is centred on the MPS, the approaches developed by South Wales Police (SWP) and Essex Police, the only two other forces currently deploying LFR, are largely similar.

This chapter focuses on how the intended utility of LFR deployments is justified by police in the policy documentation. Central to this analysis are the core principles of a human rights-compliant due diligence framework—the 'what', 'why', 'how', and 'why facial recognition' questions set out in Chapter 4—and the degree to which they are addressed by the police. While this human rights due diligence framework is used to structure the analysis herein, the policy framework prepared by the MPS is examined in light of the applicable human rights law standards and caselaw.

5.2 Police Claims of Live Facial Recognition Utility

Clearly establishing the justification underpinning a facial recognition deployment is a core component of any human rights due diligence process. This is essential not only to ensure that the deployment parameters are clearly defined and an appropriate evidence base supplied but also because the purpose behind a deployment and the parameters of that deployment will have a significant impact on any potential human rights harm. Establishing the intended utility is therefore central to resolving any 'competing interests' at play. As discussed in Chapter 4, this should be 'convincingly established' on the basis of 'relevant and sufficient' justifications.

5.3 What Policing Purpose Is LFR Intended to Achieve?

Clearly setting out the purpose underpinning an LFR deployment—'what' it is intended to achieve—is the essential first step when articulating the intended utility of this surveillance tool. Given the centrality of the underlying database of 'suspects' (the 'watchlist') to any LFR deployment's objectives, establishing the 'what' must necessarily include a discussion as to 'who' is targeted. Translated into a policing policy framework, addressing the 'what' question must therefore address both the relevant policing purposes and the construction of the watchlist. Building on the model advanced in Chapter 4, definitional specificity is essential. Establishing overly broad objectives—such as the fulfilment of 'policing purposes' or, as the analysis below shows, catching 'wanted' people—allows FRT use across an inappropriately wide variety of situations. This breadth of use depletes the ability to identify the utility of a specific deployment and to calculate the resultant human rights harm, while also building in scope for excessive officer discretion.

The MPS state that LFR may be deployed to assist in the delivery of their 'policing purposes'. In their policy documents the MPS offer the following illustrative examples, which, presumably, set out the objectives for LFR operations:

A. Supporting the location and arrest of people wanted for criminal offences;
B. Preventing people who may cause harm entering an area (e.g. fixated threat individuals, persons subject to football banning orders);
C. Supporting the location of people about whom there is intelligence to suggest that they may pose a risk of harm to themselves or others (e.g. stalkers, terrorists, missing persons deemed at risk etc.);
D. Supporting the use of targeted preventative policing tactics in areas where intelligence suggests crime may be committed or there is otherwise a need to secure an area with a precise crime fighting tool to better deter those who may pose a threat from attending. (SWP 2021a: 3.5; MPS 2023d: 4.6)[1]

[1] The illustrative examples set out by the South Wales Police are identical.

According to their own policy, any MPS LFR deployment must be matched to one of these policing purposes. Of themselves, however, these purposes are far too general to assist in articulating 'what' a particular LFR deployment is intended to address. In the London FRT deployments studied for this book, broad and imprecise definitions allowed variations to arise in the operational purposes of the technology. An exemplar of these broadly conceived purposes can be found in the police Data Protection Impact Assessment (DPIA) of 25 July 2018:

> [LFR is used t]o support ongoing policing activity with regards to a specific problem or location: LFR can provide an additional asset to enhance a police response to address a particular issue, such as an increase of a specific crime type within a particular area. This will consist of a bespoke watch-list of wanted individuals or those with conditions not to attend an area based on intelligence and crime analysis. (MPS 2018a: 2)

By 2023, as LFR operations increased in frequency and size, the Metropolitan Police DPIA evoked intelligence as the key determinant in where the cameras would be situated: '[t]he locations used will be based on the intelligence case to Deploy LFR' (MPS 2023a: 15). Moreover, the same DPIA offered a wider range of possible uses for this technology:

> The Deployment of LFR is driven by MPS policing priorities and intelligence-led assessments, both of which determine locality and the policing purpose. It is then the locality and *policing purpose* which determine the composition of the Watchlist in line with the controls in the MPS LFR Documents. The individuals found on a Watchlist are there because there is a *policing need* to locate them, and that need fits with the *policing purpose* driving the LFR Deployment. (MPS 2023a: 6; emphasis added)

'Police intelligence', 'policing purpose', and 'policing need' are all relied on heavily to authorize and legitimate LFR deployments. While these justifications cover a range of legitimate law enforcement activities, police intelligence, purpose, and need are broadly conceived and delimited notions.

This generality—the use of LFR for 'policing purposes'—also makes it difficult to discern measurements of success. This issue was present at the inception of the current phase of FRT use in London from 2016 onwards. For example, the 'Metropolitan Police Service Live Facial Recognition Trial

Evaluation Methodology'[2] used to evaluate their own initial LFR deployments between 2016 and 2019 aspired to assess the utility of this technology as a 'policing tool' in the following way:

> Metropolitan Police Service (MPS) has an objective to trial Live Facial Recognition (LFR) Technology in order to understand its potential as a tool for operational policing . . . The trial aims to provide an evidence base for strategic decision making as to the potential effectiveness of LFR as a policing tool.

Yet the same methodology neither defined concepts such as operational policing, strategic decision-making, or effectiveness nor established specified criteria for their evaluation.[3] This ambiguity, and the lack of a distinction between research objectives and success criteria, was common across MPS documents. For example, the 2018 MPS legal mandate document—in place during the operational trials analysed here—speaks of 'identify[ing] and evaluat[ing] an *evidence base* from which the overt use and deployment of LFR technology will lead to a comprehensive assessment of LFR as a policing tactic' (MPS 2018b: 3; emphasis added).

Policy documentation developed in 2023 added two further layers of specificity, however. First, the DPIA established that 'the need for a Deployment' (MPS 2023a: 31) must be set out, with reference to an appropriate intelligence case/evidence base. Doing so is consistent with the requirements established in the Code of Practice regulating the use of LFR, the first principle of which states that: '[u]se of a surveillance camera system must always be for a *specified purpose* which is in pursuit of a legitimate aim and necessary to meet an identified pressing need' (Home Office 2021: 9; emphasis added). While the establishment of an appropriate evidence base necessarily engages the 'why' question, discussed in the next section, it does indicate that a deployment's specific objective—beyond general policing purposes—must be articulated. Second, the criteria regulating who may be included on a watchlist are set out. Specifically, the MPS Standard

[2] Unpublished. A physical copy of this document was supplied to the authors by the MPS.

[3] It is important to note that sound methodological reasons may exist for testing policing aims through an evaluation of technology. In addition, it is legitimate for the MPS to incorporate a number of open-ended research questions to accommodate unanticipated issues as they arise during the research. However, these methodological choices also hold a range of implications explored below.

Operating Procedures establish that the following individuals may be included on a watchlist:

a) wanted by the courts; and/or
b) suspected of having committed, or where there are reasonable grounds to suspect that the individual depicted is about to commit an offence or where there are reasonable grounds to suspect an individual depicted to be committing an offence; and/or
c) subject to bail conditions, court orders or other restrictions that would be breached if they were at the location at the time of the deployment; and/or
d) missing persons deemed increased risk; and/or
e) presenting a risk of harm to themselves or others; and/or
f) who are victims of an offence, a person who the police have reasonable grounds to suspect the person would have information of importance and relevance to progress an investigation, or is otherwise a close associate of an individual and that individual themselves would fall within paragraphs (a)–(e). (MPS 2023f: 6.8)

Given the broadness of the last criterion, the MPS interpretation guide is included here in full:

> 'Victim of an offence, a person who the police have reasonable grounds to suspect that person would have information of importance and relevance to progress an investigation, or is otherwise a close associate of an individual'. This criteria includes a victim, a person who the police have reasonable grounds to suspect that person would have information of importance and relevance to progress an investigation, or a close association (partner etc.) of an individual, and that individual who would themselves fall within paragraphs 6.8(a)–(e) and 6.10 (a)–(e) of the categories that may be deemed appropriate for inclusion within an LFR Watchlist. The threshold for any Watchlist inclusion is high and the use of the category will be by exception. The necessity for inclusion must be based on a specific intelligence-case with the need for the inclusion on a Watchlist being supported by a written rationale. In documenting their rationale, the applicant would need to be able to demonstrate to the AO's [authorizing officer's] satisfaction:

a) why the inclusion of each victim, person reasonably suspected of having information, or close associate is *necessary* to help locate the person who is wanted by the courts and/or the police; and/or
b) why locating each victim, person reasonably suspected of having information, or close associate person is *necessary* to advance the policing investigation; and/or
c) why locating each victim, person reasonably suspected of having information, or close associate is *necessary* to ensure their safety and/or the safety of others. (MPS 2023f: 6.19; emphasis in original)

Evidently, the MPS policy framework establishes that LFR may be deployed in a wide variety of situations and in relation to a wide category of individuals. This has implications for the 'foreseeability' of the MPS' use of LFR—in light of the degree of discretion extended to the force—and raises concerns regarding compliance with the 'in accordance with the law' requirement.

5.3.1 Legal Frameworks and Operational Realities

In *Bridges*, the Court of Appeal addressed the 'in accordance with the law' requirement in the specific context of SWP's LFR deployments. The Court's analysis focused on the precision of the policy framework, with the level of discretion extended to police officers identified as the 'critical question'.[4] The Court stated that:

> The fundamental deficiencies, as we see it, in the legal framework currently in place relate to two areas of concern. The first is what was called the 'who' question at the hearing before us. The second is the 'where' question. In relation to both of those questions too much discretion is currently left to individual police officers. It is not clear who can be placed on the watchlist nor is it clear that there are any criteria for determining where [LFR] can be deployed.[5]

[4] *R (Bridges)* v *Chief Constable of South Wales Police* [2020] EWCA Civ 1058, Case No. C1/2019/2670, 11 August 2020, para. 121.
[5] *R (Bridges)* v *Chief Constable of South Wales Police* [2020] EWCA Civ 1058, Case No. C1/2019/2670, 11 August 2020, para. 91.

This represents a relatively straightforward application of the 'in accordance with the law' test, recalling the need to protect against arbitrary rights interferences and to ensure foreseeability. At the time, SWP policy argued that those who could be included on watchlist were 'persons wanted on suspicion for an offence, wanted on warrant, vulnerable persons and other persons where intelligence is required'.[6] These categories largely mirror those set out in the Metropolitan Police's Standard Operating Procedure (MPS 2023f: para. 6.8). The Court of Appeal found that the policy framework did not satisfy the 'in accordance with the law' requirement as it granted 'impermissibly wide areas of discretion'[7] to individual police officers and was therefore in violation of the right to privacy.

Given the similarities between SWP's and the MPS's policy frameworks, at first glance it might appear that the Court of Appeal's reasoning should apply straightforwardly to the MPS, and that the MPS's current use of LFR should be considered unlawful. However, two somewhat inconsistent statements by the Court give rise to a degree of uncertainty. The Court held that,

> [w]hile we can readily understand that the first three of those categories [wanted on suspicion of committing an offence, wanted on warrant, being a vulnerable person] are objective, the final category [wanted for intelligence purposes] is not. In effect it could cover anyone who is of interest to the police. In our judgment, that leaves too broad a discretion vested in the individual police officer to decide who should go onto the watchlist.[8]

This passage could be read as implying that the Court only considered the fourth category as being too broad and that the other 'objective' categories were not problematic. However, later in the judgment, the Court concludes that the SWP's overall policy was not 'in accordance with the law' as it involved impermissibly wide discretion regarding the selection of those on watchlists, 'especially' the persons where intelligence is required category.[9]

[6] *R (Bridges)* v *Chief Constable of South Wales Police* [2020] EWCA Civ 1058, Case No. C1/2019/2670, 11 August 2020, para. 123.

[7] *R (Bridges)* v *Chief Constable of South Wales Police* [2020] EWCA Civ 1058, Case No. C1/2019/2670, 11 August 2020, para. 152.

[8] *R (Bridges)* v *Chief Constable of South Wales Police* [2020] EWCA Civ 1058, Case No. C1/2019/2670, 11 August 2020, para. 124.

[9] *R (Bridges)* v *Chief Constable of South Wales Police* [2020] EWCA Civ 1058, Case No. C1/2019/2670, 11 August 2020, para. 152.

This suggests that concern vis-à-vis the level of discretion extended to all categories but was heightened with respect to the 'intelligence required' category.

This interpretation, whereby concerns exist in relation to the level of discretion associated with all four categories, is arguably more consistent with the application of the human rights law limitations regime to facial recognition. Objective criteria are important to ensure the foreseeability of police activity. However, foreseeability is only one part of the 'in accordance with the law' test, and the legal framework must also ensure that the overall scope of police activity is limited to that which is 'necessary in a democratic society'. This means that the establishment of objective criteria is insufficient in and of itself. It is the scope of activity made permissible by those objective criteria that is decisive. In this regard it is recalled that a high level of justification is required for the use of facial recognition, and so while 'wanted on suspicion of an offence', 'wanted on warrant', and 'vulnerable persons' may appear to be objective criteria,[10] they may also be overly broad and permissive. To determine whether facial recognition is necessary in a democratic society, and to ensure that officer discretion is limited accordingly, other factors will also be relevant, such as the degree of suspicion linking an individual to an offence and the seriousness of the offence itself.

That such a vital element of the Court's reasoning can be interpreted in two quite divergent ways—as problematizing only 'subjective' criteria or as incorporating the overall degree of permissiveness—gives rise to an unfortunate degree of uncertainty. For the operation of FRT, the impact of this uncertainty manifests through the database used to drive and focus the deployments.

5.3.2 Watchlists: Where Biometrics and 'Dataveillance' Meet?

Common to any 'one-to-many' facial matching process, LFR depends on a reference database to function (the 'watchlist'). Watchlist construction is an often-opaque process and, accordingly, constitutes the area where scrutiny is most difficult to apply. Most debate on facial recognition watchlists turns on several core questions concerning who is enrolled onto watchlists and

[10] As argued in this chapter and in Chapter 6, determining 'suspicion' also constitutes a subjective exercise.

for what purpose. Considering these questions together reveals a deeper issue at the heart of surveillance deployments, and one central to their impact in human rights terms: that of the nature of the link between the individual and the deployment objective (the 'what').

Analysing the technical and legal questions relating to the construction of watchlists is complex. To facilitate this examination, the discussion is divided into two broad areas of analysis. The first, discussed below, focuses on the criteria for enrolment onto an LFR watchlist. It assesses the rationale and approach stated in MPS policy documentation and considers the human rights compliance of the MPS policy framework in light of both the relevant case law of the European Court of Human Rights (ECtHR) and the *Bridges* decision. Given the similarities to the categories addressed in *Bridges*, the MPS's 'wanted by the courts', 'suspected of committing an offence', and 'of interest to the police' (criterion (g)) categories will each be addressed in turn. The more tactically and operationally relevant aspects of watchlist construction—such as data sourcing and information handling—are examined in Chapter 7.

Facial recognition deployments are human and technical endeavours. Accordingly, and common to policing uses of other technologies, operational practice generates new conditions and possibilities that may not be captured in strategy and policy documents. To address these wider implications, this section uses multiple forms of analysis. It draws on interviews with officers involved in compiling watchlists, analysis of key documentation, attendance at planning meetings and pre-operational briefings, and observations of the facial recognition operations themselves to reveal a complex picture of the 'who', 'why', and 'on what basis' of watchlist construction. Added to this are fundamental questions concerning the size of watchlists and detail over the text and image-based source material used for facial recognition databases (analysed in Chapter 7).

5.3.2.1 Enrolment onto watchlists: wanted by the courts

During the observed operational trials, and for all FRT operations since, the MPS have consistently reported that the main criterion for being included on a police watchlist was that the individual was 'wanted' (see 'To identify individuals shown as wanted by the police and the courts', MPS 2018a: 2). This sense of a clearly defined criterion was reinforced by the MPS's use of the Emerald Warrant Management System (EWMS) (see Chapter 7)—the database of individuals with outstanding warrants—as a foundational data source for developing watchlists. However, despite the seeming clarity of this term, definitions of 'wanted' were expansive and subject to interpretation.

Most commonly held understandings of 'wanted by the police and courts' would likely involve an outstanding arrest warrant or breach of conditions; for instance, an individual has breached a non-custodial licence, failed to appear in court, 'skipped bail', or even escaped custody. Such examples involve formal judicial proceedings or the existence of sufficient evidence to charge someone. Arrest warrants may also be issued for individuals wanted for questioning. Such warrants also require court authorization and thus independent scrutiny of the evidence.[11] The designation of 'wanted', in this sense, implies a connection to an independent court process.

This understanding of 'wanted' also corresponds with the Privacy Impact Assessment issued for the joint MPS–Humberside Police LFR operation in June 2018, which elaborates that '*Wanted on warrant* means the individual is circulated on the Police National Computer (PNC[12]) after a court has issued a warrant for the police to arrest an individual' (Humberside Police 2018). There is a clear policing, and indeed rule of law, interest in locating such individuals. As noted by the MPS: '[t]he courts have already given consideration as to the necessity to locate this category of person and given a direction that they should be apprehended' (MPS 2023f: 6.14).

Despite the benefit associated with apprehending such persons, this category may, however, highlight the distinction between the 'utility' and the 'necessity' of a measure. Relevant here is the fact that the category of persons wanted by the courts may be incredibly broad. It includes 'those with outstanding arrest warrants or who are otherwise required by the courts' (MPS 2023f: 6.14) and could therefore feasibly include a wide range of categories such as those subject to an arrest warrant for a violent offence or for shoplifting, or individuals who have breached the conditions imposed by a Community Order. It seems difficult to support the MPS claim that all individuals falling within this spectrum 'pose a risk to the public in general' (MPS 2023f: 6.14). The question then is whether the use of LFR to locate all individuals wanted by the courts could be considered 'necessary in a democratic society'. Absent any indication that an individual is likely to be

[11] Of course, arrest warrants may be issued for many other matters, but these could be called the core purposes.

[12] The Police National Computer was established in 1974. It holds formal records of encounters of individuals with the police and other criminal justice agencies. For example, it holds data on arrests, charges, court decisions, and a range of licensing records (such as driving and firearms).

present in an area, and given that *all* offences are included (i.e. without any limitation as to their seriousness), it is difficult to see how deploying LFR for the purposes of searching for *all* individuals wanted by the courts could satisfy the 'high level' of justification required for facial recognition deployments. Limitations with respect to the seriousness of the offence, and the likelihood that the individual will be present at the deployment location, are still required. Absent such limitations, the extent of the rights interference is extremely broad and the possibility of identifying an individual extremely uncertain. Such deployments are, in effect, speculative. This dynamic—where technologies claimed to bring precision and certainty are themselves predicated on speculative justifications and vague deployment criteria—is a central theme of the analysis that follows.

5.3.2.2 Enrolment onto watchlists: wanted in relation to an offence

The above definition of 'wanted by the courts' aligns with commonly understood notions of 'wanted' in a law enforcement or criminal justice context. However, the police documentation overseeing the operational trials—and all subsequent deployments—also reveals a second category of 'wanted' persons:

> *Wanted by police* refers to individuals who are suspected of a crime and have been circulated as wanted on Police National Computer after an inspector has reviewed the case and satisfied themselves that the individual should be arrested in the interests of detecting and preventing crime. (Humberside Police 2018)

In July 2018, the MPS produced a DPIA and legal mandate to oversee the remaining operational trials. This documentation retained significant ambiguity with respect to who could be placed on watchlist. Both documents refer to the deployment of LFR to 'identify individuals who are shown as wanted by the *police and criminal justice systems*' (MPS 2018a, 2018b; emphasis added). No further definition is provided, and discussion with officers during the observed deployments suggested that a wide range of individuals, and not just those wanted consequent to an arrest warrant, were included. Current documentation sets out similar criteria (MPS 2023a, 2023c).

Once again, the difficulty with respect to the foreseeability of police action is the broad range of individuals that may be included in this category.

At least two further and specific issues arise here. First, common to the 'wanted by the courts' rationale, the gravity of an offence is not defined and could therefore include any offence on the statute books, from a road traffic offence to burglary, sexual assault or murder. Given the 'high level' of justification required for LFR deployments, it is likely that only the most serious offences would ever be capable of satisfying this threshold. The MPS policy documentation does note that LFR will be used to focus on policing priorities and that these include 'tackling serious crime, with a particular regard to knife and gun crime, child sexual exploitation, violence against women and girls, and terrorism' (MPS 2023c: 5.2, 5.5). However, adhering to police priorities is not an explicit requirement. Moreover, policing priorities are themselves liable to change.

Second, no guidance is given—at least in public-facing documents—as to how the level of suspicion is to be determined. This means that the degree of suspicion required for an individual to be 'wanted in relation to an offence' and included on a watchlist is not set, again leaving extensive discretion to police officers. Ultimately, different authorizing officers may have inconsistent understandings as to what constitutes serious crime or an appropriate level of suspicion. The 'in accordance with the law' test requires that the policy framework limit the scope for officer discretion, but at no point does the MPS policy framework relating to the 'suspect' category establish any objective limitations. This intersection of categorical imprecision and police discretion constitutes a major theme of this book and is analysed further below.

5.3.2.3 Enrolment onto watchlists: of interest to the police

This broad understanding of 'wanted' extends further still, and in the MPS policy documentation includes 'persons of interest', at potentially significantly varying levels both of suspicion and of connection to the actual commission of an offence. In the MPS policy documentation covering the operational trials, this was included in the 'wanted by the police' component of the 'wanted by the police and courts' criterion (MPS 2018a: 1). According to the most recent and currently applicable policy documentation, this third category of 'wanted' offers the MPS's authority to use LFR to identify potential victims of an offence, those who may have information relevant to the investigation of an offence, or close associates of someone falling within the other objectives (MPS 2023f: 6.8). The Standard Operating Procedure does specify that the threshold for inclusion of this category is high, should be exceptional, and should be linked to an intelligence-based written rationale

(MPS 2023f: 6.19). However, as stated by the courts, the inclusion of *any* individual on a watchlist should be linked to an intelligence-based rationale,[13] and *any* use of LFR should be subject to a 'high level' of justification.[14] The difficult is that this category could be interpreted as including *anyone* 'of interest' to the police, once *any* link to advancing an investigation, or locating an individual, can be made. The level of discretion extended to individual police officers in this regard is extensive. Most significantly, the inclusion of this category of persons appears to be in direct conflict with the decision of the *Bridges* Court of Appeal, on any interpretation.

5.3.2.4 Vernaculars of 'wanted'

Taken together, stripping away superficially precise language of 'wanted' reveals considerable malleability of the concept, and the associated potential for arbitrary action with significant human rights consequences. This breadth of definition also generates a space for enrolling more individuals onto LFR watchlists. For example, during the planning stages for one London operation, Metropolitan police officers expressed a desire to construct a watchlist of 'all wanted people in London'. The same officers expressed that using this source for watchlist construction would have implicated more than 17,000 individuals. Watchlist sizes through 2023 and 2024 reveal that this ambition may have been realized.

The impact of such imprecise criteria for inclusion on the watchlist became apparent through the ethnographic fieldwork. For the two Stratford operations, lead operational officers repeatedly responded that 'missing and wanted people' constituted the basis for inclusion. This was reflected in the pre-trial briefings for both test deployments where 'known, missing and wanted' were mentioned. The four operations at Soho and Romford abandoned any mention of 'missing' as a criterion for enrolment on the watchlist. Nevertheless, the 'missing and wanted' couplet is regularly used to legitimate FRT operations in other police jurisdictions (Fussey et al. 2021) and to justify uses of other digital policing tools more generally. From a policing perspective, 'missing and wanted' are often considered in tandem for sound operational reasons. As one senior officer explained,

[13] See reasoning in *R (Bridges)* v *The Chief Constable of South Wales Police* [2020] EWCA Civ 1058, para. 130.

[14] *Glukhin* v *Russia*, Judgment, ECtHR, App. No. 11519/20, 4 July 2023, para. 86.

> sometimes 'mispers' [missing persons] are missing *and* wanted. And often our focus in on their wellbeing even when wanted. This is particularly true of county lines situations,[15] which occupies much of our focus. (Interviewed March 2019)

The threshold for inclusion on a watchlist at the two Stratford operations was not clear and responses to questions from the researchers (acting in the capacity of independent observers) over the type and seriousness of the crime were somewhat ambiguous. Violence was almost always stated as a reason for an individual's presence on a watchlist. Yet this was regularly supplemented by reference to additional 'other' undefined offences or factors of 'local interest'. While this loose definition may be accommodated under the third criterion listed on the July 2018 MPS DPIA—'to support ongoing policing activity with regards to a specific problem or location'—it lacks specificity and allows for extensive discretion in the use of such a potent and intrusive surveillance capability. From the Soho operations (December 2018) onwards, the criteria for 'wanted' became more defined and was established as 'wanted in relation to violent offences'. This conveyed a sense of confinement and specificity to the criteria as the operations grew in number. However, even within this narrower definition ambiguity persisted. Key issues here concern whether the individual is suspected of committing a violent offence, and if so, the degree of suspicion or whether they are wanted because they may have useful information in relation to the investigation of a violent offence. Furthermore, on at least one occasion during these later operations, requests were made by officers at the pre-trial briefing to add names to the watchlist in the minutes preceding deployment based on the introduction of 'local intelligence'—particularly if a prior history of aggression towards the police was highlighted.

This definitional flexibility and imprecision increases the scope for arbitrary uses of intrusive surveillance technology and fundamentally alters the necessity calculation, given the significantly different 'need' to find individuals wanted for questioning compared to those wanted on warrant for serious violent offences. As just highlighted above, the ambiguity over watchlist enrolment criteria pervading these foundational operations

[15] Situations where those involved in large metropolitan urban drug markets travel to control supply and distribution in other parts of the country. Although a national phenomenon, 'county lines' holds particular preoccupation for policing in London. Many interviewed officers also stressed the safeguarding element of these activities given the age of many young Londoners identified and arrested in cross-county drug markets.

persists in current LFR deployments in London. The current policy framework is insufficiently precise, resulting in the granting of excessive discretion to police officers and raising significant concerns vis-à-vis compliance with the 'in accordance with the law' test.

Of additional importance is how widening the eligibility criteria for enrolment on a police database also risks selective police action. Such possibilities hold important resonance with the practice of 'pretext stops', as highlighted in Alexander's (2010) peerless study of discriminatory policing in the US. In its US formulation, pretext stops arise from the US Supreme Court ruling in *Whren* v *United States*[16] which held that any traffic violation could be used as legitimate grounds to stop and then search a vehicle without breaching Fourth Amendment rights. Alexander's point is that is generally impossible for urban drivers to adhere to all traffic rules at all times. This ruling therefore offers enormous latitude to justify police searches and, consequently, scope to act on any pre-existing prejudices. In a striking point of coherence, a similar example was given by one intelligence officer several hours into an LFR operation in London:

> [Ethnographic note, London 2019[17]] Day-long LFR operation on a cold London winter's day. The street is sparsely populated and anti-FRT protestors outnumber passers-by in the vicinity of the cameras. The sparseness of the street is contrasted with how crowded the van—the mobile FRT control room housing intelligence unit—has become. The van is packed, partly due to the cold, but also because of a growing number of interested police 'observers' present at each LFR operation. Little has happened for several hours, and the conversation became expansive to stave off the ennui always present as the less glamourous feature of surveillance operations. After wide-ranging discussions taking in the professional and the personal—covering parenting conundrums, running times, and mutually recognized distain for public sector management—I fell into a lengthy conversation with a specialist covert officer. He described one of the most significant operational challenges his team faced was one of 'attribution', establishing the identities of individuals that had become of interest through the course of an investigation. Responding

[16] *Whren* v *United States*, 517 U.S. 806 (1996).

[17] Specific data, time, and location removed to protect participant anonymity. However, the context is significant here. Ethnographic research of this nature—particularly in circumstances where boredom prevails—presents unique opportunities for rapport and trust building, in this case offering access to unfiltered reflections on covert worlds.

> to my question of how this problem is addressed, the officer was proud of the range of strategies he had cultivated during his long experience in the covert realm. Yet, for him, the most mundane remained the most effective: the pretext traffic stop and request for ID. It was on this point that his evangelism for facial recognition turned. 'Imagine never having to stop people for bogus reasons again', he said.

This account not only highlights a specific reason driving police enthusiasm for FRT, it also signals a deeper point over the subtle yet significant ways the technology reconfigures suspicion. For these digital 'pretext' stops to occur, a wide pool of candidate files has to already exist: a dilated watchlist provides a platform for such ambitions. From a covert policing perspective, realizing this added yet hidden functionality of FRT, then, is made possible through expanded watchlists with poorly defined enrolment criteria.

Adding to more recognized variants of surveillance creep (see Marx 2002), these expansionary dynamics—dilating watchlists to realize this extended surveillance capability—highlight an additional and less visible means by which FRT alters the dynamics, classification, and hermeneutics of suspicion.[18] Moreover, as the following ethnographic chapters reveal, this ambiguity—one that enables additional surveillance capability—manifests across the whole lifecycle of FRT operations.

Fundamental to the way FRT reconfigures suspicion is this incorporation of strategic ambiguity[19] and how this nuances existing socio-legal framings of surveillance practice. From a legal perspective, the rationale for much policy in this area—and for human rights standards specifically—is the specification and limitation of surveillance activities. For example, Directed Surveillance Authorities—the authorization of covert surveillance under the Regulation of Investigatory Powers Act 2001—relies on specifying the operational and temporal limits to surveillance operations. In terms of the targets of surveillance, criminological analyses have implicated security technologies in actuarial and other risk-based processes for over three decades. As Ericson and Haggerty (1997) argued in their landmark analysis of

[18] A central argument of this book is that FRT brings subtle yet significant changes to the (socio-technical) construction of suspicion. These various dynamics are brought together in Chapter 9.

[19] The strategic gains accrued through the ambiguous formation of FRT watchlists resonate with McGoey's (2012) promulgation of the 'strategic ignorance' concept. In her analysis of pharmaceutical regulation in the US, McGoey argues that rather than being a barrier to authority, ignorance 'serves as a productive asset, helping individuals to command resources, deny liability . . . and to assert expertise in the face of unpredictable outcomes' (2012: 533).

'policing the risk society', risk-based approaches categorize the future to anticipate and reduce the universe of possible threats, 'taming the landscape of fear'. Collectively, these framings depict a *narrowing of ambiguity*; both the scope of surveillance and the possibilities of what the technology might address are focused and framed. By contrast, the development of open-ended criteria for facial recognition watchlists (i.e. to include individuals 'of interest' to the police) accommodates uncertainty to enable new possibilities. Such embrace of possibility resonates with Fussey and Sandhu's (2022) observations of a similar process occurring across other forms of digital policing, particularly covert investigations staged online. Uniting Lurry's observations on 'abductive reasoning' with Amoore's (2014) 'politics of possibility', they note that this approach marks a subtle shift where

> [t]he digital practices outlined here, however, point to an additional principle at play, one that dilates, accommodates and embraces uncertainty. These future-oriented surveillance authorizations involve inferences that recognize many potential outcomes. These approaches are also hewn into a specific form of reasoning: an informed speculation, a logic of abduction . . . [T]his form of precaution, replete with 'reasonable inferences' and 'informed guesses', becomes a staging post for many other conditions of possibility that invite further action. It constitutes the acceptance of an 'arraying of possibilities such that they can be acted upon', as Amoore (2014: 23) puts it. Rather than standard forms of probability to constrict and 'tame chance in the landscape of fear' (Ericson and Haggerty, 1997: 450), such digital practices *embrace* uncertainties. (Fussey and Sandhu 2022: 14; emphasis in original)

Here, facial recognition operates in a way that differs from its fêted (and unsubstantiated) role as an 'efficient' and 'precise crime fighting tool' (MPS 2023g). Here, uncertainty is intentionally encoded into facial recognition operation in order to realize its potential. To extend Stan Cohen's (1979) net-widening metaphor, facial recognition provides the opportunity for speculative fishing expeditions.

5.3.3 An Overly Malleable Concept

Overall, the concern with the 'what' component of the MPS policy framework is that it is framed in an exceptionally broad manner that introduces significant potential for discretion, as evidenced by the operational reality just discussed. The 'in accordance with the law' test requires that the policy framework be drafted with sufficient precision to limit the scope of permissible activity to that which is necessary in a democratic society. However, the MPS policy framework does not appear to impose any concrete limitations or restrictions vis-à-vis the offences for which facial recognition can be deployed or who is included on the watchlist. Notably, in *Glukhin*, the Court expressed concern over the quality of the domestic law regulating LFR and RFR, noting that it was 'widely formulated' and that examples of restrictive interpretation were not available.[20] Three concerns have been highlighted: a degree of subjectivity is introduced in relation to the level of suspicion required to justify an LFR deployment; the policy framework allows for LFR to be deployed—at least in principle—to identify *any* individual 'of interest' to the investigation of *any* offence, again introducing extensive scope for subjectivity; and the range of offences for which LFR can be deployed is broad, essentially covering all offences.

These concerns suggest that the decisive factor in determining whether an LFR deployment can go ahead will not be the policy framework—which does not offer any real curb on authority[21]—but rather the discretion of the authorizing officer. The fact that facial recognition can be deployed in relation to *any* offence is also unlikely to establish the high level of justification needed for the necessary in a democratic society test. These concerns apply equally to the use of RFR, as the grounds for using RFR mirror those for LFR (MPS 2023e).

The above demonstrates how such processes fall short of established human rights standards and tests. Yet, in alignment with decades of insights yielded from sociologies of policing, analysing the practice of implementing policies and standards reveals how such ambiguity yields operational benefits. In such circumstances, ambiguity over the parameters of facial recognition watchlists may be considered both strategic and instrumental.

Overall, detailed attention to the 'what' of FRT reveals both obvious and subtle processes that reshape the scope of surveillance activities. The analysis of such reveals how the processes governing the institution and application of FRT enable its adaptation for novel purposes. What is at stake is a form of compounded 'surveillance creep', where both the affordances

[20] *Glukhin* v *Russia*, Judgment, ECtHR, App. No. 11519/20, 4 July 2023, para. 83.

[21] See, e.g., *Gillan and Quinton* v *the United Kingdom*, Judgment, ECtHR, App. No. 4158/05, 12 January 2010, para. 79.

of the technology itself and the policy ecosystem that surrounds it intersect and invite its adaptation and growth into new domains. Here, vaguely formulated justifications allow LFR technologies to be adapted towards myriad purposes while ostensibly servicing a more general policing need. Such a move is evident in the shift from deploying LFR for serious and violent crime—the stated justification for many 2018–2019 deployments observed by the authors—to more broadly conceived uses following the re-establishment of operations after the COVID-19-related lockdowns of 2020–2021. In 2023, for example, a number of LFR operations were explicitly geared towards protecting high-profile events from 'disruption'. This includes LFR deployments at the coronation of King Charles III and the British Grand Prix to prevent disruption from anti-monarchy protestors and climate activists, respectively. Interestingly, a 2023 Freedom of Information Act request by Big Brother Watch revealed how two thirds of those enrolled on the Northamptonshire Police watchlist for the British Grand Prix were not wanted for arrest or suspected of criminal activity, raising suspicion that suspected climate protestors populated the majority of the database (The Guardian 2023). Adding to vital questions around surveillance creep, necessity, and proportionality, this signifies a subtle yet fundamental shift in the temporal focus of LFR operations: from identifying those suspected of serious and violent offences to a more pre-emptive—and speculative—application.

5.4 Efforts at Establishing an Evidence Base: 'Why' Is a Live Facial Recognition Deployment Required?

Addressing the 'why' question requires an evidence base to justify LFR use. Establishing this evidence base will typically implicate two central issues: (a) the extent of the problem to be addressed (i.e. 'why' is there a need to locate a specific individual?) and (b) whether individuals on the watchlist are likely to be at the deployment location.[22]

[22] Interestingly, both of these questions also help to establish a justification for the expenditure of the resources required for an LFR deployment and whether these resources could be more effectively spent in pursuit of other policing objectives.

5.4.1 'Smart' Surveillance and Police Intelligence

Substantiating the extent of the problem to be addressed depends upon factors such as the prevalence of a certain type of crime in an area and the harm associated with that crime. Evidencing these factors is not straightforward. The police are, of course, required to address all forms of crime, and all crimes cause a certain degree of harm. Yet the realities of policing complex environments mean that possibilities for identifying and pursuing possible criminal activities are unlimited. By extension, as generations of social scientists have observed, crime is not only inevitable; both the selection of certain behaviours for action, and the types of responses that follow, are shaped by social and cultural dynamics (inter alia, Christie 2004).[23] Such action is, therefore, necessarily selective.

Human rights-informed socio-legal analyses of the longstanding concern over selective police action bring additional considerations into play. Here, the 'necessary in a democratic society' test requires criminal justice agencies to provide clarification, justification, and quantification to support their actions. If a highly intrusive measure such as LFR is to be introduced, a good reason must exist for doing so, and this reason needs to be evidenced. This human rights requirement again exposes the legal illiteracy of the 'nothing to hide, nothing to fear' justification for surveillance: the evidentiary emphasis rests on those seeking to apply surveillance measures, not those subject to them. At a minimum, the interest in addressing the harm caused by the crime in question must outweigh the potential harm caused by the LFR deployment.[24] Any calculation in this regard must inevitably address issues such as the seriousness of the crime, its frequency, and its scale (such as the number of people affected).

A reason must exist to believe that individuals on a watchlist will be present at the deployment location. The importance of this criterion was highlighted by the Court of Appeal in *Bridges*: 'it will often, perhaps always, be the case that the location will be determined by whether the police have reason to believe that people on the watchlist are going to be at that location'.[25] Using the human rights due diligence framework developed above

[23] Such considerations have, of course, been foundational to the sociology of crime and punishment since its inception.

[24] This is an over-simplification of the necessity test for the purposes of explanation. For further detail, see Chapter 3.

[25] Para. 96.

as an analytical tool, this criterion becomes somewhat self-evident. It will be difficult to establish an evidence base or intelligence case to justify an LFR deployment if those on the watchlist are unlikely to be present at the proposed location.

The importance of using LFR in an intelligence-led manner is consistently claimed in police documentation. For instance, the MPS Standard Operating Procedures clearly state: '[w]atchlists must be driven by a policing need and based on the intelligence case' (MPS 2023f: 6.2). The MPS facial recognition DPIA adds further specificity:

> There are a number of requirements that help to ensure the Deployment is relevant to its legitimate aim and to ensure the relevance of the data being processed. These include:-
>
> 1. The need for a Deployment, and the location of the Deployment to be supported by intelligence and other policing information to confirm the need for the Deployment and the prospects of locating those sought; [p. 30]
> 2. The inclusion of an individual(s) on a Watchlist is to be:
>   a. *Supported by intelligence* or other information which supports the need to locate these individuals (such as a court warrant having been issued for their arrest); *and*
>   b. A policing decision is made as to the prospects of locating them through the use of LFR. (MPS 2023a: 31)

The documentation clearly articulates the need to establish an evidence base in relation to both the problem (or crime) to be addressed and the likely presence of individuals included on the watchlist. However, despite the above claims, very little information is provided as to how an intelligence case should be established (or evidenced). Indeed, the example given in the DPIA refers to a court warrant and not an intelligence case at all. This emphasis on intelligence without detailing its credibility is also reflected in the MPS Standard Operating Procedures, which states in relation to persons who pose a risk of harm:

> The risk of harm will be informed by the intelligence case and/or the considerations set out in the applicable LFR form. This will need to inform the AO as to how the individual or group of individuals present(s) a risk of harm to themselves or to others and:

> a) how using LFR to facilitate their location is *necessary* to manage the risk of harm identified; and
> b) why the significance of the harm identified means it is *necessary* for the police to take action in order to manage the risk. (MPS 2023f: 6.17)

Similarly, with respect to victims of an offence, or others who can help to progress an investigation, the Standard Operating Procedures state that:

> the necessity for inclusion must be based on a specific intelligence-case with the need for inclusion on a Watchlist being supported by a written rationale. In documenting their rationale, the applicant would need to able to demonstrate to the AO's satisfaction:
> A. Why the inclusion of each victim, person reasonably suspected of having information, or close associate is *necessary* to help locate the person who is wanted by the courts and/or the police; and/or
> B. Why locating each victim, person reasonably suspected of having information, or close associate person is *necessary* to advance the policing investigation; and/or
> C. Why locating each victim, person reasonably suspected of having information, or close associate is *necessary* to ensure their safety and/or the safety of others. (MPS 2023f: 6.19)

Repeating a consistent issue, this documentation highlights the importance of establishing an intelligence case, yet no real guidance is given as to how this should be developed and evidenced. This lack of detail is problematic in light of the nature of intelligence itself. Intelligence is a label applicable to a wide range of information with a similarly wide spectrum of reliability, from hunches to material capable of meeting the evidential standard required for legal proceedings. In the UK, police intelligence reports are graded on reliability of the source and credibility of the information, among other criteria (National College of Policing 2022). However, these gradings are initially made by those submitting the intelligence material and are therefore themselves vulnerable to subjectivity. This issue holds particular significance in relation to the scrutability of the 'intelligence case' for regulators and other external overseers of police activities. For example, research into the authorization of surveillance warrants under the Investigatory Powers Act 2016 suggests that although warrants are authorized on the basis of police intelligence, the nature of that underpinning intelligence often remains unscrutinized and therefore taken at face value (Murray et al. 2021). Despite its moniker, 'intelligence' can range from the speculative to the reliable while holding equal markers of credibility. In such circumstances, it is particularly important that the police set out the supporting evidence/intelligence base in sufficient depth, and with sufficient clarity. As noted in Chapter 4, 'relevant and sufficient' evidence should be presented, such that the need for an LFR deployment can be 'convincingly established'.

Such uses of intelligence also expose deeper linkages between social and technical elements of FRT use. These in turn resonate with longstanding ideas over the mutually constructive socio-technical relationships articulated across different manifestations of science and technology studies explored in Chapter 2. Here, as deployments of technological surveillance tools are shaped by intelligence, intelligence material is also itself shaped by technological forms of surveillance. As other studies have revealed, capturing and cataloguing intelligence through digital platforms affords it a sense of durability and credibility (Amnesty International UK 2018; Sandhu and Fussey 2020). In a context where external processes to authorize LFR deployments do not exist, these questions of how intelligence becomes used to justify facial recognition operations in London attain greater importance.

5.4.2 Siting Surveillance: Linking the Individual to the Deployment Location

The second criterion when demonstrating 'why' an LFR deployment is necessary involves linking the individuals on the watchlist to the location of the deployment. As indicated by the Court of Appeal in *Bridges*, 'reasonable grounds'[26] should exist to believe that those on the watchlist will be present at the deployment location. This clearly suggests that for each individual included on the watchlist, the likelihood that they may be present at the deployment location should be justified. By contrast, the MPS legal guidance for officers responsible for authorizing facial recognition operations is ambiguous:

[26] Para. 130.

> Watchlist composition is normally restricted to individuals suspected to be in the proximity of an area, and therefore where there is some possibility or likelihood of an individual passing through an LFR Deployment. How great that likelihood needs to be will vary between cases for inclusion, but in any case should be considered against a number of factors. This means that an AO may deem it necessary and proportionate to authorize the inclusion of people to be included in a Watchlist, *even though there may not be specific intelligence to say where in London they might be found* (MPS 2023d: 10.6 emphasis added).

This passage is both significant and revealing. First, it marks an explicit decoupling of credible intelligence from necessity. It also presents a stark contradiction to the repeated claims that facial recognition deployments are 'intelligence-led'. The same MPS guidance offers further elaboration on this point and achieves the dual outcome of increasing confusion and widening the eligibility criteria for enrolment on a facial recognition watchlist. A number of 'factors for consideration' when establishing the likelihood that an individual will be present in the area are set out:

> a) Severity of offence in question; this will often be relevant to the level of urgency associated with locating and arresting an individual. Many individuals change their behaviour, including the places they reside and frequent when they know that they are wanted for a serious offence;
> b) Risk; the level of risk associated with an individual or the offence type sought, whether that risk is to the public or themselves;
> c) Crime trends; Where there is evidence of wider organisation, repeat offending, methodologies being replicated or numbers are exponentially rising. Emerging or specific crime issues may require a broader approach in order to reassure the public and increase community safety through the use of a precision crime-fighting tactic in order to effectively respond to crime issues.
> d) Deployment location; the specific characteristics of the Deployment location may increase the possibility or likelihood of an individual passing through as well as informing the scope and nature of the Watchlist. For example, areas around transport hubs have a lot of

> people transiting from place to place and other areas of London have 'pull factors' that make it likely that people from across London and beyond may frequent that area. (MPS 2023d: 10.6)

Rather than establishing limits on watchlist enrolment based on a 'reasonable ground' to believe they will be present where the cameras are, the policy creates significant exceptions. Several issues emerge here. First, no guidance is given as to how these exceptions should be evaluated. Instead, exceptions could be made in a manner that is permissive, subjective, and highly discretionary, and ultimately feed the net-widening potential of FRT. Second, it appears that the guidance permits surveillance on categories of persons for whom no reasonable ground exists linking them to the deployment location, and that these people are included as an 'add-on'. Taking point (a), 'severity of the offence', as an example, it appears that persons suspected of committing a certain category of offence—but who have no connection to the reason justifying this specific LFR deployment—may be included on the watchlist. Point (d), 'deployment location', all but permits the addition of *anyone* to a watchlist for operations at London's transport hubs, given the likelihood that people travel. It would be extremely difficult to argue that these represent an intelligence- or evidence-based rationale for including people on facial recognition databases. Together, these factors constitute a clear risk that membership on facial recognition watchlists extends beyond the circumstances of the deployment and starts to resemble a fishing exercise.

The outcome of this loosening of criteria for being enrolled on watchlists is reflected in recent facial recognition operations. MPS records from April to December 2023 record an average watchlist size of approximately 11,425 individuals, a significant increase from the pre-pandemic operations. This resulted in a total of 56 confirmed alerts across the 23 deployments, from a total of 326,392 individuals subjected to biometric processing. This means that, on average, during each deployment there were just under 2.5 confirmed alerts from a watchlist of 11,425 and approximately 14,190 individuals scanned (MPS 2024b). This is a ratio of one watchlist entry for every 1.24 faces scanned. Put another way, for every passer-by's face scanned by facial recognition systems in London, the MPS has a watchlist of an almost equal number of people. These results raise serious questions vis-à-vis the evidence base and intelligence case justifying the eligibility criteria for the watchlists. With 56 alerts from 326,392 individuals scanned—a success rate of 0.0001716 per cent—it stretches credibility to claim sufficient attention was paid to evaluating whether individuals on the watchlist would actually be present.

5.4.3 Evaluating Necessity or Utility?

This lack of clarity (or direct guidance) regarding the evidence base supporting facial recognition operations is further complicated by how the MPS frames the necessity calculation. The legal mandate states:

> Necessity is a demanding requirement to justify any interference with Article 8. It requires the action to lie somewhere between 'indispensable' and more than something that is merely 'desirable'. In this respect, LFR will be used in response to a pressing social need by helping the MPS to fight crime in areas where LFR has the greatest potential to assist. It is a tool that helps the MPS to discharge its operational authorities, primarily to help it prevent and detect crime. (MPS 2023c: 3.11)

The first half of this statement is consistent with human rights caselaw which affirms that to satisfy the necessity test, a deployment must be more than just 'desirable' or 'useful'. However, as discussed below, this is not reflected in the examples given. The documentation provided undermines this straightforward articulation of the relevant legal principle and presents contradictory guidance to police officers. Equally, the second half of the statement makes several claims regarding the utility and necessity of LFR, replete with technologically deterministic framing, which arguably invite an authorizing officer to approve its use. This suggestion is reinforced in subsequent, and more developed, guidance:

> Authorising Officers need to decide the use of LFR is *necessary* and not just desirable to enable the MPS achieve its legitimate aim. In deciding if the use of LFR is necessary, consideration should be given to the intelligence case as this will be important in outlining the need to deploy to a particular location and the composition of the Watchlist. Consideration should also be given to whether there is an alternative, including the viability and intrusiveness of the alternative.

The issue with this example—the 'key point' for authorizing officers—is that the focus rests on whether the deployment is necessary in light of the intelligence case and the legitimate aim pursued. These are valid considerations but they only form one half of the overall necessity test. No consideration is given to the potential harm linked to the deployment. This omission of guidance on how to identify harm is a notable absence throughout the MPS legal documentation. Without a consideration of harm, the necessity test is, in effect—and despite the clear articulation of principle referred to above—reduced to a test of utility or desirability, a formulation that is incomplete, inaccurate, and insufficient. The outcome is that the guidance given to authorizing officers—who are not legally trained individuals with human rights expertise—is skewed in favour of permitting facial recognition deployments. They are led to ask, 'will the deployment meet an evidence-based policing need?' (i.e. is it demonstrably useful?) and not, 'is the deployment necessary, when the competing interests of intended utility and potential harm are taken into consideration?' As the ethnographic material presented in the following chapters relays, this inaccurate framing of necessity in terms of meeting 'policing need' is reflected through other areas of operational practice.

While it may be challenging for a policy framework to list types of appropriate evidence, and while some forces may be reluctant to disclose information on intelligence gathering, more consistent and detailed guidance could be provided. Indeed, such evidence is routinely provided to authorize other forms of intrusive surveillance and, arguably, in more sensitive security contexts, including that used by intelligence agencies.[27] For proponents, a common means of justifying facial recognition operations is the use of hypothetical examples. While examples could play a useful illustrative role in this regard—by setting out factors such as how the importance of an objective should be evaluated, what degree of reliability is acceptable when determining when and where to situate a deployment, how a clear link between the intelligence and the deployment can be demonstrated, how potential harm might be identified, and so on—they are yet to be used in this way. Instead, hypothetical examples are regularly used in a more rhetorical sense, ostensibly to convey a sense of legitimacy. Typical in this approach and the justification of other digital technologies is the celebrated role of facial recognition in tacking the twin bête noires of terrorism and sexualized abuse against children. The examples used in MPS legal documentation

[27] This has been confirmed repeatedly to the authors through ongoing research and collaboration with the principal body responsible for the oversight of UK intelligence agencies (see IPCO 2022).

neglect to discuss building an intelligence case in any meaningful way. Instead, they typically assume the intelligence case as a fait accompli. For instance, the MPS's legal mandate gives the following examples:

> **Terrorism example:** The use of LFR will assist the MPS in fighting terrorism. By way of example, LFR could be deployed at international borders. This can be part of tailored security measures to keep people safe as LFR can act as a valuable tool to assist police officers to identify those of interest to the police for terrorism reasons including those who may be travelling on false documentation. (MPS 2023c: 3.11)
>
> **Child sexual abuse and exploitation example:** The use of LFR will assist the MPS in fighting child sexual abuse and exploitation. LFR could be deployed based on intelligence to find vulnerable individuals who are missing and believed to be at risk of child sexual abuse and exploitation. (MPS 2023c: 3.11)
>
> **Example:** The use of LFR can assist the MPS to ensure public safety, including at a place of worship where the intelligence case has identified a threat to the public. (MPS 2023c: 3.13)
>
> **Example:** The use of LFR can assist the MPS in policing an assembly or demonstration, particularly when there is an intelligence case supporting there being a risk to public safety. (MPS 2023c: 3.13)

These, and other similar examples, are framed in an overly permissive manner. They do not include any guidance on how to determine the strength (or quality) of the underlying intelligence or how to evaluate the likelihood of an event occurring. Technological determinism pervades such language. Indeed, in two of the examples, the utility of LFR is unequivocally affirmed. Equally, any consideration of the potential harm linked to a deployment within the examples provided is minimal. It is noted that a deployment at a place of worship, or at a protest, may engage the rights to freedom of religion, expression, or assembly but no guidance is given as to how the degree of interference might be calculated or even considered. This lack of detail, and the overly permissive framing, is compounded by the fact that no examples are provided indicating instances where LFR might not be considered necessary. Moreover, while terrorism and the victimization of children are routinely offered as emotive justifications for FRT, these offences were not the focus of operations analysed here. Overall, such examples operate as rhetorical devices aimed at legitimating the technology rather than providing a meaningful analysis of necessity.

As discussed in Chapter 4, human rights law requires that 'relevant and sufficient' reasons be provided so that the necessity of an LFR deployment can be 'convincingly established'. The necessity calculation is complex. If the guidance provided is skewed, and if very little detail is provided as to how to undertake the calculation, then shortcomings are inevitable. Moreover, the absence of clear parameters and detailed guidance governing the use of FRT offers excessive discretion to individual authorizing officers when establishing the extent of the problem to be addressed, and why addressing it in this specific manner is necessary.

The establishment of an appropriate evidence base is essential to setting out 'why' an LFR deployment is required. This should address both the prevalence and nature of the crime or harm to be addressed and the likelihood that an individual will be present in the vicinity of the deployment location. However, while it highlights the importance of an evidence/intelligence base, the policy framework provides no guidance as to how this should be constructed. As it stands, the guidance is either skewed in favour of authorization—undermining the necessity test—or overly ambiguous, leaving too much scope for discretion and undermining the 'in accordance with the law' test. The same problem applies vis-à-vis RFR. The policy framework does not include any clear information as to the nature of the intelligence case/evidence base required for the use of RFR or how this will be evaluated to ensure human rights compliance (MPS 2023d).

5.5 Setting Parameters: 'How' Will Live Facial Recognition Technology Be Deployed?

This component assesses 'how' an intended LFR deployment aims to achieve the specified, intelligence-informed objective. Addressing such questions draws considerations of the 'what' and the 'why' together to define the intended circumstances of use and the appropriateness of deploying facial recognition for such specific ends. At the heart of such considerations are longstanding debates over the relationship between the prior justifications for how surveillance technologies will be used and the operational realities of their actual deployment. It is in this respect that the ethnographic data revealing embedded operational practices and environments intersects with the analysis of policy documents undertaken here.

The most enthusiastic adopters of LFR in the UK have been SWP and the MPS. Policy documents for both forces specify largely similar circumstances for how LFR will be deployed. The characteristics of deployments are as follows:

- LFR will deployed using dedicated camera systems, at a fixed location, for a specified period of time (SWP 2021c: 5.1; MPS 2023a: 15)
- LFR is a 'closed system', this means that it can only be used in relation to those on the watchlist, and the broader police force will not have access to the LFR system, or to the product of surveillance (MPS 2023c: 3.12)
- LFR is not deployed in an automated manner, and so any alert will always be checked by a police officer, prior to an engagement (SWP 2021c: 10.8; MPS 2023f: 10.8) (although see Chapter 8 for further discussion in this regard)
- Visible signage will indicate the use of LFR (SWP 2021c: 5.2; MPS 2023f: 5.8)
- Refusing to walk through a camera's zone of recognition should not, of itself, be treated as suspicious (SWP 2021c: 5.3; MPS 2023f: 5.9)
- There is protection against 'function creep', in that if an additional law enforcement purpose is identified, after authorisation of the initial LFR deployment, this will require specific additional authorisation. (SWP 2021c: 4.8; MPS 2023f: 4.8)

At face value, such statements appear to articulate the intended circumstances and limitations of LFR use in a relatively clear manner.[28] However, this only contends with one component of the 'how' question. The unaddressed aspect concerns how LFR will achieve the specific, intelligence-case-supported objective. The examples provided in the MPS policy framework are not overly useful in this regard. For instance, two prominent examples offered by the MPS are ambiguous regarding how LFR can effectively address the specified policing objective.

> **Example:** Areas particularly focused on providing facilities or attractions aimed at children would typically attract greater privacy expectations over an area that typically sees attendance from the public more broadly. The public would not typically expect LFR to be sited outside

[28] This is not, however, to downplay the significant concerns raised in relation to the 'what' and 'why' questions as outlined above, as deficiencies here will have a significant impact on how LFR deployments take place.

> a toyshop or school that may disproportionately see children passing the LFR system if the LFR system could be sited elsewhere. There may nevertheless be instances where the intelligence case, and the need to protect children makes it necessary and proportionate to deploy LFR to these areas. For example if it is known that wanted sex offenders are targeting those that visit the location and it [sic] not possible to locate them by siting LFR elsewhere or using other less intrusive policing tactics. If it is necessary to use LFR at the location, mitigations to reduce the privacy impact should be used wherever possible. This could include extra measures to ensure that the signage and information about the LFR Deployment is accessible to children who pass through the Zone of Recognition. (SWP 2021b: 12; MPS 2023c: 3.12)
>
> **Example:** If there was a necessity and proportionality case, based on intelligence, to deploy LFR in a residential area to locate a group of violent robbery offenders, then we understand that there may be a greater expectation of privacy in this area. To mitigate this, depending on the circumstances we may provide additional communication about the use of LFR, for example by leafleting local residents or posting on local neighbourhood social media groups. (SWP 2021b: 12; MPS 2023c: 3.12)

Aside from the questionable statements regarding expectations of privacy, returned to below, these are problematic examples as to 'how' LFR could be deployed to contribute to policing objectives. As noted above, all LFR deployments are fixed in location and time, must involve visible signage highlighting the presence of LFR cameras, and a decision not to pass through an LFR camera's field of vision cannot be treated as suspicious of itself. Under these circumstances, and in light of the fact that the police must have photos on file of the suspected burglars—indicating that, in most cases at least, those individuals will be aware that they are known to the police—it seems highly unlikely that LFR deployments set out in the examples are likely to succeed in identifying and locating the individuals included on the watchlist. Instead, it seems more likely that such individuals would take note of the visible police presence—or, potentially, the pre-deployment communication—and simply choose to avoid the area. Similarly, the child sexual abuse and exploitation example does not set out how LFR will assist but instead focuses on a comparison with one alternative measure, namely a public call for information. The intelligence case setting out 'why' LFR is necessary in this instance should have been set out previously; what is missing here is any real detail as to 'how' LFR will address the problem.

A similar problem arises as with the burglary example: in light of the highly visible police presence, will wanted sex offenders simply choose not to visit deployment locations? Other examples in the policy documentation are similarly vague, setting out hypothetical situations—such as a threat to public safety at a place of worship or assembly—but without discussing the specific role that LFR will play in any detail.

Overall, MPS policy documentation consistently offers little detail on 'how' LFR will actually help to address the identified problem. This is significant because the absence of such information depletes any linkage between the specific application of technology and the objective it is intended to address, thus weakening any claims to necessity. In each of the examples provided, a statement is made, but reasoning or justification is not provided.

5.6 Why Facial Recognition? Police Evaluation of Alternative Measures

The evaluation of alternative means is a central component of the 'necessary in a democratic society' test. It requires that if a less intrusive means capable of achieving the same overall objective can be identified, then that measure should be chosen. Of course, any alternative measures remain subject to satisfying the 'necessary in a democratic society' requirement.

The importance of evaluating alternative measures is clearly recognized in the MPS's policy framework. For example, the MPS DPIA states that:

> The use of LFR as a tool to locate persons of interest to the MPS will be considered alongside other policing tools and tactics. Consideration will be given as to the effectiveness and intrusiveness of other viable methods that might produce the same result, with the least intrusive, viable method being adopted to progress an investigation. (MPS 2020a: 38)

This statement demonstrates a clear understanding of the importance of considering alternative means and is broadly in line with the human rights law requirement. The question then turns to whether the alternative means test is implemented correctly.

The terrorism example provided by the MPS—where border officials are looking for individuals with suspected links to terrorism—appears to be an illustration of how alternative measures can be considered appropriately. Here, the human checking documents constitutes the alternative means capable of achieving the same objective. The viability of that alternative means can then be evaluated in light of the officer's ability to access a reference database of suspects and sufficiently recognize when individuals may take measures to prevent their identification.

Other references to alternative measures in MPS documentation indicate a substantially more restrictive understanding of the concept. These are unlikely to be of sufficient rigour to satisfy the 'necessary in a democratic society' test. A problematic example is given in the MPS's legal mandate:

> **Example: alternative policing methods to prevent threats to public security:** LFR may be deployed to police a high profile well-attended public event. When considering alternatives, in this example, other measures such as extra CCTV may be considered. However, they will not always be a viable less intrusive alternative in the circumstances. For example:
>
> 1. Whilst CCTV can help ensure event safety, it lacks the ability to actively Alert officers to the potential presence of individuals of interest to them.
> 2. It may not be practical to expect officers to recognise large numbers of people of interest to the Police given the nature and scale of the event, the number of officers available to police the event and the flow rate and numbers of people passing the CCTV system. This is especially relevant where the importance of making such identification supports the use of a more suitable alternative such as LFR.
> 3. Where LFR is thought to offer further important protection to the public as opposed to other policing methods. For example, this may apply where the law enforcement purposes for a Deployment include wider public safety considerations. These may include the need to locate those wanted by the courts. Such persons may attend such a high profile event, and in line with the decision of the courts to require their arrest, pose a risk to the public generally. (MPS 2023c: 5.2)

The issue here is that, although the example is intended to discuss alternative measures, the text fails to engage with the issue. Instead, the example—in effect—shuts down the possibility of viable alternatives, largely by highlighting perceived qualities of LFR and comparing other tools unfavourably in the absence of any discussion of the context. Alternative means are not presented because the discussion is focused on the specific virtues of one tool rather than the wider possibilities for addressing an objective. Here we encounter a circular logic, one almost synonymizing with Orwellian syntax, in an argument that effectively states, 'LFR has specific abilities to prevent threats to public safety. There are no better alternatives to the specific abilities of LFR in preventing threats to public safety.'

Moreover, and common to many intellectual journeys in surveillance studies, an initial flirtation with Orwell attracts one to Foucault. Yet rather than revisiting the overworn furrow of the 'Big Brother to the panopticon' journey, both had (arguably) more profound things to say about the nature of truth. Resonant with the specific means of digital knowledge production discussed in Chapter 2, the logical framings presented to justify LFR start from a presumption of efficacy and legality, which are then justified with arguments that resemble the form, but not substance, of legal reasoning.[29] Such practices represent subtle modes of justifying facial recognition, a technology that remains controversial. Here, truth claims are asserted that draw on legal (and scientific) language for their legitimacy, are seemingly authoritative, and, while insubstantial, require detailed arguments to challenge. In a highly mediatized society, such claims, and their modes of production, have become continually repeated through public and parliamentary arenas of discourse. In so doing, a renewed relevancy for the digital age is offered to Foucault's (2008) astute observation of a transition from 'regimes of jurisdiction' to those of 'veridiction'.

Returning to assessments of alternative measures, the above also appears indicative, at least in MPS documentation, of a reluctance to genuinely engage with the issue. Instead, the focus is on ill-matched like-for-like replacements whereby the only alternative to LFR considered is a lower-capability form of visual identification at the deployment location. For example, the MPS Equality Impact Assessment states that a 'key benefit' of LFR is that:

> LFR will assist officers where traditional policing methods can struggle to yield results. An individual officer cannot possibly remember all the faces of wanted persons on a Watchlist. (MPS 2024a: 2)

Again, the comparison made here is against tasks at which LFR is deemed effective rather than how a specific issue is addressed, a determination that

[29] A similar dynamic is also evident with respect to technical evaluations of LFR performance, particularly those focused on how the technology performs over different visible ethnicities. As elaborated in Chapter 2, one example is the overfitting of one narrow and highly specific study (National Physical Laboratory 2023) to dress unsubstantiated claims about the entirety of LFR performance in the language of 'scientific' legitimacy.

(obviously) has only one likely outcome. It is, of course, true that no police officer can possibly compete with the identification potential of LFR running a large watchlist. The point here is that officers are not commonly tasked with identifying people by acting like LFR systems, asked to watch cameras observing a street while memorizing vast watchlists.[30] Instead, noticeably absent from the determination above is an entire suite of law and practice geared towards identifying wanted people through covert and other investigative means, as well as significant experience with respect to the policing of protest. The issue is that these examples do not engage with other policing techniques, including those that were used in similar situations prior to LFR. Moreover, the reason large watchlists are used in this way arises from the affordances of FRT itself. The technological capability of facial recognition allows large numbers of facial images to be processed, and so policing practices have emerged that are shaped to this capability. In this framing, there are no less intrusive alternatives because there are no alternatives to the specific way LFR works. Alternatives do exist for addressing a problem, however. Overall, the comparison is invalid and, in any objective sense, the exercise is pointless.

Overall, the key problem with the MPS's discussion of alternative means is that it fails to consider alternative means. It establishes a scenario whereby officers attempting to replicate LFR is the only real alternative, without making reference to other policing techniques including those traditionally used in the same or similar scenarios.

5.7 Conclusions

As it stands, the legal and policy framework prepared by the MPS—and, indeed, all other UK forces deploying LFR—is overly broad. These documents leave too much scope for interpretation and allow room for excessive discretion on the part of individual police officers. Given that the problem of excessive discretion was so clearly emphasized by the only judicial review into facial recognition surveillance to date, it is difficult to see how current police policy documentation can satisfy the 'in accordance with the law' test or limit police action to that which is 'necessary in a democratic society'.

[30] See Chapter 3 and the 'police spotter at a football match' example for further consideration of why police actions that resemble LFR tasks are not analogous.

The analysis of MPS legal positioning above reveals three overarching issues central to human rights considerations of facial recognition use in London. First, the policy framework is extremely permissive with respect to the purposes for which LFR can be deployed. Notable here is the absence of how 'suspicion' is quantified, the lack of any explicit limitation on the category of offences for which LFR may be deployed, and the open possibility for including non-suspects (i.e. individuals 'of interest' to the police) on the watchlist. Without meaningful limitations in the policy framework, excessive discretion is enabled throughout the operational lifecycle, introducing a risk of arbitrariness and undermining the 'foreseeability' of the framework. Second, the approach to the 'necessary in a democratic society' test is problematic. While the test itself is correctly set out as being less then 'indispensable' but more than 'useful', the approach taken to the necessity test within the policy documentation itself is partial. Here, the police focus rests solely on the intelligence case and the legitimate aim pursued. No real mention is made of the potential harm to human rights. Without an examination of harm—the 'competing interest' at play—any evaluation is essentially reduced to one of utility. This incompleteness renders the 'necessary in a democratic society' test ineffective. Third, the overall approach taken to the drafting of the policy framework is deeply problematic. No policy framework can hope to be comprehensive. What it can do, however, is set out examples capable of informing officers how they might approach different situations and noting the factors that might be taken into consideration when deciding to authorize, or refuse, an LFR deployment. In this regard, it is striking that no examples are given where an LFR deployment would not be authorized, that few means of evaluating the intelligence case/evidence base linked to a deployment are provided, and that negligible engagement with the different forms of human rights harm exists. This means that police officers are not provided with the tools, information, and approach to effectively examine different situations, and that the policy framework reads more like an advocacy document than a guide. These concerns, and the first point in particular, apply equally to the use of RFR.

6
Metropolitan Police Service Efforts to Identify Potential Harm to Human Rights Associated with Live Facial Recognition Deployments

6.1 Introduction

A proper evaluation of the potential human rights harms linked to a facial recognition deployment is an essential component of the 'necessary in a democratic society' test, and is central to any human rights due diligence process. Harm to human rights is the 'competing interest' against which the intended utility of a deployment must be evaluated. It is therefore incumbent on those using this technology to evidence that such evaluations have taken place, and that they have addressed the range of rights at play. Within policing generally, an evaluation of potential harm typically takes the form of a 'risk assessment' or an 'impact assessment'. In the UK, relevant legislation requires that police forces undertake two specific impact assessments, a Data Protection Impact Assessment (under the Data Protection Act 2018)—which incorporates data protection and privacy concerns—and an Equality Impact Assessment (under the Equality Act 2010). Other potential harms to human rights are also highlighted (albeit partially) as part of the overall Metropolitan Police Service (MPS) policy framework.

The approach set out in legislation, and applied by the MPS and other police forces, presents several problems in the context of facial recognition technology (FRT). First, the statutory requirements focus police attention on an overly narrow subset of rights, namely data protection-related rights (including the right to privacy) and the prohibition of discrimination. These rights are, of course, important and relevant to facial recognition deployments. However, as discussed in this chapter, the concern is that inadequate

Facial Recognition Surveillance. Pete Fussey and Daragh Murray, Oxford University Press.
 DOI: 10.1093/9780191979927.003.0006

attention is paid to other rights, such as the rights to freedom of expression or freedom of assembly, or indeed to broader 'compound' human rights harms. Partial engagement with potential harm undermines the quality of the necessity test and risks bias in favour of authorizations: if only a subset of the actual harm is addressed, this will inevitably tilt the scales of any utility versus harm/competing interests calculation. Additionally, holding these considerations over multiple police policy documents, many of which address overlapping issues, as is currently the case with police FRT policy, is confusing. Even with relatively longstanding subject-matter expertise, navigating and understanding this policy framework is difficult, making it harder both to determine how live facial recognition (LFR) will be deployed and to discern the quality of human rights harm assessments.

In recognition of these problems, the (then) UK Surveillance Camera Commissioner recommended the development of a single integrated impact assessment to provide a comprehensive approach to facial recognition-related issues (Surveillance Camera Commissioner 2020: 3.86).[1] One explicit aim of this approach was to improve the focus of human rights assessments while reducing duplication and bureaucracy and avoiding any gaps in the decision-making process. This recommendation marks a positive move in bringing more wide-ranging human rights considerations into the heart of FRT policy processes. However, there is a risk that framing the process as an 'impact assessment' focuses on evaluating risk. As established previously, an articulation of intended utility is equally essential to the necessary in a democracy society test. Moreover, and reflecting a consistent theme highlighted by other analyses of surveillance authorization processes, in the absence of meaningful external oversight, there is a clear danger that impact assessments become a tool for superficial compliance. With this in mind, reconfiguring the current policy landscape and transitioning towards a more process-orientated due diligence framework may be appropriate.

The next section will first examine how the MPS engages with the impact assessment process before looking at the evaluation of specific rights. Section 6.3 looks at the right to privacy, Section 6.4 looks at the prohibition of discrimination, and Section 6.5 looks at broader human rights impacts, including the concept of 'compound human rights harms' as set out in Chapter 3. To recap, this term is used to refer to harms associated with

[1] The authors played a significant role in drafting this national guidance, which itself built on insights arising from research undertaken for this book.

surveillance that simultaneously affect a number of rights, such as freedom of expression, freedom of assembly, and freedom of religion, often in an interconnected manner. These rights are typically brought into play as a result of surveillance 'chilling effects'.

6.2 Pre-Deployment Impact Assessments

The Data Protection Act requires that '[w]here a type of processing is likely to result in a high risk to the rights and freedoms of individuals, the controller must, prior to the processing, carry out a data protection impact assessment' (Data Protection Act 2018: 64(1)). This should include:

(a) a general description of the envisaged processing operations;
(b) an assessment of the risks to the rights and freedoms of data subjects;
(c) the measures envisaged to address those risks;
(d) safeguards, security measures and mechanisms to ensure the protection of personal data and to demonstrate compliance with this Part, taking into account the rights and legitimate interests of the data subjects and other persons concerned. (Data Protection Act 2018: 64(3))

Facial recognition deployments are internationally recognized as 'high risk' and therefore as requiring a Data Protection Impact Assessment.[2] Understandably, this impact assessment focuses primarily on data protection-related concerns, such as the storage and processing of data. The relevant rights of the data subject include: the right to be informed; the right of access; the right of rectification; the right to erasure or restrict processing; and the right not to be subjected to automated decision-making (Information Commissioner's Office). The right to privacy is also addressed within the MPS's data protection impact assessments, although somewhat obliquely. This is returned to below.

A parallel Equality Impact Assessment is required by the Public Sector Equality Duty (PSED). This requires that the police 'must have due regard to the need to . . . eliminate discrimination, harassment, victimisation and

[2] This categorization of facial recognition as 'high risk' is also accepted internationally, as evidenced by the technology receiving the highest risk classification in the European Union AI Act 2023.

any other conduct that is prohibited by or under this Act' (Equality Act 2010: 149(1)(a)). This focuses on the need to prevent discrimination in relation to one or more of the protected characteristics, which in the context of FRT are most likely to be age, race, or gender.[3] This duty to eliminate discrimination applies both to the actual FRT used—for example, whether the technology exhibits performance bias vis-à-vis any of the protected characteristics—and to the nature of the deployment, such as whether it is used in a discriminatory manner against certain demographic groups. These issues are examined in detail below.

As this analysis demonstrates, the nature and execution of these impact assessments reveals them to be narrowly focused on selected issues/rights and insufficient in scope to adequately cover the overall human rights impact of LFR. This is problematic. As Chapter 3 sets out, LFR implicates a wide range of human rights beyond just the right to privacy or the prohibition of discrimination. For instance, using LFR at a protest will also engage the rights to freedom of expression and freedom of assembly, while an operation in the vicinity of a religious establishment may bring into play the right to freedom of religion.[4] Any shortcomings in these pre-deployment human rights assessments will inevitably undermine the human rights compliance of an operation.

The MPS Equality Impact Assessment does acknowledge the importance of a comprehensive human rights impact assessment. For example, it refers to a report of the European Union Fundamental Rights Agency which notes that:

> A fundamental rights impact assessment is an essential tool to ensure a fundamental rights compliant application of facial recognition technologies, whatever the context in which it is employed. Such an assessment needs to evaluate all affected rights, including those listed in this paper, in a comprehensive manner. To enable them to carry out such assessment, public authorities need to obtain all necessary information from the industry which is required to assess the technology's impact

[3] These are the characteristics most associated with FRT performance bias. However, depending on the nature of the deployment, other protected characteristics—such as religion or sexual orientation—may be relevant. This may occur, for example, if facial recognition deployments occur in the proximity of particular religious establishments.

[4] These are just illustrative examples. A deployment may engage a number of different rights, requiring a case-by-case assessment. For example, depending on its nature, a deployment in the vicinity of a religious establishment may also engage the right to freedom of assembly.

on fundamental rights. Trade secrets or confidentiality considerations should not hinder this effort. (MPS 2024a: 12)

Similarly, the MPS legal mandate notes that the 'Surveillance Camera Commissioner has recognized that there are potential impacts on other human rights. These include the right to freedom of assembly, freedom of thought, belief and religion, freedom of expression, freedom of association, and the protection of discrimination in respect of those rights and freedoms' (MPS 2023c: 3.5).

However, despite recognizing the importance of a more holistic or comprehensive approach to evaluating human rights impacts, the policy framework fails to engage with the practice. This again connects with a more enduring theme where signifiers of human rights compliance are offered—in this case, recognition of the need for comprehensive human rights assessment—yet not engaged with in detail.

6.3 How Do the Police Understand the Right to Privacy?

The right to privacy is the principal right addressed by the MPS. However, the understanding of this right—at least as presented in public-facing documentation—is incomplete, resulting in an inadequate assessment of the manner in which LFR use engages the right to privacy. This problem manifests in two key ways. First, the MPS's approach is anchored in the 'reasonable expectation' of privacy concept which, as formulated in the documentation, rests on a flawed assumption affecting the necessary in a democratic society calculation. Second, the understanding of the privacy implications associated with being included, or not, on a watchlist is inappropriately narrow. Ultimately, the documentation does not engage in a meaningful way with the evaluation of potential harms to privacy and offers insufficient guidance to those deploying the technology.

6.3.1 A 'Reasonable Expectation of Privacy'?

The 'reasonable expectation of privacy' concept is a central component of the MPS's right to privacy analysis. According to the force's understanding, individuals' expectation of privacy is different dependent upon where, in public, an individual is. For example, the MPS Standard Operating Procedures state that: '[s]ome places by their nature attract greater privacy expectations than others with, for example, the expectations at a busy Zone 1[5] central thoroughfare being typically different to a quiet suburban park or backstreet' (MPS 2023f: 5.4). The legal mandate document expresses this in further detail:

> The public's expectation of privacy will be different in different public spaces. In Central London, the public has historically been protected by initiatives such as the 'ring of steel'.[6] The public is also accustomed to an extensive use of similar systems such as CCTV, police patrols and other crime fighting/public safety systems deployed in order to ensure public safety. By comparison, there could be a higher expectation of privacy in a quiet outer London suburban street, albeit the public would still expect the police to conduct investigations to prevent and detect crime. (SWP 2021b: 12; MPS 2023c: 3.12)

While the reasonable expectation of privacy concept is a feature of the European Court of Human Rights' (ECtHR's) caselaw, the police's interpretation of the concept is inaccurate. The key issue from a right to privacy perspective is not where an individual is in public—whether they are in a city centre, a suburban area, or a supermarket—but whether their presence there is recorded (or subject to some other form of analysis). For instance, in *Lopez Ribalda and Others* v *Spain* the Grand Chamber held that:

> As to whether the applicants had a reasonable expectation that their private life would be protected and respected, the Court observes that their workplace, a supermarket, was open to the public and that the activities filmed there, namely the taking of payments for purchases by the customers, were not of an intimate or private nature. Their expectation as to the protection of their private life was thus necessarily limited. However, even in public places, the creation of a systematic or

[5] London vernacular for central areas of the city (originating from classifications of transport pricing).

[6] The 'ring of steel' is a colloquial term for the physical and digital security infrastructure encircling the city's financial district. This was instituted in response to Provisional IRA bombing in the early 1990s. Reaffirming the trend of experimenting surveillance technology on the capital's inhabitants, the 'ring of steel' hosted the first urban civilian deployment of Automatic Number Plate Recognition (ANPR) surveillance in the world (see Coaffee 2009 for an authoritative overview).

> permanent recording of images of identified persons and the subsequent processing of the images thus recorded could raise questions affecting the private life of the individuals concerned.[7]

This distinction, between observation and recording/processing, is the key issue arising in the ECtHR's caselaw concerning whether the right to privacy is engaged.[8] Applied to FRT, it is the processing of information—specifically the remote biometric identification of every individual passing through a camera's field of vision—that gives rise to an interference with the right to privacy, regardless of location. Whether this interference occurs in an urban or a suburban setting will exert minimal influence vis-à-vis the extent of the interference.[9] Application of the MPS's policy framework will therefore result in an inaccurate right to privacy analysis, placing excessive emphasis on the location of the LFR operation and insufficient emphasis on the consequences of that deployment, namely the recording of information and biometric processing. The MPS understanding that less privacy protections arise in urban areas—where LFR deployments are more likely to occur—also means that application of the policy framework is likely to be biased in favour of authorization. Of further note, therefore, is how 'privacy' becomes selectively formulated in a manner that gives a superficial sense of human rights compliance yet ultimately legitimates MPS surveillance activities. This is a recurrent issue in police facial recognition operations, one that occurs at many stages of the deployment process, and is a central theme of this book's analysis.

6.3.2 Privacy Considerations Arising in the Context of Live Facial Recognition Deployments

It is now generally accepted that being subject to facial recognition processing engages an individual's right to privacy, irrespective of whether they are on a watchlist or not. This was confirmed by the High Court in *Bridges*[10]

[7] *Lopez Ribalda and Others* v *Spain*, Grand Chamber, ECtHR, App. Nos. 1874/13 and 8567/13, 17 October 2019, para. 93.

[8] See, e.g., *Perry* v *The United Kingdom*, Judgment, ECtHR, App. No. 63737/00, 17 July 2003, para. 40; *P.G. and J.H.* v *The United Kingdom*, Judgment, ECtHR, App. No. 44787/98, 25 September 2001, para. 57; *S and Marper* v *The United Kingdom*, Judgment, ECtHR, App. Nos. 30562/04 and 30566/04, 4 December 2008, para. 82, referring to *Friedl*.

[9] More relevant is the context; i.e. does the deployment take place in the vicinity of a religious centre or activist HQ, at a protest, or near a cultural event?

[10] *R (Bridges)* v *Chief Constable of South Wales Police* [2019] EWHC 2341 (Admin), para. 62.

and by the ECtHR in *Glukhin*.[11] The issue at hand, therefore, is determining the extent of the rights interference.

6.3.2.1 Privacy considerations of non-watchlisted individuals

In *Bridges*, the Court of Appeal suggested that in the context of current LFR deployments—which are temporally and geographically limited, and where data relating to individuals not on the watchlist is deleted immediately after biometric processing—the extent of the right to privacy interference for individuals not on the watchlist is 'negligible'.[12] Importantly, the Court held that this 'negligible' impact was not given greater weight—in terms of the necessity calculation—by the overall number of people not on the watchlist but who pass through the camera's field of vision and are therefore subject to biometric processing. From the Court's perspective, the extent of the privacy interference is the same whether facial recognition is applied to 1 or 10,000 non-watchlisted individuals. Given that the Court did not have to address this issue,[13] and so dealt with it summarily, the broader application of this finding is debatable. However, analysis of law enforcement documentation suggests that UK police forces' approach is in line with this reasoning. For example, the South Wales Police (SWP) Data Protection Impact Assessment dismisses the rights interference arising from those not on the watchlist as follows:

> For those not on the Watchlist who are in an area where LFR is deployed there will be no impact—*there will be no intrusiveness* unless there is an Alert, whereby an officer will compare the images and if necessary can speak with the identified individual. (SWP n.d.: 13; emphasis added)

A similar statement is made in the Essex Police Data Protection Impact Assessment (2023: 7). Surprisingly, the MPS's position vis-à-vis the right to privacy impact of those not on the watchlist but who pass through a camera's field of vision is not stated.

Treating the privacy impact of those not on the watchlist as 'negligible' is problematic, as it underestimates the overall human rights harm.[14] Two

[11] *Glukhin* v *Russia*, Judgment, ECtHR, App. No. 11519/20, 4 July 2023, para. 69.
[12] *R (Bridges)* v *The Chief Constable of South Wales Police* [2020] EWCA Civ 1058, para. 143.
[13] *R (Bridges)* v *The Chief Constable of South Wales Police* [2020] EWCA Civ 1058, para. 131.
[14] As stated in multiple ECtHR rulings, the processing of personal data gives rise to an interference with the right to privacy in and of itself. See, e.g., *Lopez Ribalda and Others* v *Spain*,

concerns, relating to the nature of remote biometric identification and the chilling effects of surveillance, illustrate this point.

First, as a type of remote biometric identification, the application of FRT is equivalent—in effect, if not in form—to a physical identity check (see Chapter 2). The procedures are similar, with police analysing each individual who passes through a particular area, checking their identity, and allowing them to proceed, with no record of their having been stopped if they are not on the watchlist. Were it not done remotely, and often without the subject's knowledge, this form of direct physical identification would be widely regarded as a serious interference with the right to privacy, affecting as it does the ability to be in public anonymously. To suggest that there is no interference with the right to privacy, or that this is negligible, just because there is no physical contact is not convincing. As noted by Purshouse and Campbell, the decisive factor as to whether a surveillance measure is considered intrusive or not should not be physical contact but rather 'the significance of the intrusion with the person's liberty to use public space unmolested' (2021: 222). It is suggested that the Court of Appeal's reasoning in finding the privacy interference to be 'negligible' fails to fully acknowledge the surveillance and identification capability made possible by FRT, while placing inappropriate emphasis on the non-physical, remote nature of this capability. Relatedly, and as argued throughout this book, the remote nature of this identification brings additional considerations which are subtle in their visibility, yet significant in their implications. These include the realignment of police–citizen relationships and the fundamental reconfiguration of how suspicion is formulated through the growing adoption of FRT.

Second, neither the Court of Appeal nor UK police forces effectively consider the chilling effects of surveillance which may affect those not on the watchlist but who are nonetheless concerned by police surveillance. The emergence of surveillance-related chilling effects will vary depending on the context, which in turn attenuates the extent of any rights interference. Relevant factors include: the location of the LFR deployment, with chilling effects likely to be more pronounced at protests, areas of historic over-policing, or other 'sensitive' locations; levels of trust in the police, particularly among impacted communities; and the aforementioned lack

Grand Chamber, ECtHR, App. Nos. 1874/13 and 8567/13, 17 October 2019, para. 93; and Chapter 3 generally.

of clarity over who is included in the watchlist which, when coupled with limited public information (see Chapter 7), gives rise to uncertainty regarding the scope of police surveillance. To dismiss the chilling effects, or at a minimum to minimize their potential harm, is to ignore—or at least selectively audit—the actual impact of surveillance. Given the significant impact of surveillance chilling effects on individuals (inter alia, Stevens et al. 2023), it is therefore of concern that this issue is not engaged with in any substantive manner.

These two points are inter-related. In the first instance, it is important to recognize the enduring impact of surveillance, despite its remoteness: remote surveillance remains surveillance. The impacts of surveillance are not lessened by a reduction in proximity between observers and observed. Indeed, the enduring impact of distanced surveillance relations has long been recognized, and thus indicates the durability of existing conceptual and legal frameworks aimed at understanding and mitigating the impacts of these practices. In a trend since augmented by IP-enabled remote monitoring, McCahill (2002), Smith (2004), and others argued more than two decades ago that technologically mediated 'disembodied relationships between watchers and watched' (Smith 2004: 280) across dispersed networks have become a defining feature of twenty-first-century camera surveillance. In turn, this arraying of remotely connected elements aligns with observations of wider, enduring trends in social arrangements throughout late modernity, as captured by Gidden's (1981) theory of 'time-space distanciation' and (older) ideas of 'time-space convergence' in human geography. The point here is not that social relations are 'diluted' by remoteness but that they are reconfigured (see also Harvey 1990). Indeed, for FRT, the remoteness of monitoring may *add to, rather than reduce*, the intensity of surveillance—as evinced by the introduction of doubts over the purpose of deployments among surveillance subjects. Taken collectively, even for those individuals not on a watchlist, the right to privacy impact of a LFR deployment is not altered by remoteness and it is the fact of this surveillance that is likely to induce chilling effects, resulting in potential human rights harm. This suggests that, even for those individuals not on a watchlist, the right to privacy impact of a LFR deployment is non-negligible.

6.3.2.2 Privacy considerations of watchlisted individuals

Myriad privacy considerations also arise in relation to those individuals on the watchlist. In this regard, a previous version of the MPS Data Protection Impact Assessment stated that:

> It is the view of the MPS that Article 8(1) provides limited protection to the criminal and it is not intended to bar lawful and proportionate law enforcement activities. (MPS 2018b: 4)

While applicable to the operations analysed for the purposes of this book, this position was not reproduced in the most recent MPS documentation, perhaps due to a restructuring of the overall documentation framework. Whatever the reason for inclusion, the use of the word 'criminal' is significant here. It is uncontentious to state that privacy considerations of individuals *subject to a court decision* will not override normal attempts to locate them. This is not the case, however, with respect to *all* individuals on the watchlist. As discussed above, MPS watchlists may include individuals wanted for their intelligence value as well as those merely suspected of committing an offence. The right to privacy of these individuals remains highly relevant, and holds pertinence for the 'necessary in a democratic society' calculation. The decision in *S and Marper* is relevant:

> Of particular concern in the present context is the risk of stigmatization, stemming from the fact that persons in the position of the applicants, who have not been convicted of any offence and are entitled to the presumption of innocence, are treated in the same way as convicted persons.[15]

As highlighted in the vignette that opens this book, and the many episodes of FRT-facilitated street encounters that continue, stigma represents an important, yet underacknowledged element of enrolment into the ecosystem of facial recognition surveillance. The role of surveillance cameras in this dynamic was also established in Norris and Armstrong's (1999) classic study of CCTV operators' targeting preferences over twenty-five years ago. Evidencing operators' preference for targeting minoritized groups, they argue how the act of observing is never benign and, instead, asserts a suspicion that communicates unmistakable social messaging about inclusion, eligibility, and acceptance.

Notable about FRT is the multiple entry points to a classification of 'suspicious'. These include the biases built into the technology, the actions of street-based officers, and, for the purposes of this discussion, the

[15] *S and Marper* v *The United Kingdom*, Grand Chamber, ECtHR, App. Nos. 30562/04 and 30566/04, 4 December 2008, para. 122.

promiscuity of watchlist eligibility criteria. The status of suspects, or individuals of interest to the police, is markedly different to that of those subject to a court order, yet is not reflected in the necessity calculation. The fact that any engagement by the police occurs in public reinforces the need to ensure that these individuals' privacy rights are adequately considered. In *Gillan and Quinton* v *The United Kingdom* the European Court asserted the following in relation to police stop and searches:

> Although the search is undertaken in a public place, this does not mean that Article 8 is inapplicable. Indeed, in the Court's view, the public nature of the search may, in certain cases, compound the seriousness of the interference because of an element of humiliation and embarrassment.[16]

This concern regarding the embarrassment and humiliation associated with a stop and search clearly translates to an engagement triggered by a facial recognition alert during the course of a highly visible police operation. Indeed, across the surveillance operations observed for this book, the MPS repeatedly cited the Police and Criminal Evidence Act 1984—the legislation guiding street-based police–citizen encounters—as legal authority to stop those recognized by facial recognition cameras on the street. It is therefore important that the right to privacy of all those included on a watchlist—in a process that addresses the different circumstances of inclusion rather than offering a blanket determination—is taken into consideration. In this sense, any right to privacy analysis must draw a distinction between individuals subject to a court order and those who are merely suspicious or of interest. Unfortunately, the only example given in relation to the right to privacy of a watchlisted individual concerns a missing person, and the comparator given solely refers to sharing their information on social media (MPS 2020b: 7).

6.3.2.3 Summary

The MPS's engagement with the right-to-privacy implications of LFR deployments gives rise to three issues of particular concern. First is the inappropriate emphasis placed on 'the reasonable expectation of privacy'

[16] *Gillan and Quinton* v *The United Kingdom*, Judgment, ECtHR, App. No. 4158/05, 12 January 2010, para. 63.

at the expense of examining the impact of recording and identifying individuals in public. Second is the absent examination of distinct context-dependent privacy intrusions—that is, if LFR is deployed at a protest or a cultural event—and the minimization of any resultant chilling effects. Third is the downplaying of privacy considerations with respect to individuals on the watchlist but who are not subject to a court order. Ultimately, the right-to-privacy impacts are not fully addressed within the existing policy framework. This issue is compounded by the absence of any guidance as to how officers should actually assess potential harm to the right to privacy. This is a striking omission, which invites police decision-makers to overlook, or underestimate, potential harms and to favour authorizing FRT use.

As the above analysis shows, the right to privacy involves complex and nuanced analysis. Its formulation extends beyond traditional conceptions of the 'right to be let alone'. Privacy intersects with other rights in complex ways and is fundamental to core features of the human experience, including the formation of identity and one's meaningful engagement with the outside world (Cohen 2012; Richards 2013; Penney 2022). A fuller articulation of the content of the right, including a discussion of the chilling effects, would allow a more consequential assessment of how facial recognition affects these fundamental considerations, better prepare officers to make more informed decisions, and, ultimately, contribute to an appropriately rigorous calculation of necessity. Moreover, policy documentation could be invested with proper guidance on how to evaluate the potential harm of facial recognition surveillance. This could illustrate scenarios where a decision was taken to refuse authorization, something notably absent in the existing approaches. As currently formulated, all examples provided within all police policy frameworks make claims as to why LFR deployments are useful or necessary. Such deliberations start from a position that justifies the existence of the technology. This, in effect, renders LFR as a technology seeking a purpose.

6.4 Police Efforts to Engage with the Prohibition of Discrimination

Issues of racial bias have long been a point of contention in the history of policing London. Although the 1999 MacPherson report into the police investigation of the murder of Black teenager Stephen Lawrence—the first to assign the label 'institutionally racist' to the MPS—marked a watershed, this moment had deep antecedents stretching back decades. Since then, episodic independent reviews by David Lammy (2017) and Baroness Casey (2023)[17] have highlighted the MPS's continuing struggle to escape this label. While debates persist over the degree to which racism is 'institutional' in the MPS, current chief Mark Rowley acknowledged its extensive nature within the organization as recently as 2023 (*The Guardian* 2023b).

At the same time, and as highlighted throughout the book, the embedding of racial and other biases in technology has been established comprehensively (see Chapter 2). This is particularly true of FRT, where the most methodologically robust performance analyses have categorically shown disproportionate performance across different demographic groups (NIST 2019). That FRT performs inconsistently across different visible ethnicities, ages, and genders is a scientific and evaluative fact.

Of course, facial recognition—like other technologies—is socio-technical in character, providing an arena for different biases and value judgements to emerge. What is at stake, therefore, is not only the inherent biases embedded into coding, training data, and other elements of digital architecture (see McIlwain 2019) but also the social ecologies of how these tools are used and, crucially, the emergent outcomes arising from these human–technology interactions (a pertinent issue given the history of discriminatory policing). Relevant to facial recognition practices today, human interpretations of digitally manufactured information are particularly affected by this dynamic. For example, in analysing the over-surveillance of African American men in the US, Fiske (1998) finds racism in such conjunctions. Here—and perhaps unwittingly resonating with T. S. Eliot's (1937) aforementioned meditation on information, knowledge, and wisdom—Fiske (1998: 85) implicates the epistemologies in how technologically sourced 'information' becomes translated into 'knowledge': 'technology can determine only what is seen, it is society and its politics that determines what is known'.[18]

Uses of technology conjoins human and digital biases. Such dynamics are discernible across the range of law enforcement technologies. They have

[17] Baroness Casey's report went further than MacPherson, classifying the MPS as institutionally racist, sexist, and homophobic (Casey 2023). The mayor of London and de facto police oversight commissioner, Sadiq Khan, accepted this classification.

[18] Such observations potentially bring an epistemological and digital nuancing to Foucault's (1980) famous power/knowledge dynamic. While Foucault stresses the indivisibility of these two phenomena, in this context the epistemologies of how such 'knowledge' arises—a parallel and core concern of Foucault's writing (e.g. 1970)—hold a particular character, one shaped by encounters with digital information.

also been empirically documented with respect to the two technologies most apposite to facial recognition practices, as evidenced in the racialized character of surveillance camera operators targeting choices (Norris and Armstrong 1999) and of 'suspect' databases, such as London's Gang Matrix (Amnesty International UK 2019).

From an equality and human rights law perspective, LFR deployments implicate the prohibition of discrimination both directly and indirectly. Direct discrimination can arise if LFR is deployed in a deliberately discriminatory manner: if it is used, for example, to discriminatorily target particular communities or groups. Indirect discrimination can arise through inherent biases in the facial recognition algorithm itself, such that it gives rise to discriminatory outcomes (i.e. discrimination is not an intended outcome of the deployment). This applies, for instance, when the algorithm produces different false positive or false negative rates on the basis of protected characteristics such as age, gender, or race.

The first possibility—direct discrimination—is a concern associated with policing in general and has received extensive criminological interest, particularly with respect to disproportionate police stop and search practices (inter alia, Head 2022), the re-examination of which lies beyond the scope of this book. The second possibility is highly relevant and attends to both the disparate performance of facial recognition across demographic groups and how that information becomes translated through practice (see Chapter 2). Assessment of a facial recognition algorithm's operational characteristics should form a core part of any pre-deployment human rights due diligence framework. Situated against these wider scientific and intellectual debates, this section discusses how the MPS addresses indirect discrimination. The analysis looks first at how indirect discrimination is examined in the legal mandate before examining the police's obligations under the PSED to assess any bias in the operation of the algorithm itself. As this analysis is linked to the algorithm's performance, the issues raised in this section apply equally to both live and retrospective facial recognition.

6.4.1 Addressing Indirect Discrimination

The MPS legal mandate acknowledges the potential for indirect discrimination arising from algorithmic bias, highlighting the concern that persons of a particular demographic may be more or less likely to see a false positive generated against them. In addressing the relevant human rights law considerations, under Article 14 of the European Convention on Human Rights, the legal mandate states that

> there are two points to consider in relation to the MPS LFR system (i) does the LFR system's demographic differential performance vary by a particular demographic such as it results in a person suffering a discriminatory effect and (ii) if there is a difference in treatment, is this capable of an objective and reasonable justification. (MPS 2023c: 15)

This is an accurate statement of the relevant caselaw; it is well established that 'objective and reasonable' justifications may allow some form of discrimination. For instance, the ECtHR has held that

> the principle of equality of treatment is violated if the distinction has no objective and reasonable justification. The existence of such a justification must be assessed in relation to the aim and effects of the measure under consideration, regard being had to the principles which normally prevail in democratic societies. A difference of treatment in the exercise of a right laid down in the Convention must not only pursue a legitimate aim: Article 14 (art. 14) is likewise violated when it is clearly established that there is no reasonable relationship of proportionality between the means employed and the aim sought to be realised.[19]

Accordingly, in determining whether differential treatment is lawful or not, the objective and reasonable justification provided *must link to a legitimate aim*, and there must be *a '"reasonable relationship" of proportionality between the means employed and the aim sought to be realised'*.[20] An example of an objective and reasonable justification is the correction of 'factual inequalities',[21] whereby—for instance—one group is disadvantaged in relation to other groups with respect to the provision of education. However, the MPS legal mandate states that:

[19] *Case 'Relating to Certain Aspects of the Laws on the Use of Languages in Education in Belgium'* v *Belgium (Merits)*, Judgment, ECtHR, App. Nos. 1474/62, 1677/62, 1691/62, 1769/63, 1994/63, and 2126/64, 23 July 1968.

[20] *D. H. and Others* v *The Czech Republic*, Grand Chamber, ECtHR, App. No. 57325/00, 13 November 2007, para. 196; *Molla Sali* v *Greece*, Grand Chamber, ECtHR, App. No. 20452/14, 19 December 2018, para. 135; emphasis added.

[21] *D. H. and Others* v *The Czech Republic*, Grand Chamber, ECtHR, App. No. 57325/00, 13 November 2007, para. 175.

> In relation to an objective justification, the questions to ask are (i) does LFR pursue a legitimate aim and (ii) are the means employed reasonably proportionate to the aim pursued? (MPS 2023c: 15)

This is a misstatement of the relevant requirements, and one that is dangerously misleading for those whom the mandate is designed to inform. The question, with respect to Article 14, is not 'does LFR pursue a legitimate aim?', it is 'does the *differential treatment* arising from the use of LFR pursue a legitimate aim?'. This is a crucial and fundamental difference. It is not whether the technology itself pursues the legitimate aim but whether the discriminatory outcome is in pursuit of a legitimate aim. By accepting the MPS formulation above, any discriminatory outcome could potentially be justified provided the use of the technology itself pursued a legitimate aim. Such a formulation is clearly inadequate for addressing algorithmic and other digital bias. According to the dynamic apparent in the development of watchlists above, this also provides another example of how apparent—yet superficial—compliance with human rights law processes is implicated in facilitating surveillance activities.

With respect to the legitimate aim that the MPS analysis relies on, the legal mandate then states:

> Article 14 does not prohibit differences in treatment that are based on a public interest. What constitutes a legitimate aim is an area where the case law continues to develop with the courts having recognised a wide range of purposes including a number of actions within the ambit of criminal justice. (MPS 2023c: 16)

It is correct that the caselaw does continue to develop in this area. However, the two ECtHR cases cited by the MPS address matters fundamentally different from the circumstances relating to LFR. *Sejdić and Finci* v *Bosnia and Herzegovina* concerned a requirement to be affiliated with a defined 'constituent group' to become a member of parliament in a post-conflict society, resulting in the discriminatory exclusion of certain groups, such as the Roma and Jewish communities.[22] The legitimate aim identified was the restoration of peace in a post-conflict context. The second cited example, *Konstantin Markin* v *Russia*, concerned unlawful discrimination

[22] *Sejdic and Finci* v *Bosnia and Herzegovina*, Grand Chamber, ECtHR, App. Nos. 27996/06 and 34836/06, 22 December 2009, paras. 42–50.

with respect to different parental leave entitlements granted to military servicemen and servicewomen.[23] The legitimate aim identified was the protection of national security.

As the difference in treatment arising from the operation of a facial recognition algorithm may arise from performance bias, it is exceptionally difficult to see how this could be said to pursue a legitimate aim. There is no purpose to the differential treatment inherent to FRT, such as the restoration of peace or the protection of national security, nor is it intended to remedy a pre-existing inequality, such as the discriminatory provision of education. Rather, differential treatment is the result of a flaw arising from the operation of the algorithm itself. As such, and despite the formulations expressed in MPS documentation, it is highly unlikely that algorithmic bias would be found compatible with Article 14. In this sense, the guidance presented in the MPS legal mandate is based on an arguably incorrect reading of human rights law that may in turn mislead those it is intended to inform.

6.4.2 The Public Sector Equality Duty

The PSED is established in section 149(1) of the Equality Act 2010. It requires that public authorities—in this case, the police—pay 'due regard' to the need to eliminate discrimination. In light of known issues affecting facial recognition algorithms (as discussed in Chapter 2), the concern is that deploying FRT may give rise to indirect discrimination on the basis of race, sex, or age. As such, *before* deploying FRT the police must take 'reasonable steps' to ensure that the operation of the algorithm does not result in unacceptable bias, either themselves or by way of independent verification.[24]

The MPS and SWP have sought to satisfy this obligation by commissioning the National Physics Laboratory to test the operation of their chosen facial recognition algorithm. On the basis of this testing, the police claim that the false-positive rate 'is found to be equitable between gender, race and age. There is no statistically significant imbalance between demographics' (NPL 2023a: 38). However, as discussed in greater detail in Chapter 2, the methodology adopted in this evaluation is deeply flawed. For

[23] *Konstantin Markin* v *Russia*, 2nd Chamber, ECtHR, App. No. 30078/06, 22 March 2012, paras. 131–152.

[24] *R (Bridges)* v *Chief Constable of South Wales Police* [2019] EWHC 2341 (Admin), para. 199.

example, and among a litany of other methodological shortcomings, it is difficult to claim with any serious credibility that the seven cases assessed in this evaluation could represent a tool that has scanned over three million faces in London with any 'statistical significance'. Ultimately, the methodological deficiencies in this test mean that it must be regarded as inadequate as a form of independent verification, and that the police's positive obligations under the PSED must be regarded as unfulfilled.

The MPS policy documentation does establish that, in light of the potential for discrimination, a 'fail-safe' position will be put in place:

> No Engagement will occur with a member of the public unless at least one officer has reviewed an LFR system potential match and reached their own opinion that there is no probable match between the member of the public and the Watchlist image. (MPS 2023c: 18)

However, in *Bridges* the Court of Appeal unambiguously stated that:

> We do not consider the 'human failsafe' sufficient to discharge the PSED. As a matter of principle, it is not material to the PSED, which as we have observed, is a duty as to the process which should be followed, not what the substance of the decision should be. Secondly, as was acknowledged at the hearing before us, human beings can also make mistakes. This is particularly acknowledged in the context of identification.[25]

Indeed, concerns regarding human adjudication (including a 'presumption to intervene') are discussed in greater detail in Chapter 8.

6.5 How Do the Police Examine the Overall Impact of Live Facial Recognition Deployments?

Building on the analysis developed in Chapter 3, facial recognition surveillance can give rise to compound human rights harms whereby a number of different rights are affected, often simultaneously. This form of harm is most commonly understood by reference to the 'chilling effects' phenomenon, whereby individuals modify their behaviour due to the fear of surveillance.

[25] *R (Bridges)* v *Chief Constable of South Wales Police* [2019] EWHC 2341 (Admin), para. 185.

In turn, chilling effects implicate multiple other fundamental rights. For instance, use of facial recognition at a protest could bring the rights to privacy, freedom of expression, and freedom of assembly into play.

As previously discussed, chilling effects are difficult to quantify and evidence. This brings complexity to human rights determinations conducted prior to the use of facial recognition. However, such difficulties of assessment do not mitigate their importance. The harms associated with chilling effects can be severe, potentially affecting the means by which individuals develop their identity and participate politically. Significantly, although the short-term impact of a chilling effect may be difficult to perceive, the long-term effects can be profound, contributing to the stagnation of democratic life.

The use of facial recognition is likely to give rise to chilling effects in myriad ways. Two are particularly prominent: first, if facial recognition is used at sensitive locations, such as at a protest; second, if either live or retrospective facial recognition is used in more 'advanced' configurations, for instance through integration into a surveillance camera network via the application of AI tools to create pattern-of-life profiles or through its assimilation into other digital assemblages. Each of these will be discussed in turn.

6.5.1 The Use of Facial Recognition at 'Sensitive' Locations

The MPS legal mandate contains references to the impact that LFR deployments may have on the rights to freedom of religion, expression, and assembly, and to chilling effects. For example:

> *Article 10 and 11* have particular relevance when considering the policing of assemblies and demonstrations and any use of LFR which may impact on an assembly or demonstration. Article 10 is especially pertinent should people have reservations about expressing themselves as a result of an LFR Deployment. Article 10 is also relevant should the use of LFR deter people from attending an assembly or demonstration at all or otherwise cause people to minimise their involvement. (SWP 2021b: 13; MPS 2023c: 3.13).

The following example is then given:

> **Example:** The use of LFR can assist the MPS in policing an assembly or demonstration, particularly where there is an intelligence case supporting there being a risk to public safety. Specifically, LFR can support police officers by efficiently searching for perpetrators of violence in crowded locations where it might otherwise be difficult to locate them. In deciding the use of LFR is necessary and proportionate, regard should be had to an individual's Article 10 and 11 rights and the risk of having a 'chilling effect' on the exercise of such rights. There may be expectations of anonymity in a crowd and individuals may choose to alter their means of demonstration because of the LFR Deployment. Article 10 and 11 rights must be weighed against the need to use LFR to enable an assembly that might otherwise be disrupted by the risk to public safety. In making this decision, consideration should be given to factors which could minimise the impact of LFR. These include limiting the use of LFR in time and scope to the minimum need to ensure safety. They could also include there being focus placed on ensuring the public understand the use of LFR is to help them safely undertake their assembly. (SWP 2021b: 14; MPS 2023c: 3.13)

Broadly similar statements and examples are given with respect to freedom of religion (MPS 2021: 14; SWP 2021b: 13). Three issues arise. First, recent United Nations (UN) human rights standards for policing protest are clear that '[d]igital technologies should not be used to . . . remotely identify individuals, including by biometric means, during protests given that they are discriminatory and inconsistent with the obligation of law enforcement officials to facilitate peaceful protests' (Model Protocol: para. 32). The possibility of chilling effects is a key factor underpinning this conclusion. In determining whether the use of LFR to police a protest could be considered necessary in a democratic society, the availability of proven alternative measures is likely to play a decisive role mitigating against LFR use: policing protests, and addressing violence in the context of protests, are relatively routine policing activities. Moreover, and in alignment with UN standards, police deployment of facial recognition in such environments on public safety grounds would require a high level of justification. This justification in turn would require a robust evidence base and explanation as to why facial recognition is the most appropriate means of dealing with a specified threat, including a full consideration of alternative measures.

Second, it is the very presence of police surveillance that gives rise to chilling effects. As such, minimizing the time or scope of the deployment is likely to exert only a marginal mitigating effect, as is the argument that police surveillance is present for participants' safety. This latter argument is unlikely to hold much persuasive force in situations where a disconnect exists between those protesting and the police. It also positions public notification as something more polemical, used to convince protests participants of the virtues of the technology.

Third, and most importantly, no analysis is undertaken by the police on the nature of chilling effects or how they should be assessed. This is a significant omission. Any evaluation of chilling effects is complex but it is precisely for this reason that police decision-makers require more detailed guidance. Addressing chilling effects in a meaningful way would also attend to the important roles played by freedom of expression and freedom of assembly. The police's obligation to facilitate the right to peaceful assembly is relevant here. As stated in the 2024 UN Model Protocol for Law Enforcement Officials to Promote and Protect Human Rights in the Context of Peaceful Protests:

> States and their law enforcement agencies and officials have a positive obligation to facilitate peaceful assemblies, including protests by ensuring that those taking part can safely conduct their activities without discrimination or abuse . . . while respecting participants' rights and agency and making it possible for participants to achieve their objectives. (Model Protocol: para. 14)

This is particularly important. The principal obligation placed on the police is to facilitate the right to peaceful assembly, not to 'prevent disorder or crime', as emphasized in the MPS legal mandate. This issue reflects an enduring theme: that of the selective audit of the harms and benefits of facial recognition across MPS legal and policy analysis. Such partial framings necessarily—and inappropriately—skew the identification of the 'competing interests' at play and ultimately diminish the completeness and meaningfulness of MPS human rights necessity calculations.

6.5.2 Changes to How Facial Recognition Is Used

Current LFR deployments in England and Wales represent an initial, if accelerating, mainstream use of the technology. As such, they remain, for now, comparatively limited in scope. For instance, LFR deployments are currently limited in time (typically to a police shift) and do not yet occur on a 24/7 or rolling basis. Deployments are also limited to a specific location or set of locations. Typically, these operations involve a relatively limited number of cameras and are not yet diffused, for example, across a public transport surveillance camera network, through police body-worn cameras, or on a city-wide basis. Additionally, the use of the surveillance material produced is limited in several important ways. Deployments may only be used to identify those on the watchlist and not to identify unknown persons present at an event (although, as demonstrated in *Glukhin*, retrospective facial recognition (RFR) has the capacity to do this).

Representing an example of Amoore's (2014) observation that digital security is pivoting away from hardware towards adaptable software, FRT is a highly adaptable tool. As such, it holds the capability for deployment in a more pervasive manner and to be integrated with other surveillance and intelligence sources. Intentions to realize this capability are evident in the (then) policing minister Chris Philp's public ambition to embed facial recognition into all police body-worn cameras, expressed in 2023 (Fussey and Webster 2023), and in Cheshire Constabulary's stated intention to use RFR for 'profiling, monitoring, and tracking' (Cheshire Constabulary 2021b: 1). Such latent capability may give rise to a particularly severe chilling effect, potentially affecting large sections of the population and holding the possibility of transforming any public–police encounter—or indeed any journey through a public space—into a surveillance event. As highlighted throughout this book, such shifts in the application of technology have profound implications for the form, practice, and impact of law enforcement activity. As examined through the ethnographic material presented in the following chapters, this affects longstanding procedural approaches to the formation of suspicion and the accountability of police decision-making. One notable casualty here is the inversion of traditional forms of 'suspicion' facilitated by AI technologies. While previously individuals' behaviour—such as an act of violence or the commission of a crime—brought them to the attention of the police, advanced technologies now allow for the suspicion-less surveillance of large sections of the population, with AI-driven monitoring and assignation of potentially suspicious behaviour. Such tools integrate with existing praxis of network mapping (Fussey and Sandhu 2022) and pattern recognition (Murray and Fussey 2019; Brayne 2020) that have become staple features of policing in the digital age. For example, the deployment of FRT across a city-wide surveillance camera network on a 24/7 basis enables the tracking of individuals' movements, use of space, associations, financial activity, entertainment choices, employment, and other personal information. Increasing interoperability between data sources and—with the onset of multimodal AI systems—automated integration of text and image data may penetrate deeper into the intimate spheres of life. This may indicate, for example, information on health, professional and social networks, mobility, sexual orientation, sexual preferences, exercise habits, one's political beliefs, and one's membership of any groups or organizations. This information is obviously incredibly revealing in isolation, yet when brought together it gains exponential potency. In this sense, when data sources are added together, the surveillance harms that arise become multiplicative. As highlighted above, the abundance of data on any individual also facilitates the justification of subsequent surveillance activity.

The most obvious physical presence of surveillance is typified by the image of a surveillance camera, a favoured motif of Banksy and Ai Weiwei as a signifier of surveillance and reproduced ad nauseum elsewhere. Yet a discernible surveillance presence is not required for chilling effects to occur. In the UK, previous police practices have involved the infiltration and surveillance of non-violent groups challenging the status quo. Prominent examples include the MPS 'spycops' scandal, involving the placement of undercover officers across a range of social and environmental campaign groups. Among many candidates, perhaps the most egregious example of such was the MPS spying on Baroness Doreen Lawrence when campaigning to seek justice for her son, Stephen Lawrence, himself murdered by racists and whose death the MPS failed to adequately investigate (a failure later described in the public enquiry as a result of institutional racism within the organization) (*The Guardian* 2019). The fallout of such revelations is a likely fear among activists that such surveillance may result in criminal charges given the state's eagerness to prosecute protestors.[26] A prominent example is the 2020 decision of the justice secretary to 'fast track' those involved in the 2020 Black Lives Matter protests (Vice 2020). Surveillance is both political and politicized. As such, the possibility that more widespread facial recognition surveillance will result in chilling effects is extremely high,

[26] There are numerous cases where the prosecution of protestors has been pursued by police yet failed or was dropped in the courts. Examples include: www.independent.co.uk/news/uk/crime/extinction-rebellion-protest-appeals-prosecutions-b1897399.html; www.amnesty.org.uk/press-releases/northern-ireland-prosecution-dropped-black-lives-matter-protestors; www.globaltimes.cn/page/202201/1245283.shtml?id=11.

particularly if such surveillance is incorporated into a broader AI-assisted surveillance assemblage.

These same concerns apply to, and are potentially amplified by, RFR. However, while LFR is yet to become deployed in the more 'advanced' manner discussed here, it is likely that RFR is. The framework applicable to RFR is permissive, and—unlike LFR—no limitation is established with respect to how it can be used or whether it can be combined with other surveillance techniques or analytical tools.

6.6 Conclusions

This chapter has demonstrated significant shortcomings with respect to how the MPS both conceptualize harm and incorporate legal analysis of harm into their policy frameworks. Highlighted was the inappropriate emphasis on the 'reasonable expectation of privacy' at the expense of privacy concerns related to the recording of information in public; the failure to examine distinct context-dependency privacy intrusions and the de-emphasis of any associated chilling effects; and the downplaying of privacy considerations for individuals on the watchlist but not subject to any court order. These concerns are compounded by the absence of any guidance as to how officers should actually assess potential harm, both to privacy and to broader rights brought into play by the chilling effects of surveillance (encapsulated here by the compound harm approach). This is a striking omission, which invites police decision-makers to overlook, or underestimate, potential harms and to favour authorizing FRT use. It is hard to avoid the conclusion that harm is selectively recognized and only partially addressed. In each formulation, FRT emerges as a justified tool, absent any real critical engagement.

7
Deploying Facial Recognition Technology in London
Techno-Certainties and Operational Ambiguities

7.1 Introduction

This chapter draws on empirical data analysing the operational activities that preface the deployment of facial recognition surveillance. The analysis draws on ethnographic observations of pre-operational meetings and activities, unrestricted access to the operations themselves, interview data with police planners, and analysis of police documentation. This offers a rare insight into the operational practices that accompany facial recognition technology (FRT) deployments. A core focus of this chapter concerns how principles and strategic intentions shift as FRT moves from policy to the pavement and is implemented in practice. Emerging from this analysis, a principal finding addresses the disconnect between the stated aims and principles of FRT operations, and the operational realities of how such tools are used in public. As highlighted by the data, much of the emerging lexicon surrounding the technology shifts and gains new meaning as operations progress. Terms such as 'intelligence case', 'policing need', 'wanted', and 'human-in-the-loop' become modified as FRT deployments transition from planning to practice. These shifts further underscore the importance of analysing technologies such as live facial recognition (LFR) in their situated social, organizational, and operational environments to fully understand their deeper implications and outcomes. While this chapter emphasizes the pre-deployment activities surrounding FRT operations, Chapter 8 analyses FRT during its active operational use.

Cutting across these operational and pre-operational spheres of action is the role of human decision-making in the form of police discretion.

Facial Recognition Surveillance. Pete Fussey and Daragh Murray, Oxford University Press.
 DOI: 10.1093/9780191979927.003.0007

Despite often being positioned as an objective and value-free alternative to imperfect and biased modes of human policing, FRT amplifies and elevates subjective human discretion throughout all stages of the deployment lifecycle. Analysis of police legal and policy documents in previous chapters has demonstrated how discretion becomes central to the siting of cameras through loose definitions of 'policing need', uses of 'intelligence', and, crucially, the permissive classifications of behaviour deemed suitable for inclusion on a watchlist. This chapter builds on the analysis to highlight how discretion manifests, expands, and becomes central to how facial recognition is used in operational practice. Contrary to the scientific discourse accompanying FRT, this growing discretion brings further inconsistency and subjectivity into technologically mediated practices.

Central to the analysis presented here are three areas of discussion. The first concerns police intelligence handling and how this both shapes and is shaped by the digital surveillance tools it is used to justify. A second, related issue regards information sources and the creation of 'watchlists' and how disparate data architectures sources are brought together into data assemblages that drive the operation of LFR. The third section examines a further issue where the discretionary choices of observers and the observed meet and, in doing so, create a flashpoint for a particularly controversial element of facial recognition operations: the absence of consent as people choose to avoid cameras and the way such actions are cast as suspicious.

7.2 Intelligence Validates Digital Surveillance: Digital Surveillance Reifies Intelligence

> Facial recognition to identify unknown suspects from CCTV images is showing immense potential. The results that we're getting are beyond what I expected and I think are going to transform investigative work, potentially, in the way that DNA transformed investigative work 30 years ago.
>
> (Sir Mark Rowley, commissioner of the London Metropolitan Police Service, in an address to the think tank 'Policy Exchange', 2023)

Justifications for LFR operations routinely start from a position that assumes the efficacy and legitimacy of technology and then recruits selective interpretations of law, statistics, and science to confirm this view.

As Chapters 2 and 5 establish, unevidenced claims of FRT's crimefighting abilities are commonplace. These relay a technological determinism redolent of the way the rapid expansion of CCTV throughout the 1990s and early 2000s was heralded by many supporters as a policing panacea (Fussey 2007). FRT is credited with a range of impressive powers in advance of objective evidence to justify such claims. It identifies the 'wanted' and reassures the fearful while provoking panic among would-be offenders, all while meeting variously formulated 'policing needs'. This fêted adaptability of FRT to address a wide range of crime and policing issues is not only unevidenced, it may also be used for performative purposes. For instance, recent (unsubstantiated) public claims by the Metropolitan Police Service (MPS) director of intelligence regarding LFR's utility in tackling 'robbery and violence against women and girls' (*The Guardian* 2023e) were made in the wake of multiple public scandals involving serious offences committed by MPS officers against women, and follows a public report identifying serious levels of misogyny in the organization (Casey 2023). It also demonstrates the highly politicized narratives surrounding this technology.

Present throughout many of the justifications underpinning LFR is the role of police intelligence. Intelligence establishes the overall objective (often described as 'policing purpose') to be addressed and the grounds for doing so. Police intelligence is therefore key to establishing the evidence base required to demonstrate the necessity of LFR deployments (see Chapter 5). One of the challenges here—one perennial to analysing the legitimacy of police activity and of growing importance in an age of intrusive AI-driven surveillance—is the contrast between the inscrutability of such intelligence and its importance in justifying police activity. As cited in Chapter 5, 'intelligence' covers a spectrum of information of varying form and reliability. In many cases, reliance on the opaque rationale of intelligence allows justifications to emerge that are both unverifiable and unfalsifiable.

Ethnographic research, including attendance at police facial recognition planning meetings, pre-operational briefings where intelligence was presented, and observations of the operations themselves, offers access into the often hidden practice of how intelligence material becomes recruited to justify surveillance operations. As the discussion below reveals, accessing this world allows analysis of the specific connections between intelligence, the overall policing objective, and the surveillance tools intended to address it.

7.2.1 'All Watched Over by Machines of Loving Grace'? Applying Facial Recognition Technology to a Panoply of Policing Objectives

Worsening levels of violence in London became a central narrative accompanying the LFR deployments observed in this research.[1] Increased knife crime had generated particular public concern and became a priority focus for the MPS. While (then) chairperson of the National Police Chiefs Council Sara Thornton labelled the rise 'a national emergency' in 2019, it was London that experienced the most acute offending levels (BBC 2019, 14 March). The MPS also faced significant political pressure to address this issue, with the city's mayor, Sadiq Khan, funding a new Violent Crime Taskforce and (then) Home Secretary Sajid Javid publicly committing additional Treasury funds to tackle the issue.

Criminologists have long recognized the power of politicized language around 'law and order' (Pratt 2007; Reiner 2007), and such emotive topics provide powerful justificatory narratives for advanced surveillance technologies such as LFR. Yet while this discourse may help establish a *legitimate aim* for the technology, it does not automatically follow that associated LFR deployments are *necessary in a democratic society*. This very point was highlighted by the MPS in the legal mandate they developed to support LFR operations in the capital: '[t]he fact that the suspected offence may be serious will not alone render intrusive actions proportionate' (MPS 2018c). Determining necessity/proportionality requires an evaluation of the link between LFR technology and the purpose motivating its deployment in light of the potential harm to human rights. This is, of course, difficult when the purpose is ambiguously defined.

During the observed operations, the specifics of 'what' was being addressed by LFR shifted over time. While initial justifications for LFR were anchored in addressing 'violent crime', including knife crime, justification frequently drifted to cover other roles. This occurred most obviously

[1] 'All watched over by machines of loving grace' refers to the 1967 poem of the same name by Richard Brautigan. The poem hinges on the connection of words depicting technology and nature in the same phrase (e.g. 'cybernetic ecology'). This yoking of the technological and the organic holds particular resonance for considering the socio-technical imbrications of FRT. Also appropriate for this context, commentators have variously argued that the poem can be read either as a utopian statement of how technology may transform the human experience or, conversely, as a more cynical critique of such Panglossian visions. Despite the romance such an enigmatic and pluralistic meaning might bring, reading the poem in the twenty-first century strongly invites the latter interpretation.

when attempts were made to enrol people onto facial recognition watchlists for purposes other than those originally specified. For example, a senior officer with a leadership role for one Stratford operation told researchers that the criterion for enrolment on the watchlist was being 'wanted in connection with violent offences', before stating that other 'locally relevant' offences also constituted a basis for inclusion. Moreover, it became increasingly commonplace to hear of LFR being recruited for additional purposes and claimed benefits. These included the use of LFR for detection, deterrence, intentional crime displacement, disruption, reducing fear of crime, and enhancing public confidence. No attempts were made to evidence or measure the impact of LFR in relation to any of these objectives, thus abandoning such statements to the realm of rhetoric. As LFR operations evolved, then, the technology became justified on an ever-expanding range of justifications. These expanded far beyond the original headline justification of how the tool would tackle 'serious crime', and the link between LFR operations and the defined policing objective diminished.

This diversification of purpose also illustrates how concerns regarding overly broad policing purposes articulated in the MPS policy frameworks become exacerbated as the technology is deployed. Changes to the stated purpose of a LFR deployment can have significant implications in terms of surveillance creep (see Marx 1989 and others) and the necessity calculation (put simply, while LFR may be necessary for one purpose—such as certain instances of violence crime—this may not be the case for other purposes). Also affecting necessity considerations is the effectiveness of LFR stated objectives and the availability of an evidence base to support any claims in this regard. Regarding the justification that LFR deterred offenders, for instance, no evidence was ever presented demonstrating the effectiveness of the technology in this regard. As decades of criminological literature attest, even when deterrence effects may be apparent, they are often difficult to substantiate (Akers 1990; Hayward 2007). Moreover, other research has established how attributing deterrence impacts to a specific measure is additionally complex when considering the effects of surveillance cameras (Tilley 1998).

A similar dynamic applied to police claims that LFR deployments reduced fear of crime in the local area, and the absence of any substantiation for these claims. Indeed, considerable debate exists over the degree to which security measures, notably visible surveillance cameras, reduce or exacerbate public fears. For example, early US evaluations of surveillance cameras could not attribute their presence to any positive impact on fear of crime (Musheno et al. 1978). Other studies reveal a more complex relationship between surveillance cameras and crime, such as Gill and Spriggs's (2005) assertion that surveillance cameras tend to enhance feelings of safety only among those that already felt secure. Of course, a key complicating factor concerns the way both fear of crime and trust in the police relate to social location. Such complexities demonstrate the problems with making blanket statements on behalf of any community. This is particularly problematic when those statements are made on behalf of one of the most diverse communities in the world, such as the London Borough of Newham where Stratford is located (Fussey et al. 2011), and when no meaningful pre-deployment consultation was undertaken.

Claims of LFR-induced deterrence are further complicated by their often-contradictory nature. For example, in 2023 evidence to the House of Commons Science and Technology Committee, an MPS representative made unevidenced and unchallenged claims that the technology exerted a deterrence effect on potential offenders while denying the possibility of any chilling effects on others (SITC, 'Oral Evidence' (n 369) Q447). This claim speculatively presupposes the psychology of social groups (i.e. LFR only deters the people the police intend it to, all others are unaffected, and thus no chilling effects take place). It also fails to acknowledge that if LFR did in fact act as a deterrent, as claimed, it would undermine the operational objective of identifying people because they would have been dissuaded from being in the vicinity. This very issue played out in one of the earlier LFR operations in east London. As noted above, during the Stratford operations, LFR was claimed to have utility across crime control, investigation, deterrence, and public reassurance goals. These claims were repeated during all planning meetings and consistently stated during both operations in the area. However, offers assigned to street-based intervention teams regularly expressed frustration that public engagement activities—such as publicizing the operations on social media, leafleting, and on-street police–public engagement—critically undermined the detection capabilities. This frustration was apparent at the second Stratford operation, where a ten-hour operation yielded a solitary facial recognition alert which turned out to be a false positive. As one plain-clothes officer deployed to a covert unit explained to the authors, 'by the afternoon everyone in the neighbourhood knew about the trial. Information had gone out on local networks and social media'.

These unchallenged inconsistencies echo those written into the LFR policy framework, as discussed in Chapter 5 (e.g. in relation to the pursuit of sex offenders). Similar to the hyperbole accompanying the growth of CCTV surveillance around the millennium, surveillance-as-panacea discourses are not only incorrect, they are also internally contradictory. These issues further underscore both the politicized nature of much discourse surrounding FRT and, crucially, the paucity of evidence to support many claims over its effectiveness. That such claims are made via recourse to 'the intelligence picture' demonstrates the fallibility of solely relying on unscrutinized 'intelligence' as a suitable basis to implement intrusive surveillance technology. While some techno-evangelism surrounding facial recognition represents a clear appeal for public legitimacy and support, it also affects how the necessity and proportionality calculations are approached. If FRT is considered effective in all applications, then it becomes easier to make claims as to necessity and proportionality.

These dynamics demonstrate how the policing purposes for facial recognition are not necessarily 'intelligence led' as often claimed. Enhanced through the allure of clandestinity, 'intelligence' lends a sense of purpose and professionalism to LFR narratives, yet it is unaccountable and unfalsifiable. The secrecy with which 'intelligence' is cultivated does not necessarily invest information with reliability or meaning. Through more detailed scrutiny of how intelligence is used to drive LFR deployments—in terms of the location and timing of operations—the misapplications and fallibility of existing intelligence-based processes become further revealed. In such circumstances, LFR becomes a technology seeking a purpose. In such circumstances, facial recognition deployments are not intelligence led. They are technology led.

7.2.2 Locating Offenders, Positioning Surveillance

The 2020 Court of Appeal ruling addressing the legality of South Wales Police's (SWP's) use of FRT held that excessive discretion had been afforded to the police in relation to 'who' was placed on a watchlist and 'where' deployments took place. The former issue was addressed in Chapter 5. Regarding the latter, high levels of discretion over the location of surveillance operations were discernible in planning meetings observed for this book. While police public statements regularly present LFR as a 'precise crime fighting tool' (MPS 2023g), deployed on an 'intelligence-led' basis, observations of planning and strategy processes revealed how deployment decisions were shaped by multiple factors. As the examples below demonstrate, rather than placing cameras to respond most effectively to the intelligence-based objective, decisions over camera placement became influenced by affordances of politics, public relations, and the technology itself. The following discussion charts the location of MPS facial recognition deployments during the current phase of operations relying on AI-driven surveillance capabilities. This current era begins in west London at one of the world's largest urban gatherings.

7.2.2.1 Carnival: from Bakhtin to biometrics

In a famous essay by Russian literary theorist Mikhail Bakhtin, carnival is characterized as a moment of permissibility, where licentious behaviour becomes normalized and social orders inverted (see Carrabine 2008). Such public assemblies have readily attracted epithets of judgement, disorder, and immorality. Historically, they have also (predictably) drawn highly moralized forms of censure, first from the church and more latterly from the state. Carnivals, then, commonly exist as sites of contestation over social order.

West London's Notting Hill Carnival is one of the largest public assemblies in the world. Taking place over three days each August, 'Carnival' draws over two million visitors in a celebration of (mainly) Caribbean cultures and their enormous contribution to the cultural, social, and economic life of the UK. The event has a history of longstanding conflicts over the policing of diversity. Most recently, communities–state tensions escalated following the UK government's illegal detention and deportation of many among the lawfully settled Caribbean diaspora (known as the 'Windrush Scandal'). Publicly surfacing in 2018 but widely known for years prior, this event can be contextualized as an unequivocally racist manifestation of the government's 'hostile environment' to migrants.[2] It was in this context that the MPS chose to stage their first two LFR operations, during August 2016 and again the following year.

From an MPS perspective, this event constitutes one of the most challenging policing events of the calendar. As one officer described of colleagues,

[2] The part of the UK government initiating and overseeing these actions was the Home Office, the same department that funds the MPS. While the Immigration Enforcement command is fiscally and operationally separate from the MPS, their union under the same administrative department holds deep symbolism for many. Such tensions were further stoked by the vindictiveness, racism, and, according to the public review laid before parliament, 'institutional ignorance and thoughtlessness' (Williams 2020) with which such punitive measures were carried out. These included passport confiscations and, despite their legal entitlement to it, the denial of healthcare to the elderly.

'you can always instantly tell which unlucky soul has "done carnival". The sheer exhaustion is etched into their faces' (interviewed January 2019). As such, incentives exist for the police to find new ways of policing the event. Yet the history of police–communities conflict, coupled with decades of public reports repeatedly evidencing racism within the organization (MacPherson 1999; Lammy 2017; Casey 2023), mean the deployment of experimental police surveillance technology in this setting is hardly uncontroversial. Moreover, and according to MPS statistics, the LFR operation at the 2017 Notting Hill Carnival remains one of the largest deployments of this technology in Europe and—excluding China—possibly the world (see Chapter 8).

LFR deployments at the Notting Hill Carnival laid the foundation for future uses of the technology across London. Yet examining police justifications of LFR performance at these operations reveals selective use of statistics that, irrespective of how the technology actually functioned, presents the technology as effective. As the analysis reveals, different data sets were used depending on the argument being made. In every single case this way of measuring FRT performance artificially presents the technology in the most positive light possible. This approach of selectively using dual data sets is repeated in subsequent MPS analysis of facial recognition performance (see NPL and MPS 2020, discussed in Chapter 8) and has implications with respect to future justifications for deployment and determinations of necessity. Amplifying facial recognition performance statistics elevates its claimed utility across a wider range of applications, increasing the justifications for, and likelihood of, deployment.

To elaborate, the MPS figures presented in Table 7.1 detail a 'true positive' rate for 'bluelist' individuals. 'Bluelist' individuals are police volunteers instructed to pass in front of the cameras. This was the statistical measure offered by the police to evidence *positive* LFR performance at the event. True positive rates for these groups tend to be higher than active operational statistics for several reasons. Principally, and without suggestion this was intentional, 'bluelist' actors are differently primed (their goal is to test identification) to other candidates (who may be indifferent to, or actively seek avoidance of, cameras). This subtle yet significant detail was evident in bluelist tests observed by the authors, where volunteers were briefed inside the control room, had prior knowledge of the camera recognition zone, and regularly walked conspicuously through it. It is notable that all official MPS reporting of the facial recognition operations analysed in this book (NPL and MPS 2020) similarly rely on this measure to advertise the benefits of the technology. By contrast, false-positive rates are derived from a combination of the 'operational watchlist'—a different database comprising police suspects where their presence is not known in advance—and an *estimate* of the total number of individuals passing in front of the camera. Using this measure can deflate a sense of poor performance.

Table 7.1 Official MPS statistics for LFR performance at the 2017 Notting Hill Carnival

Notting Hill Carnival 2017—Summary	
Duration	12 hours
Watchlist size	528
Recognition opportunities	Approx. 101,000
Alerts against operational watchlist	96
People engaged by a police officer following alert	6
Alerts confirmed correct at engagement	1
False-positive identification rate	*0.09%*
True-positive identification rate for bluelist	*71%*

Source: Data derived from NPL and MPS 2020.

These seemingly small methodological choices can exert significant impacts. For example, deeper analysis of police statistics reveals how, despite a claimed 'false-positive identification rate' of 0.09 per cent[3]—a seemingly impressive result—the cameras may have been *almost totally ineffective.* The same statistics reveal that only one alert was 'confirmed correct at engagement'. Other ways of presenting this information include '1 in every 101,000 faces scanned yields a verifiably accurate match'; '0.001 per cent of faces scanned yielded a correct alert'; '1 in 96 facial recognition alerts verified as accurate'; or '98.96 per cent of all facial recognition alerts not proven as accurate'. On these same statistics, it is equally accurate to state a 'no hit' rate of 98.96 per cent, something significantly less impressive than a false-positive rate of 0.09 per cent.

Additional caution in accepting such statistical claims is necessary. The figure for the total number of faces scanned is an estimate.[4] Estimating a

[3] 95 is 0.094 per cent of 101,000.

[4] While facial recognition software logs numbers of faces scanned, estimates of crowd sizes are used for sound methodological reasons. For example, as observed in the Soho operations,

slightly different number of faces scanned significantly affects the ratio of false alerts to 'recognition opportunities' and can respectively amplify or reduce the true- and false-positive rates of effectiveness. For example, and hypothetically discounting the single 'alert confirmed correct at engagement', slightly changing the estimated number of 'recognition opportunities' (the number of faces scanned) is decisive in concluding whether the technology worked at all. If at Notting Hill the evaluators had estimated that 102,000 rather than 101,000 faces were scanned (a slight difference of 0.98 per cent in the estimate), this would mean all 96 people could have been wrongly identified.[5] Moreover, using this methodology, the system could still be presented as accurate and successful. It would have been possible to claim a 0.09 per cent false-positive rate even though 100 per cent of facial recognition watchlist alerts for the 2017 Notting Hill Carnival were incorrect.

Whether by accident or design, every statistical and methodological choice presents the technology more favourably. This approach is continued in the collaborative, and then independent, studies the National Physical Laboratory (NPL) conducted into MPS facial recognition algorithms in 2020 and 2023, respectively (NPL and MPS 2020; NPL 2023).

A common, and technologically deterministic, counter-argument to criticisms of LFR performance is that innovation will inevitably make the systems more accurate. There is truth in one specific element of this point in that lab testing indicates that the algorithms supplied by NEC have become more accurate over time. While this approach to evaluating FRT performance is used more widely (and is adopted by National Institute of Standards and Technology (NIST) standards), it does not translate seamlessly to other considerations of FRT operation. For example, when justifying the tool for policing purposes or evaluating the human rights implications of the technology, such calculations of false positives inherently conceal the impact of the technology on wrongly identified individuals. Moreover, and while important, technical capability is not necessarily equivalent to overall system performance. LFR system performance relies on a range of socio-technical and environmental factors including human decisions over the location of

lagging caused by processor overload (image analysis is an intensive computational activity) meant many faces were not logged. 'Recognition opportunities' therefore exist, even if the computer is not acting on them. This use of estimates persists until at least 2023 and is a core part of that year's NPL analysis of bias in MPS facial recognition algorithms (NPL 2023).

[5] As stated above, 0.094 per cent of 101,000 is 95. However, 0.094 per cent of 102,000 is 96.

cameras, how watchlists are populated, how system sensitivity is set, camera aspect ratios, and whether computer-suggested matches are credible.

Even when performing well, the enormous labour of deploying facial recognition often results in moderate outcomes. In 2023, for example, the MPS conducted their second largest facial recognition operation, using three different camera sites, each equipped with technology far more advanced than the S17 algorithm deployed at the 2017 Notting Hill Carnival. According to the official MPS statistics, the LFR operation at the coronation of Charles III in central London scanned an estimated 70,000 faces and yielded 2 matches, of which 1 resulted in an arrest (MPS 2024b). That is, LFR outcomes at Notting Hill in 2017 and the coronation in 2023—on the basis of verifiable outcomes—were essentially the same.

7.2.2.2 Of crime and place

Decisions over the location of cameras at observed operations were additionally influenced by technical and operational considerations. These included the possibility to park a surveillance van in a particular location, the cameras' field of view, possibilities for situating intervention teams, risks to the public, risks to the police, and so on. Thus, the practical realities of positioning a van and teams of officers along with considerations of how to optimize technical performance became prominent considerations.

For example, the second Stratford LFR deployment was intended to complement a Newham Borough-wide initiative targeting violence. Pre-operational intelligence briefings highlighted violent crime statistics for the London Borough of Newham and its unfavourable comparison to other regions of the capital. At the time, Newham experienced the fourth highest rate of violence of thirty-two London boroughs, the fifth highest rate of robbery and the tenth highest rate of knife crime. The LFR deployment took place in Westfield Shopping Centre. However, local intelligence data and crime mapping statistics used to plan the operation identified offences concentrated some distance away at Stratford Broadway, the other side of London's busiest train station, a large carriageway, and another shopping centre. Indeed, the Westfield mall has been consistently regarded as materially and symbolically distinct from its urban setting; furnished with some of the most advanced environmental security measures in the world and (to paraphrase Hamlet) part of a 'sterile, hygienized promontory' parachuted in and fortified as part of the London 2012 Olympic development (Fussey et al. 2012: 264). What the Westfield Centre did offer, though, was excellent camera sightlines along a bridge that funnelled shoppers past the cameras and into the retail spaces beyond. The positioning of LFR cameras to optimize their scope of view thus became a crucial factor.

The affordances of LFR technology, and the way environments can optimize the technology, thus trumped the value of intelligence regarding where operations were located. While such considerations are inevitable to a degree, they also decouple specific 'intelligence-led' priorities from the tool deployed to address them. In such circumstances, it is not police intelligence that shapes how LFR is operated but the operation of LFR that shapes how intelligence is used.

Furthermore, factors other than an exclusive intelligence focus may also be discerned in the siting of LFR cameras. For example, the final two deployments of the 'trial period' took place in Romford, east London during January and February 2019. Romford is located in the London Borough of Havering, one of the least diverse municipalities in the capital (ONS 2022) and part of an outer-London area holding a longstanding reputation for far-right support. Several officers expressed surprise at this choice of location, with a typical view being that it represented an 'overcompensation for Notting Hill and Newham for PR' (interviewed January 2019).

7.2.3 Temporalities of Intelligence and Surveillance

Assessing how LFR deployments align to intelligence-based justifications also requires a consideration of time. In Soho, pre-deployment briefings strongly emphasized the clustering of serious violent offences. However, these offences were overwhelmingly connected to central London's night-time economy. The prevalence of offences intensified at weekends and between the hours of 23:00 and 04:00. By contrast, and in recognition of the depleted performance of LFR in low-light conditions, the MPS operations took place on a Monday and Tuesday roughly between the hours of 08:00 and 16:00. A similar disconnection applied at the Romford operations in January and February 2019. For the Soho operations, several important tactical, operational, and technological reasons informed the decision to divorce the operation from the temporalities identified by police intelligence. These included the availability of officers, operational priorities, and the undesirability of redeploying stretched night-time teams on a weekend before Christmas. Despite the cameras being used for active operations, with a 'live' watchlist actively intended to identify individuals for arrest, this temporal disconnect was justified on the grounds that the technology was being 'trialled' as a 'research' enterprise. Notwithstanding the absence of a clear operational methodology, positioning such activities as a trial would have required capability testing (e.g. performance in low light), whereas a deployment needs to evidence the necessity of the particular intervention, including its ability to address the identified aim.

Overall, the above analysis demonstrates how issues of time and place may often indicate linkages to the intelligence case but, on closer analysis, such connections may be tenuous and superficial. This unmooring of the intelligence picture from the specific temporalities and spatialities of LFR deployments means the technology is less capable of meeting its objectives. This in turn critically undermines arguments that seek to justify and claim necessity for its use.

7.3 Watchlists in Practice: Where Biometrics and 'Dataveillance' Meet

Analysis of MPS legal and policy documents in Chapter 5 revealed the myriad ambiguities surrounding the construction of facial recognition watchlists. Here, a lack of precision coupled with shifting criteria for eligibility for enrolment on a watchlist offered significant scope for inconsistent and discretionary practices to shape the development of facial recognition reference databases. This chapter develops the analysis by examining the manifest practices involved in physically building and applying a watchlist. It draws on interviews with those involved in compiling watchlists and observations at facial recognition planning meetings, pre-operational briefings, and LFR operations to examine the human act of synthesizing text- and image-based information into a single reference database. It argues that the human labour involved brings further subjectivity, complexity, and uncertainty into the FRT operational cycle.

7.3.1 Types of Watchlists and the Form of Images

It is common for facial recognition operations to use several watchlists simultaneously. The MPS used two separate watchlists for each observed deployment: an operational list made up of images of individuals they were seeking to locate and a 'bluelist' comprising police volunteers and other staff put in place to monitor technical performance. It is important to recognize that different watchlists are normally developed to varying technical standards. For example, operational watchlists populated by persons of police interest are normally sourced from police custody images of suspects. Most custody images are captured with a degree of optical consistency, including lighting and the positioning of subjects. 'Bluelist' database images are collected in a variety of circumstances including, as observed on several operations, outdoor smartphone photographs on the day of a given deployment. This varying quality of source material undermines comparisons of performance across 'operational' and 'bluelist' cohorts as official MPS evaluations have done (NPL and MPS 2020). These differences also raise questions of ecological validity that challenge the degree to which selective data—such as bluelist images—can be generalized to assess FRT performance more broadly as the MPS's report on LFR bias claims to do (NPL 2023). While it is difficult to assess the performance of facial recognition algorithms with respect to each database, the point remains that they use different data sources of varying quality and are therefore not directly comparable. In anticipating this criticism, some evaluators have claimed bluelists adhere to the common benchmarks for custody image capture. This is the 2007 'Police Standard for Still Digital Image Capture and Data Interchange of Facial/Mugshot and Scar, Mark & Tattoo Images' (NPIA 2007) (see NPL 2023). However, and to put it mildly, this 2007 standard is unequivocally anachronistic in the era of advanced digital imagery. It therefore offers a very low bar for quality control that most digitally captured images are likely to achieve irrespective of the significant variations in quality between them.

In accordance with legal data protection obligations, most observed operations created a fresh bespoke watchlist. There were two exceptions. The second Soho deployment, which took place on the day following the previous operation, was considered by the police to be the same operation with similar levels of data currency for data protection purposes. The other exception was the second Romford operation that took place almost two weeks after the first. According to the accounts of those involved in the operation, the retention of the same watchlist was justified on the grounds that the second Romford operation was postponed due to forecasted snow (that never arrived) and limited police resources available for compiling a new database. As detailed below, reusing watchlists in this manner resulted in individuals being unnecessarily and incorrectly stopped on the basis of outdated data. This also risked contravention of the Data Protection Act

2018[6] and the Surveillance Camera Code of Practice established under the Protection of Freedoms Act 2012.[7] Concern over limited police resources cannot justify non-compliance with legal obligations.

7.3.2 The Data Ecosystem

Despite the considerable surveillance possibilities brought about by FRT, its potency as a law enforcement tool is critically dependent on the data architecture that supports it. The size and form of watchlists were also impacted by affordances of the data that forms part of the LFR ecosystem and, ultimately, shapes its operation. And, contrasting with the intrusive, often dystopian, symbolism of the technology, empirical analysis of how the foundational data to support FRT operations is assembled reveals a complex and inconsistently performed task, and one that undermines the functionality of the tool.

Across the observed operations, senior officers consistently highlighted how compiling a watchlist constituted one of the most significant challenges of an operation. This complexity largely originated from the need to draw information from different databases and from the incompleteness of these origin data sets. For example, custody records were often incomplete and missing vital details that needed to be sourced from elsewhere. Understanding these issues in detail requires an understanding of the different data sources and the relationships between them.[8]

Interviews conducted with those compiling facial recognition watchlists revealed that the principal data source used by the MPS was the Emerald Warrant Management System (EWMS). While the name might suggest that only individuals with outstanding arrest warrants were included on any watchlist, officers highlighted how this was not always the case in practice. At both the second Stratford operation and the final Romford deployment, senior officers stated that records from the Crime Report Information System (CRIS) were entered directly into watchlists. This difference is

[6] §38(1)(a): 'personal data processed for any of the law enforcement purposes must be accurate and, where necessary, kept up to date'.

[7] §2.6.12 of the 2013 Code in operation at the time of these deployments: 'Any information used to support a surveillance camera system which compares against a reference database for matching purposes should be accurate and kept up to date.'

[8] While descriptions of these data practices are accurate for the operations analysed here, it is important to recognize that the MPS has more recently invested in a new data infrastructure system. See below regarding the implications of these plans.

crucial for several reasons. Primary among them is that, despite the name, CRIS records are unfiltered reported victim and witness statements. CRIS records therefore constitute intelligence reports pertaining to criminal incidents and therefore do not denote people who are 'wanted' in a judicial sense. The previous chapter revealed the vagaries around who becomes eligible for enrolment on a watchlist; here, these surveillance lists dilate further through the data sources used to populate them.

An additional, and unrecognized, dimension to how data infrastructure influences the scope and reach of FRT operations concerns the relationship between watchlists and other repositories of police information. Two separate incidents in central London, occurring hours apart, demonstrate the significance of this issue. The following ethnographic note pertaining to the first of these is illustrative in this regard:

> Charing Cross Road, London, 17/12/2018, 11:24: Facial recognition 'red hit'/passer-by wearing a red camouflage jacket and a baseball cap with an image of knuckle duster on the front matched the watchlist. IC3 Black male. 0.55 threshold score. Extremely fast intervention. Information immediately radioed through to the intervention teams stationed further (south) down Charing X Road. Match radioed through because the mobile devices issued to street-based teams were not working. Individual stopped and gave a name that did not match any police computer records. Intervention teams suspected a false name and believed they had reasonable grounds to check identify under PACE.[9] One officer used a mobile fingerprint scanner to confirm identity. The individual was not on the watchlist but was 'wanted' in connection to his status as wanted in relation to malicious communications and taken to the police station for processing. Fifteen minutes later the street-based undercover officer

[9] Police officers interviewed for this research established an approach where the legislation most relevant to police–citizen street encounters—the Police and Criminal Evidence Act (PACE) 1984—was relevant to FRT operations in two important ways. First, an LFR match was deemed sufficient grounds to claim reasonable suspicion and therefore stop a matched individual in the street and establish their identity. This was normally achieved through the use of 'Mobile Ink', a portable fingerprint scanner. Second, officers considered that s24 of PACE gave officers the legal power to arrest individuals refusing to submit to a street-based fingerprint check on the grounds that they were reasonably believed to be wanted. This exact scenario occurred in the second Romford operation, when a matched individual refused to unclench their fist and submit to a fingerprint scan. They were subsequently arrested and taken to the local police station for processing. While ostensibly separate episodes in an intensifying sequence of police procedure, these events demonstrate how, regardless of whether they are correct or not, computational matches have significant ramifications throughout the criminal justice process.

(also a trained 'super recognizer') enters the van to review the footage. He takes one look at the surveillance feed and (correctly) declares 'that's not him'. Interestingly, and by his own account, if this officer had been equipped with a working mobile device, and therefore seen the initial match, he probably would have advised against stopping the suspect.

This account reveals many dimensions shaping how LFR operates in practice. Among these is how LFR technology intersects with other digital tools and how, somewhat counterintuitively, failure in any of these parts of the assemblage extends the reach and scope of surveillance. The above demonstrates how individuals not enrolled on watchlists, yet 'wanted' with respect to offences that fall below the threshold for FRT surveillance, may still be arrested as a result of this technology. In this episode the individual was wanted on the grounds of malicious communication, something not reaching the severity of 'serious violence' reportedly required for enrolment on the watchlist for this LFR deployment. In other words, it is possible for individuals stopped on the basis of a verified incorrect LFR match to be then arrested for another reason. Manifold implications arise from this event. In one respect, FRT is deployed on a proportionality calculation regarding serious crime but, in a form of surveillance creep, also operates below that threshold to broker arrests for more minor offences.

A second incident occurring shortly after at nearby Leicester Square also reveals the complex relationship between 'FRT-specific' databases and the wider informational infrastructure:

Leicester Square, London, 17/12/2018, 13:20: Facial recognition 'red hit'/ passer-by. 0.56 threshold score. Adjudicated as a credible match and identity confirmed by street-based intervention teams as an individual on the watchlist. The matched individual claimed the offence listed on the watchlist had been dealt with by the criminal justice system for the offence in question. Police National Computer checks revealed this to be true. The watchlist was out of date and the offence had been entered incorrectly on the Emerald database. However, the individual was wanted in relation to malicious communications. This is a lesser offence and one that would fail to meet the threshold for inclusion on the operational watchlist.

This episode represents a variation on the theme whereby those 'wanted' with respect to crimes not sufficiently serious for enrolment on watchlists may still be implicated in LFR surveillance. Several issues apply here. First is the aforementioned lack of compliance with both the Data Protection Act and the UK government's Surveillance Camera Code of Practice stipulations on data currency. Here, the inaccuracy of digital identification, poor source information quality, and the outdated nature of the watchlists themselves generated multiple impacts including an arrest for a lesser offence. From a policing perspective, this may be considered a value added or diffusion of benefit. However, while these events demonstrate how LFR may play a wider role in apprehending offenders, extending surveillance beyond those on the watchlist generates significant concerns. The first is that the stated purpose of FRT operations is extended. From a human rights perspective, surveillance creep of this kind inappropriately extends the reach of deployments and disrupts compliance with the necessity calculation. This also expands police powers beyond those for which they are authorized for the purposes of the deployment. Furthermore, questions are raised over the presence of LFR and its potential to interfere with individuals' ability to move freely.[10]

As the data richness of policing environments increases, so opportunities to link watchlists to other information sources will grow. With increased emphasis on logging data through routine police work where 'every patrol becomes a data-gathering mission', as Ferguson (2017: 104) puts it, police stops are increasingly likely to yield information 'of interest' on any individual. Accordingly, LFR-initiated stops are similarly prone to extending the net-widening tendencies of digital policing. A further parallel—and amplification—may exist regarding 'pretext stops' discussed in Chapter 5. Given that police data sources also overrepresent specific demographic groups—notably young Black males (inter alia, Lammy 2017; Amnesty International UK 2018)—and the established algorithmic biases when recognizing ethnicity, LFR-initiated stops that link to these wider data sources are likely to affect some demographics more explicitly than others.

7.3.2.1 The secret source?

The most obvious database when considering police intelligence and other investigative information is the Police National Database (PND). It is important to note that, despite their similar names, the PND is a distinct and

[10] Relatedly, see below and Chapter 8 for examples of how the presence of LFR may trigger conditions for other offences to occur.

separate entity from the Police National Computer (PNC). Established in 1974, the PNC is a national system recording formal criminal charges and other interventions. The PND captures intelligence. Established over thirty years later, and more heavily implicated in the operation of FRT, the PND includes both image- (such as custody images) and text-based (such as intelligence reports) data. The PND serves as both a repository and data-sharing facility for police intelligence. It was introduced in response to the 2004 Bichard Inquiry review of child protection following the murder of two schoolgirls by Ian Huntley, a school caretaker in Soham, Cambridgeshire. Much of the inquiry focused on the deletion of, and failure to share, information between police organizations about prior investigations into Huntley for a series of alleged sexual offences, which would have prevented his employment at the girls' school. The PND was subsequently established as a means to share intelligence, improve vetting, and avoid similar tragedies in the future. In the time since the operations observed for this book, both the PND and the PNC systems are being progressively merged into a new national Law Enforcement Data Service (known colloquially, and more commonly, as LEDS). While LEDS started to offer limited capability from March 2022, its growth and replacement is gradual (Home Office 2018, 2022). Moreover, interviews with Home Office employees connected with the LEDS scheme (in April 2019) revealed that integration is far from straightforward with particular technical difficulties arising over the identification and removal of irrelevant photographs including those deemed by the High Court as being held by the MPS unlawfully.[11] At the time of writing, MPS facial recognition policies still refer to the PND.

However, during the observed operations the MPS did not make use of the PND database of already processed gallery images or any other PND custody images at all. According to senior officers responsible for planning the facial recognition operations, this was because the MPS had ceased populating the PND since before 2013. Sound operational reasons support this decision, which include 'lack of quality control over who inputs the PND data' and 'different forces upload their intelligence on different timescales' (interviewed January 2019). This reflects a broader view that much PND intelligence was out of date, a view expressed by police in other forces

[11] See *RMC and FJ* v *Commissioner of Police for the Metropolis and Secretary of State for the Home Department* [2012] EWHC 1681(Admin) and Chapter 3.

(Hadjimatheou and Fussey forthcoming). In conversations held throughout the ethnographic fieldwork officers consistently noted how national (PND) and local (MPS) databases operated on different temporal cycles, with the latter being updated on a more continuous basis. Officers also complained about the poor quality of custody images on the PND. Added to this were a range of data duplication and consistency issues.

Operational planning for facial recognition deployments in London instead drew watchlist data from more localized (London-centric) information sources. As the discussion below relays, while this strategic decision conferred benefits in terms of the potential to access more up-to-date material, it also entailed disadvantages, most pointedly the time-consuming task of manually re-keying information into watchlists from multiple databases, each of varying completeness and quality.

7.3.2.2 Local databases

The most prominent data source for facial recognition watchlists in London was the EWMS.[12] In essence, EWMS functioned as an MPS system for logging and processing warrants. However, overlap exists between the EWMS database and the PNC.[13] Indeed, EWMS was perhaps described most clearly to researchers as an MPS *implementation* of the PNC. It therefore adopts similar functions to the PNC, although there are key differences (such as timescales for updating information) that have an impact on watchlist formulation.[14]

The principal shortcoming with using the EWMS to identify 'wanted' individuals for the watchlist was that the database contained no image data. Therefore, images matching the profiles of 'wanted' individuals selected for each watchlist needed to be sourced from elsewhere. A further difficulty involved how data was structured in different databases. For example, filters

[12] More detail on the EWMS data architecture can be found here: www.governmentcomputing.com/police-bluelight/news/newsthe-met-explains-thinking-behind-new-integrated-policing-system-4862503.

[13] Note this was the Police National *Computer*, not the Police National *Database*. This represents a further fracture in police data infrastructure. The Metropolitan Police also developed a parallel approximation of the PND, discussed in the following sections.

[14] The complex relationships between local and national databases also apply to other forms of facial recognition technology. For example, both retrospective facial recognition (RFR) and operator-initiated facial recognition (OIFR) check against local custody image databases first before accessing the PND. The compound implications of data deficiencies in either of these databases have yet to be researched.

(such as 'violent crime') could be applied to some databases to reduce the number of records returned by a search. Yet these filters did not exist in all the databases used for each operation. The resulting activity of watchlist construction was therefore complex and laborious. The following description is a distillation of many hours of conversations with those responsible for organizing facial recognition operations including officers with delegated responsibility to construct watchlists. The complexity of these conversations, and the data infrastructure they discussed, are thus brought together in a single description for the purposes of explanation.

When officers applied a filter to search for specific crime type (such as 'violent crime'), the EWMS returned a 'front page' offering information such as the name and date of birth of an individual, but records routinely omitted other vital data. The incompleteness of this information meant that it became necessary to retrieve relevant missing data (such as custody images, Identity Code (IC) used to denote ethnicity (hence 'IC1, IC3', and so on), and offence detail) from other sources. Original EWMS information was therefore manually entered into other databases in order to obtain the required information. These included the aforementioned MPS-owned CRIS, the local Criminal Intelligence (CRIMINT), and their custody image databases. Notable here are the 'intelligence' and 'information'—not 'criminal'—record-handling purposes of these databases. In an earlier attempt by the MPS to harmonize dispersed data sources, these three local databases were brought together in a federated platform called EAPPs (DP). While the purpose of the EAPPs (DP) platform was to synthesize these smaller databases, their differences meant they were not easily integrated. As a result, information from these smaller databases became lost when transferred to EAPPs (DP). Critical among this lost information for the functioning of LFR were custody images. These were not always automatically uploaded from the MPS custody image database to the EAPPs (DP) platform. This created a dilemma for officers working on creating facial recognition watchlists: crucial image data—the faces the LFR system was intended to match to—was missing from many text files. Officers created two workarounds to rectify this limitation. One involved officers returning to the smaller MPS custody image database to manually identify and export each missing facial image. Relating this process, officers described how this limited interoperability meant they had to manually search the source database, physically take screen shots, then crop and export images into the watchlist before reconciling with the text data gained from other sources. Another workaround was to use a similar approach but to draw records held on the PNC. Once synthesized, the watchlist images were subjected to biometric processing by the facial recognition software. With watchlists of over 2,000 people, this laborious process took weeks to complete. This issue gains further significance when considering that LFR operations often ran two weeks after watchlists had begun to be compiled.

The arduous and time-consuming nature of this process clearly undermines arguments claiming the efficiency of LFR, especially those that only focus on one narrow aspect of its operation (such as identifying faces in crowds). Moreover, distinct irony exists concerning how a technologically advanced reverse image analysis system (LFR) only becomes functional once officers spend days manually matching images, crime numbers, and crime record data points to build the system's data architecture. Such hidden labour undermines claims that FRT necessarily offers operational efficiency and is a factor always missing from selective audits of LFR benefits. Moreover, these operational inefficiencies often metastasized, creating problems affecting how LFR worked in practice (Chapter 8).

While the process varied across different LFR operations, a simplified and indicative example of how watchlists were constructed by the MPS is set out in Figure 7.1.

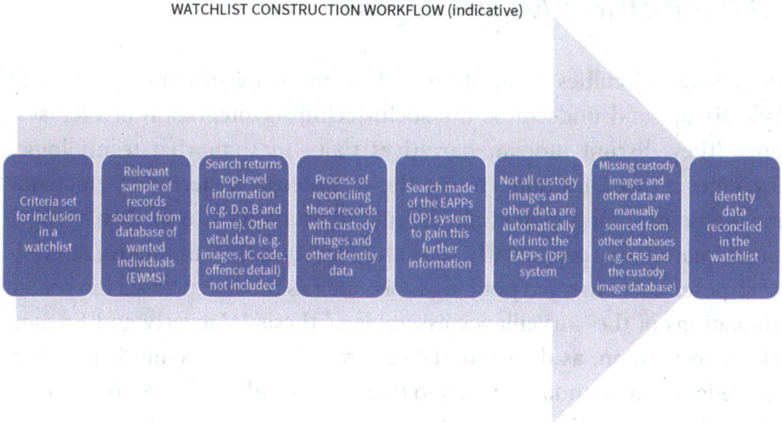

Figure 7.1 Indicative workflow for constructing the facial recognition watchlist (Fussey and Murray 2019).

Figure 7.2 also illustrates how, according to accounts of those involved in their construction, the different databases are drawn together for the construction of LFR watchlists for the observed period.

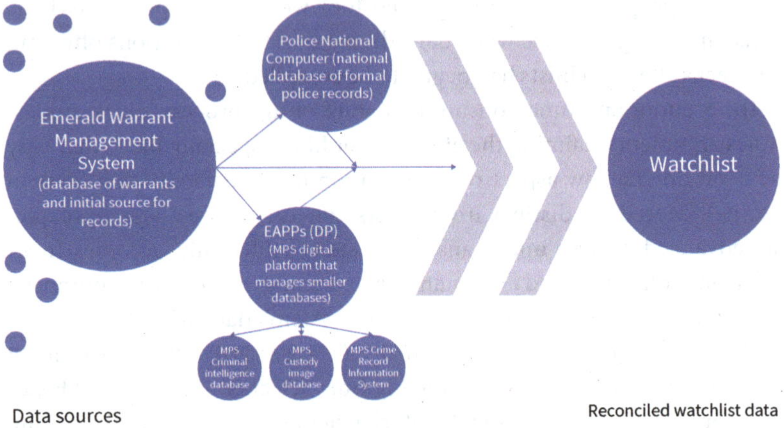

Figure 7.2 Representation of the relationship between different data sources involved in the population of face recognition watchlists (Fussey and Murray 2019).

7.3.3 Fractured Assemblages

The above difficulties in locating and synthesizing disparate sources of data disrupt and undermine the socio-technical integration of FRT systems. They disrupt utopian narratives that—in somewhat technologically deterministic fashion—frame the technology in terms of efficiency and 'game-changing' potential. Yet such limitations also challenge more critical narratives, particularly those highlighting the cumulative surveillance potential of merged policing tools, such as those expressed in specific adaptations of the 'surveillance assemblage' thesis (Haggerty and Ericson 2000). In London, as disparate data sources became assembled together, their edges and boundaries asserted themselves and differences became reinforced. Such frontiers may undermine the overall possibilities of surveillance networks. As in his definitive analysis of assemblage theory, DeLanda (2016: 10, 13) encourages us 'to conceive of emergent wholes in which their parts retain their autonomy' and to discard the ontological sense of 'seamless totalities and transcendent essences'. The sum, to paraphrase Latour et al. (2012), may be less than its parts.

Such outcomes do not simply translate in binary terms as successes or failures. Consistent with foundational theoretical formulations of assemblage—of *agencement*, or 'emergence'—new possibilities and outcomes arise from the merger of old policing databases with the new of AI-driven technologies. For example, the arduous and time-consuming nature of their construction meant watchlists were outdated at the moment they became assembled. This lack of data currency (and accuracy) led to individuals being stopped, unnecessarily and thus arbitrarily, after being matched by FRT systems. This problem was compounded by the perspective that an FRT match offered sufficient legal grounds to establish reasonable suspicion, and thus authorize police to stop someone, under PACE 1984, regardless of how poorly the system was performing or how outdated its information was. A disconnect therefore existed between the different temporal cycles—and data recency—of databases used in the facial recognition ecosystem.

Outdated information can also complicate the measuring of system effectiveness. At one of the Romford test deployments a fifteen-year-old male was matched to the watchlist as he walked past the cameras. A decision was made to intervene and the individual was questioned. This was a verified correct match but, similar to the case above, he had already been dealt with by the criminal justice system in the time between watchlist compilation and the LFR test deployment. The inclusion of this individual—and an unknown number of others—on a watchlist during the weeks of its construction breached the broader policies that guide the scant regulation and oversight of FRT. These include the UK government's Surveillance Camera Code of Practice which unequivocally states that all 'reference database[s] for matching purposes should be accurate and kept up to date' and that 'underlying data [must be] fit for purpose' (Home Office 2013: 11). Similar provisions are laid out in the UK's post-Brexit data protection legislation, which is upheld by the only oversight body with any meaningful regulatory power, the Information Commissioner's Office (ICO).[15] Moreover,

[15] The Information Commissioner and ICO have the legal authority to initiate investigations, issue significant fines, and compel data controllers to cease activities. Despite being vocal on the issue, the meaningfulness of ICO regulation of facial recognition should be considered in the context that it has not issued any such notices for public surveillance schemes since 2013; has launched zero investigations into police uses of surveillance technology since the European General Data Protection Regulation was enacted; and has a stated position of not fining public bodies for data protection breaches (ICO 2022a).

the MPS themselves pledged that watchlists would be 'reviewed again no more than 2 days prior to the operation to ensure that it only contains relevant and actionable data' (MPS 2018b: 14). Given the complexity involved in constructing watchlists in this way, such a review would evidently be a difficult—if not impossible—task.

7.3.4 Futures

Being one of the largest metropolitan police forces in the world, the size of the MPS and its ageing databases meant it necessarily encountered greater difficulties in managing and merging data into FRT watchlists than smaller forces (Fussey et al. 2021). In response to the above issues, the MPS has sought a £44 million investment to enhance the integration of their disparate information ecosystem. The intention is to develop an adapted version of the 'CONNECT' police data management system used by SWP and elsewhere (TechMonitor 2018). Officers expressed a hope that this would simplify the process of constructing watchlists. While this may bring operational efficiencies, two caveats are important to note. First is the technological determinism of assuming new digital assets will necessarily have the desired benefits and not generate new affordances, complexities, and challenges. Second, is the unremittingly poor record of UK state agencies in successfully implementing large-scale information management projects. Central to the many high-profile failures in this area have been the endlessly documented shortcomings in UK public procurement, outsourcing, and oversight arrangements (see Brown et al. 2014; *New Statesman* 2024). Such problems reached their tragic nadir in the largest miscarriage of justice in British legal history, the wrongful—and malicious—prosecution of over 900 Post Office workers for fraud based on inaccurate data from Fujitsu's inadequate and flawed accounting technology.

More broadly, while data integration is identified as an issue above, the wider point is that security assemblages, particularly those relying on socio-technical systems, are necessarily replete with similar fractures, boundaries, and points of friction (Fussey 2013). As Bigo (2001: 91) presciently noted on the (metaphorical) eve of 9/11, security 'is a boundary function'.

7.4 Manufacturing Consent?

7.4.1 Consent and Overt Surveillance

UK police forces classify FRT as a form of overt surveillance. This designation holds manifold implications, not least with respect to reduced authorization and oversight processes and the central role of 'consent' by those affected in legitimating overt surveillance practices. These are explored below. Before doing so, it is important to recognize debate over whether such complex technology can be classified with such simplicity. This issue involves several considerations.

Contrasting legal regulatory procedures surround covert and overt surveillance, overt practices receive little regulatory scrutiny, and clear advantages exist for those conducting surveillance to label their operations thus. Central to this practice is consideration of how surveillance practices are authorized and regulated differently depending on whether they are designated to take place overtly or covertly. For covert surveillance, certain independent assessment is required for its authorization under the Regulation of Investigatory Powers Act (RIPA) 2000. This authorization is normally conducted by a senior officer independent of the operation. More intrusive forms of covert surveillance (such as those covered by the post-Snowden Investigatory Powers Act 2016) require independent judicial authorization. No such assessments exist for 'overt' surveillance.

Section 26(9)(a) of RIPA sets out as follows the conditions for surveillance to be regarded as covert:

> surveillance is covert if, and only if, it is carried out in a manner that is calculated to ensure that persons who are subject to the surveillance are unaware that it is or may be taking place.

In response, the UK government's Surveillance Camera Code of Practice governing open street surveillance systems defined overt surveillance as 'any use of surveillance for which authority does not fall under RIPA 2000' (Home Office 2021). Also relevant is the government guidance on RIPA that forms the code of practice for covert surveillance:

> The use of overt CCTV cameras by public authorities does not normally require an authorisation under the 2000 Act. Members of the public

> should be made aware that such systems are in use. For example, by virtue of cameras or signage being clearly visible, through the provision of information and by undertaking consultation. (Home Office 2018a: 27)

Two issues are pertinent here. The first concerns the roles of consent and consultation over overt systems (discussed below). Second is the role that 'cameras . . . being clearly visible' has in garnering consent. For LFR, the difficulty here is that while the cameras themselves may be visible, it is their function and role that are not. Regardless of how noticeable the cameras are, it is highly unlikely that anyone passing LFR-equipped cameras has detailed knowledge of whether they could be enrolled onto a watchlist or not. LFR relies on a hidden database of suspects, and the covert processing of that information, to function. Elements of FRT operation are visible while other aspects are not. Put another way, aspects of public FRT uses can be considered *both* overt *and* covert. This disparity also amplifies the knowledge asymmetries of surveillance, the differences between observers and the observed concerning what is known about how surveillance operates. Such impacts are amplified in other facial recognition systems, notably RFR. In this case, while the surveillance cameras themselves may be visible, the fact that the recorded data may later be analysed using RFR is not. Additional complexity is added when one considers that RFR may be used not only to identify those present but also for targeted surveillance purposes, to facilitate tracking, monitoring, and profiling (Cheshire Constabulary 2021a: 1).

Police[16] and politicians[17] have routinely argued that FRT equates to seemingly more benign, and accepted, forms of visual surveillance, such as open street surveillance cameras. Yet these claims are critically undermined by the operational and technical realities of facial recognition deployments. Indeed, successive domestic and European legal rulings have held that FRT asserts a higher level of intrusion than standard forms of camera surveillance.[18] Moreover, not only does FRT rely on a hidden database, the form and handling of the information it requires makes it different from other forms of surveillance. Most obviously, FRT relies on biometric data, itself a special category of information, which is seen as a more sensitive form of data due to its highly personalized nature. Uses of such data thus hold

[16] *R (Bridges)* v *Chief Constable of South Wales Police* [2019] EWHC 2341 (Admin).

[17] Kit Malthouse, (then) policing minister (House of Commons 2020, para. 549).

[18] Respectively, *R (Bridges)* v *The Chief Constable of South Wales Police* [2020] EWCA Civ 1058; *Glukhin v Russia*, Judgment, ECtHR, App. No. 11519/20, 4 July 2023.

greater scope for intrusiveness and are legally subject to higher legal standards for data management (see Chapter 3). Additionally, unlike other forms of video surveillance, FRT requires the capture *and* processing of data for it to function. It is in the processing (alongside the structuring and retention) of data that additional intrusion occurs[19] (see Chapter 3).

Overall, despite different treatment by legal and regulatory processes, simple delineations between overt and covert surveillance are often subjective and unsatisfactory, particularly in circumstances when techniques could be argued to be either. As surveillance technologies become more complex in form and function, particularly in cases of novel AI-driven surveillance tools such as facial recognition, this tension is likely to amplify.

7.4.2 Public Consent

Classifying FRT as overt elevates the importance of acquiring consent from those subjected to surveillance. The UK government's Surveillance Camera Code of Practice[20] in operation at the time of the operations analysed here is clear on this point:

> The government considers that wherever overt surveillance in public places is in pursuit of a legitimate aim and meets a pressing need, any such surveillance should be characterized as surveillance by consent, and such consent on the part of the community must be informed consent and not assumed by a system operator. Surveillance by consent should be regarded as analogous to policing by consent . . . It denotes that the legitimacy of policing in the eyes of the public is based upon a general consensus of support that follows from transparency about their powers, demonstrating integrity in exercising those powers and their accountability for doing so. (Home Office 2013: S1.5 p. 3)

This issue becomes more pertinent when considering that domestic courts have recognized that FRT engages the rights of all those passing the cameras, not just those enrolled on the operational watchlists.[21] It is here that

[19] *Catt v The United Kingdom*, Judgment, ECtHR, App. No. 43514/15, 24 January 2019.
[20] A document singled out by the Court of Appeal as a policy from which FRT may derive legal basis (*R (Bridges)* v *The Chief Constable of South Wales Police* [2020] EWCA Civ 1058).
[21] *R (Bridges)* v *Chief Constable of South Wales Police* [2019] EWHC 2341 (Admin).

a contradictory argument was often expressed by law enforcement officials during the fieldwork. This asserted, on the one hand, that LFR operations were overt, yet operational secrecy obviated the need to acquire consent because of the clandestine nature of the watchlists. Similarly, one senior officer leading LFR operations in Wales expressed the following justification in court proceedings:

> It is important to ensure that a balance is maintained between transparency and engagement whilst not unduly impacting on the effectiveness of the deployment . . . at times it may be appropriate to advertise a deployment so that individuals of concern are deterred from attending. At other times it may be more appropriate to encourage attendance by not disclosing deployment specifics so that an individual is more likely to attend and be detained. (*Bridges* 1, para. 30)

The MPS facial recognition Standard Operating Procedure also offers significant latitude for subjective interpretation:

> In considering the level of awareness raising measures, whilst a baseline needs to be maintained to ensure that any Deployment is overt, the objectives for the Deployment and its use a policing tactic will also be relevant if the policing need to deploy is to be realised. For example, unduly extensive signage may undermine the effectiveness of a Deployment seeking locate persistently outstanding offences. (MPS SOP, §5.8)

While such comments may make sense from an operational perspective, they are more complicated when considering the legal and regulatory implications. The overall claim of such arguments is that police reserve the right to deploy a surveillance tool in which significant numbers of people are wholly unaware that their sensitive biometric data is being captured and processed, and then to (self-)define such practices as overt.[22] In addition to the obvious contradiction, further difficulties with such arguments include the selective and arbitrary judgements over the degree to which individuals

[22] Resonating with this analysis, the relevant district court summed up this argument as follows, 'Whilst deployment of AFR is not covert, it is reasonable to suppose, however, that a large number of people whose facial biometrics are captured and processed by SWP's use of AFR are unaware of this taking place.' *Bridges* 1, para. 39.

are informed about 'public' surveillance, the scope for arbitrary use, and the way such decisions are not exposed to any form of meaningful independent oversight.

The following sections analyse the approaches taken by the MPS to acquire consent. Examination of these processes reveals a common conflation between attempts to gain consent and attempts to promote public reassurance, test public opinion, and communicate more broadly. This discussion is structured around core conditions deemed necessary for consent to be meaningful. These are: that consent is sufficiently informed; that clear alternatives exist for non-consenting individuals to exercise a different choice; and that such alternative choices may be exercised without fear of penalty. Empirical analysis of how the MPS undertook public engagement activities reveals a range of varied and complex issues affecting consent and FRT operations.

7.4.2.1 Informed consent

The data reveals how the MPS adopted multiple strategies to acquire informed consent. These can be loosely grouped into three categories: uses of social media, deploying uniformed officers, and positioning information boards. Taking these in turn, the MPS would usually advertise deployments on Twitter/X forty-eight hours in advance. Police social media activity accompanying operations across 2023 and 2024 reveals this policy has changed and is largely abandoned, with information being released only within hours, and sometimes at the commencement, of deployments.

Uniformed officers were deployed at all the operations observed for this research. These officers were briefed to engage with the public, explain the role of the technology, and signpost further information (such as the public LFR website). Given the divisive nature of FRT, and its deployment in sites of longstanding police–community tensions, such engagements were repeatedly met with hostility and the task of public reassurance was not straightforward and often proved challenging for officers. Uniformed officers were also issued with leaflets for distribution to the public. For example, 1,400 leaflets were printed in advance of the second Stratford trial. Pre-operational briefing sessions placed significant emphasis on the importance of leafleting.[23]

[23] On file with authors.

An important distinction, and one not made by MPS processes, is that between public communication and consent gathering. Reviewing the information on each leaflet reveals how, if this was a sole source of information, it would be difficult to acquire sufficient information to meaningfully consent to having one's biometric data processed by police FRT schemes. For example, the information provided transparency regarding the time and location of the operations, but held no detail on the purpose of the deployment and who was likely to be the subject of surveillance, thus pointing to the above complexity over neat distinctions between overt and covert surveillance. Also notable was the provision of an email address for queries. When officers were asked about the volume of emails, they responded that they had yet to receive any. Reflecting a more enduring theme, offering a means of communication signifies consultation, yet without more this remains symbolic.

Also resonating with the theme of symbolic consultation is how public communication materials contained less information over time. This is apparent when comparing the 2018 Stratford operations with the deployment at the 2017 Notting Hill Carnival, which contained more information on the purpose and likely subjects of surveillance.

Text from 2017 Notting Hill Carnival leaflet:

> **Police Trial of Facial Recognition Technology.** The Metropolitan Police Service (MPS) is currently trialling the use of facial recognition technology in the identification and arrest of wanted individuals and those with bail conditions not to attend Notting Hill Carnival.
>
> The trial will involve the use of mobile cameras installed with facial recognition software at Notting Hill Carnival.
>
> The camera scans the faces of individuals as they pass by and identifies potential matches with uploaded custody images of individuals currently wanted for arrest or on bail not to attend Notting Hill Carnival.
>
> When a match is made police officers will be alerted, who will then stop the individual, verify their identity, and if necessary arrest them.
>
> The deployment of these cameras at Notting Hill Carnival will be intelligence-led and temporary. Only images which come up as a match to a wanted individual will be retained.
>
> The use of facial recognition technology aims to support standard policing activity to ensure everyone has a safe and enjoyable carnival.

Text from 2018 Stratford deployment leaflet:

> **Police Trial of Facial Recognition Technology.** The Metropolitan Police Service (MPS) is currently trialling the use of facial recognition technology in the identification of specific individuals at various events and locations.
>
> The trial will involve the use of mobile cameras installed with facial recognition software.
>
> The cameras scan the faces of people as they pass by and alerts [sic] police officers to potential matches of specific individuals.
>
> The deployment of these cameras will be intelligence-led and temporary. Only images which come up as a match to a targeted individual will be retained for a limited period.
>
> The use of facial recognition technology aims to support standard policing activity to ensure everyone's safety.

Public signage is a cornerstone of data protection compliance for standard street-based surveillance cameras (see ICO 2022b). For their LFR operations, the MPS also relied on signs as an attempt to obtain informed consent. These were mainly intended as a means to inform the public they were entering an area of camera coverage. Signs were often positioned in an ad hoc manner that, in turn, depleted their potential to elicit meaningful consent. As the fieldnotes from one deployment in central London relay:

> Central London, 17.12.18: LFR van used as a control room stationed in Cambridge Circus, at a busy intersection between Shaftesbury Avenue and Charing Cross Road. No markings on the van to advertise its purpose. A sign is placed at knee height to inform pedestrians of the LFR operation. Assessing the cameras' field of view from the monitors inside the van, it is clear that any pedestrian could only read the 'warning' sign once they had passed through the zone of recognition and already had their faces scanned.

Figures 7.3. and 7.4 show the relationship between surveillance cameras and the signage designed to inform pedestrians of the operation. In such circumstances it is difficult to consider such consent-gathering mechanisms as anything other than gestural.

Figure 7.3 Positioning of information boards in relation to LFR van, first Soho test deployment (morning deployment at Cambridge Circus, 17/12/2018). Photograph by Pete Fussey, 2018.

Figure 7.4 Positioning of second information board next to LFR van, second Soho test deployment (additional to information boards placed outside the zone of recognition) (Leicester Square, 18/12/2018). Photograph by Pete Fussey, 2018.

Broader questions also apply to whether signage can ever provide sufficient information from which informed consent can be claimed. In addition to the problems of street-level signs containing sparse information is that in complex urban settings such as central London, visual and audible distractions comprise the urban experience. The inevitable response, as Georg Simmel famously wrote in his examination of the psychology of urban life, is to continuously screen out the cacophony of stimuli competing for one's attention; to develop a blasé attitude, as Simmel put it. This operation took place in Leicester Square, the tacky heart of London's tourist district, a location with aspirations to reference Times Square and Shinjuku, replete with stimuli that would overload the senses of any seasoned urban flâneur. Here, attention is rarely grabbed without concerted effort. Unmarked police vans and knee-high signs may exist in plain sight, but they are also routinely ignored. The same dynamic applies for the Metropolitan Police's propensity to deploy facial recognition amid those congregating at London's 'cathedrals of consumption' (Ritzer 2010), at Oxford Street and Stratford's Westfield mall. The point here is not to suggest attempts to gain consent are futile but that existing attempts are little more than symbolic at best.

This view on the absence of meaningful consent was also recognized by members of civil society organizations actively protesting at each facial recognition deployment. Here, director of Big Brother Watch, Silkie Carlo, challenged the extent to which consent is informed or meaningful, and focused especially on the data-processing and biometric-processing aspects:

> No, there's no consent. No, there's no information, so people aren't informed. They're not in any meaningful sense of the word, even the vernacular word or the legal meaning of the word, there's no meaningful consent process whatsoever. You certainly can't withdraw consent. It has real-life significance and legal impacts as well, serious risks to individuals involved. Data collection that people aren't informed about. And biometric data processing . . . We've [probably spoken to] more people than anyone, members of the public, than any other group because we've been at every deployment except the first one in Stratford, we've been at every deployment since the announcement of the trial, when we were in Notting Hill Carnival, the second one, and then Stratford, Romford, Leicester Square, all the rest of it, and we've been there beginning to end handing out leaflets, talking to people. I would struggle to recall anyone who said to me, 'Oh, yes, I know about this.' The people see the sign and go, 'That's good' or 'That's bad', but in a responsive way and . . . I could count on one hand the amount of people we've spoken to

> that seemed to be really informed about what it actually is. (Interviewed March 2019)

A conflation between the delivery of (scant) public information and modes of acquiring consent is at the heart of these practices. At a time of well-publicized declining public support, and a consequent crisis of legitimacy for London's police (see Casey 2023), it is understandable that officials will seek public support for their activities. Consistent across planning meetings was a sense that public support for FRT was important. However, also consistent was an assumption that support for this technology within the police was, in a utilitarian sense, reflected across society,[24] and that others could be persuaded once the benefits were articulated. As such, public information, engagement, and consent gathering—all respective components of data protection, equalities, and human rights legislation—were conflated into simple, and inadequate, public information strategies.

7.4.2.2 Withdrawal of consent without penalty

A less-publicized but nonetheless vital element of meaningful consent concerns the availability of alternative choices and the ability to take them without penalty. This issue has many components. The first, and more benign, element concerns practical inconvenience reaching the same destination while avoiding cameras. This ranged from crossing the street to, in one operation at Stratford, having to take an eighteen-minute walking detour. In this latter case, any notion of consent is heavily caveated by the inconvenience of not consenting.

More controversial was how the police responded to individuals who refused consent by avoiding the camera's gaze, either through covering their faces, actively avoiding the cameras, or otherwise refusing to walk through the zone of recognition. Police responses to such avoidance behaviour

[24] These affective dynamics—principally, the anxiety over persuading the public over FRT's supposedly inherent benefits—manifested in other ways. As described in the Introduction, this research is founded on the authors' appointment by the MPS to conduct an independent human rights review of their LFR operations. On concluding the report, the authors supplied a draft to the MPS with the offer to include a right to reply or to raise any disagreement over matters of objective fact (but not of inference or analysis). Over the five weeks with which the MPS held a pre-publication copy of the report, officials failed to identify a single matter of objective fact yet used a variety of strategies to repeatedly petition the authors to change the 'tone' of the report. As research notes from the time relay (29 May 2019), this included requests to 'include a few lines giving the authors' opinion over the enormous policing benefit of facial recognition', which, at the time, had not been proven by the MPS's own data. While, for obvious reasons, all police attempts to change the content of an independent public report were rejected, it is notable that concerns were focused on the tone rather than substance of public reporting.

varied and, at times, became arbitrary and subjective. As the accounts below reveal, such inconsistencies intersect with complex issues around suspicion and surveillance creep, where the presence of cameras themselves may exert a criminalizing effect.

During the Stratford operations, police planners made an initial attempt to systematize the response to individuals actively avoiding the cameras. However, these attempts served to create rather than remove confusion. During pre-trial briefings, officers were told that anyone avoiding the cameras was 'not an indicator of suspicion' in itself, on account of an individual's right to privacy in a public space (notes from attended pre-operational briefing, London, 26/7/2018). Yet mixed messages were the norm. The same briefings also expressed how a 'turnaround' constituted evidence of LFR working as a 'crime disruption strategy'. Such re-framing allowed refused consent (camera avoidance) to be interpreted as grounds for reasonable suspicion, and hence possible intervention under PACE powers.[25]

Further attempts at clarity were made at the following operations in central London. Here, officers were advised to consider stopping those individuals considered to be 'intentionally' avoiding the cameras. Officers were also instructed to exercise discretion assessing what counted as 'intentional' and the degree to which any camera avoidance could be deemed suspicious. Moreover, this advice further illustrates the complexity, and superficiality, of claims that LFR was operating as an overt form of 'surveillance by consent'. Such guidance opens a further avenue for subjectivity and individual discretion to shape digital facial recognition practices. In reality, this guidance gave officers licence to apprehend any individuals withdrawing their consent to biometric surveillance.

As the following analysis details, these assertions of police discretion hold further practical and legal implications. Taking these in turn, the added workload of processing those avoiding the cameras may undermine arguments that AI-driven surveillance is more efficient and effective than other forms of policing. From a legal and rights-based perspective,

[25] S24 of PACE 1984 was regularly invoked as the legal justification for police to stop someone on the street following a facial recognition match. This was on the grounds that a camera alert established sufficient 'reasonable suspicion' of an individual's criminal involvement. Of additional interest here is that suspicion of 'turnarounds' is foundational to other forms of covert policing. As Maguire and Fussey (2016) document, covertly observing how 'suspects' respond when sighting security assets (armed patrols, police dogs, etc.) from afar is a fundamental part of 'behavioural detection' strategies that seek to identify suspicious behaviour. In other policing contexts, and for clear operational reasons, turning around to avoid FRT cameras *would* be classified as suspicious.

guidance that seemingly imposes limitations on police activities may, in practice, invite the opposite by legitimating more intrusive forms of surveillance. These in turn impact on considerations of necessity and proportionality and, relatedly, of purpose limitation and surveillance creep. This arises through the latitude officers were given to apprehend those avoiding the cameras on the basis of 'intelligence or policing need' (fieldnotes, January 2019). For example, at one of the LFR operations in Romford, east London, three individuals were arrested for clearly attempting to avoid the cameras. As the fieldnotes relay:

> Romford 31/1/2019. Two individuals walked towards the surveillance van along the high street. On spotting the information boards they immediately ran down the side street between the signs and the van. Two officers set off in pursuit and the individuals were detained for a stop and search. Both arrested for drug possession.
>
> Shortly after, a third individual was searched by police after avoiding the LFR van and subsequently arrested for drug-related offences.

Such incidents demonstrate a wider application of LFR beyond the targeting of those directly enrolled on the operational watchlists. Resonating with the arrest for lesser communications offences on Charing Cross Road months before, these incidents could be used to argue how LFR asserts 'diffusion of benefit' (see Tilley 1998). However, two significant arguments exist to challenge such claims; one legal, one operational. From a legal and human rights perspective, LFR was justified and legitimated on the grounds that it was targeting 'serious and violent offenders'. The above episodes demonstrate that when police action is justified on an individual's *reaction to* (not *identification by*) facial recognition, the technology becomes directly implicated in the policing of more minor offences. This in turn complicates the necessity and proportionality calculations surrounding its use. For example, the necessity calculation involved in scanning tens of thousands of passers-by for the purposes of detecting drug possession will be markedly different to that associated with serious violent crimes, which was the basis used in Romford. Moreover, it is beyond argument that the drug possession objectives could be achieved via less intrusive means. In fact, six of the eight arrests connected with this LFR operation were related to individuals avoiding the cameras rather than detections by the technology itself (fieldnotes from operational debrief meeting, 1 February 2019), and thus represent the principal policing outcome of the day. It could be argued that policing outcomes in this regard would have been met regardless of whether the cameras were switched on. Overall, treating LFR camera avoidance as suspicious not only undermines the premise of informed consent; these practices also reveal how LFR use results in an extension of police powers and of 'surveillance creep' (Marx 1989).

In a practical and operational sense, the affordance of LFR technology invites interventions whereby officers become diverted to process these more minor offences. This disrupts police tasking and drains resources. This in turn raises questions over whether other areas of policing are adequately covered. Indeed, the first Romford operation collapsed before its conclusion due to depleted resources. Resources were depleted because officers were tied up processing individuals who had avoided the cameras and therefore were not available to intervene on the street when the FRT system alerted police to a possible match.[26] These less obvious yet significant drains on police resources challenge the much-rehearsed argument that AI-driven surveillance is more efficient and effective than other forms of policing.

Another episode witnessed during this eventful operation received national media attention and reveals a set of deeper issues pertaining to one of the fastest-growing applications of FRT: OIFR. The version of events reported in the media was of a white male issued with a £90 fixed penalty fine for a public order offence after he covered his face to avoid the LFR cameras stationed on the street. Media stories at the time largely ventriloquized social media postings by civil society actors, with the implication that fines were issued for those avoiding the cameras. Author observations and interviews with police present at the time reveal a more nuanced picture, with the individual expressing frustration at being stopped for covering his face, but then proceeding to shout racial abuse in the street. This crucial context was edited from many mainstream media accounts (including by the BBC). According to the police, this, rather than avoiding the cameras, was the reason for the fine. Nevertheless, the existence of FRT generated the environment that escalated the conflict and was not immaterial to its outcome.[27] Also important was the seemingly minor role played by OIFR in

[26] Another factor compounding the scarcity of resources was that an MPS violent crime unit was scheduled to arrive during the afternoon to support the LFR operation. This unit never arrived. When senior officers were asked why this had happened, they explained that the head of the unit 'forgot'.

[27] Individuals working for human rights and other civil society organizations identified other instances of members of the public being stopped by police on the basis that face coverings were deemed suspicious. As Big Brother Watch director Silkie Carlo stated in an interview, 'We saw that at Leicester Square [a Soho trial] as well. We saw a young man who was

this episode. While the individual was being questioned by police, his face is scanned by another officer with a handheld device equipped with OIFR capability. In another superficial and meaningless pretence at gathering consent, this officer informed the subject they were being photographed for comparison to the watchlist as they were taking the photograph. No match was issued because no warrant for this individual existed. This episode also reveals how, as FRT technology becomes available to increasing numbers of operational officers, and given inconsistent understandings of the law as it relates to complex technologies outlined in this chapter, standards of use and compliance with legal basics, such as consent gathering, will become increasingly varied.

made late for work because where it was cold he'd put the scarf over his face and he was ID'd' (interviewed 5 March 2019). This issue is set to intensify given legislation tabled in 2024 that aims to give police additional powers to remove face coverings from protestors under the 2024 Criminal Justice Bill. At present, police officers have the power to demand individuals remove items of clothing intended to conceal their identity if an area is under a (temporary) s60AA order ('section 60 order') of the Criminal Justice and Public Order Act 1994. Similar to street-based identity checks under PACE, failure to comply may give grounds for an arrest. The new legislation will extend this power and give police the authority to make the absence of face coverings a condition under which a protest becomes authorized. Such provisions and conditions run counter to recent United Nations human rights standards on police protest (UNSR 2024), co-drafted by the authors.

8
Human–Technology Interaction during Advanced Surveillance Operations

8.1 Introduction

This chapter examines operational practices associated with live facial recognition (LFR) operations in London. In doing so, it further highlights how, despite the repeated framing of facial recognition technology (FRT) as an objective and precise policing tool, its use is contingent on complex and dynamic human–computer relationships. Moreover, and resonating with issues affecting the creation of watchlist databases, the operational use of FRT surfaces, animates, and is predicated on human subjectivity and discretion.

Rather than offering an advanced and value-neutral capability for law enforcement, FRT is better understood as involving a series of trade-offs. Identification, detection, and recognition technologies work by balancing competing demands. Perhaps central among these is the trade-off between accuracy and efficiency. Optimizing one function of the system may sub-optimize another. For FRT a central trade-off occurs between the numbers of alerts generated and the accuracy of these identifications. When a facial recognition system is deployed, operators have a choice to set a 'similarity score', a sensitivity threshold above which the FRT system will issue alerts. Broadly analogous to a correlation coefficient that statistically measures confidence in a relationship, the sensitivity of FRT systems is set at a value between 0 and 1.[1] A '0' score would mean no confidence in a relationship, a '1' would mean full confidence in the match. Sensitivity thresholds can

[1] This statistic is sometimes incorrectly expressed as the percentage to which the FRT system has matched the source and probe images. The confusion is understandable given the language of 'similarity scores', yet the difference is significance when considering issues of accountability: '*similarity scores* cannot be interpreted as likelihoods, probabilities, or a "percentage match." This is true because each developer emits scores on their own proprietary interval'. See Consensus Study Report (2024: 40).

Facial Recognition Surveillance. Pete Fussey and Daragh Murray, Oxford University Press.
 DOI: 10.1093/9780191979927.003.0008

be increased to gain more accurate results (more 'true positives') but the system would make fewer matches overall. Alternatively, the sensitivity could be reduced to acquire higher numbers of matches, yet many of these are more likely to be inaccurate (more 'false positives'). In the London police FRT deployments analysed here, algorithm developers NEC recommended a threshold score of 0.55. While threshold scores were a source of near-constant debate among operational teams, this threshold remained in place for all surveillance operations observed for this book.[2]

Another trade-off for LFR operations concerns the relationship between system performance and a camera's field of view (the 'zone of recognition'). Selecting a wider-angle view allows cameras to scan larger numbers of faces. Yet the consequence of this decision is to place additional load on computer processing and potential depletion of system performance (see below)[3] as it attempts to analyse this larger quantity of data. However, a more constrained, cropped view also incurs compromises. Most obviously, it will result in fewer faces being scanned, but a cropped image may also exclude vital information useful for engaging with identified suspects. This issue surfaced during the Leicester Square operation of 18 December, as detailed in the ethnographic fieldnotes:

> 18/12/2019, 13:50pm, Leicester Square, London: LFR alert, 0.55 threshold score. A clear image of the face captured by the system but the rest of the suspect's body was outside the frame. A description was radioed through to officers on the ground yet, despite attempts to intercept, it was impossible to provide meaningful detail beyond limited reference to ethnicity and hair colour. The interception space is extremely crowded. Intervention teams could not act because no information on clothing or other useful features could be provided beyond 'male, blond, mid-20s'.

Such incidents point to two important issues affecting LFR performance. The first concerns the inevitable trade-offs that occur once technologies are deployed in practice. For example, choices over how the field of view is framed affect the technological capability of LFR. As Fussey et al.

[2] Davies et al.'s (2018) research into SWP deployments of the same technology reveal more experimentation with FRT sensitivity thresholds. In more recent deployments, the MPS have set their threshold at 0.6.

[3] As noted in Chapter 2, FRT became a more viable law enforcement tool because AI-driven digital architecture allowed image processing to become far more efficient. Operational choices can compromise such efficiency gains.

(2021: 337) argue, 'such decisions rendered some faces visible to the machine yet, in doing so, rendered others invisible'. Second, while emphasis on FRT performance tends to emphasize technical aspects, the resolution of these digital practices requires more traditional aspects of policework; in this case, descriptions of appearance and clothing to facilitate interception.

These trade-offs are not only inherent in digital policing strategies such as FRT, they also highlight how algorithmic processes themselves can be manipulated by human calibration. As such, technological processes cannot be considered outside of their relationship to the socio-technical contexts they are deployed in. Moreover, while such technological outcomes are shaped by their social environments, these environments are themselves simultaneously shaped by the introduction of technology. As discussed below, LFR matches accompanied by a high similarity score often primed human decision-makers to accept the computer's suggestion of a suspicious person.

This chapter draws on ethnographic data to trace through the embedded practices of facial recognition surveillance. Through the empirical analysis of six observed facial recognition operations in London, the chapter argues that policing discretion becomes elevated through all stages of the process. It first examines the highly selective ways seemingly objective measurements of performance are utilized to justify and drive LFR deployments, and how LFR's capabilities are communicated to officers involved in its operation. The majority of the chapter then examines how human operators are brought in to adjudicate algorithmic processes. This theme is particularly significant for attempts to regulate technology and for auditing its suggestions. For example, the perceived ability of humans to judge the validity of computational decisions—a 'human in the loop'—has become an article of faith in recent developments in AI regulation and law. As the data and analysis below reveal, rather than removing error, these combinations may serve both to reinforce error and extend the scope of surveillance operations. Furthermore, human judgement is highly performative and symbolic in these contexts. It offers the appearance of scrutiny yet regularly fails to fulfil this role. In so doing, such attempts may serve to *reduce* accountability because they signify regulation, yet the task is executed inadequately. In other respects, examining LFR *in practice* reveals how measures intended to introduce accountability resulted in the extension of surveillance practices across scale, scope, and space. Taken together, current faith in human–machine accountability mechanisms generates a dual disadvantage: they may extend surveillance and reduce the effectiveness of its oversight.

8.2 Live Facial Recognition Performance in London

As the discussion above relays, objective and consensual understandings of LFR performance are often difficult to ascertain. The study closest to the research presented here is the review of South Wales Police's (SWP's) FRT operations between 2017 and 2018 (Davies et al. 2018). Both SWP and the Metropolitan Police Service (MPS) used the same NEC facial recognition algorithms, initially adopting NEC's 'M17' algorithm before transitioning to the much better-performing 'S20' algorithm during 2018. Notwithstanding the methodological differences that deplete the meaningfulness of direct comparisons between South Wales and London, the SWP evaluation claimed a 3 per cent 'confirmed true positive' rate for the M17 algorithm and an improved 26 per cent performance for the M20 algorithm (Davies et al. 2018).

The data presented here mostly focuses on six MPS LFR deployments between June 2018 and February 2019 where ethnographic research was conducted. Averaging the published statistics from the MPS's self-evaluation of these deployments, the MPS claim an overall 'false positive identification rate' of 0.085 per cent and a 'true positive identification rate' of 73.5 per cent (National Physical Laboratory and Metropolitan Police Service 2020). The latter measure was used to support MPS claims in the national media that their LFR system was 'at least 70% effective' (*The Guardian* 2020). However, as noted above, the MPS used different data sets depending on the argument they advanced. In every instance, the data set selected was the one most likely to present a positive impression of LFR performance. Such statistics conceal other stories too. For example, a 0.0 per cent false-positive rate is claimed for the port of MPS–Humberside Police deployment at the Port of Hull in June 2018. Less explicit in the analysis is the fact that, during its five hours of deployment, the false-positive rate was zero because the system failed to match any faces at all. Accordingly, the unacknowledged true-positive rate for those on the watchlist was also 0.0 per cent. Relatedly, at the Stratford Westfield deployment in London during July 2018, a 0.01 per cent false-positive rate is claimed (National Physical Laboratory and Metropolitan Police Service 2020). However, this operation, observed by the authors, yielded a single alert during an entire eight-hour operation, which incorrectly matched a female student of African-Caribbean heritage to a database entry of a 'wanted' suspect. Put another way, the seeming effectiveness of this 0.01 per cent false-positive rate is undermined by the material fact that 100 per cent of LFR alerts were incorrect.

The MPS conducted ten deployments of LFR technology in London between 2016 and 2019. The authors were invited to conduct ethnographic research and to prepare an independent report covering the final six of these 'trials'. Tables 8.1 and 8.2 set out the details of these test deployments including the number of matches made by the LFR system and watchlist size.[4]

Table 8.1 MPS LFR deployments occurring before research commenced

Trial	Date	Number of LFR matches	Watchlist size	Facial recognition algorithm
Notting Hill Carnival 2016	28–29/8/2016	1	266	NEC S17
Notting Hill Carnival 2017	27–28/8/2017	96	528	NEC S17
Remembrance Sunday 2017	12/11/2017	7	42	NEC S17
Humberside Port 2018	13–14/6/2018	0	144	NEC M20

Table 8.2 Observed MPS LFR deployments

Trial	Date	Number of LFR matches	Watchlist size	Facial recognition algorithm
Stratford 1	28/6/2018	5	489	NEC M20
Stratford 2	26/7/2018	1	306	NEC M20
Soho 1	17/12/2018	5	2226	NEC M20
Soho 2	18/12/2018	9	2226	NEC M20
Romford 1	31/1/2019	10	2401	NEC M20
Romford 2	14/2/2019	16	1996	NEC M20

The MPS facial recognition system matched forty-six passers-by to watchlist entries over the course of the observed operations. Four of these matches are excluded from the analysis. One of these was excluded because it was a duplicate alert. This occurred during the January 2019 operation

[4] The first four test deployments were not observed by the researchers; data was provided to the authors by the MPS facial recognition technical evaluation team.

in Romford, London. Here, the same individual was matched twice at separate times the same afternoon. While this was a correct match to someone on the watchlist, the watchlist itself was out of date. This individual had been processed by the courts and was therefore in no sense 'wanted' during the weeks it took to compile the watchlist and launch the LFR operation.[5] The second match was discounted by the intelligence teams adjudicating the LFR images in light of the knowledge that the database was out of date. A further three matches were also discounted. Here, alerts occurred after the MPS facial recognition van was deployed and technical infrastructure switched on. However, the street-based intervention teams tasked with stopping and checking the identities of matched individuals were not in place. Therefore, no capacity existed to confirm any alerts.

Overall, forty-two matches are included in the analysis that follows. MPS officers judged computer-generated LFR matches sufficiently credible to stop individuals and perform an identity check on twenty-six of these occasions. Four of these twenty-six attempted interventions were unsuccessful. This usually occurred because the matched individual was lost in a crowd. Of the remaining twenty-two stops, fourteen were verified as incorrect matches following an identity check. Eight were verified as correct matches following an identity check (Table 8.3).

Table 8.3 Numbers and percentages of correct and incorrect matches from completed identity checks

Attempts to stop an individual following (i) a computer-generated match and (ii) human adjudication as credible	Individuals **actually stopped** for an identity check	**Incorrect matches** among individuals stopped for an identity check	**Correct matches** among individuals stopped for an identity check	Percentage of incorrect matches among individuals stopped for an identity check (14 of 22 stops)	Percentage of correct matches among individuals stopped for an identity check (8 of 22 stops)
26	22	14	8	63.64%	36.36%

[5] This case was also excluded by the MPS in their own analysis of the same operations (National Physical Laboratory and Metropolitan Police Service 2020: 20). In the interests of balance, it is important to note that, had the MPS included this in their analysis, it would have presented a more positive picture of the LFR deployment. A duplicate match also occurred at Stratford in June 2018. This incident is included in the analysis because the police treated each alert as separate and tried to apprehend the same individual on both occasions despite it being a confirmed false match the first time.

This should not be interpreted as showing that computer-generated matches were *only* correct on eight occasions, but that they were only *verifiably correct* on eight occasions. Without checking the individual's identity, for example when a matched individual is subsequently lost in the crowd, it is impossible to know if a match adjudicated to be credible was a true or false positive.

In sum, the MPS LFR system made forty-two matches eligible for analysis here. Twenty-six of these were judged as credible by a human operator. Sixteen were judged as non-credible. Of these twenty-six matches deemed credible, twenty-two suspects were stopped and had their identities checked. Fourteen were discovered to be incorrect matches once their identity was confirmed by other means. Judging LFR outcomes on the actual numbers of alerts and factual numbers of verifiably correct and incorrect matches reveals significantly more modest performance than the above evaluations that dilute these statistics with estimates of populations flows. For example, using the same data,[6] the official MPS report of these same operations claimed an averaged false-positive rate of 0.08 per cent (NPL and MPS 2020).[7] This claim was made despite 63.64 per cent of alerts being verifiably *incorrect* and only 19.05 per cent of alerts being verifiably *correct*. Such assertions demonstrate how poorly suited the standard lab-based framing of false-positive statistics is for meaningfully conveying the operational, social, and human rights impacts of FRT.

8.2.1. Algorithmic performance and database size

As discussed in Chapter 5, considerable controversy accompanies the issue of watchlists. Among these debates, the criteria for inclusion and the size of the watchlists are particularly prominent. The former issue is discussed in the previous chapter. The size of watchlists was a key topic of discussion in MPS planning meetings ahead of each LFR operation. Such deliberations incorporated many considerations including, notably the labour involved in compiling watchlists and the availability of potential candidates. For example, early in the fieldwork, one tactical MPS planner suggested

[6] Researcher and operational MPS data was compared and corroborated during debriefing sessions following each deployment.

[7] MPS published the following false-positive statistics for Stratford 1 (0.05), Stratford 2 (0.01), Soho 1 (0.1), Soho 2 (0.1), Romford 1 (0.10), and Romford 2 (0.13) (NPL and MPS 2020).

that around 17,000 individuals could be classified as 'wanted' across the Greater London area, and that these should be eligible for enrolment on a facial recognition watchlist. Such ambitions encountered both practical and legal challenges. The former are detailed in Chapter 7 while specific human rights considerations are addressed in Chapter 6. While these limitations persisted, watchlists prepared for the full operational launch of LFR in 2022 often exceeded 9,000 individuals (MPS 2022). More recently, since June 2024, watchlists of over 15,000 individuals are routine, with deployments in East Ham (2 August) and Stratford (8 August) exceeding 16,000 (MPS 2024b).

It was often argued during MPS facial recognition planning meetings that larger watchlists would result in increased numbers of matches. This reasoning was used on several occasions and was instrumental in driving substantial increases in watchlist size throughout the research period. Such deliberations were not necessarily grounded in any evidence or analysis of LFR performance. As the data below establishes, this relationship is complex. To illustrate, the proportion of matches to watchlist size was highest at the first Stratford trial, despite the watchlist being comparatively smaller than that used in other test deployments. Interestingly, this trial was also the shortest of any of the observed deployments, leaving less available time for matches to be made (Table 8.4).

Table 8.4 LFR alerts and watchlist sizes

Trial	Date	Number of computer-generated LFR matches	Watchlist size	Ratio of LFR matches to watchlist size
Stratford 1	28/6/2018	5	489	1:97.80
Stratford 2	26/7/2018	1	306	1:306.00
Soho 1	17/12/2018	5	2226	1:445.20
Soho 2	18/12/2018	9	2226	1:247.33
Romford 1	31/1/2019	10	2401	1:240.10
Romford 2	14/2/2019	16	1996	1:124.75

Taken together, the data reveals how any firm conclusions over LFR performance and watchlist size are difficult to establish. It is also important to recognize how such calculations, outcomes, and ratios are influenced by a range of additional and unaccounted for variables. Most obvious is the absence of any statistical calibration depending on whether such matches are accurate or not. Other considerations include the time in which the LFR system was active and the density of crowds passing the cameras. The recent wave of LFR deployments in London also demonstrates the absence of a correlative relationship between watchlist size and numbers of alerts.[8]

8.3 Human Adjudication of Algorithmic Processes

In an operational law enforcement setting, computer-issued alerts are one element of a much larger sphere of practice shaping the use of FRT. Even within the short temporal parameters of an active operation, much happens between an FRT alert and the resolution of activity it inspires.

Particularly important to this process is how LFR matches are adjudicated by human operators. Here, the human in the loop has been consistently advanced as a corrective to concerns over the unaccountability of algorithmic processes. Human assessment of computational processes is not only seen as an essential solution to perceived threats of algorithmic power, they also resonate with a powerful narrative of the triumph of human over machine and offer relief from nightmares of powerful unaccountable and unintelligible technology. Human arbitration of digital policing processes is expressed in many forms. For example, one common refrain is that technology constitutes a 'decision support rather than decision-making' mechanism or, as (then) Home Secretary Priti Patel claimed, 'decisions about people will always be made by people' (House of Lords 2021: 47). These framings have since extended to include the modifying adverb, adding that human review of digital processes must be conducted *meaningfully*.

Recognition of the need to interpose meaningful human deliberations into automated processes is reflected in a suite of existing and emerging international legal and regulatory provisions. These including the European Union (EU) General Data Protection Regulation (GDPR) and Law Enforcement Directive, the EU AI Act 2024, and New York City's Algorithmic Accountability Bill of 2018. In the UK, section 49 of the 2018

[8] In 2024, LFR deployments in London utilized watchlists of between 12,000 and 15,000 individuals. Alert rates ranged from a minimum of zero to a maximum of sixteen, with no discernible relation to the size of the watchlist.

Data Protection Act holds that a 'significant decision' over individuals may not be made exclusively on the basis of an automated decision 'unless that decision is required or authorised by law'. Predating this, and with additional relevance to law enforcement FRT operations, the role of meaningful human intervention was highlighted in the first iteration of England and Wales's Surveillance Camera Code of Practice of 2013:

> Any use of facial recognition or other biometric characteristic recognition systems needs to clearly justified and proportionate in meeting the stated purpose, and be suitably validated. It should always involve human intervention before decisions are taken that affect an individual. (Home Office 2013: 4)

This notion is developed in national guidance, tailored specially to police uses of LFR technology:

> 4.53. A fundamental ingredient of the lawful use of LFR as part of a police operation is that there can be no decision making by the technology. Decision making should only be made by a human decision maker and not an algorithm . . .
>
> 4.59. Human decision making should be meaningful and guard against a tendency to defer to an algorithm by simply agreeing with or endorsing all outcomes of the LFR system. To do so would simply be to render decision making as being essentially automated. (Surveillance Camera Commissioner 2020: 49–50)

The above stresses how meaningful human intervention is a legal and regulatory requirement for police uses of computer-driven processes. Yet this stipulation for human involvement also generates several crucial issues, one of which holds significant human rights implications: it is not only *whether* human intervention takes place; the *nature* of the adjudication is also of significance. Accordingly, to what degree is human scrutiny of digital processes meaningful? What is the definition or threshold for a 'significant' or meaningful (human) decision? Is it possible to separate computer and human decision-making processes in this way?

The following sections empirically analyse human and technical interactions in live police operational uses of facial recognition. The data reveals the complex interrelationships between algorithmic classifications of suspicion and human discretion in policing contexts. The analysis is driven by the theoretical thrust of this book concerning the intricate interplay—and co-construction—of digital policing tools and their operational environments. A central argument here is that human adjudication of technological processes does not occur in a vacuum. These two 'human' and 'digital' realms do not exist in isolation, uncontaminated by the other. Consequently, the data also shows how faith in human operators' ability to moderate algorithmic bias and other digital errors is overstated and predicated on an oversimplified view of human–machine interaction. Simple human–machine binaries, where an operator is considered an objective arbitrator of technological processes, somehow untouched by normative and subjective values, are thus considered inadequate for understanding and mediating technologies such as FRT in their live operational environments. As science and technology studies (STS) have long established, and as demonstrated here, a complex dialogue exists between technology and its environment. Indeed, dismantling such human–computer binaries has been a core project in the philosophy of science over several decades. As Latour argued in his critique of Heidegger's concept of technology,[9] 'the myth of the Neutral Tool under complete human control and the myth of the Autonomous Destiny that no human can master are symmetrical' (Latour 1999: 178). There is no binary opposition between the human and the technical, and neither elicit decisions in a value-free realm.

8.3.1 From Alert to Resolution

The MPS's approach to addressing computer-issued facial recognition alerts is set out in Figure 8.1. Ethnographic observation of both the control room-based intelligence units and street-deployed intervention teams for these same operations reveals a more complex picture. Discrete parts of the workflow often became combined and, in the process, reshaped. Additionally, the 'agreed protocols' guiding the resolution of alerts were highly inconsistent, at times chaotic, and consistently impacted by individual, environmental, technological, and operational factors (detailed below). Taken together, these complex interactions demonstrate the ways FRT becomes shaped and conditioned through its live operational environments.

[9] Latour's essay is positioned as an attack on Heidegger's concept of technology. However, as Riis (2018) accurately argues, despite his critique Latour's argument owes a debt to Heidegger.

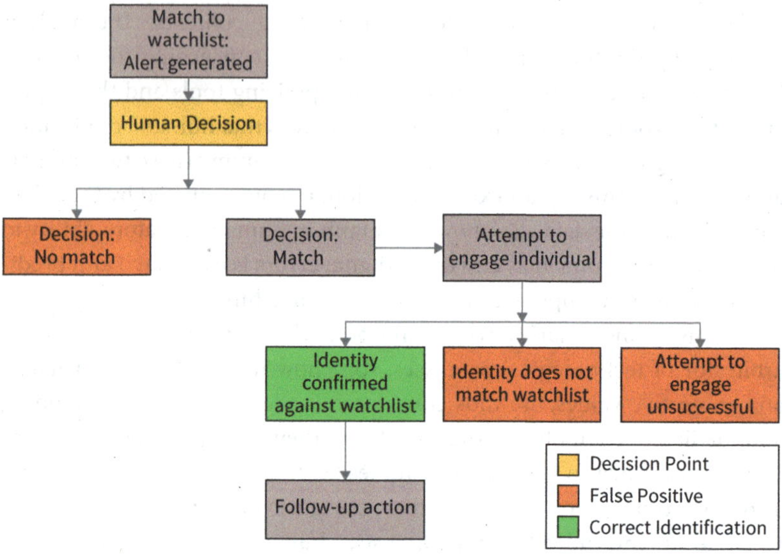

Figure 8.1 Flowchart detailing MPS action plan following a facial recognition match (derived from NPL and MPS 2020: 15).

While deployment practices are sometimes complex in nature, three key moments define operational LFR processes. One is the computer-issued alert itself. Yet it is the latter two events that bring human and computational decision-making together. The first of these is the review of computer-generated matches to watchlist images by intelligence officers. This element has received particular attention in commentaries on facial recognition considering the claimed potential for human adjudication as an appropriate safeguard. The second of these socio-technical moments has thus far received scant consideration, yet is key to both the overall outcome of FRT practices and their human rights implications: how confirmed matches are resolved on the street.

For the purposes of explanation, it is helpful to set out the two distinct policing teams involved in this operation. The first is the 'intelligence unit' stationed in the FRT-equipped control room (normally a van). These receive the initial computer alert and conduct the initial assessment of its credibility. The second group are street-based intervention teams tasked with intercepting the matched individual, assessing their identity, and pursuing any further action. A variety of tools are used to connect these two units. Most frequently, teams communicated through two-way radio and verbal descriptions of matched individuals. As the operational trials progressed, street-based intervention teams were equipped with mobile devices that would receive LFR alerts at the same time as the intelligence units.

FRT systems are designed to alert operators to someone of potential interest passing the cameras. As such, the FRT system suggests an identity which, for intelligence units, offers grounds for suspicion. The intended process for the MPS operations was: once an alert was deemed credible by the human operator, action would be taken to confirm a 'suspect's' identity, an activity normally tasked to downstream intervention teams. Under these circumstances an individual would be approached and asked for identification. Pre-operational briefings given to intervention teams advised that if matched individuals did not possess, or refused to provide, credible identification, s24 of the Police and Criminal Evidence Act (PACE) 1984 could be used to offer power of arrest. This was based on the interpretation that an LFR alert established sufficient 'reasonable suspicion' that the individual was involved in the commission (or attempted commission) of an offence. This is a fundamentally problematic assumption for a number of reasons. First, the prevalence of incorrect matches was a well-known phenomenon and one that was evident from any basic analysis of operational statistics. This means an often significant number of those stopped would be individuals with no connection whatsoever to any watchlist-related offence. Second, not everyone on the watchlist is there because they have committed, or are suspected of committing, an offence. As discussed in detail in Chapter 5, the watchlist includes much wider categories of people than suspected offenders, including missing persons and persons of intelligence interest to the police (potentially as a witness to an offence or individuals who may provide information relevant to the investigation of an offence). S24 PACE does not provide legal authority to determine these individuals' identity.

8.3.2 The Human Adjudication of Digital Facial Recognition Matches

In line with applicable standards, and signalling an intent to bring human oversight into the FRT operational process, all observed officer briefings were clear on the importance of human adjudication. Particularly common was a variation of this instruction issued for the first Stratford operation:

> an alert is never treated as a sole indication that a positive match has been secured. Officers are expected to conduct further checks to confirm [the matched individual's] identity including the use of INK technology [for on-the-spot fingerprinting]. (Facial Recognition Pre-Operational Briefing, Stratford, London, 16/6/2018)

Officers were instructed that a computer-derived match was not sufficient to confirm an identity in and of itself. Given the poor performance and significant error rates observed, such caution appears appropriate. However, the stated importance of human adjudication of LFR matches—typically phrased as variants of 'human engagement is critical' and 'generation of an alert should never be treated as a sole indicator of suspicion'—was regularly undermined by expressions of techno-evangelism. Resonating with the above theme of the politicizing of technical evaluations to portray LFR in its most positive light, pre-operational briefings often eulogized the presumed capabilities and policing value of the technology. For example, in two operational briefings for street-based intervention teams, messaging on the importance of human judgement was undermined with misleading and incorrect statements that 'it is 100 per cent effective in spotting those uploaded into the system' (senior MPS officer, 28 June 2018) and 'the technology is very accurate, despite misinformation' (senior MPS officer, 24 July 2018). Not only did such mixed messages undermine important emphasis on, and the legal requirement for, meaningful human adjudication, they also contradicted some of the more nuanced views of those actually operating the technology. This tendency to advance unevidenced claims as to LFR's effectiveness and utility persists into the contemporary policy framework (Chapter 5).

It is also possible to identify a deeper and more enduring issue operating across the whole lifecycle of FRT deployments here. This involves the introduction of policy with the ostensible goal of governing the operation of FRT. Yet, in the process of doing so, these policies assert a different role, one that advocates for, rather than governs, the technology. From planning to deployment, these policies subtly frame the technology in a way that underscores and reinforces its effectiveness before it has been deployed and tested. This works as a more unobtrusive form of technological determinism, delivering strategic narratives that legitimate its use and prime its users.

Pre-operational briefings also provided street-based intervention teams with a script with which to recite when requesting an identity check with a matched individual. This was:

> The MPS are conducting facial recognition trials in this area (here is a leaflet). You have passed through the area and an alert has been generated. As such we are requesting your name so that we can verify your identity and the accuracy of the alert. (Ethnographic fieldnotes from pre-operational briefings, Saville Row Police Station, London, 17/12/2018; Romford Police Station, London, 31/1/2019)

Identity checks typically involved an initial request for matched individuals to produce an identity document.[10] If this was not provided, officers used mobile fingerprint scanners ('Mobile Ink' technology). Reliance on s61(6A) PACE to authorize the use of mobile fingerprint scanners in this context gives rise to the same problems raised above in relation to s24 PACE. Specifically, there are known issues with false positives (giving rise to a likelihood that it is the FRT system, and not the individual, that is providing a false name), and more importantly only some of the individuals on the watchlist are suspected of committing an offence.[11] Moreover, in the heat of an LFR operation, when street-based intervention teams are tasked with quickly locating individuals in a crowd, the supply of information from the control room is focused and limited to physical descriptions and their movement through space. Across all observed operations, the reason for someone's membership on the watchlist was never communicated. Hence, while the law discriminates on who is eligible to have their fingerprints taken without consent, in practice on-street officers did not.

Refusal to comply with a request for fingerprinting was interpreted as legal grounds for arrest based on reasonable suspicion that an individual was wanted (as indicated by the FRT system). This precise issue arose at

[10] Unlike other European countries, the obligation to carry identity documentation is not a legal requirement in the UK.

[11] S61(6A) PACE authorizes a constable to take fingerprints without consent, if 'the constable reasonably suspects that the person is committing or attempting to commit an offence, or has committed or attempted to commit an offence' and '(a) the name of the person is unknown to, and cannot be readily ascertained by, the constable; [or]

(b) the constable has reasonable grounds for doubting whether a name furnished by the person as his name is his real name'.

one of the Romford operations when a matched individual refused to have their fingerprints taken on the street. Officers then elected to arrest the individual and escort them to a police station for additional identity checks. This facilitates a self-reinforcing process. Any incorrect FRT match could be interpreted as giving rise to suspicion that a matched individual was offering a false name, and thus offer (potential) grounds to perform an identity or fingerprint check, regardless of the accuracy of the system.

Several corollary effects emerge from the overall identification process. Many are demonstrated by the incident relayed in Chapter 7 on Charing Cross Road in central London. In this case, an individual was wrongly identified by the cameras and gave a name that did not match the watchlist record when questioned. Using PACE powers, officers then obligated the individual to submit to a mobile fingerprint scan, which revealed he was wanted for a lesser offence. The offence related to malicious communications and would have fallen below the threshold of seriousness required to be enrolled on the operational watchlist. This episode demonstrates the ways in which technologies such as FRT are mediated by their relationship to other digital infrastructure. The availability of one related biometric technological instrument (mobile fingerprint scanner) enabled what was for the police a serendipitous arrest. As explored below, other elements of the digital assemblage also acquire significance during the course of LFR deployments. For example, failures in other components of the digital ecosystem, such as mobile tablets issued to intervention teams, were also critical to the outcome of facial recognition operations.

Overall, human assessment of computer-issued facial recognition alerts was a near constant across all observed operations. The first human judgement to overrule a computational match occurred midway through the third observed LFR operation.[12] This was judged as a non-credible match on the basis that the computer matched a passer-by with a database image of a much older female. While definitive trends are difficult to ascertain from small frequencies, the rate of disconfirming alerts became more frequent following this initial occurrence, and may suggest that as human users habituate to a technology, the confidence to scrutinize it may grow.

[12] Alert 3 of the first Soho test deployment, 17 December 2018.

Table 8.5 Human adjudication rates for facial recognition alerts in London

Total number of computer-issued LFR matches eligible for analysis	Cases adjudicated as credible by police officers	Cases conclusively adjudicated as non-credible by officers
42	26 (61.9%)	16 (38.1%)

However, as Table 8.5 shows, a discernible tendency existed for operators to accept computer-issued suggestions and use this as a basis for intercepting someone on the street. Particularly notable is how humans tended to be deferential to the algorithm *even though the computer was not verifiably correct, and was known to be not verifiably correct, on most occasions*. In other words, the majority of computer-suggested matches were judged as credible, even though they were not accurate and, as operations progressed, were known to be not accurate. As such, across different operations and decision-making arrangements a discernible 'presumption to intervene' existed. Here, human discretion became ceded to algorithmic identifications of suspicious individuals regardless of their accuracy. Such outcomes raise significant questions over the way human adjudication is framed as a means of ensuring algorithmic accountability.

Significant here is the consideration of why such deference to the computer may occur. However, rather than assuming human operators automatically cede agency to algorithmic suggestions, closer inspection reveals complexity surrounding the human decision-making process. As the data below reveals, myriad digital affordances and environmental, cultural, individual, and operational factors assert themselves to condition police discretion in relation to digital facial recognition processes. To adequately address this complexity, it is first necessary to set out the considerable variance in the sites and arrangements that formed the environments in which such human decisions were made.

8.3.2.1 Varied human-in-the-loop regimes and the presumption to intervene

A central argument of this chapter questions the degree to which human scrutiny of AI-driven processes is meaningful. A related, yet underexplored, element of this issue concerns the composition of human-in-the-loop practices, the ways in which human adjudication is practised. Together, these points raise questions over whether objective and meaningful human adjudication is possible in current LFR operational contexts, particularly when considering the temporal, operational, and environmental factors at play.

Moreover, decision-making processes varied across operations. Particularly significant was inconsistency over where primary decision-making authority rested. For example, primacy regularly shifted between decisions made by intelligence units in a control room and, on other occasions, by street-based intervention teams. While human adjudication practices were highly inconsistent, three distinct arenas for decision-making were discernible: multiple human adjudicators in the control room; simultaneous street-based and control room adjudication; and street-based adjudication using mobile technologies. It is also important to note that these shifts also occurred in the context of other changes, such as increases in watchlist sizes, differing availabilities of support teams, diverse geographical settings, and the inconsistent performance of communications technology (see below).

A key outcome of these human–technical interactions is, regardless of how decision-making arrangements were structured, different regimes of human scrutiny routinely *exacerbated rather than mitigated* algorithmic inaccuracy. Moreover, additional forms of scrutiny tended to reproduce and reinforce computer-generated grounds (the 'alert') for intercepting someone on the street. This regression *from* the mean brought by different human-in-the-loop arrangements elevated the likelihood that suggested matches would be confirmed, rather than challenged, a processes characterized here as 'the presumption to intervene'.

The first category of human scrutiny of LFR comprises multiple adjudicators in the control room. The intelligence teams reviewing LFR footage varied in number and location. The standard practice involved at least two officers monitoring surveillance camera feeds and alerts from laptops equipped with facial recognition software. These 'ideal' arrangements often varied during long, often cold, and frequently eventless operations. For example, at times, a solitary officer remained at this post. On other occasions, particularly on very cold days, the surveillance van was extremely crowded. The central London deployments also saw the occasional inclusion of MPS 'super recognizers'.[13] While the role of 'super recognizers' was mostly focused on street-level intervention, had they been involved in control room decision-making, an interesting question would arise over the credence

[13] See Chapter 1.

given to such perceived expert knowledge when disagreements arose over the veracity of computer matches.

Adding to numbers in the LFR control room was a frequent stream of 'visitors'. These included curious members of MPS staff and officers seeking respite from the near-constant presence of media and members of civil society organizations staging protests and counter-leafleting campaigns at each operation. The headline-grabbing nature of FRT also brought repeated attempts from outside parties to fleetingly observe proceedings inside the control room. These included brief visits from regulators such as representatives from the Information Commissioner's Office (ICO) and Biometrics Commissioner's Office. While some visits fell within regulatory duties, others were born from different motivations. On one occasion in central London, the intelligence unit was 'doorstepped' by an interested member of the House of Lords who, on overcoming initial objections to access the van, proceeded to occupy the adjudicator's chair to interrogate officers on basic questions long since answered on the FAQ section of the MPS website. The visitor then took to social media to inaccurately describe his self-proclaimed role in holding the police to account. Such episodes no doubt added distraction and difficulty to adjudication tasks.

Each LFR alert punctuated the typical ennui of police surveillance operations. Ensuing excitement and activity often brought more individuals into the adjudication process. While multiple operators are often considered a means to bring additional scrutiny to LFR alerts (see NPL and MPS 2020), this also raised the likelihood of disagreements within the same adjudication team. A question then arises of how such disparities are resolved.

Across all different human-in-the-loop configurations, contrasting opinions were most often resolved with a decision to *confirm* rather than challenge computer decisions and attempt to apprehend the matched individual. This phenomenon resonates with a central argument advanced by this book, that the combination of different approaches to algorithmic auditing offers an impression of accountability. However, the operational realities of implementing these measures result in an extension of surveillance. In this setting, the operational reality of reconciling differences gives the impression of meaningful supervision, yet the default towards accepting computer-issued matches means human adjudication serves to reproduce and amplify errors.[14]

[14] An interesting conceptual parallel exists here with psychological concepts of 'risky shift' and its replacement 'group polarization', where oppositional views become reconciled into one extreme position rather than a compromised average. Using this lens to consider how

An example of the way different adjudication processes may reinforce, rather than mitigate, incorrect matches is evident in the events following one LFR match in Leicester Square, London:

> 17 December 2018, Leicester Square, London, 14:22pm: Fourth match of the day (0.57 score). The officer adjudicating images attempts to radio a request to observe a suspect. Responding to failures of both the radio and mobile tablets, he leant out of the van and tried to radio again. When this failed, he took off after the suspect on foot. By this time the individual had crossed almost the length of Leicester Square. Limited adjudication time. Decision-making was near instant. Meanwhile, the second adjudicating officer with more time identified significant differences between the probe and gallery images. The gallery image had moles on the suspect's face, the probe image had none. While difficult to ascertain at first, most tellingly they had different-colour eyes. A false positive.

A second category of adjudication involved the simultaneous, rather than sequential, decision-making by control room-based intelligence units and street-based intervention teams. This involved intelligence officers radioing through a description of an LFR match *while they were still in the process of deliberating over the credibility of the alerted match*. A decision to trigger the street intervention teams to keep sight of a matched individual may arise from sound operational reasons. For example, it may buy intelligence officers important 'thinking time' when under pressure to decide on the veracity of computer matches while allowing the intervention team to start looking for the matched individual before losing sight of them. Indeed, this tactic formed a core approach for one observed SWP LFR operation in Swansea during July 2019. Here, matched individuals were tracked by traditional street-based surveillance cameras while intelligence units came to a decision. In London, however, every single instance in which this simultaneous approach was adopted led to an attempt to engage a matched individual. In other words, every time an intervention team was tasked to watch someone to buy adjudication time resulted in an active attempt to intercept a matched individual. This includes instances when intelligence units ultimately adjudicated that the LFR system had not supplied a credible match,

aggregation of human-digital knowledge regimes compound, rather than mediate, error in digital policing contexts could constitute a fecund area of enquiry. For example, a key driver of this phenomenon is likely to relate to the diffusion of responsibility across human and computer 'actants' in LFR processes.

for example when the adjudication decision came after someone was apprehended or was overruled by teams on the street. Alerting the street team always resulted in an engagement, irrespective of the control room adjudication decision. Such episodes underscore two enduring themes inherent in the facial recognition operations: the presumption to intervene and the coercive outcomes of multiple possible adjudication points. Regarding the latter, operational arrangements of multiple adjudication points, again, did not lead to one to correct another but, rather, provide a further opportunity for interceptions to take place.

As currently formulated, existing framings of 'human-in-the-loop' remedies for algorithmic bias contain an inherent ontological fallacy: that the human and the technical audit and correct each other towards an apotheosis of an objective 'truth'. Such critiques resonate with Foucault's (2008) emphasis on the way truth claims are produced, sanctioned, and valorized through 'regimes of veridiction' as discussed in Chapter 2. Yet, in addition to overstating the capacity of human scrutiny, this framing of human–computer interaction as a mode of accountability, where the former corrects the latter, also offers detail on how such truth claims are constituted, reproduced, and legitimized. Indeed, further insights could be drawn from Foucault's tutor, Georges Canguillhem (1979), whose major intellectual project critiqued the ways highly normative truth claims become constituted in science. This again underscores how FRT may be considered as both political and politicized. The former is evidenced through its uneven demographic focus, the latter through its positioning as an objective science, and one calibrated towards ever-increasing precision by its human overseers. Indeed, statements such as 'Live Facial Recognition technology is a precise community crime fighting tool', as the MPS director of intelligence stated in mid-2023 (MPS 2023g), have become commonplace as the FRT deployments expand.[15] Yet the complexities, affordances, and normative practices that condition facial recognition use challenge these politicized appeals to scientific objectivity. As Monahan (2022: 7) elegantly argues in his analysis of the 'cultural production of surveillance',

> objective vision is a violent parsing of the world that constructs elements as separate from context and subject to manipulation. Even if its

[15] Such claims would also invite the question of whether something so precise would require extensive correction by human agents.

> modalities shift over time, objective vision is a political achievement masquerading as a disinterested scientific posture.

As documented throughout this book, this politicization of scientific (and legal) discourse is a common feature in the legitimating narratives surrounding facial recognition. This is further evidenced in the polemical aggrandisement of inadequate evaluative studies that claim an absence of ethnic and gendered algorithmic bias in police facial recognition systems (e.g. NPL 2023). Accordingly, in the context of facial recognition surveillance practices, notions of scientific objectivity can be considered an oxymoron.

8.3.2.2 From adjudicating to amplifying suspicion

The third variety of human adjudication occurred through the use of mobile technologies issued to street-based intervention teams. These devices have become a common feature of facial recognition operations, now often referred to as operator-initiated facial recognition (OIFR). These smartphone or mini-tablet handheld devices were equipped with software that had the capacity to receive alerts and—when data records were complete—access the watchlist. Further demonstrating the influence of the socio-technical contexts of FRT, how these technologies were deployed and used in real-time operations significantly impacted the scope and impact of deployments. Understanding the implications of these technologies requires a more precise explanation of how they were used in practice.

While often presented as a distinct technology, OIFR has become an integral part of LFR deployments. In later operations, the LFR system would send alerts to the adjudication operators in the control room and to the intervention team's OIFR handheld devices at the same time. One significant difference existed in the digital architecture the technology used by each group. Alerts sent to the intelligence units would only occur if a match exceeded the threshold score (described above), set at 0.55 in conformity with the manufacturer's recommendations. The system would show these groups one image, that of the matched individual. The mobile devices used by street-based officers also received the same alerts when this threshold was triggered. However, the handheld devices were configured in a way to receive a range of possible matches, including the records of others listed on the watchlist below the 0.55 threshold. Matches given the highest confidence score were at the top of the list. This meant watchlist records hidden to the intelligence units because they did not reach the requisite threshold of similarity would become visible to street-based police teams. Despite both units being implicated in human-in-the-loop adjudication processes, street-based intervention teams were thus receiving information and images for computer-issued LFR matches in a far less filtered form. Handheld devices also had the added functionality where they could be used to take photographs of individuals and compare against the custody image database directly. The affordances and implications of these varied capabilities are examined below.

It is also important to note the variation with which these devices were used in London and their differential impact on LFR processes. In the four Stratford and Soho operations, small tablet-sized devices were issued to members of the intervention teams on the street. Yet technical failures—typically problems with poor data connectivity beyond 20 metres and constant network dropouts—led to street-based officers complaining over being encumbered with poorly performing kit. This resulted in their abandonment, with tablets handed back to the technical team and lying unused on a desk for much of these operations. Officers were then unable to view images of suspects and became reliant on radioed descriptions of individuals they were pursuing. As such, analogue equipment became crucial to fulfilling the promise of cutting-edge digital law enforcement tools. These devices were replaced with smaller smartphone-sized devices in the two later Romford test deployments, where they were used extensively.

While various uses and perceived benefits of these devices were expressed in operational briefings and other MPS planning meetings, two principal applications were most prominent. The first was the claim that handheld devices would assist street-based intervention teams with the location of individuals matched by the LFR system. As outlined above, a typical scenario would be that once a computer-generated match was adjudicated as credible, intelligence teams would radio through a verbal description to street-based intervention teams who would then seek to intercept the matched individual. One intended purpose of issuing handheld devices was so that intervention teams had access to both the source and watchlist image of those they were seeking on the ground. The second approach was to use mobile devices as an additional 'check' on the original decision by intelligence units that an LFR match was credible. This was the most common justification for the use of handheld devices, one commonly articulated during the planning and execution of LFR operations and set out in the 'Metropolitan Police Service Live Facial Recognition Trial Evaluation

Methodology' supplied to the authors by the MPS. As detailed below, this task became significantly more complex to achieve once the tools were deployed in an operational setting, thus questioning the degree to which this practice offered an additional site of adjudication.

Once issued in the smaller smartphone format, handheld devices were used extensively for the two later operations in Romford, London. Signifying a broader evolution of the technology, a similar practice using app-enabled smartphones also became a common feature of later LFR trials by SWP (Davies et al. 2018).

In practice, this activity complicated where the primary site of decision-making lay. Moreover, the data reveals how additional adjudication points reinforced, rather than mitigated, overall deference to the original algorithmically generated decision. For example, during the second Romford operation the decisive choice to apprehend a matched individual was made by street-based officers with handheld devices on at least five occasions. Most of these decisions took place while intelligence units, the stated primary decision-makers, were still deliberating over the credibility of a computer-generated match. Moreover, the decisions of the control room-based intelligence units to intercept a matched individual subject were *never* rejected by mobile-equipped officers. However, decisions by control room-based intelligence units to disregard computer-issued matches *were frequently 'overruled'* by street-based mobile-equipped officers on the basis of their separate access to imaging information. Most of these matches were confirmed as false positives following an identity check. Of further note here is how the human deference to the algorithm persisted *despite evidence that the technology was performing poorly* and that the LFR system was not correct on most occasions.

As the example presented at the start of this book relays, such processes and encounters have real-world implications. Here, during one of the Romford operations a fourteen-year-old child was stopped on the street and questioned by four officers. This occurred when street-based intervention teams responded independently to an LFR alert transmitted to their handheld devices despite the same alert being adjudicated as non-credible by intelligence teams in the control room. Here, a visibly distressed and clearly intimidated young Black male in school uniform was stopped and surrounded by five plainclothes officers around 20 metres from the van, and led by the wrists to a side street. An identity check confirmed the inaccuracy of this stop yet this occurred too late to prevent the child's clearly visible distress and ensuing conflict on the streets, with an adult female shouting at the officers and complaining about police racism and the persecution of young Black males.

This incident surfaces problematic aspects of LFR deployment, starting with the problem of on-the-street officers not waiting for control room adjudication—a clear example of the presumption in favour of intervention, which in turn provides a further example of 'surveillance creep'. Moreover, this episode illustrates difficulties surrounding how LFR alerts are resolved through engagements with the public, particularly when it involves the police handling of young people. Of further significance are the views of senior officers surrounding this incident. In subsequent discussion with the researchers, senior officers appeared well informed about the implications of such incidents. However, several senior officers pointed to the (organizational) cultural difficulties surrounding those in senior ranks telling uniformed officers how they should act in street-based settings. Hostility aimed against senior officers was expressed in many conversations during the course of the ethnographic fieldwork. Senior officers were both aware of, and sensitized to, this phenomenon and had elected to be strategic when challenging their subordinates. On this issue, senior officers privately conceded that lower-ranking colleagues were acting in an overly zealous manner yet decided not to act and thereby avoid conflict. The bearing of organizational cultures on police–citizen street encounters is well documented in the sociology of policing and its presence is reflected in these advanced surveillance operations too, albeit in more complex form. Such influences again challenge any notion that human operators act as objective arbitrators of digital processes.

8.3.3 Extending Surveillance through 'Humans in the Loop'

The presumption to intervene is one, albeit important, component of the wider human rights implications arising from the human-in-the-loop adjudication of algorithmic decisions. As highlighted through the data, one difficulty with this discourse is that it conveys a misplaced sense of accountability. This overstates the meaningfulness of human review and, accordingly, the capacity of humans to conduct such a review. Human adjudication is assumed to be an adequate mechanism, yet the quality of decision-making is never evaluated. A corollary is that, for surveillance practitioners, human-in-the-loop requirements are easy to fulfil in superficial ways, opening the possibility for highly gestural forms of regulatory compliance.

The London FRT operations also reveal another important component to this debate. Somewhat counterintuitively, the enactment of human-in-the-loop adjudication manifestly extended the surveillance potential of facial recognition surveillance. This dynamic was further apparent in the Romford deployments through the use of mobile devices by street-based intervention teams. While justified on the grounds of providing an additional level of human review, on-the-ground uses of this technology created new affordances that facilitated the creep of surveillance practices into new arenas. For example, during the first Romford deployment several individuals were detained as a direct result of law enforcement officers accessing the facial recognition database outside of the operational and geographical footprint of the LFR deployment. In one instance, this led to the arrest of an individual with an outstanding warrant for discharging a firearm in London:

> 31/1/2019, Romford town centre, London, 11:20am: Arrest of an individual not matched by the LFR cameras and was identified outside of the camera's zone of recognition. Identity was confirmed by an officer on the street photographing the suspect with a mobile device and comparing against the database. This revealed an outstanding warrant for firearms offences. When asked what the grounds for the initial pre-identification stop were, one street-based officer claimed the suspect was 'spotted by a super recognizer' who had previously seen the watchlist. With 2,401 individuals enrolled on the watchlist, this explanation seemed to stretch credibility. Further enquiries revealed that the individual was stopped and photographed for avoiding the cameras.

This incident raises several important questions over the parameters of how advanced surveillance technologies such as LFR are used in public. On one reading, a suspect wanted in relation to a serious offence was apprehended and arrested due to the additional capability brought about by FRT-enabled smartphones. This undoubtedly supports the legitimate aim justification for the use of this technology. However, as this book has argued, the lawful basis and rights-respecting uses of FRT extend beyond such appeals to legitimacy. These justifications fall short when used as a synecdoche for the permissibility of FRT as a whole. Taken to its conclusion, such a justification would delimit the use of FRT in public. For example, questions of necessity and, by extension, proportionality remain relevant with uses of FRT extending beyond the established geographical and operational limits of the deployment. Indeed, the foundational purpose of defining deployment parameters is to ensure that the 'in accordance with the law' and 'necessity' requirements for surveillance operations are met. If LFR is approved for one purpose, and under certain circumstances, then it is difficult to justify that these conditions can be adapted by officers on the ground acting outside the scope of the deployment. For officers acting outside these parameters, at best, the technology becomes used incorrectly. At worst it becomes used unlawfully.

Moreover, and as explored in Chapter 7, targeting those avoiding cameras complicates the role of consent. Given that consent to engage with the cameras could not be withdrawn without penalty, such incidents critically undermine any claim that these active police operations were a 'trial' in any meaningful sense. This issue becomes compounded when considered in relation to the MPS legal and policy documents governing their use of facial recognition. Here, procedures are explicit in stating that avoiding cameras should not be treated as suspicious of itself. Yet if avoiding cameras results in apprehension, then this statement becomes meaningless, thus, again, indicating superficial attempts to demonstrate legitimacy, legality, and proper procedure.

A relevant incident earlier in the day also raises concerns regarding compliance with the 'necessity' test when officers act in an extra-procedural manner:

> 31/1/2019, Romford town centre, London, 11:00am: Two individuals apprehended for shoplifting by private security guards in a nearby retail mall. The shopping centre is located far outside the camera zone of recognition and beyond the range of the LFR van communications. On apprehending the subjects, the shopping centre guards issued a call for assistance. Many officers were available because of the scale of the nearby LFR operation. One officer assigned to the LFR operation responded and visited the site with his handheld facial recognition device, which he used to check the identities of the two suspected shoplifters against the watchlist. On questioning over the sequence of events and data sources used, officers explained that the suspects were listed on the CRIS (MPS intelligence) database. However, this information had not been uploaded onto the Emerald Warrant Management System (the database of wanted individuals, i.e. those with warrants out against

them). They were therefore not on the watchlist but were nonetheless arrested following being subjected to a face recognition scan.

These incidents demonstrate how providing advanced surveillance capability to street-based officers generates conditions for surveillance creep. In this sense, surveillance practices extended not only beyond the geographical footprint of the facial recognition operation but also its operational parameters. Significant here is that these boundaries were established precisely in order to ensure compliance with the 'in accordance with the law' and the 'necessary in a democratic society' tests. This further questions whether uses of FRT in this way meant that offending behaviour (e.g. shoplifting) that would not meet the threshold of seriousness to be enrolled on the watchlist ('wanted for serious violence') became targeted by the technology once it was deployed in practice. Moreover, the different data architecture of the mobile facial recognition app—depending on whether faces were matched by control room cameras or through handheld devices—allowed suspect identities to be pursued beyond the operational watchlist, the data source listed in all legal and data protection justifications for the operation. The issuance of these handheld devices therefore allowed the parameters of the facial recognition deployment to be circumvented and extended. The more visible LFR operation also served as a basis for officers to act extra-procedurally on their own 'initiative'. Moreover, these events demonstrate how handheld devices became used in an entirely unregulated way.[16] Of further importance is how these handheld OIFR tools that allowed this surveillance creep to happen were publicly justified on the grounds that they provided human auditing of, and overall accountability for, algorithmic decisions. In addition to these extra-procedural uses of the technology, these actions also raise questions over whether the legal and policy frameworks themselves are adequate tools for governing the use of facial recognition in practice.

Another episode on the same day further underscores these themes of surveillance creep, extra-procedural applications, digital affordances, and consent. The incident, one widely reported in the UK national media (inter alia, *The Independent* 2019), relates to an individual who was apprehended by the street-based intervention teams for 'suspiciously' avoiding the LFR cameras. The encounter resolved with the individual being issued a £90

[16] At the time of writing, the MPS did not have any publicly accessible policy governing use of OIFR in place.

fixed penalty fine on the grounds of a public order offence and an example of surveillance overreach that galvanized opponents of LFR. An eyewitness working for a civil society organization relays her experience:

> So, the first day in Romford, a man was actually fined for having a scarf over his mouth and chin, and then goaded by police. And then he said an expletive, apparently. I didn't hear it, but apparently he did and then he was given a public order fine of £90. (Interview with Silkie Carlo, director, Big Brother Watch, May 2019)

National media stories of the incident expressed an almost verbatim repetition of views of the same civil society observers on Twitter. The police version is that the individual arrested became aggressive and abusive to officers when confronted, and the public order fixed penalty was issued in accordance with standard procedure for addressing such behaviour. The independent (unreleased) media video footage reveals an escalating confrontation between the police intervention teams and this individual. At one point, and in a detail edited out of media reports, the intercepted individual can be heard shouting in unequivocally racist terms. While it is unsurprising such behaviour attracted a sanction, the role of FRT in priming and staging the entire situation cannot be ignored.

The denial of any choice to withdraw consent from the LFR 'trial' also holds significance. Relevant here is how the independent media footage shows an officer taking this individual's photograph with one of the FRT-enabled smartphones early in the altercation. The officer mentions he is taking the individual's photograph *while triggering the shutter*. There is no dialogue between the two people, and hence no opportunity to meaningfully consent. Aside from its decorative and performative function, such displays of 'consent-gathering' are ultimately meaningless.

From a legal perspective it is also important to note how these officers were operating outside the established bounds of the LFR trial. The individual was not flagged as—or particularly suspected of—being on the watchlist, and so the offices' decisions were made entirely outside the parameters of the deployment. These actions were also inconsistent with instructions that a decision to avoid cameras was not to be treated as suspicious. The wider adoption of FRT will necessarily implicate greater numbers of officers in its use and thus heightens the likelihood of extra-procedural use. Across public communications and their own policy documentation, the MPS were clear in stating that LFR was 'only' used to trace those wanted for serious violence. Yet the realities of facial recognition operations, the affordances the technology offers, and the propensity for surveillance creep mean that, in actuality, crossing the street to avoid a camera was sufficient to be compared to the LFR database.

The extension of surveillance in this manner not only removes any meaningful sense of 'surveillance by consent', it may also undermine public safety and the policing goals of those using the technology. For example, during this operation, the aggressive pursuit of those avoiding the cameras tied up large numbers of officers in questioning suspects and processing those charged with offences below the stated threshold for inclusion on the watchlist, such as being in possession of illegal substances. If LFR was effective in arresting those wanted for serious violence, as claimed in MPS documentation (e.g. MPS 2023g), then its creep into addressing more mundane offences undermines the very public safety argument deployed to legitimize its use and away from the pursuit of such serious offenders. The absence of a clear legal basis to operate outside the established deployment parameters also raises significant concerns vis-à-vis human rights law compliance.

Such evolution, adaptation, and, ultimately, creep of FRT resonates with deeper issues concerning the oversight of surveillance more broadly. Much current surveillance regulation emphasizes the initial stages of an operation, including its permissibility, authorization, and parameters for use, such as warrants for covert and targeted surveillance. However, uses of leading-edge technologies such as LFR bring further complexity given the scope of such tools is not well understood in advance. Added to this, as the above data of actual LFR operations demonstrates, uses of this technology evolve once it becomes deployed. New affordances and conditions of possibility emerge through its application. These novel adaptations and 'creep' indicate clear limitations in the focus and reach of existing surveillance regulation processes.

Of further note here is how law enforcement uses of facial recognition continue to expand. Indeed, in 2024 alone, the MPS used LFR 117 times between January and August, up from 32 times between 2020 and 2023 (FT 2024). This expansion in scale brings an increased portability and diversification of surveillance tools, most notably in the issuing of handheld OIFR, which functions both as an integral part of LFR operations and as a surveillance tool in its own right. This in turn enables larger numbers of officers to conduct facial recognition searches for a wider range of purposes.

8.3.4 Spatial, Technical, and Affective Influences on Human Adjudication

Adding to the above are the range of environmental, technological, and affective elements shaping the use and creep of LFR. As discussed throughout this book, FRT is deployed in complex socio-technical environments. It necessarily operates in concert with myriad technological, operational, and spatial variables that affect the capability and outcome of LFR. One cross-cutting theme arising from each is that of time pressure. By definition, LFR operations happen in real time, yet, as the data below demonstrates, multiple elements influence the temporal frames and quality of human decisions of use.

8.3.4.1 Spatial dynamics

Among these influences, the physical characteristics of an operational environment, particularly choices over the positioning of intervening officers, had significant bearing on adjudication processes and the interception of matched individuals. Indeed, the data reveals the significance of how space is organized *behind* the FRT zone of recognition. Key here were how complex crowd dynamics affected the time available for human decision-making and the likelihood matched individuals could be located. For example, during the two Stratford operations intervention teams were stationed very close to, and sometimes within, the camera 'zone of recognition'. This physical proximity dramatically compressed the time available for intelligence teams to weigh up the accuracy of any computer matches. Within a few seconds of an FRT alert, any matched individual would have since walked beyond the line of officers responsible for intercepting them. While the number of alerts across these two days were small (five), and therefore difficult to draw generalizations from, these spatial dynamics exerted a decisive effect on the decision-making process. During the first Stratford operation two alerts in near succession triggered an immediate attempt to intercept the matched individual with zero time attributed to adjudication. More problematic was that both computer matches were of the same individual who had already been stopped for an identity check and disconfirmed as a wanted suspect.

A variation on this theme also played out in the two Soho operations. Here, the surveillance van carrying the two LFR-equipped cameras was stationed in Leicester Square for three half-day sessions. Not only is this one of the most congested areas in western Europe's most populous city, the LFR operations took place shortly before Christmas, at one of the busiest times of year. The spaces surrounding the intervention teams were extremely crowded, natural light was poor, and most people wore heavy coats to protect against the December elements. This placed intervention teams in a challenging operational environment and added pressure to make rapid assessments on the credibility of computer-issued matches. Responding to this problem, one of the senior officers in the control room argued that 'if we are not sure, we should stop [people]' (fieldnote, Leicester Square, 18/12/2018). Such statements express a direct affirmation of the above findings regarding the default human deference to the algorithm. Overall, the spatial characteristics of the area under surveillance and choices about the deployment of cameras and intervention team officers significantly condition the quality of officers' ability to adjudicate computer-suggested matches.

8.3.4.2 Assemblages and ensembles of surveillance technology

Despite its seeming potency, it is important to recognize that FRT does not operate in isolation. It functions as a component in a wider ensemble of surveillance-enabling technology. Critical interconnections and interdependencies between FRT and other technological infrastructure thus exist for the technology to operate. Moreover, any weaknesses in individual components of this wider ensemble critically affect the functioning of FRT. As the empirical data details below, overall performance of the wider ensemble is contingent on specific elements and, crucially, how they interconnect. The nature of these relationships between different technologies in the surveillance ecosystem also holds theoretical as well as practical significance. For example, longstanding theorizations of 'surveillance assemblage' (discussed in Chapter 1) tend to emphasize the coalescence of different technologies in generating highly potent surveillance tools; the sum being greater than its parts. While such accounts are accurate for many contexts and hold value for identifying the amplification of surveillance potential tools once brought together, these technologies are not necessarily enhanced by such unions. Limitations in specific technological components can restrict the overall ability of LFR. Single points of failure inhibit the network and reduce overall surveillance possibilities. The sum may, in fact, be less than its parts.

Principal among the wider technologies crucial to LFR functioning is communications technology. Two communications processes are critical to the LFR operational process. One is the transmission of LFR-matched images to handheld devices possessed by the street-based intervention teams. Separately, intelligence units would also seek to radio through a matched individual's details to intervention teams. Both activities depended on sufficient communications bandwidth to function. A common issue across the deployments involved difficulties in transmitting images from the control room to intervention teams. In both Stratford and Soho, problems with poor data connectivity beyond 20 metres, constant network dropouts, and officer complaints over being encumbered with another piece of kit led to officers disengaging from this technology. For these operations, the result of this dissatisfaction was a pile of unused tablets lying on a desk, with street-based officers unable to review suspect images and thereby reliant on radioed descriptions of matched individuals they were tasked with intercepting.

Additional to the transmission of digital images, analogue police radio technology also worked poorly in central London, with limited reception inside the LFR van.[17] These technical difficulties not only limited the effectiveness of LFR, they also reduced the time available for humans to meaningfully adjudicate computer-issued matches. Analogue equipment became crucial to fulfilling the promise of cutting-edge digital law enforcement tools. Moreover, the performance of technology manifestly conditions the operational choices made be human practitioners.

Technical issues were not limited to inconsistent communications systems. Despite the high-end optics of LFR-equipped camera systems, problems with image resolution in one market-leading camera led to its replacement during the second Stratford operation. The following LFR deployment in Soho encountered problems with both hardware and software. In particular, the system was unable to process the large numbers of passers-by, with 'red boxes' capturing faces for only some of the monitored image. Both Soho operations encountered problems with computer processing capability. On the morning of the second of these, the FRT-equipped computers struggled under the heavy processing load needed to analyse live video. Adding to the limits on 'red boxing', caching problems meant laptop

[17] For a global city of this size, it is notable how poor communications technology has dogged emergency service responses in London for decades. The functionality of 'Airwave' radio, a bespoke network intended to offer reliable integrated communication between the city's emergency services, was singled out for criticism in a review of emergency responses following the 7 July 2005 terrorist attacks (London Assembly 2007), and its limited functionality was a source of frustration for security workers at the 2012 London Olympics (Fussey et al. 2012).

processes were taking significant time to work. At the initial start of the deployment some 'bluelist' hits (police officers testing the system by intentionally walking in front of the cameras) were coming through late. As a result, batches of alerts came through at the same time, some 45 minutes after the camera had identified someone.

This technical shortcoming is particularly significant when reconsidering how effectiveness is measured. If effectiveness is formulated as a comparison between the absolute numbers of faces processed and the ratio of accurate matches, as described above, limited processing holds two significant implications. It may skew the ratio so that correct matches are compared against a smaller number of processed images, and therefore offer a statistic that could inflate the effectiveness of LFR. Additionally, this limited processing means any claim of LFR effectiveness is, at best, based on an estimate of overall numbers of passers-by. Both factors undermine the seeming objectivity of 'technical' statistics on LFR efficacy.

8.3.4.3 Affective influences

Less tangible yet also significant are the affective and ergonomic aspects of LFR operations. For the most part, police surveillance operations are dull and uneventful affairs punctuated by brief and intensive periods of activity. Common to other ethnographic studies of surveillance operations (Norris and Armstrong 1999; McCahill 2002; Smith 2015), ennui was both a presence and influence in these operational environments. Given the contrast between dullness and drama, it is important to recognize how the atmospheres and affective states change when an FRT alert is triggered.

This was particularly apparent at the second Stratford trial where one sole alert was generated late in the day, towards the end of an uneventful 10-hour deployment. Under these circumstances the alert rapidly transformed a setting of boredom to one of activity where one adjudicator immediately left their station to track down the matched individual themselves. Yet the matched individual had already merged into the crowded adjacent retail mall and emphasis then shifted from adjudicating on the veracity of the match to tracing the individual by other means.[18] While the matched individual was initially lost among the throng of the shopping centre, they were eventually located and identified as an incorrect match. Common to other forms of human decision-making, emotive and affective contexts can be

[18] The individual was eventually tracked down using the shopping centre's surveillance camera network. An identity check revealed this to be a false match.

identified as key conditioning agents for both the concretization of suspicion and the human-in-the-loop adjudication processes designed to audit computer-issued decisions.

8.4 Conclusions

Examining the experiences of facial recognition operations demonstrates a series of emergent practices that arise as the technology is deployed. Common to other qualitative research of law enforcement technology-in-practice (inter alia, Brayne 2020), many of these elements are only revealed through observation, analysis, and understanding of how digital tools are deployed in operational settings.

This emphasis on the creative and emergent practices also holds significant theoretical resonance. Two such interconnected themes are particularly important here: the conjoining of human and technical elements and, relatedly, the way surveillance practices become active. Many of the theoretical approaches relevant to advanced surveillance operations discussed in Chapter 1, for example, stress the kinetic and animating qualities of socio-technical arrangements. For Foucault, power was productive. It did not lie in a potential state awaiting activation. Assemblage theorists emphasized how the coming together of different elements creates something new, an effervescent 'emergence'. Here, parallels may be drawn with foundational concepts advanced in Martin Heidegger's canon. While specific technologically focused elements of his thought were criticized in STS (Latour 1999), links may be drawn between STS and Heidegger's (1978) work on technology ('Technik') alongside his wider philosophical approach. Regarding technology, neither theoretical approach recognizes boundaries between subject and object or, in this context, the human and the technological (see also Riis 2008). Each only makes sense when considered with the other. Moreover, Heidegger's more enduring philosophical project emphasizes how substance and meaning come into being through engagement and use. Such theoretical insights are not decorative: surveillance occurs in its 'doing'. Accordingly, analyses of surveillance technologies are less about what they might do than how they realized through practice. Crucial to understanding the realization of surveillance outputs, then, is accounting for these complex techno-social relationships and environments.

In the context of FRT, the human and technical are brought together with particular intensity at the point at which a computer matches the face of a passer-by to an image on the source database. Such computer-driven acts trigger a chain of human action; the adjudication of images followed by a possible physical intervention of an individual on the street. As this chapter has shown, many accompanying narratives place the human and technical realms as separate and in opposition to each other. In doing so, an ontological assumption becomes asserted in the belief that one (the human) will correct the other (inaccurate computational decisions). The data and analysis presented above challenges such assumptions.

Rather than providing a corrective to inaccurate matches, such mergers routinely compound and reinforce error. The human does not correct the digital but, instead, is implicated in complex techno-social interrelationships. Such deep-seated ontological considerations hold resonance for practical matters of law and rights. Human-in-the-loop adjudication is consistently advanced as a way of bringing accountability and oversight to computer-issued decisions. It is an approach encoded in law and regulation designed to make such tools auditable or, at least, curb excessive harm arising from their errors.[19] Yet the complex ways operators engage with the LFR technology are irreducible to human–computer binaries. Humans are both regularly deferential algorithmic decisions and, as the data shows, human adjudications may also extend the range, scope, and intrusion of surveillance practices.

[19] See, e.g., the GDPR, the EU Law Enforcement Directive, and the Data Protection Act 2018.

9
Conclusion
Facial Recognition as a Complex Socio-Technical Surveillance System

9.1 Introduction

This book has traced the origins of police biometric surveillance from nineteenth-century preoccupations with identity and urban legibility through to operational uses of AI-driven incarnations on the streets of London today. In doing so, the analysis has sought to both frame the discussion surrounding current uses of this technology and identify pressing issues concerning intensifying police uses of AI-assisted surveillances tools. To properly address the changed nature and degree of surveillance, and its complex impacts on individuals, the book advances the concept of 'compound human rights harm'. This idea is formulated to more effectively encapsulate the true impact of surveillance and to properly account for its multifaceted, complex, and dynamic effects. In considering the practical implications of considering compound human rights harms, the book draws on the most recent human rights theory and practice to additionally specify a due diligence framework specifically tailored to the police use of facial recognition technology (FRT). This framework interrogates the 'necessary in a democratic society' test for the specific context of FRT. The framework is centred on understanding and evaluating the 'competing interests' at play in any police use of FRT and is argued to hold particular value for assessing the claimed utility and the potential harm of this technology. In doing so, the framework sets out the key considerations that should be taken into account prior to, and in the evaluation of, any deployment.

Such legal considerations are informed by detailed empirical and theoretical analysis of how facial recognition surveillance manifests through operational practice, thus bringing legal scholarship into dialogue with the computational and social sciences. In drawing these strands together, the book concludes by asserting five key contributions that emphasize an understanding of FRT not only as a technical tool but as a socio-technical

Facial Recognition Surveillance. Pete Fussey and Daragh Murray, Oxford University Press.
 DOI: 10.1093/9780191979927.003.0009

system capable of changing the fundamental nature of policing. These are: FRT and the extended surveillance gaze; the complex human–technical imbrications of AI-driven surveillance; the reconfiguration of suspicion; new dimensions of surveillance creep; and the instrumental and selective use of legal and scientific discourse to legitimize FRT. Each is addressed in turn.

9.2 Facial Recognition and the Extended Surveillance Gaze

FRT represents a step change in police surveillance capability, one exerting policing, social, and legal effects. With respect to policing, three aspects of FRT are highlighted here. First is the fact that FRT is a tool of remote surveillance. This distance between watcher and watched exacerbates the asymmetries of surveillance. By its nature, the activity of watching through FRT requires hidden databases and barely decipherable AI-driven computational processes. By contrast, the heightened intrusion elevates the visibility of the watched. The remote nature of FRT further allows for highly intrusive surveillance technology to become used in the absence of physical friction, and potentially without the knowledge of those surveilled. Although the surveillance infrastructure FRT depends on may be visible—and therefore classified as 'overt'—the surveillance capability itself runs in the background, and so the remote nature of the technology engenders opacity through its core nature and purpose. Second is the scale of surveillance made possible by FRT. The resource-intensive nature of 'traditional' physical surveillance demanded that it only be applied selectively and in a targeted manner. FRT, however, can be used to surveil large segments of the population—potentially everyone in a public space—with heightened efficiency. Third is the future surveillance potential facilitated by FRT. As a foundational surveillance tool, FRT can be augmented by further analytical technologies, such as tools to track, monitor, geo-fence, or profile.

Turning to the social effects, participation in social and public life is attenuated by the use of FRT. The above factors combine to transform the mere fact of participation in public life into continued possibilities for highly intrusive surveillance. A principal means of presenting the self in public and a fundamental attribute of identity—the face—becomes a means by which privacy becomes subverted in public. In so doing, the deeply personal nature of the body becomes reconfigured into something more visible, more public. In addition to availing oneself for future scrutiny through retrospective facial recognition (RFR) and other biometric identification tools, the nature of police–citizen encounters is altered by subtle yet significant shifts in the application of suspicion and what it means to be in public, as discussed below.

From a legal perspective, two factors are prominent. First is that the transformative surveillance capability of FRT poses significant challenges to current approaches to human rights law. This is most clearly demonstrated by reference to the chilling effects of surveillance. Chilling effects are perhaps the paradigmatic example of diffuse harms that are often not immediately apparent yet manifest in complex ways. Human rights law, as currently framed, is not well suited to encapsulate or address this harm. Human rights law analysis is typically conducted on a right-by-right basis and, as the analysis has shown, is not well suited to incorporating the compound multi-rights impacts linked to chilling effects, at least as things currently stand. This risks downplaying FRT harm, resulting in an inappropriate imbalancing of the human rights analysis and bias in favour of authorization. In essence, and if appropriate responses are not developed, the step change in surveillance capability brought about by FRT may exceed human rights law's more traditional analogue-centric frame of analysis. Second, FRT is currently deployed in the absence of an appropriate legal framework. This presents a serious challenge to the rule of law. An advanced surveillance capability, with the potential to shift the accepted balance of power between the state and its citizens, is deployed at the exclusive discretion of the police. As discussed in Chapter 6, and elaborated upon below, even the intervention of the courts—and a finding that certain FRT uses are unlawful—has not resulted in any discernible change in police policy. In fact, it has resulted in the codification (and therefore routinization) of those same uses judged to be unlawful and a dramatically expanded rollout.

UK policing has long been at the forefront of adopting experimental technology. At its epicentre is London and the Metropolitan Police Service (MPS), one of the world's largest urban police forces. This study offered a detailed insight into one of the most controversial AI-driven policing tools at a critical moment on the cusp of its mass adoption. As the MPS was one of only two UK police forces experimenting with this technology at the time, the template for how live facial recognition (LFR) has come to be used nationally was forged during the research period. This study is predicated on unique access to MPS planning, processes, and operations and, to date, represents the only independent study of LFR in its operational environment. Crucial to the analysis is the scrutiny of how FRT works in practice, alongside the affordances of this technology and socio-technical contexts it is situated within. The outcomes of facial recognition surveillance become realized through the value-laden and politicized socio-technical environments it is deployed within. Interrogating the emergent practices that arise from these contexts exposes detailed insights crucial to the theory, practice, and legal governance of this technology.

Equally central to the analysis was the application of international human rights law. Three key contributions relevant to the study of FRT were advanced. First, the concept of compound human rights harm was developed in order to more effectively encapsulate the complex, multifaceted, and diffuse harm associated with surveillance, and with surveillance-related chilling effects in particular. Second, a novel due diligence framework tailored to police use of FRT was established and set out. This framework is centred around a before-the-fact application of the 'necessary in a democratic society' test, and is positioned towards resolving the 'competing interests' at play, namely the potential utility and potential harm linked to a specific use of FRT. The framework establishes the key questions that law enforcement policies should be judged against prior to deploying FRT, and in doing so also provides a means of evaluating the lawfulness of a deployment after the fact. This framework was then applied to the MPS's approach to FRT, demonstrating how human rights law analysis can be used to evaluate both the policy framework put in place to regulate FRT and LFR deployments themselves. The research reveals several additional themes that emerge from the operational use of FRT.

9.3 Human Adjudication of AI Systems

The research offers a key contribution in examining how humans interact with advanced surveillance technologies in live operational settings. Understanding how human operators engage with this technology allows ideas about AI governance to be stress-tested in the context of their real-world applications. Prominent among such approaches is faith in human oversight of technology. Much law and policy focused on the regulation and responsible use of AI places dependence on the role of human overseers to correct the biases, errors, and unfavourable outcomes of computational decision-making. As LFR operations evolved, sites of human oversight over the veracity of computer-issued matches varied. The ethnographic analysis identified a discernible deference to the algorithm—a 'presumption to intervene'—across these assorted arrangements. Discretion became ceded to algorithmic identifications of 'suspicious' individuals, regardless of their accuracy. That human adjudication takes place is not in question. The issue at stake is the form it takes and the degree of meaningful scrutiny applied. These events reveal several shortcomings in the efficacy and scope of human review as it applies both to FRT and to the human attenuation of AI systems more generally.

Faith in human-in-the-loop mediation of digital decisions contains several brittle assumptions. The first overstates human objectivity. The philosophy of science has taught us that the separation of 'human' and 'technical' contains an inherent ontological fallacy: that the human and the technical inhabit separate realms and that the former can objectively assess the latter. Instead, analysing the operation of FRT reasserts the naivety of assuming human action is somehow inoculated from the influence of technology. FRT implicates human actors in complex ways, elicits affordances that invite specific actions, and creates conditions that make others possible. The repeated human deference to computer-issued facial recognition alerts does not imply humans unthinkingly concede their agency to the machine. Instead, FRT frames and structures suspicion, and *primes* operators, in advance of any human adjudication. Ensuing decisions over the veracity of FRT matches also occur in an environment that holds consequences for human actors. Professional liability accompanies any decision not to accept a computer-issued alert of a potential suspect. This incentive structure not only conditions any sense of objectivity, it also resonates with deeper questions over how responsibility, liability, and agency become laundered through digital technology (see Rubel et al. 2019; Fussey et al. 2021).

A related assumption supposes, deterministically, that human involvement will inevitably ameliorate flaws in technological decision-making; that humans and machines audit and correct each other towards apotheosis of an objective 'truth'. Resonating with Foucault's (1977c: 13) critique of 'the techniques and procedures which are valorised for obtaining truth' and his broader project on 'regimes of veridiction', this analysis shows that human-in-the-loop mediation introduces new modes of endorsement for computational decisions. A key outcome is that biases and other digital deficiencies become reproduced and, crucially, legitimated.

Excessive faith in the capacity of humans to moderate algorithmic decisions holds additional significance for how FRT and other AI systems are regulated. Signalling the presence of human scrutiny offers the appearance of holding algorithmic decisions to account, yet is limited in its purpose. In such circumstances, interposing a 'human in the loop' risks ceding oversight to a performative and symbolic form of regulation. This is not to argue that human intervention is unnecessary or should be abandoned, but to caution that its sufficiency may be overstated. Of further importance is how such performative forms of oversight deliver net-widening consequences. As the ethnographic data demonstrated, the very mechanisms claimed to bring accountability to algorithmic processes—the human review of computational decisions—served to extend the scope of surveillance and facilitate its creep into new domains.

9.4 The Hermeneutics of Suspicion

Technological innovation has been part of law enforcement practice for generations. However, the speed and reach of current AI-driven surveillance tools have accelerated this trend and brought profound changes to the theory and practice of today's digital policing activities. When applied to the use of FRT, these changes assert particular significance for how suspicion is assumed, constructed, and addressed. This outcome resonates strongly with a long tradition in the sociology of policing that has emphasized the range of structural (Bowling and Phillips 2002; Campbell 1999), bureaucratic (Matza 1969), and individual (Davis 1971; Dworkin 1977; Norris et al. 1992) factors that shape suspicion formation in law enforcement. This book has argued that the accelerated adoption of FRT and other AI-driven surveillance tools brings a further, techno-social, component to police suspicion formation. While subtle, such changes are far-reaching in their implications. The impact of this techno-social conditioning of suspicion may be considered sufficiently fundamental that the foundational principles and legal frameworks governing state surveillance practices become challenged and, in some cases, subverted. Specifically, this book identifies how FRT impacts suspicion in five distinct ways:

i. *Technologically structured suspicion.* As discussed in earlier chapters, for over half a century sociologies of policing have identified the complex environmental, organizational, and individual factors that inform how suspicion becomes constructed. In turn, the robustness of evidence used to inform classifications of suspicion varies significantly, comprising unverified tipoffs and hunches at one end of the spectrum to legal standards of evidence at the other. The ethnographic data reveals how the adoption of FRT digitally structures, validates, and affirms a form of suspicion. Two observations are particularly salient. First is the role of facial recognition alerts in priming officer decision-making, which in turn influences the 'deference to the algorithm' detailed in Chapter 8. A second area of importance is how initial suspicion does not originate from the officer exercising discretion. In London, a computational facial recognition match justified a street-based stop and search. Humans do not generate the initial and decisive grounds for suspicion. Instead, as Fussey et al. (2021: 329) argue, the officers' role becomes relegated to something more akin to intermediaries, 'interpreting and then acting upon a (computer instigated) suggestion originating outside of, and prior to, their own intuition'. Of further note is that, because authored by AI-driven processes, these initial formations of suspicion are neither accountable nor explainable. The origins of such decisions are not scrutable to humans.

ii. *Subverting the sequence of surveillance.* Foundational to all legal frameworks that permit surveillance is a clear sequencing of activities. In the simplest terms, this refers to the requirement that a sufficient threshold of suspicion needs to exist before intrusive surveillance can be authorized. In effect, 'suspicion' needs to exist before 'surveillance'. FRT—particularly its 'live' and 'operator-initiated' variants—reverses this dynamic. The faces of *all* who pass the cameras are scanned and biometrically processed before being discounted. A form of surveillance therefore occurs in advance of suspicion. The remoteness and speed of this transaction is regularly cited as a means to minimize the intrusion. However, remoteness does not translate easily into benignity. As sociologies of surveillance and policing have consistently revealed, the application of scrutiny asserts powerful corollary effects. These include the surveillance chilling effects documented throughout the book. In other respects, the act of surveillance has long been argued to communicate unambiguous messages over exclusion and denied citizenship (Norris and Armstrong 1999).

iii. *Disrupting distinctions between covert and overt surveillance.* Legal and policy approaches to governing intrusive surveillance draw a distinction between 'overt' and targeted 'covert' uses. Covert surveillance is largely attributed with greater intrusion, thus implicating higher levels of oversight and more stringent authorization procedures, such as those outlined in the Regulation of Investigatory Powers Act 2001 and the Investigatory Powers Act 2016. This distinction is maintained in other democratic jurisdictions, albeit often upheld through different mechanisms, such as the judicial authorization approach of FISA [Federal Intelligence Surveillance Act] courts in the US. The MPS (self-)designated their LFR operations as 'overt'. In one sense, this designation accurately reflects the public and publicized nature of deployments. However, analysis of the operational practice of FRT reveals how the technology resists such clear categorization. For example, while the presence of cameras *may* be overt, the use of FRT (particularly RFR) is not, nor is the application of any additional analytical tools (such as those to facilitate profiling or tracking) visible. FRT relies on a hidden database of suspects. The technology also functions on the basis that individuals are not aware they are enrolled onto this database and will therefore pass the cameras. Furthermore, overt systems can be easily adapted to conduct surveillance typically associated with covert capabilities. Such dynamics highlight the inadequacies of binary partitions of 'overt' and 'covert' surveillance when considering the operational use of FRT.

iv. *Individual and categorical suspicion.* At one scale of operation, comparing data extracted from individual faces to a database record, FRT constitutes an individualized form of surveillance. However, its source data, operation, and functionality are heavily shaped by categorical forms of surveillance. Watchlists are developed from police records, which themselves reflect arenas of police attention. That the digital architecture of FRT performs differently across demographic groups is an established scientific fact. Through unequal performance across categories of race and gender, the technology is likely to influence whether someone is subjected to unnecessary police stops by virtue of their membership of a demographic group. Added to this are other categories of unequal technical performance. As the computer science literature highlights, the physiological structure of one's face may be sufficient to increase the chances of being misidentified by the cameras.

v. *Facilitating a shift from suspicion to pre-emptive policing.* Recent FRT deployments at mass gatherings have demonstrated an intensifying use of this technology to mitigate against what *might* happen and to isolate individuals that *may* cause disruption. During November 2017, an early MPS deployment stationed LFR at the Whitehall Cenotaph, the epicentre of the UK's Remembrance Sunday commemorations. The comparatively tiny watchlist of forty-two people contained what was later revealed in a Freedom of Information request to contain 'fixated individuals'. These referred to people deemed by the police to be capable of disrupting the ceremony despite not necessarily being 'wanted' for any offence. Years later, this initial approach has become a mainstream principle of FRT operations in the UK. For example, in one of the largest operations in the world outside China, the triple LFR deployment surveying crowds at the 2023 coronation of Charles III in London was part of an MPS strategy where 'tolerance for any disruption, whether through protest or otherwise, will be low', with their stated ambition to 'deal robustly with anyone intent on undermining this celebration' (*The Guardian* 2023d). Changes in legislation covering protests during 2023, elements of which have since been ruled unlawful by the courts, also enabled arbitrary classifications of 'legal' and 'illegal' protestors to be made. Targeting this latter category has become an explicit justification of FRT deployments. For example, as a Freedom of Information request by Big Brother Watch revealed, two thirds of those enrolled onto the Northamptonshire Police watchlist for the British Grand Prix of that year were not wanted for arrest or suspected of criminal activity (Big Brother Watch 2023). At a time of heightened climate justice activism, it is believed that FRT was thus used to facilitate the pre-emptive identification and interception of suspected protestors. Paralleling debates in other areas of digital policing, this temporal shift, from targeting those after being suspected of an offence to those who might offend, brings heightened levels of speculation into the process.

This shift in the modalities of suspicion dovetails with another core concern of surveillance scholarship, the adaptation and creep of surveillance tools into other domains and applications.

9.5 An Anatomy of Biometric Surveillance Creep

Surveillance creep is traditionally formulated as the reapplication of a surveillance tool for other purposes (inter alia, Marx 2002). A standard example of such would be the installation of Panasonic's cameras in Beijing's

Tiananmen Square for 'traffic monitoring' during the mid-1980s and their later use to track down protestors after the 1989 uprising (Fussey et al. 2011). Detailed analysis of the planning and operation of FRT in London, however, reveals how creep happens at all stages of the deployment process. Creep is therefore not just the outcome of redeployed technology but rather something layered into its application at multiple stages.

At the planning stage, FRT surveillance creep arises from the varying thresholds adopted for deployment. The data reveals how the criteria for being enrolled on a facial recognition watchlist routinely crept to include not only individuals wanted in relation to 'serious violent crime' but also two further categories of individuals: those 'of interest' to the investigation of *any* offence and, as outlined above, the pre-emptive prevention of potential offences. Particularly significant is how this practice occurs despite the Court of Appeal for England and Wales explicitly finding that including persons 'of interest' to the police granted excessive discretion to officers, and was unlawful on this basis.

The affordances of FRT also invite surveillance creep. This occurs through the privileging capability of technology over the intelligence case justifying an operation. For example, the ethnographic data revealed how cameras were positioned to maximize sight lines rather than to respond to the location of offences highlighted by intelligence. Similarly, the camera's diminished optical capability in poor lighting led to operations aimed at tackling offences linked to the nighttime economy being staged in daylight. Such operations could be accurately described as 'technology-led' rather than 'policing-led'.

The realities of live operations also generated elements of surveillance creep. False positives, inaccurate watchlists, and 'suspicious' behaviour in the vicinity of LFR deployments all prompted engagement by officers and, in many cases, formal sanctions. Outcomes included falsely identified people being arrested for offences that fell below the threshold of severity established to justify the LFR operation in the first instance. Others were searched and sanctioned for avoiding cameras. Collectively, these outcomes result in surveillance, and policing, extending beyond the stated purposes of an operation. The issuing of additional handheld technology as part of later surveillance operations led to some of the most explicit forms of operational surveillance creep. This included officers using the tools outside the scope of the operation to scan faces for issues unrelated to the purposes and boundaries of the deployment.

9.6 Valorization and Veridiction: Using Policy, Law, and Science to Legitimate FRT

What has become apparent over the course of the analysis conducted for this book is that law and scientific discourse is consistently recruited as a tool to legitimize the use of FRT in and of itself. Such narratives obfuscate and override both the actual scientific evidence base and the applicable law. The policy framework currently in place gives the impression of legitimacy and legal compliance, and in doing so indicates the role of a governance structure. On detailed reading, however, this policy framework serves—in effect—as an advocacy piece, underscoring the often unevidenced virtues of the technology without incorporating any caution or critique.

The testing regime put in place by the MPS is a case in point. In reference to work a commissioned to analyse algorithmic bias, the MPS assert that:

> The NPL [National Physical Laboratory] report gives us an impartial, scientifically underpinned and evidence-based analysis of the performance of the facial recognition algorithm currently used by the Met and SWP [South Wales Police]. It tells us . . . [t]here are settings our algorithm can be operated at where there is no statistical significance between demographic performances. (MPS website)

This suggests compliance with the Public Sector Equality Duty and clearly presents a scientific underpinning for claims that the algorithm can be operated in a non-discriminatory manner. Indeed, NPL testing has become a cornerstone of the public-facing discourse surrounding the expanded rollout of FRT, and in this regard serves a clear legitimizing function. The testing regime is discussed in detail in Chapter 2. Simply put, however, it cannot be claimed with any degree of credibility that the seven facial recognition matches the analysis relies on can result in 'statistically significant' results.

A similar legitimizing function is evident in the legal analysis underpinning the policy framework (discussed in detail in Chapter 5). The approach to the 'necessary in a democratic society' test is emblematic. The test itself is correctly set out as being less than 'indispensable' but more than 'useful', and reference is made to the relevant case law. The approach actually set out in the documentation, however, is selective and partial. The focus in the documentation rests solely on the intelligence case and the legitimate aim pursued, absent an incorporation of the potential harm to human rights.

As the necessity test is dependent upon the resolution of the competing interests at play—that is, utility versus harm—this results in a fundamental imbalance. Despite stating that a deployment must be more than just 'desirable' or 'useful', the policy guidance in effect reduces the necessity test to one of utility. The approach taken to the prohibition of indirect discrimination, itself based on a misstatement of the relevant law, is equally problematic. The legal mandate suggests that discriminatory outcomes associated with LFR may be permissible if the use of LFR itself is in pursuit of a legitimate aim. For discrimination to be permissible, however, the discrimination itself must be in pursuit of a legitimate aim. This apparently slight difference in approach fundamentally alters the legal analysis, legitimizing the otherwise illegitimate.

This legal inexactitude is compounded by the overall framing of the policy documentation. No policy framework can hope to be comprehensive. What it can do, however, is set out examples capable of informing officers' approach to different situations, while noting the factors that might be taken into consideration when deciding to authorize, or refuse, a LFR deployment. The policy framework in place, however, is characterized by an absence of any critique. The utility of LFR is justified on the basis of assertion. The legal mandate states, for example, that LFR '*will assist*' the MPS in fighting terrorism and child sexual abuse and exploitation (MPS 2023c: 3.11). A variety of examples are then presented, working through use cases relating to potential LFR deployments. It is striking, however, that no examples are given where a LFR deployment would not be authorized. Rather than informing police officers' decision-making so that they can effectively engage with the complex issues arising in relation to FRT, the policy framework instead implicitly but inevitably guides towards the authorization of LFR. The result is a framework that suggests in-depth engagement with applicable legal frameworks, and ultimately legal compliance, but which inexorably works towards the legitimization of FRT.

This conclusion is underscored by the fact that key parts of the current policy framework directly replicate the framework that was found to be unlawful by the Court of Appeal in *Bridges*. As discussed in Chapter 3, the High Court and Court of Appeal judgments give rise to an unfortunate degree of ambiguity, which leaves the precise legal requirements governing FRT somewhat unclear. What is unambiguous, however, is the Court of Appeal's conclusion that the 'wanted for intelligence purposes' category could 'in effect cover anyone who is of interest to the police' and that this leaves too broad a discretion to police officers. This was a central component in the

Court's finding that SWP's use of FRT was unlawful. The MPS policy framework directly replicates this. The MPS are authorized to use LFR to identify potential victims of an offence, those who may have information relevant to the investigation of an offence, or close associates of someone falling within the other objectives (MPS 2023e: 6.8). That is, precisely those wanted for intelligence purposes. Interestingly, in the immediate aftermath of the *Bridges* Court of Appeal judgment, SWP removed this criterion from their policy framework. It has now been reinstated.

In such contexts, law and policy play a paradoxical role, offering the appearance of regulating surveillance while actually serving to extend it. Observing a similar trend, Loftus (2019) notes how covert policing strategies, once a last resort, became mainstreamed by the introduction of the Regulation of Investigatory Powers Act (RIPA) (2000). RIPA was originally designed to put covert policing on a legal footing following the passing of the Human Rights Act (1998), specifically to ensure authorization and oversight procedures for directed surveillance. For Loftus (2019) and others (inter alia, Harfield and Harfield 2018), the existence of such processes has made directed surveillance much more accessible and thus more extensively used. A similar dynamic is evident in the Investigatory Powers Act (2016), which established legal parameters around the acquisition of digital data following Edward Snowden's (2013) revelations of the National Security Agency (NSA) and GCHQ illegally spying on their own citizens (Murray and Fussey 2019). In effect, the Investigatory Powers Act extended surveillance powers that were used only by intelligence agencies such as GCHQ (albeit unlawfully) to public authorities, such as local councils. A similar dynamic may be evident in the development and adoption of policy documentation to regulate the use of FRT. Initially developed by the MPS and SWP, this policy documentation has spread and become largely replicated by other forces—including Northamptonshire, North Wales Police, and Essex Police—as they begin to deploy LFR.

Resonant with the analysis of digital knowledge production discussed in Chapter 2, it is hard to avoid the conclusion that the logical framings presented to justify LFR start from a presumption of efficacy and legality, which are then justified with arguments that resemble the form, but not substance, of legal reasoning. A similar dynamic is also evident with respect to technical evaluations of LFR performance, where partially substantiated efficacy claims are dressed in the language of 'scientific' legitimacy and applied across all forms and uses of the technology. Such practices represent subtle modes of justifying facial recognition, a technology that remains controversial. Here, truth claims are asserted that draw on legal and scientific language for their legitimacy, they are seemingly authoritative, and, while insubstantial, they require detailed arguments to challenge. In a highly mediatized society, such claims, and their modes of production, have become continually repeated through public and parliamentary arenas of discourse in arenas where scope for nuance and detailed rebuttal is constricted. The elevation of these forms of knowledge, and their epistemological underpinnings, brings a renewed relevancy to Foucault's (2008) astute observation of a transition from 'regimes of jurisdiction' to those of 'veridiction' for the digital age.

9.7 Final Thoughts

Prior to the policing operations empirically studied for this book, FRT constituted a faltering and unreliable policing tool that appeared in sporadic and discontinuous experiments. At the end of this experimental phase, FRT had become mainstreamed, with 147 deployments of LFR in London between April 2023 and September 2024 (MPS 2024b) alone, increased adoption by SWP, Northamptonshire Police, North Wales Police, and Essex Police, and near universal use of RFR. The speed and alacrity of police FRT adoption has legitimated its deployment in other contexts, most notably through its increasingly routine—and uncounted—use in entertainment and retail spaces. The intrusive nature of this technology, the extension of surveillance asymmetries, its capacity to radically reconfigure police–citizen relationships, the inherent tendency for creep, and the regulatory vacuum it operates within render the current moment as a critical juncture in the analysis of AI-driven law enforcement. Moreover, the unregulated growth of this technology for both 'the police' and in 'policing' more generally has created new sites of control, of arbitrary rights interferences and bias in spaces of everyday interaction.

Not only does this herald the extension of surveillance infrastructure into new domains but a foundation is created whereby these surveillance tools can be adapted for future, and as yet unanticipated, applications. The current policy and technical infrastructure for FRT was enabled through the proliferation of urban surveillance cameras more than two decades ago. In another parallel, both technologies attained article of faith status at the point of introduction. Both were bestowed with expectations of transforming the landscape of offending despite the absence of any meaningful evidence at the time. This existing surveillance infrastructure also provides copious image data, which becomes available for analysis via RFR algorithms and could become applied to almost any public assembly or interaction. In other respects, future adaptations of FRT could increasingly link identity with spurious ascriptions of emotional states or intention through overhyped affect technologies. While appearing innovative by virtue of its AI architecture, such digital mergers of physiology and physiognomy also resonate with Victorian-era positivist criminology. As the myriad histories of police surveillance repeatedly remind us, such developments generate tangible consequences for those subjected to these tools. Hidden from meaningful oversight, as technologies proliferate, so disadvantage multiplies. As such, the realities of non-regulated, non-transparent expansion of FRT are significant and consequential.

A pressing question therefore emerges: what do we do about this? One immediate human rights law response is to legislate, and to establish a clear legal basis to regulate the use of FRT. Yet caution is required here too. It is not enough that any legislation satisfies the 'in accordance with the law' requirement of the three-part human rights test (relating to the quality and foreseeability of law). As discussed above, many examples attest to how legislation authored with the intention of restricting surveillance has inadvertently served to extend it. A key risk in legislating, therefore, is the establishment of overly permissive legislation that fails to uphold human rights obligations, provides scope for surveillance expansion, and is misapplied to permit extra procedural activity. Any legislation developed to permit such intrusive surveillance, therefore, must restrict use to that which is necessary in a democratic society. A key challenge here is ensuring that the overall harm associated with FRT is effectively taken into account—including the incorporation of potential chilling effects—to ensure that any necessity calculation is not inappropriately imbalanced. Meaningful independent oversight is also a key element to ensure compliance with the law both in principle and in practice. Without such oversight, responsibility for the deployment of FRT is handed solely to its users.

One difficulty affecting FRT, and experimental police technologies more generally, is the absence of clarity over the potential benefits or the potential harm of this technology. Seeking precision in this regard is further complicated by the deluge of unevidenced politicized and polemical claims. These combine to frustrate the ability to make appropriately informed decisions as to whether, and under what circumstances, FRT could ever be used in a human rights law-compliant manner. At present, the case for using FRT has yet to be established, the true extent of potential harms is unknown, and the mechanisms to ensure respect for human rights law obligations are absent. Under such circumstances, the evidence overwhelmingly supports arguments made by the UK Parliamentary Science and Technology Committee, the European Union, parts of the United Nations, and civil society organizations across the world: advocating a moratorium on this technology until these shortcomings are resolved, if they ever can be.

References

ACLU. 2002. *Drawing a Blank: The Failure of Facial Recognition Technology in Florida, an ACLU Special Report*. Washington, DC: ACLU. www.aclu.org/report/drawing-blank-report-tampa-police-records-reveals-poor-performance-face-recognition.

Ada Lovelace Institute. 2022. *The Ryder Review: Independent Legal Review of the Governance of Biometric Data in England and Wales*. London: Ada Lovelace Institute.

Agamben, G. 2008. 'No to Biopolitical Tattooing', *Communication and Critical/Cultural Studies* 5(2): 201–202.

Ainsworth, P. 1998. *Psychology, Law and Eyewitness Testimony*. Chichester: Wiley.

Akbari, A. 2025. 'The Birth of Code/Body', in V. Steeves and B. Roessler (eds.), *Being Human in a Digital World: Interdisciplinary Perspectives*. Cambridge: Cambridge University Press.

Akers, R. 1990. 'Rational Choice, Deterrence, and Social Learning Theory in Criminology: The Path Not Taken', *Journal of Criminal Law and Criminology* 81: 653–676.

Alexander, M. 2010. *The New Jim Crow: Mass Incarceration in the Age of Colorblindness*. New York: New Press.

Ali, A. 2016. 'Citizens under Suspicion: Responsive Research with Community under Surveillance', *Anthropology & Education Quarterly* 47: 78–95.

Amnesty International. 2023. 'Automated Apartheid: How Facial Recognition Fragments, Segregates and Controls Palestinians in the OPT'. London.

Amnesty International UK. 2018. *Trapped in the Matrix: Secrecy, Stigma and Bias in the Met's Gang Database*. London: Amnesty International UK.

Amoore, L. 2007. 'Vigilant Visualities: The Watchful Politics of the War on Terror', *Security Dialogue* 38(2): 139–156.

Amoore, L. 2009. 'Algorithmic War: Everyday Geographies of the War on Terror', *Antipode* 41(1): 49–69.

Amoore, L. 2014. *Politics of Possibility*. Durham, NC: Duke University Press.

Anderson, B. 2010. 'Security and the Future: Anticipating the Event of Terror', *Geoforum* 41(2): 227–235.

Anderson, Lord. 2015. *A Question of Trust: Report of the Investigatory Powers Review*. London: HMSO.

Andrejevic, M. and Selwin, N. 2022. *Facial Recognition*. Cambridge: Polity Press.

Apple Corp. 2017. *Face ID Security Guide*. www.apple.com/business/site/docs/FaceID_Security_Guide.pdf.

Arendt, H. 1963. *Eichmann in Jerusalem: A Report on the Banality of Evil*. New York: Viking Press.

Arendt, H. 1973 [1951]. *The Origins of Totalitarianism*. London: Harcourt, Brace & World.

Armstrong, G. and Norris, C. 1999. *The Maximum Surveillance Society: The Rise of CCTV*. London: Routledge.

Aston, V. 2017. 'State Surveillance of Protest and the Rights to Privacy and Freedom of Assembly: A Comparison of Judicial and Protester Perspectives', *European Journal of Law & Technology* 8: 2–19.

Atkinson, R. 2003. 'Domestication by Cappuccino or a Revenge on Urban Space? Control and Empowerment in the Management of Public Spaces', *Urban Studies* 40(9): 1829–1843.

Atkinson, R. and Helms, G. (eds.). 2007. *Securing the Urban Renaissance*. Bristol: Policy Press.

Bailey, Jane and Valerie Steeves (eds.). 2015. *eGirls, eCitizens: Putting Technology, Theory and Policy into Dialogue with Girls' and Young Women's Voices*. University of Ottawa Press, JSTOR, http://www.jstor.org/stable/j.ctt15nmj7f.

Bannister, J., Fyfe, N. R., and Kearns, A. 1998. 'Closed Circuit Television and the City', in C. Norris, J. Moran, and G. Armstrong (eds.), *Surveillance, Closed Circuit Television and Social Control*. Aldershot: Ashgate, pp. 21–41.

Barad, K. 2003. 'Posthumanist Performativity: Toward an Understanding of How Matter Comes to Matter', *Gender and Science* 28(3): 801–831.

Bate, S. et al. 2018. 'Applied Screening Tests for the Detection of Superior Face Recognition', *Cognitive Research* 3: 1–19.

Baudrillard, J. 1994. *Simulation and Simulacra*. Ann Arbor, MI: University of Michigan Press.

Bauman, Z. 1998. *Consumerism, Work and the New Poor*. Buckingham: Open University Press.

Bauman Z. 2004. *Identity, Conversations with Benedetto Vecchi*. Cambridge: Polity Press.

Bauman, Z. 2008. *Identity: Conversations with Benedetto Vecchi*. Cambridge: Polity Press.

Bauman, Z. and Lyon, D. 2012. *Liquid Surveillance: A Conversation*. Cambridge: Polity Press.

BBC. 2015, 15 June. 'Download Festival: Leicestershire Police Defend Facial Recognition Scans', *BBC News*.

BBC. 2019, 14 March. 'Ten Charts on the Rise of Knife Crime in England and Wales', *BBC News*.

BBC. 2019, 16 May. 'Facial Recognition', *BBC News*.

BBC. 2023, 8 April. 'Facial Recognition Tech: Liberty "Police Racism" Claim', *BBC News*.

BBC. 2024, 13 February. 'Met Police Scraps Controversial Gang Database'. www.bbc.co.uk/news/uk-england-london-68283487.

Benjamin, R. 2019. *Race after Technology: Abolitionist Tools for the New Jim Code*. Cambridge: Polity Press.

Benjamin, W. 2015 [1968]. 'The Work of Art in the Age of Mechanical Reproduction', in H. Arendt (ed.), *Illuminations*. London: Penguin Random House, 211–245.

Bhagwat, A. 2008. 'Associational Speech', *The Yale Law Journal* 120: 982–1028

Big Brother Watch. 2018. 'Face Off: The Lawless Growth of Facial Recognition in UK Policing'. London

Big Brother Watch. 2023, 28 October. '*The Guardian*: Two-Thirds of People on Facial Recognition List Were Not Wanted for Arrest'. London.

Bigo, D. 2001. 'The Möbius Ribbon of Internal and External Security(ies)', in M. Albert, D. Jacobson and Y. Lapid (eds.) *Identities, Borders, Orders: Rethinking International Relations Theory*. Minneapolis: Minnesota University Press.

Bijker, W., and Law, J. 1992. *Shaping Technology/Building Society*. Cambridge, MA: MIT Press.

Birhane, A. 2022. 'The Unseen Black Faces of AI Algorithms', *Nature* 610(7932): 451–452.

Bobak, A. K., Pampoulov, P., and Bate, S. 2016. 'Detecting Superior Face Recognition Skills in a Large Sample of Young British Adults', *Frontiers in Psychology* 7: 1–11.

Bowling, B. 1999. 'The Rise and Fall of New York Murder: Zero Tolerance or Crack's Decline?', *The British Journal of Criminology* 39(4): 531–555.

Bowling, B. and Phillips. C. 2002. *Racism, Crime and Justice*. Harlow: Pearson Education Ltd.

Boykoff, J. 2014. *Celebration Capitalism and the Olympic Games*. London: Routledge.

Boykoff, J. and Fussey, P. 2014. 'London's Shadow Legacies: Security and Activism at the 2012 Olympics', *Contemporary Social Science* 9(2): 253–270.

Bradford, B. and Fussey, P. 2023. 'Security and Smart Cities', in A. Liebling, S. Maruna, and L. McAra (eds.), *The Oxford Handbook of Criminology*. Oxford: Oxford University Press, pp. 609–631.

Braidotti, R. and Bignall, S. (eds.). 2019. *Posthuman Ecologies: Complexity and Process after Deleuze*. London: Rowman & Littlefield.

Brantingham, P. and Brantingham, P. 1981. 'Notes on the Geometry of Crime', in P. J. Brantingham and P. L. Brantingham (eds.), *Environmental Criminology*. London: Sage, pp. 27–54.

Brayne, S. 2020. *Predict and Surveil: Data, Discretion, and the Future of Policing*. Oxford: Oxford University Press.

Brewer M. B. and Silver M. D. 2000. 'Group Distinctiveness, Social Identification, and Collective Mobilisation', in S. Stryker, T.J. Owens, and R. W. White (eds.), *Self, Identity, and Social Movements*. Minneapolis: University of Minnesota Press.

Brown, A., Fishenden, J., and Thompson, M. 2014. *Digitizing Government: Understanding and Implementing New Business Models*. London: Palgrave Macmillan.

Brown, S. 1995. *CCTV in Town Centres: Three Case Studies*. Police Research Group Crime Detection and Prevention Series Paper No. 68. London: HMSO.

Brown, S. 1998. 'What's the Problem, Girls? CCTV and the Gendering of Public Safety', in C. Norris, J. Moran, and G. Armstrong (eds.), *Surveillance, Closed Circuit Television and Social Control*. Aldershot: Ashgate, pp. 207–220.

Browne, S. 2015. *Dark Matters: On the Surveillance of Blackness*. Durham, NC: Duke University Press.

Bullock, K. and Johnson, P. 2012. 'The Impact of the Human Rights Act on the Police Service in England and Wales', *British Journal of Criminology* 52(3): 630–650.

Buolamwini, J. 2019, 25 January. 'Response: Racial and Gender Bias in Amazon Rekognition—Commercial AI System for Analyzing Faces', *Medium*.

Buolamwini, J. and Gebru, T. 2018. 'Gender Shades: Intersectional Accuracy Disparities in Commercial Gender Classification'. *Proceedings of Machine Learning Research* 81.

Burrows, R. and Gane, N. 2006. 'Geodemographics, Software and Class', *Sociology* 40(5): 793–812.

Calhoun, C. 1998. 'Community without Propinquity Revisited: Communications Technology and the Transformation of the Urban Public Sphere', *Sociological Inquiry* 68(3): 373–397.

Callon, M., Lascoumes, P., and Barthe, Y. 2009. *Acting in an Uncertain World: An Essay on Technical Democracy*. Cambridge MA: MIT Press.

Campbell, E. 1999. 'Towards a Sociological Theory of Discretion', *International Journal of the Sociology of Law* 27: 79–101.

Canguilhem, G. 1979. *Le normal et le pathologique*. Paris: PUE.

Canning, V. and Tombs, S. 2021. *From Social Harm to Zemiology: A Critical Introduction*. London: Routledge.

Carrabine, E. 2008. *Crime, Culture and the Media*. Cambridge: Polity Press.

Casey, Baroness. 2023. 'An Independent Review into the Standards of Behaviour and Internal Culture of the Metropolitan Police Service'. www.met.police.uk/SysSiteAssets/media/downloads/met/about-us/baroness-casey-review/update-march-2023/baroness-casey-review-march-2023a.pdf.

Chandrasekaran, R. 2007. *Imperial Life in the Emerald City: Inside Baghdad's Green Zone*. London: Bloomsbury.

Cheshire Constabulary. 2021a. 'Retrospective Facial Recognition Technology (RFR) Data Protection Impact Assessment'. 7 September 2021.

Cheshire Constabulary. 2021b. 'Data Protection Impact Assessment'. 7 September 2021.

Christie N. 2004. *A Suitable Amount of Crime*. London: Routledge.

Christopherson, S. 1994. 'Fortress City: Privatizatised Spaces, Consumer Citizenship', in A. Amin (ed.), *Post-Fordism: A Reader*. Oxford: Blackwell, 409–428 .

CISCO. 2023. *Managed Stations Smart Analytics: Service Realisation*. Internal document revealed through freedom of information request. https://s3.documentcloud.org/documents/24757665/2executive-summary-managed-stations_service-realisation_report_redacted.pdf.

Coaffee, J. 2005. 'Urban Renaissance in the Age of Terrorism: Revanchism, Social Control or the End of Reflection?', *International Journal of Urban and Regional Research* 29(2): 447–454.

Coaffee, J. 2009. *Terrorism, Risk and the Global City: Towards Urban Resilience*. Farnham: Ashgate.

Coaffee, J. and Fussey, P. 2015. 'Constructing Resilience through Security and Surveillance: The Politics, Practices and Tensions of Security-Driven Resilience', *Security Dialogue* 46: 86–105.

Cohen, J. E. 2000. 'Examined Lives: Informational Privacy and the Subject as Object', *Stanford Law Review* 52: 1373–1438.

Cohen, J. E. 2012. *Configuring the Networked Self: Law, Code and the Play of Everyday Practice*. New Haven, CT: Yale University Press.

Cohen, S. 1979. 'The Punitive City: Notes on the Dispersal of Social Control', *Contemporary Crises* 3: 339–363.

Cohen, S. 1985. *Visions of Social Control*. Cambridge: Polity Press.

Coleman, R. 2004. 'Reclaiming the Streets: Closed Circuit Television, Neoliberalism and the Mystification of Social Divisions', in *Surveillance and Society*, 2(2/3) pp. 293–309.

Coleman, R. and Sim, J. 1998. 'From the Dockyards to the Disney Store: Surveillance, Risk and Security in Liverpool City Centre', *International Review of Law, Computers and Technology* 12(1): 27–45.

Coleman, R. and Sim, J. 2000. 'You'll Never Walk Alone: CCTV Surveillance, Order and Neo-Liberal Rule in Liverpool City Centre', *British Journal of Sociology* 51(4): 623–639.

Collier, S. 2009. 'Topologies of Power: Foucault's Analysis of Political Government beyond "Governmentality"', *Theory, Culture and Society* 26(6): 78–108.

Consensus Study Report. 2024. *Facial Recognition Technology: Current Capabilities, Future Prospects, and Governance*. Washington DC: National Academies Press.

Davies, B., Innes, M., and Dawson, A. 2018. *An Evaluation of South Wales Police's Use of Automated Facial Recognition*. Cardiff: Universities' Police Science Institute.

Davies, S. 1996. 'The Case Against: CCTV Should Not Be Introduced', *International Journal of Risk, Security and Crime Prevention* 1(4): 327–331.

Davis, J. P. et al. 2016. 'Investigating Predictors of Superior Face Recognition Ability in Police Super-Recognisers', *Applied Cognitive Psychology* 30(6): 1–51.

Davis, K. 1971. *Discretionary Justice: A Preliminary Inquiry*. Baton Rouge, LA: Louisiana State University Press.

Davis, M. 1990. *City of Quartz: Excavating the Future of Los Angeles*. London: Verso.

Davis, M. 1992. 'Fortress Los Angeles: The Militarization of Urban Space', in M. Sorkin (ed.), *Variations on a Theme Park: The New American City and the End of Public Space*. New York: Hill and Wang, pp. 154–181.

Davis, M. 1998. *Ecology of Fear: Los Angeles and the Imagination of Disaster*. New York: Metropolitan Books.

Davis, J. L., Love, T. P., and Fares, P. 2019. 'Collective Social Identity: Synthesizing Identity Theory and Social Identity Theory Using Digital Data', *Social Psychology Quarterly*, 82(3): 254–273.

de Goede, M. and Randalls, S. 2009. 'Precaution, Preemption: Arts and Technologies of the Actionable Future', *Environment and Planning D: Society and Space* 27(5): 859–878.

DeLanda, M. 2016. *Assemblage Theory*. Edinburgh: Edinburgh University Press.

DeLanda, M. 2018. *Assemblage Theory*. Edinburgh: Edinburgh University Press.

Deleuze, G. 1988. *Foucault*. Minneapolis, MN: University of Minnesota Press.

Deleuze, G. 1995. 'Postscript on Control Societies', in G. Deleuze, *Negotiations 1972–1990*. New York: Columbia University Press, pp. 177–183.

Deleuze, G. and Guattari, F. 1987. *A Thousand Plateaus: Capitalism and Schizophrenia*. Minneapolis, MN: University of Minnesota Press.

Dick, C. 2020. *RUSI Annual Security Lecture*. London: RUSI.

Ditton, J. 1998. 'Public Support for Town Centre CCTV Schemes: Myth or Reality?', in C. Norris, J. Moran, and G. Armstrong (eds.), *Surveillance, Closed Circuit Television and Social Control*. Aldershot: Ashgate, pp. 221–228.

Douglas, M. 1966. *Purity and Danger: An Analysis of the Concepts of Pollution and Taboo*. London: Routledge.

Douglas, M. 1992. *Risk and Blame: Essays in Cultural Theory*. London: Routledge.

Dworkin, R. M. 1977. *Taking Rights Seriously*. Cambridge, MA: Harvard University Press.

Dyb, K. and Halford, S. 2009. 'Placing Globalizing Technologies: Telemedicine and the Making of Difference', *Sociology* 43(2): 232–249.

Edmund, G. and Wortley, N. 2016. 'Interpreting Image Evidence: Facial Mapping, Police Familiars and Super-Recognisers in England and Australia', *Journal of International and Comparative Law* 3(2): 473–523.

EFF. 2009, 10 December. 'Google CEO Eric Schmidt Dismisses the Importance of Privacy'. www.eff.org/deeplinks/2009/12/google-ceo-eric-schmidt-dismisses-privacy.

Eliot, T. S. 1934. *The Rock*. New York: Harcourt Brace and Company.

Ericson, R. and Haggerty, K. 1997. *Policing the Risk Society*. Oxford: Clarendon Press.

Essex Police. 2023. 'Live Facial Recognition Data Protection Impact Assessment'.

European Commission. 2012. Article 29 Data Protection Working Party. Opinion 3/2012 on developments in biometric technologies. 00720/12/EN WP193. Brussels. https://ec.europa.eu/justice/article-29/documentation/opinion-recommendation/files/2012/wp193_en.pdf.

European Union Fundamental Rights Agency. 2020. 'Facial Recognition Technology: Fundamental Rights Considerations in the Context of Law Enforcement'. Vienna: EU FRA.

Evening Standard. 2019. *Face-scanning CCTV Approved for London Hot-Spots Despite Privacy Storm*, 2 September. https://www.standard.co.uk/news/tech/facescanning-cctv-approved-for-london-hotspots-despite-privacy-storm-a4226661.html.

Fassin, D. 2013. *Enforcing Order: An Anthropology of Urban Policing*. Cambridge: Polity Press.

Ferguson A, 2017. *The Rise of Big Data Policing: Surveillance, Race, and the Future of Law Enforcement*, New York: New York University Press

Financial Times. 2019, 12 August. 'London's King's Cross Uses Facial Recognition in Security Cameras'.

Financial Times. 2024, 2 October. 'Met Police Use of Facial Recognition in London Surges'.

Fiske, J. 1998. 'Surveilling the City: Whiteness, the Black Man and Democratic Totalitarianism', *Theory, Culture and Society* 15(2): 67–88.

FISWG. 2012. *Guidelines for Facial Comparison Methods*. www.fiswg.org/fiswg_guidelines_facial_comparison_methods_v1.0_2012_02_02_archived.pdf.

FISWG. 2018. 'Facial Image Comparison Feature List for Morphological Analysis'. https://fiswg.org/FISWG_Morph_Analysis_Feature_List_v2.0_20180911.pdf.

Forensic Science Regulator. 2019. 'Code of Practice for Forensic Gait Analysis'. https://assets.publishing.service.gov.uk/government/uploads/system/uploads/attachment_data/file/918878/137_Forensic_Gait_Analysis_Issue_2.pdf.

Foucault, M. 1972. *The Archeology of Knowledge and the Discourse on Language*. New York: Pantheon

Foucault, M. 1977a. *Discipline and Punish: The Birth of the Prison*. London: Penguin.

Foucault, M. 1977b. 'Nietzsche, Genealogy, History', in D. Bouchard (ed.), *Language, Counter-Memory, Practice: Selected Essays and Interviews*. Ithaca, NY: Cornell University Press, pp. 139–165.

Foucault, M. 1977c. 'The Political Function of the Intellectual', *Radical Philosophy* 17.: 12–15.

Foucault, M. 1980. *Power/Knowledge: Selected Interviews and Other Writings 1972–1977*. C. Gordon, ed. Brighton: Harvester Press.

Foucault, M. 1982. 'Space, Knowledge, and Power', in P. Rabinow (ed.), *The Foucault Reader*. New York: Pantheon, pp. 239–257.

Foucault, M. 1984. 'Life: Experience and Science', in P. Rabinow and N. Rose (eds.), *The Essential Foucault: Selections from Essential Works of Foucault, 1954–1984*. New York: The New Press, pp. 6–18.

Foucault, M. 1991. 'Governmentality', in G. Burchill, C. Gordon, and P. Miller (eds.), *The Foucault Effect: Studies in Governmentality*. London: Harvester Wheatsheaf, pp. 87–104.

Foucault, M. 1994. Life: experience and science. In Paul Rabinow and Nickolas Rose, eds., *The Essential Foucault: Selections from Essential Works of Foucault, 1954-1984*. New York and London: The New Press, pp. 6–18.

Foucault, M. 2007. *Security, Territory, Population, Lectures at the Collège de France 1977–1978*. Basingstoke: Palgrave.

Foucault, M. 2008. *The Birth of Biopolitics: Lectures at the Collège de France 1978–79*. Basingstoke: Palgrave.

Frontex. 2020. International Conference on Biometrics for Borders: Morphing and Morphing Attach Detection Methods.

Furedi, F. 2008. 'Fear and Security: A Vulnerability-Led Policy Response', *Social Policy & Administration* 42(6): 645–661.

Fussey, P. 2004. 'New Labour and New Surveillance: Theoretical and Political Ramifications of CCTV Implementation in the UK', *Surveillance and Society* 2(2–3): 251–269.

Fussey, P. 2007. 'An Interrupted Transmission? Processes of CCTV Implementation and the Impact of Human Agency', *Surveillance and Society* 4(3): 229–256.

Fussey, P. 2008. 'Beyond Liberty, Beyond Security: The Politics of Public Surveillance', *British Politics* 3(1): 120–135.

Fussey, P. 2010. 'Protecting Britain's Crowded Spaces from Terrorist Attacks: Key criminological reflections', in A. Silke (ed.) *Psychology, Terrorism and Counterterrorism*. London: Routledge.

Fussey, P. 2013. 'Contested Topologies of UK Counterterrorist Surveillance: The Rise and Fall of Project Champion', *Critical Studies on Terrorism* 6(3): 351–370.

Fussey, P. and Murray, D. 2019. 'Independent Report on the London Metropolitan Police Service's Trial of Live Facial Recognition Technology', Human Rights Big Data & Technology Project.

Fussey, P. and Sandhu, A. 2022. 'Surveillance Arbitration in the Era of Digital Policing', *Theoretical Criminology* 26: 3–22.

Fussey, P. and Webster, W. 2023. 'Policy Review: The Evolving Governance of Surveillance Cameras in the UK', *Information Polity* 28(4): 559–567.

Fussey, P., Davies, B., and Innes, M. 2021. '"Assisted" Facial Recognition and the Reinvention of Suspicion and Discretion in Digital Policing', *The British Journal of Criminology* 61(2): 325–344.

Fussey, P., Coaffee, J., Armstrong, G., and Hobbs, D. 2011. *Securing and Sustaining the Olympic City: Reconfiguring London for 2012 and Beyond*. Aldershot: Ashgate.

Fussey, P., Coaffee, J., Armstrong, G., and Hobbs, D. 2012. 'The Regeneration Games: Purity and Security in the Olympic City', *The British Journal of Sociology* 63(2): 260–284.

Fyfe, N. R. 2004. 'Zero Tolerance, Maximum Surveillance? Deviance, Difference and Crime Control in the Late-Modern City', in L. Lees (ed.), *The Emancipatory City? Paradoxes and Possibilities*. London: Sage, pp. 40–56.

Fyfe, N. R. and Bannister, J. 1996. 'City Watching: Closed Circuit Television in Public Spaces', *Area* 28(1): 37–46.

Gandy, O. H. (2009) *Coming to Terms with Chance Engaging Rational Discrimination and Cumulative Disadvantage*, London: Routledge.

Gandy, O. H. 2016. *Coming to Terms with Chance: Engaging Rational Discrimination and Cumulative Disadvantage*. London: Routledge.

GAO (US Government Accountability Office). 2017. 'Aviation Security: TSA Does Not Have Valid Evidence Supporting Most of the Revised Behavioral Indicators Used in Its Behavior Detection Activities'. www.gao.gov/assets/gao-17-608r.pdf.

Gates, K. 2006. 'Identifying the 9/11 "Faces of Terror": The Promise and Problem of Facial Recognition Technology', *Cultural Studies* 20(4–5): 417–440.

Gates, K. 2011. *Our Biometric Future: Facial Recognition Technology and the Culture of Surveillance*. New York: New York University Press.

Gates, K. 2013. 'The Cultural Labor of Surveillance: Video Forensics, Computational Objectivity, and the Production of Visual Evidence', *Social Semiotics* 23(2): 242–260.

Germain, S. 2007. 'The Rise of CCTV in France: An Analysis of a Municipal Experimentation', Paper given at the *European Society of Criminology Conference*, Bologna, Italy, 28 September.

Gibson, J. 1977. 'The Theory of Affordances', in R. Shaw and J. Bransford (eds.), *Perceiving, Acting, and Knowing: Toward an Ecological Psychology*. Hillsdale, NJ: Erlbaum, pp. 67–82.

Giddens, A. 1981. *A Contemporary Critique of Historical Materialism. Volume 1: Power, Property and the State*. London: Macmillan.

Goffman, E. 1968. *Asylum: Essays on the Social Situation of Mental Patients and Other Inmates*. Harmondsworth: Penguin.

Goold, B. 2004. *CCTV and Policing Public Area Surveillance and Police Practices in Britain*. Oxford: Oxford University Press.

Gould, S. J. 1981. *The Mismeasure of Man*. New York: W. W. Norton & Company.

Graham, S. 2005. 'Software-Sorted Geographies', *Progress in Human Geography* 29(5): 562–580.

Graham, S. 2010. *Cities under Siege: The New Military Urbanism*. London: Verso.

Graham, S., Brooks, J., and Heery, D. 1996. 'Towns on the Television: Closed Circuit TV in British Towns and Cities', *Local Government Studies* 22(3): 3–27.

Graham, S. and Marvin, S. 1996. *Telecommunications and the City: Electronic Spaces, Urban Places*, London: Routledge.

Greenwald, G. 2014. *Nowhere to Hide: Edward Snowden, the NSA and the Surveillance State*. London. Hamish Hamilton.

Grint, K. and Woolgar, S. 1997. *The Machine at Work: Technology, Work and Organization*. Cambridge: Blackwell.

Grother, P. 2019, 28 October. Presentation on Facial Recognition Delivered to the Biometrics Institute.

Hadjimatheou, K. and Fussey, P. 2025 '"The dream to know everything about everyone": Affordances of Commercial Data Systems and Digital Net Widening in Policing', *Theoretical Criminology* (accepted and in press).

Haggerty, K. 2006. 'Tear Down the Walls: On Demolishing the Panopticon', in D. Lyon (ed.), *Theorizing Surveillance*. London: Routledge, pp. 37–59.

Haggerty, K. D. and Ericson, R. V. (2000), 'The Surveillant Assemblage', *The British Journal of Sociology*, 51: 605–622.

Haggerty, K. and Gazso, A. 2005. 'Seeing beyond the Ruins: Surveillance as a Response to Terrorist Threats', *Canadian Journal of Sociology* 30(2): 169–187.

Haggerty, K. and Ericson, R. 2000. 'The Surveillant Assemblage', *British Journal of Sociology* 51(4): 605–622.

Harfield, C. and Harfield. K. 2018. *Covert Investigation*, 5th ed. London: Oxford University Press.

Harfield, C. and Harfield, K. 2023. *Covert Investigation*, 6th ed. London: Oxford University Press.

Harvey, D. 1990. *The Condition of Postmodernity: An Enquiry into the Origins of Cultural Change*. Cambridge, MA: Blackwell.

Hatherley, O. 2010. *A Guide to the New Ruins of Great Britain*. London: Verso.

Hayward, K. 2007. 'Situational Crime Prevention and Its Discontents: Rational Choice Theory versus the "Culture of Now"'. *Social Policy & Administration* 41(3): 232–250.

Head, T. 2022. The Limits of Legitimacy: Power, Racisms and the Policing of Youth in Inner-City London. Unpublished PhD thesis. University of Essex.

Heidegger, M. 1978. *The Question Concerning Technology*. London: Routledge & Kegan Paul.

Higgs, E. 2011. *Identifying the English A History of Personal Identification 1500 to the Present*. Continuum.

HM Coroner. 2011. *Coroner's Inquest into the London Bombings of July 7th 2005*. https://webarchive.nationalarchives.gov.uk/ukgwa/20120216072447mp_/http://7julyinquests.independent.gov.uk/docs/orders/rule43-report.pdf.

Hobbs, D. 1988. *Doing the Business: Entrepreneurship, the Working Class and Detectives in East London*. Oxford: Oxford University Press.

Home Office. 2013. *Surveillance Camera Code of Practice*. London: Home Office.

Home Office. 2018a. *Code of Practice for Covert Surveillance and Property Interference, Issued in August 2018 Pursuant of 71(4) of the Regulation of Investigatory Powers Act 2000*. London: Home Office.

Home Office. 2018b. *National Law Enforcement Data Programme, Law Enforcement Data Service Privacy Impact Assessment Report*. London: Home Office.

Home Office. 2021. *Surveillance Camera Code of Practice (Updated)*. London: Home Office.

Home Office. 2022. *National Law Enforcement Data Programme (NLEDP) Accounting Officer Assessment*. London: Home Office.

House of Commons. 2019. *Science and Technology Committee, Oral Evidence: Work of the Biometrics Commissioner and the Forensic Science Regulator*. HC 1970. Tuesday 19 March. http://data.parliament.uk/writtenevidence/committeeevidence.svc/evidencedocument/science-and-technology-committee/the-work-of-the-biometrics-commissioner-and-the-forensic-science-regulator/oral/98556.html.

House of Commons. 2020. Automated Facial Recognition Surveillance. Debated 27 January. https://hansard.parliament.uk/commons/2020-01-27/debates/9AEC6C71-400E-49D9-8B49-15D9ED8C693F/AutomatedFacialRecognitionSurveillance.

House of Lords. 2021. *Technology Rules? The Advent of New Technologies in the Justice System*. Justice and Home Affairs Committee, 1st Report of Session 2021–2022.

House of Lords. 2024. 'Peaceful Protests', Debated 25 April.

Human Rights Committee. 1989. 'General Comment No. 18', UN Doc. HRI/GEN/1/Rev.1. November.

Human Rights Committee. 2011. 'General Comment No. 34', UN Doc. CCPR/C/GC/34. 12 September.

Human Rights Committee. 2020. 'General Comment No. 37', UN Doc. CCPR/C/GC/37. 17 September.

Human Rights Council. 2011. 'Human Rights and Transnational Corporations and Other Business Enterprises', UN Doc. A/HRC/Res/17/4. 6 July.

Humberside Police. 2018. 'Privacy Impact Assessment for the Use of Facial Imaging Deployment at Terminal 1, King George Dock, Hull'.

Huq, A. Z. 2020. 'A Right to a Human Decision', *Virginia Law Review* 106: 611–689.

Information Commissioner's Office. 2006. 'A Report on the Surveillance Society: Public Discussion Document', London: Information Commissioners' Office, http://www.ico.gov.uk/upload/documents/library/data_protection/practical_application/surveillance_society_public_discussion_document_06.pdf

ICO. 2022a. 'Open Letter from UK Information Commissioner John Edwards to Public Authorities'. https://ico.org.uk/about-the-ico/media-centre/news-and-blogs/2022/06/open-letter-from-uk-information-commissioner-john-edwards-to-public-authorities.

ICO. 2022b. 'Video Surveillance (Including Guidance for Organisations Using CCTV)'. https://ico.org.uk/for-organisations/uk-gdpr-guidance-and-resources/cctv-and-video-surveillance/guidance-on-video-surveillance-including-cctv.

ICO. n.d. 'Guide to Law Enforcement Processing: Individual Rights', https://ico.org.uk/for-organisations/guide-to-data-protection/guide-to-le-processing/individual-rights.

Introna, L. and Nissenbaum, H. 2010. *Facial Recognition Technology: A Survey of Policy and Implementation Issues*. New York: Center for Catastrophe Preparedness and Response, New York University.

Introna, L. D. and Wood, D. 2004. 'Picturing Algorithmic Surveillance: The Politics of Facial Recognition Systems', *Surveillance and Society* 2(2/3): 177–198.

Investigatory Powers Commissioner's Office. 2022. *Annual Report 2022*. London: IPCO, https://ipco-wpmedia-prod-s3.s3.eu-west-2.amazonaws.com/Annual-Report-2022.pdf,

Jacobs, J. 1961. *The Death and Life of Great American Cities*. New York: Vintage Books.

Jencks, C. 1977. *The Language of Post-Modern Architecture*. New York: Rizzoli.

Joh, E. 2016. 'The New Surveillance Discretion: Automated Suspicion, Big Data, and Policing', *Harvard Law & Policy Review* 10: 15–43.

Jospeh, S. and Castan, M. 2013. *The International Covenant on Civil and Political Rights: Cases, Materials and Commentary*. 3rd ed. Oxford: Oxford University Press.

Kaker, S. A. 2014. 'Enclaves, Insecurity and Violence in Karachi', *South Asian History and Culture* 5(1): 93–107.

Kendrick, L. 2013. 'Speech, Intent, and the Chilling Effect', *William & Mary Law Review* 54: 1633–1692.

Kitchin, R. 2014. *The Data Revolution: Big Data, Open Data, Data Infrastructures and Their Consequences*. London: Sage.

Kleinberg, K., Vanezis, P., and Burton A. 2007. 'Failure of Anthropometry as a Facial Identification Technique Using High-Quality Photographs', *Journal of Forensic Sciences* 52(4): 779–783.

Kloppenburg, S. and van der Ploeg, I. 2018. 'Securing Identities: Biometric Technologies and the Enactment of Human Bodily Differences', *Science as Culture* 29(1): 57–76.

Kydd, A. 2022. 'Our Place in the Universe: Alexander Wendt and Quantum Mechanics', *International Theory* 14(1): 130–145.

Lammy, D. 2017. 'The Lammy Review: An Independent Report into the Treatment of, and Outcomes for, Black, Asian and Minority Ethnic Individuals in the Criminal Justice System'. https://assets.publishing.service.gov.uk/media/5a82009040f0b62305b91f49/lammy-review-final-report.pdf.

Langstone, D. 2009. 'Myths, Crimes and Videotape', in J. Burnett, K. Walker, and P. Senker (eds.), *The Myths of Technology: Innovation and Inequality*. Oxford: Peter Lang, pp. 113–130.

Lashmar P. 2016. 'No More Sources? The Impact of Snowden's Revelations on Journalists and Their Confidential Sources', *Journalism Practice* 11: 665–688.

Latour, B. 1987. *Science in Action: How to Follow Scientists and Engineers through Society*. Cambridge, MA: Harvard University Press.

Latour, B. 1999. *Pandora's Hope: Essays on the Reality of Science Studies*. Cambridge, MA: Harvard University Press.

Latour, B. 2005. *Reassembling the Social: An Introduction to Actor-Network-Theory*: Oxford: Oxford University Press.

Latour, B. 2012. 'Spaces of Transformation: Continuity/Infinity', lecture delivered at the Tate Modern, London, 3 March.

Latour, B., Jensen, P., Venturini, T., Grauwin, S. and Boullier, D. 2012. 'The Whole is Always Smaller Than Its Parts', *The British Journal of Sociology*, 63: 590–615.

Le Bon, G. 2018 [1895]. *The Crowd: A Study of the Popular Mind*. London: SMK Books.

Lefebvre, H. 2004. *Rhythmanalysis: Space, Time and Everyday Life*. London: Continuum.

Lemke, T. 2021. *The Government of Things: Foucault and the New Materialisms*. New York: New York University Press.

Lentzos, F. and Rose, N. 2009. 'Governing Insecurity: Contingency Planning, Protection and Resilience', *Economy and Society* 38: 230–254.

Levinas, E. 1985. *Ethics and Infinity: Conversations with Philippe Nemo*. Pittsburgh, PA: Duquesne University Press.

Lianos, M. 2012. *The New Social Control*. Ottawa: Red Quill Books.

Liberty. 2019. 'Stop and Search: The Facts'. www.libertyhumanrights.org.uk/tags/stop-and-search.

Liberty. 2020. 'Appellant's Replacement Skeleton Argument', 2 April. www.libertyhumanrights.org.uk/wp-content/uploads/2020/02/Appellants-Skeleton-Argument-in-the-Court-of-Appeal.pdf.

Liberty Investigates. 2023. 'Hundreds of Thousands of Innocent People on Police Databases as Forces Expand Use of Facial Recognition', 25 September. https://libertyinvestigates.org.uk/articles/hundreds-of-thousands-of-innocent-people-on-police-databases-as-forces-expand-use-of-facial-recognition-tech.

Loftus, E. 1990. *Eyewitness Testimony*. Cambridge, MA: Harvard University Press.

Loftus, B., Goold, B., and Mac Giollabhui, S. 2016. 'From a Visible Spectacle to an Invisible Presence: The Working Culture of Covert Policing', *British Journal of Criminology*, 56(4): 629–645.

London Assembly. 2007. *7 July Review Committee*. London: London Assembly. www.london.gov.uk/sites/default/files/gla_migrate_files_destination/archives/assembly-reports-7july-report.pdf.

London Police Ethics Panel. 2019. 'Final Report on Live Facial Recognition'.

Los Angeles Times. 2001, 2 February. 'Super Day for Big Brother'.

Los Angeles Times. 2008, 7 August. 'Many Eyes Will Watch Visitors'.

Lyon, D. 2001. *Surveillance Society: Monitoring Everyday Life*. Buckingham: Open University Press.

Lyon, D. 2003a. *Surveillance as Social Sorting: Privacy, Risk and Automated Discrimination*. London: Routledge.

Lyon, D. 2003b. *Surveillance after September 11th*. Cambridge: Polity Press.

Lyon, D. 2006. *Theorizing Surveillance: The Panopticon and Beyond*. London: Routledge.

Lyotard, F. 1984. *The Postmodern Condition*. Manchester: University of Manchester Press.

MacKay, C. 1841 [1995]. *Extraordinary Popular Delusions and the Madness of Crowds*. Ware: Wordsworth Reference.

Macoveciuc, I. 2020. 'The Utility of Gait as a Biological Characteristic in Forensic Investigations: An Empirical Examination of Movement Pattern Variation Using Biomechanical and Anthropological Principles'. Doctoral thesis, University College London.

MacPherson, S. 1999. *The Steven Lawrence Inquiry*. https://assets.publishing.service.gov.uk/media/5a7c2af540f0b645ba3c7202/4262.pdf.

Maguire, M. and Fussey, P. 2016. 'Sensing Evil', *Focaal: Journal of Global and Historical Anthropology* 75: 31–44.

Maguire, M., & Fussey, P. 2016. 'Sensing Evil: Counterterrorism, Techno-science, and The Cultural Reproduction of Security', *Focaal—Journal of Global and Historical Anthropology*, 2016(75): 31–44.

Manning, P. 1978. 'Rules, Colleagues and Situationally Justified Actions', in P. Manning and J. Van Maanen (eds.), *Policing: A View from the Streets*. New York: Random House, pp. 71–89.

Marcuse, H. 1964. *One-Dimensional Man: Studies in the Ideology of Advanced Industrial Society*. Boston, MA: Beacon Press.

Marjanovic, O., Cecez-Kecmanovic, D., and Vidgen, R. 2021. 'Algorithmic Pollution: Making the Invisible Visible', *Journal of Information Technology* 36: 391–408.

Marx, G. 1989. *Undercover: Police Surveillance in America*. Oakland, CA: University of California Press.

Marx, G. 2002. 'What's New about the "New Surveillance"? Classifying for Change and Continuity', *Surveillance and Society* 1(1): 9–29.

Marx, G. 2016. *Windows into the Soul: Surveillance and Society in an Age of High Technology*. Chicago, IL: The University of Chicago Press.

Matar, R. and Murray, D. 2025. 'Rethinking International Human Rights Law's Approach to Identity in the Era of AI', *Human Rights Law Review* (forthcoming).

Mathiesen, T. 1997. 'The Viewer Society: Michael Foucault's "Panopticon" Revisited', in *Theoretical Criminology* 1(2): 215–234.

Matsumoto, D. et al. 2011. 'Evaluating Truthfulness and Detecting Deception'. FBI Law Enforcement Bulletin, June. http://davidmatsumoto.com/content/Evaluating%20Truthfulness%20and%20Detecting%20Deception.pdf

Matthews, A. and Tucker, C. 2015. 'Government Surveillance and Internet Search Behavior', MIT Sloane Working Paper No. 14380.

Matza, D. 1969. *Becoming Deviant*. Englewood Cliffs, NJ: Prentice-Hall.

McCahill, M. 2002. *The Surveillance Web: The Rise of Visual Surveillance in an English City*. Cullompton: Willan Publishing.

McGoey, L. 2012. 'The Logic of Strategic Ignorance?', *British Journal of Sociology* 63(3): 533–576.

McGoldrick, D. 2018. 'Thought, Expression, Association, and Assembly', in D. Moeckli et al. (eds.), *International Human Rights Law*, 3rd ed. Oxford: Oxford University Press, pp. 210–234.

McGrath. 2004. *Loving Big Brother: Surveillance Culture and Performance Space*. London: Routledge.

McGregor, L., Murray, D., and Ng, V. 2019. 'International Human Rights Law as a Framework for Algorithmic Accountability', *International and Comparative Law Quarterly* 68: 309–343.

McIlwain C. 2019. *Black Software: The Internet and Racial Justice, from the AfroNet to Black Lives Matter*. Oxford: Oxford University Press.

Milone, M. 2001. 'Biometric Surveillance: Searching for identity', *The Business Lawyer* 57(1): 497–512.

Ministry of Justice. 2012. *Statistical Bulletin on the Public Disorder of 6th to 9th August 2011: September 2012 Update*. London: Ministry of Justice. https://assets.publishing.service.gov.uk/government/uploads/system/uploads/attachment_data/file/219665/august-public-disorder-stats-bulletin-130912.pdf.

Moeckli, D. 2018. 'Equality and Non-Discrimination', in D. Moeckli et al. (eds.), *International Human Rights Law*, 3rd ed. Oxford: Oxford University Press, pp. 152–168.

Monahan, T. 2022. *Crisis Vision: Race and the Cultural Production of Surveillance*. Durham, NC: Duke University Press.

Motsch et al. 2018. 'Modelling Crowd Dynamics through Coarse-Grained Data Analysis', *American Institute of Mathematical Sciences* 15(6): 1271–1290.

MPS. 2018a. 'Live Facial Recognition: Legal Mandate', version 1.01.

MPS. 2018b. 'Data Protection Impact Assessment for the Use of Live Facial recognition with the MPS'.

MPS. 2018c. 'Live Facial Recognition, (LFR) MPS Legal Mandate'.

MPS. 2018d. 'Live Facial Recognition, (LFR) MPS Operational Mandate'.

MPS. 2020a. 'Data Protection Impact Assessment'.

MPS. 2020b. 'Live Facial Recognition: Legal Mandate', version 2.0.

MPS. 2021. 'Live Facial Recognition: Legal Mandate'.

MPS. 2022. 'MPS LFR Deployments 2020–2022'. www.met.police.uk/SysSiteAssets/media/downloads/force-content/met/advice/lfr/new/lfr-deployment-grid-2020-2022.pdf.

MPS. 2023a. 'Data Protection Impact Assessment (DPIA)'.

MPS. 2023b. 'Facial Recognition Technology'. www.met.police.uk/advice/advice-and-information/fr/facial-recognition-technology.

MPS. 2023c. 'Live Facial Recognition: Legal Mandate', version 3.0.

MPS. 2023d. 'MPS LFR Policy Document: Direction for the MPS Deployment of overt Live Facial Recognition Technology to Locate Person(s) on a Watchlist', version 3.0.

MPS. 2023e. 'MPS Policy: Retrospective Facial Recognition System', version 1.0.

MPS. 2023f. 'Standard Operating Procedure for the Overt Operational Deployment of Live Facial Recognition (LFR) Technology', version 3.0.

MPS. 2023g. 'Statement on Release of Research into Facial Recognition Technology'. https://news.met.police.uk/news/statement-on-release-of-research-into-facial-recognition-technology-464791.

MPS. 2024a. 'Equality Impact Assessment: Steps 1 to 7'. www.met.police.uk/SysSiteAssets/media/downloads/force-content/met/advice/lfr/impact-assessments/lfr-eia2.pdf.

MPS. 2024b. 'MPS LFR Deployments 2023 to Date'. www.met.police.uk/SysSiteAssets/media/downloads/force-content/met/advice/lfr/deployment-records/lfr-deployment-grid.pdf.

Mulvey, L. 1975. 'Visual Pleasure and Narrative Cinema', *Screen* 16(3): 6–18.

Murakami Wood, D. and Monahan, T. 2019. 'Platform Surveillance', *Surveillance and Society* 17(1/2): 1–6.

Murgia, M. 2023. *Code Dependent: Living in the Shadow of AI*. London: Picador.

Murray D. 2020. 'Using Human Rights Law to Inform Sates' Decisions to Deploy AI', *AJIL:Unbound!* 114: 158–162.

Murray, D., Fussey, P., McGregor, L., and Sunkin, M. 2021. 'Effective Oversight of Large-Scale Surveillance Activities: A Human Rights Perspective', *Journal of National Security Law and Policy* 11(3): 743–770.

Murray, D. 2024. 'Police Use of Retrospective Facial Recognition Technology: A Step Change in Surveillance Capability Necessitating an Evolution of the Human Rights Law Framework', *Modern Law Review* 87: 833–863.

Murray, D. and Fussey, P. 2019. 'Bulk Surveillance in the Digital Age: Rethinking the Human Rights Law Approach to Bulk Monitoring of Communications Data', *Israel Law Review* 52: 31–60.

Murray, D. et al. 2024. 'The Chilling Effects of Surveillance and Human Rights: Insights from Qualitative Research in Uganda and Zimbabwe', *Journal of Human Rights Practice* 16: 397–412.

Musheno, M., Lavine, J., and Palumbo, D. 1978. 'Television Surveillance and Crime Prevention: Evaluation of an Attempt to Create Defensible Space in Public Housing', *Social Science Quarterly* 58(4): 647–656.

Mythen, G. and Walklate, S. 2006. 'Criminology and Terrorism: Which Thesis? Risk Society or Governmentality?', *British Journal of Criminology* 46(3): 379–398.

National Academies Press. 2024. *Consensus Study Report, Facial Recognition Technology: Current Capabilities, Future Prospects, and Governance*. Washington, DC: National Academies Press.

National Center for Border Security and Immigration. 2014. *Appraising the AVATAR for Automated Border Control*. Tucson, AZ: The University of Arizona.

National College of Policing. 2022. 'Intelligence Report'. www.college.police.uk/app/intelligence-management/intelligence-report.

National Institute of Justice. 2003. 'CCTV: Constant Cameras Track Violators', *National Institute of Justice Journal* (249):16–23.

National Physical Laboratory. 2023. 'Facial Recognition Technology in Law Enforcement Equitability Study: Final Report'. https://science.police.uk/site/assets/files/3396/frt-equitability-study_mar2023.pdf.

National Physical Laboratory and Metropolitan Police Service. 2020. 'Metropolitan Police Service Live Facial Recognition Trials'. www.met.police.uk/SysSiteAssets/media/downloads/central/services/accessing-information/facial-recognition/met-evaluation-report.pdf.

Neville, M. 2012. 'Bringing the Rioters to Justice', presentation delivered at Global MSC Security Conference , Bristol, March.

New Statesman. 2024, 3 July. 'Why Do Big Digital Projects in the Public Sector Fail?'.

NIST. 2018. *Ongoing Face Recognition Vendor Test (FRVT) Part 2: Identification*. Washington, DC: US Department of Commerce.

NIST. 2019. *Face Recognition Vendor Test (FRVT) Part 3: Demographic Effects*. Washington, DC: US Department of Commerce.

NIST. 2020. *Face Recognition Vendor Test (FRVT) MORPH Performance of Automated Face Morph Detection*. Washington, DC: US Department of Commerce.

NPIA. 2007. *Police Standard for Still Digital Image Capture and Data Interchange of Facial/Mugshot and Scar, Mark and Tattoo Images*. National Policing Improvement Agency.

Norris, C. and Armstrong, G. 1999. *The Maximum Surveillance Society*. Oxford: Berg.

Norris, C. and McCahill, M. 2006. 'CCTV: Beyond Penal Modernism?', *The British Journal of Criminology* 46(1): 97–118.

Norris, C., Fielding, N., Kemp, C. and Fielding, J. 1992. 'Black and Blue: An Analysis of the Influence of Race on Being Stopped by the Police', *The British Journal of Sociology* 43(2): 207–224.

O'Connor, K. and Elliott, S. 2014. 'Biometric Zoo Menagerie', in S. Li and A. Jain (eds.), *Encyclopedia of Biometrics*. Berlin: Springer, pp. 1–4.

O'Neil, C. 2016. *Weapons of Math Destruction: How Big Data Increases Inequality and Threatens Democracy*. London: Allen Lane.

Office of the High Commissioner for Human Rights. 2022. 'OHCHR Assessment of Human Rights Concerns in the Xinjiang Uyghur Autonomous Region, People's Republic of China', 31 August.

Olssen, M. 2021. *Constructing Foucault's Ethics: A Poststructuralist Moral Theory for the 21st Century*. Manchester: Manchester University Press.

ONS. 2022. 'Census Map'. www.ons.gov.uk/census/maps/choropleth/identity/ethnic-group.

OSAC. 2021. 'Standard Guide for Facial Comparison Overview and Methodology Guidelines'. www.nist.gov/system/files/documents/2021/12/06/OSAC_2022-S-0007_Standard_Guide_for_Facial_Comparison_Overview_and_Methodology_Guidelines_DRAFT_OSAC_PROPOSED.pdf.

Palolen, E. 2011. 'European Capitals of Culture and the Limits of the Urban Effects in Luxembourg and Sibiu 2007', *Brazilian Journal of Urban Management* 3(2): 245–256.

Parliamentary Office of Science and Technology. 2018. 'Biometric Technologies'. https://researchbriefings.parliament.uk/ResearchBriefing/Summary/POST-PN-0578#fullreport.

PEN America. 2013. 'Chilling Effects: NSA Surveillance Drives U.S. Writers to Self-Censor'.

Penney, J. W. 2016. 'Chilling Effects: Online Surveillance and Wikipedia Use', *Berkeley Technology Law Journal* 31: 117–174.

Penney, J. W. 2022. 'Understanding Chilling Effects', *Minnesota Law Review* 106: 1452–1518.

Pearson, G. 1988. *Hooligan: A History of Respectable Fears*. London: Palgrave.

Poletta, F. and Jasper J. M. 2001. 'Collective Identity and Social Movements', *Annual Review of Sociology* 27: 283–305.

Poster, M. (1990) *The Mode of Information*, London: Sage.

Poyner, B. 1992. 'Video Cameras and Bus Vandalism', in R. V. Clarke (ed.), *Situational Crime Prevention: Successful Case Studies.*. New York: Harrow and Hetson, pp. 44–52.

Pratt, J. 2007. *Penal Populism.* London: Routledge.

Purshouse, J. and Campbell, L. 2021. 'Automated Facial Recognition and Policing: A *Bridge* Too Far?', *Legal Studies* 42: 209–227.

Raco, M. 2003. 'Remaking Place and Securitising Space: Urban Regeneration and the Strategies, Tactics and Practices of Policing in the UK', *Urban Studies* 40(9): 1869–1887.

Raja, K. et al. 2020. 'Morphing Attack Detection: Database, Evaluation Platform and Benchmarking', *IEEE Transactions on Information Forensics and Security.*

Reicher, S. 2001. 'The Psychology of Crowd Dynamics', in M. A. Hogg and R. S. Tindale (eds.), *Blackwell Handbook of Social Psychology: Group Processes.* Oxford: Blackwell, pp. 182–208.

Reiner, R. 2007. *Law and Order: An Honest Citizen's Guide to Crime and Control.* Cambridge: Polity Press.

Richards, N. M. 2008. 'Intellectual Privacy', *Texas Law Review* 87, pp. 387–445.

Richards, N. M. 2013. 'The Dangers of Surveillance', *Harvard Law Review* 126, pp. 1934–1965.

Riis, S. 2008. 'The Symmetry between Bruno Latour and Martin Heidegger: The Technique of Turning a Police Officer into a Speed Bump', *Social Studies of Science* 38(2): 285–301.

Ritzer, G. 2010. *Enchanting a Disenchanted World: Continuity and Change in the Cathedrals of Consumption.* Thousand Oaks, CA: Pine Forge Press.

Robertson, D. J., Kramer, R. S. S., and Burton, A. M. 2017. 'Fraudulent ID Using Face Morphs: Experiments on Human and Automatic Recognition', *PLoS ONE* 12(3): 1–12.

Rolling Stone. 2018, 13 December. 'Why Taylor Swift Is Using Facial Recognition at Concerts'.

Rose, N., O'Malley, P., and Valverde, M. 2006. 'Governmentality', *Annual Review of Law and Society* 2: 83–104.

Rouvray, A. and Berns, T. 2013. 'Gouvernementalité algorithmique et perspectives d'émancipation. Le disparate comme condition d'individuation par la relation? [Algorithmic Governmentality and Prospects of Emancipation: Disparateness as a Precondition for Individuation through Relationships?]', trans. E. Libbrecht, *Réseaux* 177: 163–196.

Rubel, A., Castro, C., and Pham, A. 2019. 'Agency Laundering and Information Technologies', *Ethical Theory & Moral Practice* 22: 1017–1041.

Rutherford, A. 2020. *How to Argue with a Racist: History, Science, Race and Reality.* London: Weidenfeld & Nicolson.

Sandhu, A. and Fussey, P. 2020. 'The "Uberization of Policing"? How Police Negotiate and Operationalise Predictive Policing Technology', *Policing and Society* 31(1): 66–81.

Science and Technology in Policing. n.d. 'Facial Recognition: Delivering More Precise Policing'. https://science.police.uk/delivery/case-studies/facial-recognition-delivering-more-precise-policing.

Scottish Biometrics Commissioner. 2023, 12 October. 'Commissioner Responds to Statement by Policing Minister for England and Wales about UK Police National Database (PND)'.

Security Matters. 2023, 7 April. 'Facial Recognition Technology Report Finds No Risk of Bias or Discrimination'.

Sennett, R. 1990. *The Conscience of the Eye: The Design and Social Life of Cities*. New York: W. W. Norton.

Shany, Y. 2023. 'The Case for a New Right to a Human Decision under International Human Rights Law', SSRN Working Draft.

Shaw, C. and McKay, H. 1942. *Juvenile Delinquency and Urban Areas.* Chicago, IL: University of Chicago Press.

Short, E. and Ditton, J. 1995. 'Does CCTV Affect Crime?', *CCTV Today* 2(2): 10–12.

Skinns, D. 1998. 'Crime Reduction, Diffusion and Displacement: Evaluating the Effectiveness of CCTV', in C. Norris, J. Moran, and G. Armstrong (eds.), *Surveillance, Closed Circuit Television and Social Control.* Aldershot: Ashgate, pp. 175–188.

Smith, G. J. D. 2004. 'Exploring Relations between Watchers and Watched in Control(led) Systems: Strategies and Tactics', *Surveillance & Society* 4(4): 280–313.

Smith, G. J. D. 2015. *Opening the Black Box: The Work of Watching*. London: Routledge.

Smith, N. 1996. *The New Urban Frontier: Gentrification and the Revanchist City*. London: Routledge.

Smith, N. 1998. 'Giuliani Time: The Revanchist 1990s', *Social Text* 57: 1–20.

South China Morning Post. 2015, 25 October. 'The Search for "Super Recognisers" in Hong Kong: People Who Never Forget a Face'.

South Wales Police and Gwent Police. 2022. 'Policy Document for the Overt Use of Operator Inititated (sic) Facial Recognition (OIFR)'.

Starr, A. et al. 2008. 'The Impacts of State Surveillance on Political Assembly and Association: A Socio-Legal Analysis', *Qualitative Sociology* 31: 251–270.

Stephens Griffin, N. 2021. '"Everyone Was Questioning Everything": Understanding the Derailing Impact of Undercover Policing on the Lives of UK Environmentalists', *Social Movement Studies* 20: 459–477.

Stevens, A. et al. 2023. '"I Started Seeing Shadows Everywhere": The Diverse Chilling Effects of Surveillance in Zimbabwe', *Big Data & Society* 10: 1–14.

Stoycheff E. 2016. 'Under Surveillance: Examining Facebook's Spiral of Silence Effects in the Wake of NSA Internet Monitoring', *Journalism & Mass Communication Quarterly* 93: 296–311.

Sumich, J. 2023. 'Building Walls to Tame Time: Enclaves and the Enduring Power of Failure', *Economy and Society* 52(1): 137–157.

Sumner, C. 1994. *The Sociology of Deviance: An Obituary*. Milton Keynes: Open University Press.

Super Recognisers. n.d. *Media*. www.superrecognisers.com/media.

Surveillance Camera Commissioner. 2013. *Surveillance Camera Code of Practice.* London: The Stationery Office.

Surveillance Camera Commissioner. 2019. *The Police Use of Automated Facial Recognition Technology with Surveillance Camera Systems: Section 33 Protection of Freedoms Act 2012.* March.

Surveillance Camera Commissioner. 2020. *Facing the Camera: Good Practice Guidance for the Police Use of Overt Surveillance Camera Systems Incorporating the Use of Facial Recognition Technology to Locate Persons on a Watchlist, in Public Places in England and Wales.*

SWP. n.d. 'Live Facial Recognition Data Protection Impact Assessment (DPIA)'.

SWP. n.d. 'Operator Initiated Facial Recognition, Data Protection Impact Assessment'.

SWP. 2021a. 'Soth Wales Police Policy Document for the Overt Deployment of Live Facial Recognition (LFR) Technology', version 1.0.

SWP. 2021b. 'South Wales Police Live Facial Recognition (LFR): Legal Mandate', version 1.0.

SWP. 2021c. 'Standard Operating Procedure for the Overt Operational Deployment of Live Facial Recognition (LFR) Technology', version 1.0.

Taylor, A. 2018. 'The Automation Charade', *Logic* 5.

Taylor, I., Evans, K., and Fraser, P. 1996. *A Tale of Two Cities: Global Change, Local Feeling and Everyday Life in the North of England.* London: Routledge.

TechMonitor. 2018, 8 May. 'Met Police Picks Northgate for MiPS Integrated Policing Deal'.

The Danish Institute for Human Rights. 2020. 'Guidance on Human Rights Impact Assessment of Digital Activities'.

The Evening Standard. 2019, 2 September. 'Face-Scanning CCTV Approved for London Hot-Spots Despite Privacy Storm'.

The Guardian. 2002, 13 June. 'Robo Cop'. www.guardian.co.uk/uk/2002/jun/13/ukcrime.jamesmeek.

The Guardian. 2010, 11 January. 'Privacy No Longer a Social Norm, Says Facebook Founder'.

The Guardian. 2014, 12 April. 'Demolishing Glasgow's Red Road Flats for the Commonwealth Games Could Leave the City's Reputation in Rubble'.

The Guardian. 2015, 5 November. 'You Look Familiar: On Patrol with the Met's Super-Recognisers'.

The Guardian (2016) 'You look familiar: on patrol with the Met's super-recognisers', 5 November, https://www.theguardian.com/uk-news/2016/nov/05/metropolitan-police-super-recognisers

The Guardian. 2019, 16 July. 'Black Undercover Officer Who Spied on Stephen Lawrence Campaign Named'.

The Guardian. 2020, 24 February. 'Met Police Chief: Facial Recognition Technology Critics Are Ill-Informed'.

The Guardian. 2022, 28 October. '"Why Not Just Go the Full Vegas?": The Crass, Ad-Laden Reinvention of Central London'.

The Guardian. 2023a, 28 October. 'Major UK Retailers Urged to Quit "Authoritarian" Police Facial Recognition Strategy'.

The Guardian. 2023b, 21 March. 'Met Police Found to Be Institutionally Racist, Misogynistic and Homophobic'.

The Guardian. 2023c, 11 September. 'Facial Recognition Could Transform Policing in Same Way as DNA, Says Met Chief'.

The Guardian. 2023d, 3 May. 'Police Accused Over Use of Facial Recognition at King Charles' Coronation'.

The Guardian. 2023e, 5 April. 'Live Facial Recognition Labelled "Orwellian" as Met Police Push Ahead with Use'.

The Guardian. 2024, 27 January. 'Facial Recognition Cameras in Supermarkets "Targeted at Poor Areas" in England'.

The Independent. 2019, 31 January. 'Police Stop People for Covering Their Faces from Facial Recognition Camera Then Fine Man £90 after He Protested'.

The Independent. 2024, 13 August. 'Starmer Plan to Expand Facial Recognition Technology after Far-Right Riots Condemned by Charities'.

The Lammy Review. 2017. *An Independent Review into the Treatment of, and Outcomes for, Black, Asian and Minority Ethnic Individuals in the Criminal Justice System*. https://assets.publishing.service.gov.uk/government/uploads/system/uploads/attachment_data/file/643001/lammy-review-final-report.pdf.

The London Evening Standard. 2019, 2 September. 'Face-Scanning CCTV Approved for London Hot-Spots Despite Privacy Storm'.

The New Yorker. 2016, 15 August. 'The Detectives Who Never Forget a Face'.

The New York Times. 2015, 9 October. 'London Police "Super Recognizer" Walks Beat with a Facebook of the Mind'.

The New York Times. 2023, 3 January. 'Madison Square Garden Uses Facial Recognition to Ban Its Owner's Enemies'.

The New York Times. 2024, 27 March. 'Israel Deploys Expansive Facial Recognition Program in Gaza'.

The Observer. 2024, 27 January. 'Facial Recognition Cameras in Supermarkets "Targeted at Poor Areas" in England'.

The Royal Society. 2017. *Forensic Gait Analysis: A Primer for Courts*. London: The Royal Society.

Thrift, N. 2005. *Knowing Capitalism*. London: Sage.

Tilley, N. 1993. *Understanding Car Parks, Crime and CCTV: Evaluating Lessons from Safer Cities*. Home Office Police Research Group Crime Prevention Unit Series Paper no. 42.

Tilley, N. 1998. 'Evaluating the Effectiveness of CCTV Schemes', in C. Norris, J. Moran, and G. Armstrong (eds.), *Surveillance, Closed Circuit Television and Social Control*. Aldershot: Ashgate, pp. 138–154.

Töpfer, E. 2006. 'Unleashed: The FIFA World Cup 2006 as a Catalyst for the Expansion of Public Area CCTV in Germany', Paper presented at the Policing Crowds–Privatising Security, Berlin, 25–26 June.

Townend, J. 2017. 'Freedom of Expression and the Chilling Effect', in H. Tumber and S. Waisbord (eds.), *The Routledge Companion to Media and Human Rights*. London: Routledge, pp. 73–82.

Troullinou, P. 2017. 'Exploring the Subjective Experience of Everyday Surveillance: The Case of Smartphone Devices as Means of Facilitating 'Seductive' Surveillance'. Unpublished PhD thesis, The Open University.

Undercover Policing Inquiry. www.ucpi.org.uk.

UNSR. 2014. 'Report of the Special Rapporteur on the Rights to Freedom of Assembly and Association, Maina Kiai', UN Doc. A/HRC/26/29. 14 April.

UNSR. 2024. 'Human Rights Compliant Uses of Digital Technology by Law Enforcement for the Facilitation of Peaceful Protests'.

UN Human Rights Council. 2024. 'Model Protocol for Law Enforcement Officials to Promote and Protect Human Rights in the Context of Peaceful Protests'.UN Doc. A/HRC/55/60. 31 January.

UrbanEye. 2004. 'CCTV in London', Working Paper no. 6 from the *Urban Eye: On the Threshold to Urban Panopticon? Analysing the Employment of CCTV in European Cities and Assessing Its Social and Political Impacts European Commission* project. www.urbaneye.net/results/ue_wp6.pdf.

Van Brakel, R. and Govaerts, L. 2024. 'Exploring the Impact of Algorithmic Policing on Social Justice: Developing a Framework for Rhizomatic Harm in the Pre-Crime Society', *Theoretical Criminology.* 29(1): 91–109.

Van der Ploeg, I. 2012. 'The Body as Data in the Age of Information', in K. Ball, K. Haggerty, and D. Lyon (eds.), *Routledge Handbook of Surveillance Studies.* London: Routledge, pp. 176–184.

VICE. 2015, 28 January. 'Living in the Shadows of Glasgow's High-Rise Ghettos before They Get Blown Up'.

VICE. 2020, 12 June. 'UK Government Accused of Threatening to Criminalise Black Lives Matter Protests'.

Wacquant, L. 2007. 'Territorial Stigmatization in the Age of Advanced Marginality', *Thesis Eleven* 91: 66.

Waszkiewicz, P. 2007. 'The Effectiveness of CCTV (The case of Warsaw)'. Paper given at the *European Society of Criminology Conference,* Bologna, Italy, 28 September.

Waters, S. 2017. 'The Effects of Mass Surveillance on Journalists' Relations with Confidential Sources', *Digital Journalism* 6: 1294–1313.

Webber, C. 2019. *Psychology and Crime: A Transdisciplinary Perspective.* London: Sage.

Weber, M. 2001 [1904]. *The Protestant Ethic and the Spirit of Capitalism.* London: Routledge.

Webster, C. W. R. 2004. 'The Evolving Diffusion, Regulation and Governance of Closed Circuit Television in the UK', *Surveillance and Society,* 2(2/3): 230–250.

Weizman, E. 2017. *Hollow Land: Israel's Architecture of Occupation.* London: Verso.

Welsh, B. C. and Farrington, D. P. 2002. *Crime Prevention Effects of Closed Circuit Television: A Systematic Review,* Home Office Research Study 252, London: Home Office.

Wendt, A. 2015. *Quantum Mind and Social Science: Unifying Physical and Social Ontology.* Cambridge: Cambridge University Press.

Wiecek, C. and Sætnan, A. 2002. 'Restrictive? Permissive? The Contradictory Framing of Video Surveillance in Norway and Denmark', Working paper no. 4 from *Urban Eye: On the Threshold to Urban Panopticon? Analysing the Employment of CCTV in European Cities and Assessing its Social and Political Impacts European Commission* project. http://www.urbaneye.net/results/ue_wp4.pdf

Williams, W. 2020. *Windrush Lessons Learned Review*. London: House of Commons.
WIRED. 2024, 17 June. 'Amazon-Powered AI Cameras Used to Detect Emotions of Unwitting UK Train Passengers'.
Wood, M. 2019. 'Thoughts on Recent Research Paper and Associated Article on Amazon Rekognition', AWS blog post. 26 January.
World Bank. n.d. *World Development Indicators*. Washington DC: World Bank. https://datacatalog.worldbank.org/search/dataset/0037712/World-Development-Indicators.
Zuboff, S. 2019. *The Age of Surveillance Capitalism: The Fight for a Human Future at the New Frontier of Power*. London: Profile Books.
Zukin, S. 1995. *The Culture of Cities*. Chichester: Wiley.

Index

For the benefit of digital users, indexed terms that span two pages (e.g., 52–53) may, on occasion, appear on only one of those pages.

Tables are indicated by an italic *t* following the paragraph number.

The manufacturer's authorised representative in the EU for product safety is Oxford University Press España S.A. of El Parque Empresarial San Fernando de Henares, Avenida de Castilla, 2 – 28830 Madrid (www.oup.es/en or product.safety@oup.com). OUP España S.A. also acts as importer into Spain of products made by the manufacturer.

Printed in the USA/Agawam, MA
April 9, 2026

903555.153